# The Economics
# of Public Finance

# Studies of Government Finance
## TITLES PUBLISHED

# The Economics of Public Finance

*Essays by*

ALAN S. BLINDER and ROBERT M. SOLOW

GEORGE F. BREAK

PETER O. STEINER

DICK NETZER

*Studies of Government Finance*

THE BROOKINGS INSTITUTION

WASHINGTON, D.C.

*Copyright © 1974 by*
THE BROOKINGS INSTITUTION
*1775 Massachusetts Avenue, N.W., Washington, D.C. 20036*

*Library of Congress Cataloging in Publication Data:*

Main entry under title:
The Economics of public finance.

(Studies of government finance)
~~Bibliography: p.~~
1. Finance, Public—United States—Addresses,
essays, lectures.    2. Finance, Public—Addresses,
essays, lectures.    I. Blinder, Alan S.    II. Series:
Brookings Institution, Washington, D.C. National
Committee of Government Finance. Studies of government
finance.
HJ257.2.E25      336.73      74-276
ISBN 0-8157-0998-6
ISBN 0-8157-0997-8 (pbk.)


9 8 7 6 5 4 3 2 1

THE BROOKINGS INSTITUTION is an independent organization devoted to nonpartisan research, education, and publication in economics, government, foreign policy, and the social sciences generally. Its principal purposes are to aid in the development of sound public policies and to promote public understanding of issues of national importance.

The Institution was founded on December 8, 1927, to merge the activities of the Institute for Government Research, founded in 1916, the Institute of Economics, founded in 1922, and the Robert Brookings Graduate School of Economics and Government, founded in 1924.

The Board of Trustees is responsible for the general administration of the Institution, while the immediate direction of the policies, program, and staff is vested in the President, assisted by an advisory committee of the officers and staff. The by-laws of the Institution state, "It is the function of the Trustees to make possible the conduct of scientific research, and publication, under the most favorable conditions, and to safeguard the independence of the research staff in the pursuit of their studies and in the publication of the results of such studies. It is not a part of their function to determine, control, or influence the conduct of particular investigations or the conclusions reached."

The President bears final responsibility for the decision to publish a manuscript as a Brookings book or staff paper. In reaching his judgment on the competence, accuracy, and objectivity of each study, the President is advised by the director of the appropriate research program and weighs the views of a panel of expert outside readers who report to him in confidence on the quality of the work. Publication of a work signifies that it is deemed to be a competent treatment worthy of public consideration; such publication does not imply endorsement of conclusions or recommendations contained in the study.

The Institution maintains its position of neutrality on issues of public policy in order to safeguard the intellectual freedom of the staff. Hence interpretations or conclusions in Brookings publications should be understood to be solely those of the author or authors and should not be attributed to the Institution, to its trustees, officers, or other staff members, or to the organizations that support its research.

# Foreword

GOVERNMENT BUDGETS that in the aggregate exceed 30 percent of the gross national product pose hard questions for policy makers and public finance experts alike: How do taxes and government expenditures affect the stability and growth of the economy? What principles should guide decisions about whether the government should undertake or finance a given activity? Who bears the burden of the major taxes levied by modern governments to finance their expenditures? How should governmental responsibilities be distributed in a federal system and at what level of government—and with what taxes—should various public activities be financed?

These and related questions were the subjects of the program of Studies of Government Finance that was undertaken more than a decade ago by the Brookings Institution with the financial assistance of the Ford Foundation. A cooperative research effort of Brookings, various universities, and other nonprofit research institutions, the program was supervised by the National Committee of Government Finance, assisted by an advisory committee of distinguished economists and tax lawyers. It produced thirty-five books, over fifty doctoral dissertations, and numerous articles in professional and other journals. Many of the ideas presented in this voluminous literature have influenced public as well as professional opinion regarding the difficult issues of public finance. To assess the state of knowledge in public finance at the end of this sustained research effort, four essays were commissioned to review the professional literature, summarize and evaluate competing views, and identify the issues where knowledge remains insufficient.

In the first of the four essays, "Analytical Foundations of Fiscal Policy," Alan S. Blinder of Princeton University and Robert M. Solow of the Massachusetts Institute of Technology survey the theoretical and empirical underpinnings of fiscal policy. After discussing how the influence of fiscal policy on macroeconomic activity should be measured, the authors examine various budgetary rules that have been suggested to improve the stability of the economy and find that no single rule can be satisfactory for all situations. Although they believe that "money matters," they defend the efficacy of fiscal policy against the monetarist contention that it is ineffective. From an examination of the lags and uncertainties in the operation of fiscal policy and an analysis of the 1968–70 income tax surcharge, they conclude that, although much remains to be learned about the econometrics of policy multipliers, the post-surcharge experience does not undermine the theoretical foundations of fiscal policy.

Where the burdens of various taxes fall has been a matter of intensive research by public finance theorists in the last twenty years. As public expenditures—and taxpayer resistance—rise, policy makers find it increasingly difficult to use tax instruments to promote economic objectives and to distribute the burdens of taxation fairly at the same time. George F. Break of the University of California at Berkeley, in "The Incidence and Economic Effects of Taxation," explains recent innovations in the theory of tax incidence and reviews recent empirical studies of the effect of taxation on the economy. He summarizes and appraises current professional opinion on the incidence of the major taxes and on the effect of taxation on the work-leisure and consumption-saving choices, private investment, the allocation of resources, and economic growth.

In "Public Expenditure Budgeting," Peter O. Steiner of the University of Michigan surveys and synthesizes the literature dealing with the hard questions of public expenditure policy, including the theory of benefit-cost analysis and its application to public expenditure choices. Steiner reviews the various justifications scholars have offered for governmental provision or financing of particular goods and services. Although he finds none of the models wholly satisfactory, his work contributes to the debate concerning the process by which collective values are articulated and collective decisions come to be accepted as binding.

Dick Netzer of New York University, in "State-Local Finance and Intergovernmental Fiscal Relations," clarifies the debate over fiscal federalism that arose when the initial revenue-sharing proposals were made. He explores the appropriate distribution of responsibility for public services among federal, state, and local governments, the appropriate revenue systems for the subnational governments, and —in the absence of what could be only a fortuitous correspondence between ideal systems for each—the appropriate means of coordinating the two. He traces the historical responses, inertia, accidents, and traditions that have molded the present system and the new elements that demand and support change in it. In Netzer's view, the theory of fiscal federalism suggests that desirable changes in the allocation of expenditure responsibilities would involve both centralizing and decentralizing shifts.

The Steiner and Netzer papers were completed and printed for limited distribution as separate papers in 1969. They are included in this volume in their original form because the passage of time has diminished neither their analytical cogency nor their relevance to current problems.

Alan Blinder and Robert Solow wish to thank David I. Fand, Saul H. Hymans, Dwight M. Jaffee, Wallace E. Oates, William Poole, and James Tobin for helpful comments and suggestions.

George Break wishes to acknowledge the help of John A. Brittain, Harvey E. Brazer, Marian Krzyzaniak, Charles E. McLure, Jr., Peter M. Mieszkowski, Joseph A. Pechman, and Carl S. Shoup.

Peter Steiner wishes to thank Joseph C. Miller, who was co-author of the section on federal government budget planning, assembled the bibliography, and assisted in many other ways; the Graduate School of the University of Wisconsin and the Cook Foundation of the University of Michigan Law School, both of which assisted in financing his research; and Burton A. Weisbrod, Robert Dorfman, Roland N. McKean, and Lee Hanson for helpful suggestions.

Mendelle T. Berenson and Alice M. Carroll edited the manuscript; Evelyn P. Fisher verified the accuracy and consistency of the data and references; Florence Robinson prepared the index.

The views expressed here are those of the authors and should not be ascribed to the National Committee on Government Finance or its Advisory Committee, to the Graduate School of the University of Wisconsin, or to the trustees, officers, or staff members of the Brookings Institution, the Cook Foundation, or the Ford Foundation.

KERMIT GORDON
*President*

*May 1974*
*Washington, D.C.*

# Studies of Government Finance

Studies of Government Finance, a special program of research and education in taxation and government expenditures at the federal, state, and local levels supported by a special grant from the Ford Foundation, was undertaken and supervised by the National Committee on Government Finance appointed by the trustees of the Brookings Institution.

# Contents

xiii

## Public Expenditure Budgeting                                       241

### Peter O. Steiner

## State-Local Finance and Intergovernmental Fiscal Relations          361

### Dick Netzer

# Tables

# Figures

## Blinder and Solow

## Steiner

## Netzer

# Analytical Foundations
# of Fiscal Policy

ALAN S. BLINDER *and* ROBERT M. SOLOW

# Analytical Foundations
# of Fiscal Policy

OUR INTENTION IN THIS ESSAY is to survey the analytical and some
of the empirical foundations of fiscal policy. We cannot hope to catalogue completely all that is known or suspected, for there is hardly a
bit of analytical or empirical knowledge about macroeconomics that
does not bear directly on fiscal policy. Our principle of selection has
been to stick close to fundamentals, especially to those issues important for the making or evaluation of policy around which controversy
persists.

In discussing controversial matters, we have tried to expound a
consistent set of ideas, partly theoretical and partly empirical, that a
reasonable eclectic economist might hold. These ideas are our own
and they are not the only possible ones. Some of the issues are not yet
settled, and no set of attitudes would command universal agreement.
We do not believe ours to be far from the mainstream in any respect.
But we shall try to call special attention to those areas where evidence
is weak or conflicting and reasonable people may differ without being
merely contrary.

## Scope of the Survey

Our subject matter might be defined loosely as the stabilization aspect of taxes and government expenditures. But this definition is too ambiguous. Hansen has proposed the more precise definition that fiscal policy comprises all tax and expenditure transactions of governments as they affect the size of the public debt but not its composition, while monetary policy and debt management are concerned with the composition of the public debt but not with the level of or the changes in its size. Thus a government purchase and its financing can be separated into a fiscal-policy component and a monetary policy-debt management component.[1] The transaction is pure fiscal policy if it is financed entirely with taxes, so that the public debt does not change, or if the debt-financed part of the expenditure does not alter the proportions of outstanding government obligations (including high-powered money). This is a reasonable place to draw the boundary between fiscal and monetary policy, although it is not foolproof. Only in the special case in which portfolio preferences are independent of the absolute scale of wealth can an equiproportional change in the outstanding stocks of all government securities claim "neutrality."

Nothing much besides academic division of labor depends on the choice of a precise demarcation between fiscal and monetary policy. In practice the two are interconnected; wherever we place the boundary we are bound to poach across it. Moreover, in discussing the monetarist critique of fiscal policy we must necessarily analyze the two together.

In textbook terms, we can illustrate the border between fiscal and monetary policy in the context of a familiar simple model:

(1)        $Y = C(Y - T, M/P, B/P, K) + I(Y, r, K) + G$
(2)        $M/P = L(Y, r, B/P, M/P, K)$
(3)        $D = P(G - T) = dB/dt + dM/dt + X,$
where
$Y$ = real income
$P$ = the price level

[1] Bent Hansen, *The Economic Theory of Fiscal Policy* (Translation, Harvard University Press, 1958), p. 31, with a credit to Erik Lindahl, "Theory of the Public Debt," in *Studies in Economics and History,* presented to Eli F. Heckscher, Uppsala (1945), p. 92.

$M$ = the stock of outside money, somehow defined

$B$ = the value of outstanding nonmonetary public debt, somehow defined

$r$ = the appropriate interest rate

$K$ = the (fixed) stock of real capital goods

$C$ = a consumption function

$I$ = an investment or marginal-efficiency function

$L$ = a liquidity-preference function (or, if alternatively, $Y/L = V$, the velocity-of-money function)

$G$ = government purchases

$T$ = tax receipts net of transfers

$D$ = the nominal deficit

$X$ = a residual included to handle such complications as changes in the market value of debt induced by changes in interest rates, or other sources of capital gains and losses[2]

$t$ = time.

The first equation states that income is the sum of consumption, investment, and government expenditures. Consumption is related to income less taxes, public holdings of financial instruments, and real capital; and investment to income, the interest rate, and capital. The second equation determines the real stock of money in terms of income, the interest rate, public holdings of financial instruments, and real capital. The final equation specifies that the government deficit is equal to government spending minus taxes, or, alternatively, the increase in monetary and nonmonetary public debt.

In contrast with the flow variables, $G$ and $T$, which anyone would include in the realm of fiscal policy, the stocks $M$ and $B$ would clearly be assigned to the realm of monetary policy and debt management. In a more detailed model, monetary policy would also be concerned with the breakdown of $B$ into longer- and shorter-term securities, each with its own interest rate. Equation (3) states an important interrelation between stocks and flows, and between monetary and fiscal variables, by recognizing that a deficit or surplus must be financed by the creation or destruction of money or of interest-bearing public debt.[3]

---

[2] Later on we consider this relation in more detail, and are more precise about the role of interest payments on the public debt as expenditure items of government and personal income of consumers.

[3] The definitions of the stock of money and of bonds had better be compatible with this equation.

This simple model is sufficiently broad to be compatible with a variety of theories about the determination of the main aggregative quantities. A monetarist might make $V$ a quasi-constant and be uninterested in $C$ and $I$ separately. An ultra-Keynesian, on the other hand, might believe that $L$ exhibits a liquidity trap or that $I$ is very, or totally, interest inelastic, or both. Of course, $T$ and $G$ may themselves be functions of some of the other variables, depending on fiscal institutions. For instance, at a minimum, $T = T_0 + T(Y)$, with $T_0$ a shift parameter approximating a change in the level of rates, and $T'(Y)$ the marginal tax rate. Transfer items could already have been included as negative items in $T(Y)$. Even $G$, instead of being taken as exogenous, might also be related to $Y$ once a certain pattern of public expenditures had been legislated, or agreed upon, or simply observed to hold in practice.

In one sense the simple model might be said to be in the Keynesian tradition: it is set out in real terms and has to be converted to value flows through multiplication by the price level. Some modern monetarists prefer to construct a macroeconomic model so that it determines nominal magnitudes in the first instance, through their mutual interactions. A separate mechanism then has to be invoked to decompose changes in these nominal magnitudes into their real and price-level components. That difference has no significance for the matters discussed here.

Fiscal policy is an activity of the "stabilization branch" of the government, in Musgrave's terminology.[4] It is difficult in practice to separate the activities of the stabilization branch from those of the distribution and allocation branches. Suppose we let economic stabilization mean stabilization of aggregate employment. Obviously, many fiscal policies can yield the same overall level of employment. They may differ, however, in what they do to the employment of various industrial, occupational, and regional groups, as well as in what they do to the composition of real output, and perhaps its level. It would be natural, then, to broaden the definition of economic stabilization to mean simultaneous achievement of a satisfactory level of aggregate employment and of aggregate output, and perhaps other objectives as well. Provided enough effective instruments (that is, tax and expendi-

    [4] See Richard A. Musgrave, *The Theory of Public Finance: A Study in Public Economy* (McGraw-Hill, 1959).

ture parameters) are available, and provided that output and employment are not for other reasons in nearly one-to-one correspondence, there will be one or more fiscal policies capable of achieving the stabilization targets. But these policies will still yield different results as regards, say, the composition of output between consumption and investment, or between public goods and private goods; or as regards commodities that use natural resources to a greater or lesser extent. Different fiscal policies will also have different implications for the distribution of after-tax income by size, or between wages and profits. Shall we go further and define economic stabilization to mean stabilization of output and employment with 75 percent of income going to labor and 25 percent to capital? Convention suggests that we should not. The primarily allocational and distributional consequences of alternative tax and expenditure policies are left to be studied in connection with the allocation and distribution branches under the general heading of public economics.[5]

*The Main Issues*

Economic stabilization is obviously too important to be left to economists. Inevitably, public discussion of fiscal policy is carried on at two levels: by professional economists in their journals and elsewhere, and by politicians, journalists, and the interested public in speeches and the press. These two currents of discussion are not independent. One important link between them is forged by the economists who serve in the Treasury, the Council of Economic Advisers, the Federal Reserve System, or elsewhere in the federal government, and those who testify before the Joint Economic Committee and other committees of Congress when legislation is under review; and by the few specialized reporters who try to keep track of professional work. The lines of communication are not always clear, however, as witness those days in 1964 when a generation of middle-aged economists discovered that what most of them had been teaching for fifteen years, and what a few of them had actually been taught, had flowered as the "New Economics."

This essay is a survey of professional work, directed at both professionals and amateurs. But it is only proper that we focus on analytical issues that have flared up in popular discussion and that there-

---

[5] Many of these questions are discussed in other essays in this volume.

fore, one hopes, have been important in the actual formulation and appraisal of fiscal policy. There is, as there ought to be, causal influence in both directions. When some question erupts into prominence, the interested part of the profession is very likely to examine it, try to isolate its genuine intellectual substance (if there is none, that is also interesting), and see what, if anything, economics has to say about the answer. And if economics does have something to say—indeed, even if it seems to have two contradictory things to say—the results are likely to find their way into public discussion through the press, the Joint Economic Committee, and the Council of Economic Advisers. Our belief in the importance of this process has governed our choice of topics.

We begin in the following section with an analysis of the proper way to define a summary number that will answer the question, "How expansive—or contractionary—is fiscal policy this year as compared with, say, last year, or with some other policy?" This is not a question that the analytical economist *has* to answer. At a sufficiently austere level, every fiscal policy can be described in terms of its natural parameters—tax rates, specific expenditures, financial details, and so on—and a complete macroeconomic model will grind out the resulting income and employment totals. One fiscal policy is more expansionary than another if, and to the extent that, it induces a higher level of aggregate output.[6] But experience shows that for political debate this simply will not do. The public seems to need a number, traditionally a budget deficit, to view with pride or alarm as the case may be. Even if there is no one right way to provide a single number, simple models suggest that there are better and worse ways, and that is the subject of the next section.

This leads naturally to another time-hallowed subject of debate about stabilization policy. Suppose society could agree on a single satisfactory indicator of the stance of fiscal policy. Would it then be a good idea to elevate fiscal policy above the hurly-burly of vulgar political argument by legislating once and for all an automatic formula? For instance, the social contract could name the unemployment rate

---

[6] There is a terminological problem here. The language suggests that an expansionary fiscal policy ought to be one that *increases* aggregate output. Then one would need some other word to distinguish two policies, each of which leaves output stationary, one at a high level, the other at a low level. We keep to a static definition, but it should not be hard to translate into dynamic terms.

as the key measure of aggregate economic activity, and prescribe that each January the executive and the legislature should set the agreed-upon measure of fiscal influence at a level that depends in an explicitly stated way on the average unemployment rate over the preceding twelve months. One traditional view has chosen the current budget deficit as the measure of fiscal influence and urged that it be set at zero irrespective of the unemployment rate. There are, of course, much more sophisticated proposals. We tend to regard the debate between rules and discretion as more or less pointless, in the sense that it is more or less pointless to debate whether a growing boy should abstain completely from eating between meals: talk is one thing, but nobody can actually keep a young boy's hand out of the cookie jar. In any case, we discuss suggestions for fiscal rules in the following section.

Then we turn to the inevitable connection between fiscal and monetary policy generated by the need to finance any budget deficit or to dispose of the proceeds of any budget surplus. This is primarily a technical matter, and we discuss it mainly because the conventional textbook treatment of fiscal policy stops short after one budgetary period and fails to track down the consequences of the further changes in stocks of financial assets that must go on as long as the budget deficit or surplus continues. The only policy issue that surfaces here is a version of the "crowding out" hypothesis: the notion that deficit-financed government expenditures may have no effect on aggregate demand because (a) if they are financed by the sale of bonds, an equal amount of private spending is "crowded out" of existence, whereas (b) if they are financed by an increase in the money supply, it is the monetary policy that generates the expansion of aggregate demand.

This analysis leads naturally to a discussion of what is probably the main doctrinal issue in the theory of fiscal policy at present: the revival of the quantity theory of money by what has come to be called the "monetarist" school. The monetarist critique is sometimes described by its proponents as a defense of the proposition that monetary policy matters against the "Keynesian" belief that it does not. But since most contemporary Keynesians do in fact believe in the effectiveness of monetary policy, the monetarist argument usually turns out to be a defense of the proposition that fiscal policy does not matter against the Keynesian belief that it does. There are other strands in the monetarist view of stabilization policy, and we try to sort them out. We then go on to consider the notion that the econometric work of the St. Louis Federal Reserve Bank has established the correctness of the monetarist critique of fiscal policy. Finally, we ask whether monetarism has produced a complete macroeconomic model that provides a theoretical alternative to the modern Keynesian model, or that fits the econometric facts any better. We might as well break it to the reader here that we remain eclectic Keynesians.

The ultimate empirical foundation for rational fiscal policy is—or presumably eventually will be—found in econometric models of the whole economy. Several such models are now in operation, and we survey their messages. We cannot avoid superficiality here: an interpretive comparison of the various models is a major research task, which is in fact being undertaken by the model builders themselves. We ask merely what the models seem to say about the time lags between fiscal policy moves and their economic effects; in so doing, we naturally compare what they say about the ultimate size of fiscal policy multipliers. These are important matters because they suggest the sort of forecasting accuracy that is required for effective stabilization via fiscal policy. We try to give the reader some feeling for the extent to which the various models give the same answer to fiscal policy questions. This is hardly the same thing as knowing whether they give the right answer, but it is a useful preliminary.

The comparisons among the models illustrate the obvious fact that fiscal policy has to be made on the basis of uncertain knowledge about the parameters and the exogenous variables. This, therefore, is the logical place for a brief reference to some recent work that tries to take the uncertainties explicitly into account in determining the optimal dosage of fiscal policy in given circumstances.

Finally, we offer what might be interpreted as an eclectic Keynesian view of the history of fiscal policy in 1968–70. If the aftermath of the Revenue Act of 1964 made household heroes of macroeconomists, then the aftermath of the Revenue and Expenditure Control Act of 1968 bid fair to send them scurrying back to their universities with their doctrinal tales between their legs. This legislation was intended to restrain an accelerating inflation, but prices rose faster after its passage than before. In the dramatic way these things get talked about, the events of 1969–70 have been described as the failure of the New Economics. We find this picture much overdrawn. There are indeed sobering lessons to be learned from that experience, but some of them reinforce, rather than undermine, received fiscal theory.

Others, of course, warn against any enthusiastic tendency to overstate the accuracy with which even correct theory can be applied. We do not believe that the roof fell in, much less that the foundations crumbled.[7]

## Measuring Fiscal Influence

Since Keynes, a common, though by no means universal, presumption in the economics profession has held that the government budget can influence the aggregate level of income and employment.[8] If this view is correct, an attempt to quantify the impact seems a natural next step; that is, after classifying policy A as "expansive" and policy B as "contractionary," economists would like to be able to say that policy C is "more expansive" than policy A and to give some *quantitative* meaning to such a statement. Such a measure is required for at least two distinct purposes.

1. *Historical assessments of past policy.* Summary measures of the quantitative impact of fiscal policy were first used in the literature to analyze past fiscal policy.[9] As such, these measures can indicate when fiscal policy was expansionary (and how much), when it was contractionary (and how much), and when it was more or less neutral in its aggregative effects. Such investigations reveal whether the government has been a stabilizing or destabilizing force.

2. *Policy planning.* More important, measures of fiscal influence should enable the economist to prescribe the right dosage of fiscal stimulus (or restraint) when an insufficient (or excessive) level of private demand is forecast. The experience with the 1968 income tax surcharge suggests that it is still easier to talk about accurate prescription than to write one.[10]

---

[7] We do not try to reassess the theory of inflation. Though this was not actually the case, one could imagine that the 1968 fiscal policy actions might have done everything they were expected to do except stop prices from rising. We would have regarded that as good news for fiscal theory and bad news for the theory of inflation.

[8] The chief dissenters have been the monetarists. See pp. 57–58 for a critique of monetarism.

[9] The pioneering paper was E. Cary Brown's "Fiscal Policy in the 'Thirties: A Reappraisal," *American Economic Review*, Vol. 46 (December 1956), pp. 857–79. See also Wilfred Lewis, Jr., *Federal Budget Policy in the Postwar Recessions* (Brookings Institution, 1962).

[10] At this writing controversy still exists over what went wrong on that occasion. We offer our opinions in the concluding section.

None of this necessarily argues for a *single number* to be used as "the" measure of fiscal influence. Whenever one attempts to reduce a multidimensional concept—like the influence of the government on aggregate economic activity—to a single dimension, index number problems inevitably arise. Furthermore, examples abound of democratic (and even undemocratic!) countries in which the announcement of the government budget marks the beginning of a vigorous economic debate without a focus on a single number like the deficit.[11] A case can indeed be made for educating the public to a multi-budget concept just as the Council of Economic Advisers under Walter Heller educated it to the full employment surplus.[12]

However, the political realities of the day seem to dictate settling on a single index to measure the overall expansionary or contractionary effect of any proposed tax and expenditure program. If economists do not come up with one, the public or the Congress will probably invent its own, and the choice is unlikely to be the best. Instead, then, of trying to talk the layman out of seeking such a number, economists might do better to lead him to a "sensible" concept of the government deficit. Furthermore, economics is not—or at least should not be—silent on such questions as how much increase in the automobile excise tax rate it would take to cancel out the expansionary effects of defense spending. If economic models can reduce the various dimensions of the government budget to a single, common, denominator, why not use them? For these reasons, we believe that developing a single number to measure fiscal influence is a legitimate scholarly exercise.

Given the decision to embark on such a course, we are faced immediately with a choice between two distinct families of measures. A "budget" measure seeks only to supply a number summarizing the congeries of taxation and expenditure programs; it is mute on the effects of the program on the gross national product. The great virtue of such a measure, it is often said, is its independence of any particular model of the economy.[13] Its great vice is that for this very reason it

---

[11] For an argument against the use of a single number, see the comments by Warren L. Smith in Wilfred Lewis, Jr. (ed.), *Budget Concepts for Economic Analysis* (Brookings Institution, 1968), pp. 131–32.

[12] See, for example, *Economic Report of the President together with the Annual Report of the Council of Economic Advisers, January 1962,* pp. 78–82. Hereafter, this document will be referred to as the *Economic Report,* followed by the year.

[13] We shall argue below that this is not, in fact, entirely true.

may not be very informative, since it is the economy, not the budget, that is ultimately important. The ordinary budget deficit is probably the best illustration of both the virtue and the vice.

A "fiscal impact" measure is a single number indicating the effect of the total budget on the gross national product, or any other variable of interest. Basically, such a measure is derived from a suitable budget measure by applying to the latter some appropriate "multiplier." A fiscal impact measure, unlike a budget measure, will convey interesting information, but its dependence on a specific model of the economy is obvious. As a practical matter, the measure can be quite sensitive to the model employed (we demonstrate this below). After surveying some suggested measures of each kind, we shall argue that a specific measure of fiscal impact is to be preferred.

*The Actual Budget Deficit*

Those who learn their economics from the press and the speeches of high government officials could be forgiven for believing that the fiscal policy impact of a budget program is summed up entirely in the difference between revenues and expenditures—the government deficit or surplus. A deficit is supposed to be expansionary, and a surplus restrictive, because government spending "puts money into the income stream" and taxation removes it. Most students who take an elementary course in economics presumably learn that this is not so. The balanced-budget theorem shows that it is not really the deficit that matters. A dollar of government spending is more expansionary than a dollar of taxes is restrictive, so that a balanced increase in spending and taxes will increase the level of income.

Furthermore, economists have long realized that even an appropriately weighted deficit is woefully inadequate as a measure of fiscal policy since it is endogenous to all but the simplest models of income determination. As soon as the dependence of tax receipts on the level of activity is acknowledged, it is clear that increases in GNP will *automatically* reduce the deficit (or raise the surplus) unless the government takes countervailing action. Thus depressed levels of national income will *cause* large deficits even when the government is "really" being very contractionary, and vice versa. This is the central point of E. Cary Brown's pioneering paper.[14] Brown replaced the ordinary

---

[14] "Fiscal Policy in the 'Thirties."

budget deficit by the weighted deficit at full employment and showed how this change drastically altered the assessment of fiscal policy in the 1930s. Table 1 compares the actual budgetary deficits with the full employment deficits calculated by Brown. The contrast is quite dramatic. Some of the large budgetary deficits that alarmed Hoover and Roosevelt were actually sizable surpluses in the full employment budget. What is more, fiscal policy became steadily more *restrictive* between 1931 and 1933.

Brown's work raises the basic conceptual problem that has been the unifying theme of subsequent work—separating the *discretionary* aspects of fiscal policy (changes in tax schedules and spending) from the *automatic* ones. Although, in a deeper sense, no neat separation is possible—allowing the automatic stabilizers to work unhindered is, after all, a discretionary choice—such a dichotomy is needed for both historical assessment and policy planning.

### The Full Employment Surplus

The most obvious, and by now the most popular, way to separate discretionary from automatic fiscal actions is to focus on the full employment budget. If the budget would be in surplus at full employment, fiscal policy is termed restrictive; if the budget would be in deficit, it is termed expansionary. Although the idea was anticipated by Brown, and in fact goes back much further, the concept of the full

### TABLE 1. Actual and Full Employment Deficits, 1929–39

(*In billions of constant dollars*)

| Year | Actual deficit | Full employment deficit | Weighted full employment deficit |
|------|------|------|------|
| 1929 | 1.3 | 1.3 | 2.2 |
| 1930 | 3.2 | 2.1 | 3.0 |
| 1931 | 6.5 | 4.9 | 5.7 |
| 1932 | 4.7 | 1.4 | 3.0 |
| 1933 | 3.4 | −1.7 | 0.9 |
| 1934 | 4.9 | −0.3 | 2.7 |
| 1935 | 4.4 | 0.1 | 2.9 |
| 1936 | 6.0 | 2.0 | 4.9 |
| 1937 | 0.6 | −3.3 | 0.4 |
| 1938 | 4.3 | −1.0 | 2.4 |
| 1939 | 4.8 | 0.3 | 4.6 |

Source: From or computed from data in E. Cary Brown, "Fiscal Policy in the 'Thirties: A Reappraisal," *American Economic Review*, Vol. 46 (December 1956), Table 2, p. 873.

employment surplus appears to have been articulated first in testimony before Congress by Charles L. Schultze and Herbert Stein.[15] According to Schultze:

> Given existing tax rates, full employment in the economy would mean a level of income which would produce certain revenues. . . . Taken together with expenditure programs, these revenues would yield a given surplus. . . .
>
> An attempt to budget for an overly large surplus at full employment will prevent the economy from reaching full employment. . . .
>
> Thus the actual level of the budget surplus is not the best measure of the impact of fiscal policy on the economy.[16]

The focus on the full employment budget can trace its antecedents at least as far back as the work of Beardsley Ruml and the Committee for Economic Development around the time of the Second World War.[17] The CED recognized that low levels of output were bound to cause budgetary deficits, and that it would be folly to try to balance the budget by raising tax rates, as was done in Hoover's time. It recommended that tax rates be set, instead, so as to yield a balanced budget, or perhaps a small surplus, at full employment.

By 1962, the full employment surplus (FES) had been enshrined in the *Economic Report of the President;*[18] eventually it became one of the centerpieces of the New Economics under Presidents Kennedy and Johnson.

At about the same time that the CEA under Heller was introducing the FES as a policy planning tool, Wilfred Lewis, Jr., demonstrated its usefulness in historical studies of fiscal policy. Using a concept like the FES to separate the discretionary and automatic aspects of stabilization policy, Lewis concluded that "the built-in fiscal stabilizers have made a substantial contribution to the stability of the postwar economy," while deliberate discretionary policies "generally have been less helpful."[19] Table 2 summarizes Lewis's results for the

[15] Charles L. Schultze, testimony in *Current Economic Situation and Short-Run Outlook,* Hearings before the Joint Economic Committee, 86 Cong. 2 sess. (1961), pp. 114–22; and Herbert Stein, testimony in *January 1961 Economic Report of the President and the Economic Situation and Outlook,* Hearings before the Joint Economic Committee, 87 Cong. 1 sess. (1961), pp. 209–18.

[16] Schultze, *Current Economic Situation,* p. 120.

[17] See Herbert Stein, *The Fiscal Revolution in America* (University of Chicago Press, 1969), especially pp. 184–86.

[18] *Economic Report, 1962,* pp. 77–81.

[19] Lewis, *Federal Fiscal Policy,* pp. 15, 17.

**TABLE 2. Impact of Automatic Built-in Fiscal Stabilizers and Discretionary Policies on Federal Budget Surplus or Deficit, Four Recession and Recovery Periods, 1948–61**

(*In billions of current dollars*)

| Period | Surplus (+) or deficit (−) | | |
|---|---|---|---|
| | Automatic component | Discretionary component | Total |
| *Recession* | | | |
| 1948:4–1949:2 | −3.7 | −4.0 | −7.7 |
| 1953:2–1954:2 | −6.6 | +8.2 | +1.6 |
| 1957:3–1958:1 | −8.7 | −2.0 | −10.7 |
| 1960:2–1961:1 | −6.8 | −3.2 | −10.0 |
| *Recovery* | | | |
| 1949:2–1950:2 | +6.1 | +6.1 | +12.2 |
| 1954:2–1955:2 | +10.4 | −1.5 | +8.9 |
| 1958:1–1959:2 | +17.4 | −8.8 | +8.6 |
| 1961[a] | +10.8 | −7.4 | +3.4 |

Source: Wilfred Lewis, Jr., *Federal Fiscal Policy in the Postwar Recessions* (Brookings Institution, 1962), Table 4, p. 16.

[a] The last quarter for which data were available when the calculations were made was 1961:4 (see source); however, that is not considered the terminal quarter of recovery.

four business cycles from 1948 to 1961. Reading it, one should note that it is usually *changes* in a measure of fiscal impact that convey useful information. The discretionary deficit during the recovery period 1958–59, for example, was not in and of itself perverse; without it, there might have been no recovery. The real issue is whether the discretionary component of fiscal policy has been moving in the right direction, given the current economic situation.

The role of the full employment surplus can be illustrated in the context of the following rock-bottom model of income determination:[20]

$$C = C(Y - T) \quad \text{(consumption function)},$$

where $C$ is real consumer spending, $Y$ is real GNP, and $T$ is real tax receipts;

$$Y = C + A + G \quad \text{(income identity)},$$

where $A$ is real autonomous private expenditures and $G$ is real government purchases;

$$T = T(Y, \tau) \quad \text{(tax function)},$$

[20] For a mathematical version of the following, see the appendix to this section.

where $\tau$ is a tax parameter (think of it as the tax rate), or a vector of such parameters. The income determination equation is

(4) $$Y = C[Y - T(Y, \tau)] + A + G,$$

and the actual budget surplus is $T(Y, \tau) - G$, while the FES is $T(Y^*, \tau) - G$, where $Y^*$ is real GNP at full employment. The ordinary surplus is obviously an inadequate measure of the influence of fiscal policy since the first term is endogenous; that is, it fails to distinguish between the influence of the budget on the economy and the influence of the economy on the budget. The FES avoids this pitfall by measuring tax revenues at full employment.[21]

But, like the ordinary surplus, the FES runs afoul of the balanced-budget theorem: changes in tax receipts simply do not carry as much bang for the buck as changes in government purchases. Since the FES fails to weight tax receipts by the marginal propensity to consume, it is impossible to associate a given change in the FES with a specific change in income; it depends on how the change is apportioned between taxes and spending. As pointed out by Brown, the weighted full employment surplus would be a better measure.

But another problem arises with the full employment surplus, whether weighted or unweighted, which did not afflict the ordinary budget surplus. Suppose the tax regulations (that is, the vector of parameters, $\tau$) are altered when the economy is very far below full employment. The revenue yield of this change *at actual income levels* may well be very different from the hypothetical revenue yield *at full employment*. Even the sign may be different. Consider, for example, a small reduction in personal income tax rates coupled with a very large increase in corporate tax rates. At low levels of business activity, with corporate profits depressed, this change might generate a net loss of revenues, even though at high levels of employment larger tax collections might result. This ambiguity, of course, is merely a reflection of the innate difficulty of collapsing two parameters ($G$ and $\tau$) into one. There is simply no way to do this that is correct for *every* level of GNP. The weighted FES is a true measure of the impact of budgetary changes on a full employment economy; but such information may be of limited interest if the unemployment rate is 6 percent.

Whatever the educational benefits of the FES—and they appear to

---

[21] We abstract here from growth, so $Y^*$ is assumed unchanged. This restriction will be dropped shortly.

have been considerable—sophisticated investigations of fiscal influence require a different measure.[22]

## The Concept of Fiscal Drag

The chief selling point of the FES over the ordinary budget deficit is that the former indicates only *discretionary* changes while the latter includes the effects of the automatic stabilizers. However, in a growing economy, even this is not true. With unchanged tax laws, a growing economy will generate ever-increasing tax receipts at full employment (or, for that matter, at any other constant level of utilization). The more elastic the tax schedule with respect to aggregate income,[23] the more important these "automatic" increments to the FES will be. If private demand is expanding too rapidly, such an automatic increase in full employment revenues may be desirable, but in other circumstances it will not be. Instead, it will place what Heller has called a "fiscal drag" on the system. According to Heller:

... in a growth context, the great revenue-raising power of our Federal tax system produces a built-in average increase of $7 to $8 billion a year in Federal revenues ... Unless it is offset by such "fiscal dividends" as tax cuts or expansion of Federal programs, this automatic rise in revenues will become a "fiscal drag" siphoning too much of the economic substance out of the private economy and thereby choking expansion.[24]

The role of fiscal drag in our rock-bottom model is clear. Since the FES is defined as $T(Y^*, \tau) - G$, its value will change if $\tau$, $G$, or $Y^*$ changes. Movements in the FES attributable to the first two arguments are discretionary; the automatic change in the FES due to economic growth is fiscal drag, according to Heller's definition.[25]

An alternative to Heller's definition of fiscal drag may be a more useful tool, since it accounts for the fact that some automatic increase in the full employment surplus may be desirable if autonomous expenditures are rising.

[22] For a recent discussion of the pros and cons of the full employment surplus, see Arthur M. Okun and Nancy H. Teeters, "The Full Employment Surplus Revisited," *Brookings Papers on Economic Activity* (1:1970), pp. 77–110, and the discussion of the paper, pp. 111–16.

[23] This elasticity is the product of the elasticity of the tax base with respect to national income, and the elasticity of tax receipts with respect to the base.

[24] Walter W. Heller, *New Dimensions of Political Economy* (Harvard University Press, 1966; W. W. Norton, 1967), p. 65.

[25] Ibid., p. 181, note 9. For a mathematical version of what follows, see the appendix.

Suppose, for the sake of the argument, that the time path of real government expenditures is set optimally according to allocational criteria discussed in the essay by Peter Steiner in this volume, and not varied for stabilization purposes. Thus, both $A$ and $G$ can be taken as exogenous by the stabilization branch.[26] According to the model, if the economy is to expand along its full employment growth path, tax rates must be manipulated so as to maintain

$$Y^* = C[Y^* - T(Y^*, \tau)] + A + G.$$

As we show in the appendix, this equation can be used to obtain the *discretionary change in full employment taxes needed to maintain full employment*. It seems natural, then, to define *adjusted fiscal drag* as the difference between the automatic increase in full employment taxes (Heller's definition) and the total tax increase required to maintain full employment. We show in the appendix that the *size* and *sign* of the adjusted fiscal drag depend on the relative growth of private and public autonomous demand in relation to capacity, and on the relative sizes of the multiplier and the marginal propensity to consume. Specifically, the *sign* of the adjusted fiscal drag depends *only* on the relative *sizes* of the increase in capacity that would be required to meet the autonomous growth in demand relative to the actual increase in capacity. Its *size* depends also on the marginal propensity to consume. On this definition, if autonomous demand and supply expand equally, no drag is exerted and no tax cut is needed.

The preceding discussion of fiscal drag, like most of the literature on measuring fiscal influence, has ignored changes in the price level. This procedure is legitimate only if the price level in fact never changes, or a "classical dichotomy" exists so that the price level does not impinge upon any real variables. In the short run, however, with commitments made in money terms with imperfect foresight, one can hardly ignore the real consequences of a changing price level. In particular, Gramlich has pointed out that, owing to progressivity, the government's real tax receipts will depend on the level of prices, $P$, and that, since many expenditure programs are fixed in *money* terms, real spending may exhibit a similar dependence.[27]

[26] This terminological division of the government's functions comes, of course, from Musgrave, *Theory of Public Finance*.

[27] Edward M. Gramlich, "Measures of the Aggregate Demand Impact of the Federal Budget," in Lewis (ed.), *Budget Concepts for Economic Analysis*, especially pp. 117–19.

To see this, suppose the tax laws make nominal tax receipts a function of nominal income:

(5)                          $PT = f(PY, \tau)$,

where $\tau$ is again a set of tax parameters, and where the elasticity of $f(\cdot)$ with respect to $PY$ exceeds unity—that is, it is a progressive tax function. Now suppose the price level rises with real output fixed. Clearly, *real* tax receipts will rise because money income will rise in the same proportion as the price level, causing money tax receipts—by progressivity—to rise more than proportionately with $P$.[28] In other words, pure price inflation as well as real growth gives rise to fiscal drag. For example, based on Waldorf's estimate of 1½ for the income elasticity of the personal income tax, a 4 percent inflation will add 2 percent to *real* tax receipts.[29] If, in addition, the state fixes nominal expenditures, $PG$, rather than real expenditures, $G$, in its budget statement, this effect will be even more severe.

Given this possibility, there are four reasons why the full employment surplus might change. Alterations in tax parameters or in real government purchases lead to the discretionary changes in the FES that are of interest for stabilization policy. But a rise in either potential GNP or the price level will automatically raise the FES—that is, cause fiscal drag. The appendix demonstrates that we can define a new concept of adjusted fiscal drag that accounts for the automatic stabilizing effects of inflation, simply by subtracting from our previous measure of adjusted fiscal drag the product of the rate of inflation, the marginal propensity to tax, and money GNP.

We shall return to the question of correcting measures of fiscal influence to account for inflation at the end of this section.

[28] To be precise, by (5):

$$T = \left(\frac{1}{P}\right) f(PY, \tau), \text{ so}$$

$$\frac{dT}{dP} = -\frac{f}{P^2} + \left(\frac{1}{P}\right) f_1 \, Y, \text{ so}$$

$$\left(\frac{P}{T}\right)\left(\frac{dT}{dP}\right) = -1 + \left(\frac{PY}{f}\right) f_1,$$

which is positive if and only if the tax structure is progressive.

[29] See William H. Waldorf, "The Responsiveness of Federal Personal Income Taxes to Income Change," *Survey of Current Business*, Vol. 47 (December 1967), pp. 32–45. Charles J. Goetz and Warren E. Weber have shown that these inflation effects were sufficient to counter the tax cuts of 1964–65 and 1970. See their "Intertemporal Changes in Real Federal Income Tax Rates, 1954–70," *National Tax Journal*, Vol. 24 (March 1971), pp. 51–63.

## The Weighted Full Employment Surplus

Of the several problems the FES concept presents as a measure of fiscal influence, the easiest to remedy is its failure to recognize the differential strengths of taxes versus government expenditures. This was, in fact, accomplished by Gramlich in his doctoral dissertation and a subsequent conference paper.[30] In the rock-bottom model, the amendment merely requires weighting tax receipts by the marginal propensity to consume. If $W$ denotes the weighted FES, then

$$W = c\, T(Y^*, \tau) - G,$$

where $c$ is the marginal propensity to consume.

This "innovation," as we have seen, was anticipated in Brown's paper. It was also anticipated, in a slightly different form, in Richard Musgrave's concept of "fiscal leverage."[31] The main difference is that Musgrave's measure reflects fiscal impact whereas Gramlich's weighted FES is a budget measure. Essentially, fiscal leverage is the "weighted budget":

$$FL = \sum_{i=1}^{N} m_i G_i - \sum_{j=1}^{M} \mu_j T_j,$$

where $G_1, \ldots, G_N$ are different types of expenditures, $T_1, \ldots, T_M$ are different types of tax receipts, and the $m_i$ and $\mu_j$ are the appropriate multipliers suggested by some model. The leverage, $FL$, includes both discretionary and automatic changes in the budget. Musgrave notes that a purer measure of the change in fiscal policy would be obtained by calculating fiscal leverage at some fixed level of income.[32] With this done, and with full employment income used as the reference point, the result is the weighted full employment deficit multiplied by some appropriate multiplier. In the rock-bottom model with only one $G$ and one $T$, fiscal leverage at full employment would be

$$FL^* = m(G - cT^*),$$

where $m$ is the ordinary multiplier, and $T^*$ is full employment revenues. In fact, since multipliers are hard to know with any precision,

[30] Edward M. Gramlich, "The Behavior and Adequacy of the United States Federal Budget, 1952–1964," *Yale Economic Essays,* Vol. 6 (Spring 1966), pp. 99–159; and "Measures of the Aggregate Demand Impact."

[31] Richard A. Musgrave, "On Measuring Fiscal Peformance," *Review of Economics and Statistics,* Vol. 46 (May 1964), pp. 213–20.

[32] Ibid., p. 214.

Musgrave actually suggests dividing this measure by the multiplier.[33] If this is done, the result is precisely the weighted full employment deficit.

We do not find any reason to prefer a budget concept, like the weighted FES, to a fiscal impact measure, like fiscal leverage at full employment. The alleged virtue of budget measures is their independence of any particular model. This is true of the FES (apart from the need to estimate tax revenues at full employment). However, once weights are introduced, one is forced to use estimated expenditure coefficients from some econometric model. In fact, things are even more complicated. In addition to choosing a model, one must choose a time horizon, since impact multipliers differ from second-quarter multipliers and so on. And this problem arises whether interest centers on multipliers (as in a fiscal impact measure) or only on ratios of multipliers (as in a budget measure). The superiority of a budget measure is thus hard to argue since it makes only trivially less demand on the available knowledge of the economic structure.

Gramlich's work makes it abundantly clear that $W$, a budget measure, is indeed sensitive to the model chosen for its estimation. He compares time series for $W$, which he constructs using six different econometric models, with the unweighted FES as calculated by Keith Carlson.[34] The Okun model aside—it does not purport to be a full-fledged econometric model anyway[35]—all models generate weighted FES series (using long-run expenditure coefficients) that are radically different from the unweighted FES. Unfortunately, the models appear to be far from agreement among themselves. For example, for 1964:1, the estimates of $W$ (in constant 1958 dollars) range from $12.6 billion to $31.0 billion.[36] These differences are not quite so large as they look. Because all the multipliers are local, they apply only to small changes in exogenous variables. If only first differences of $W$, instead of levels, are estimated, the models agree much more closely; for 1964:1, estimated changes in the weighted FES range from $1.1 billion to $3.0 billion.[37] Secondly, if the focus is on first-quarter rather than steady-

[33] Ibid., p. 216.

[34] K. Carlson, "Estimates of the High-Employment Budget: 1947–1967," Federal Reserve Bank of St. Louis, *Review,* Vol. 49 (June 1967), pp. 6–14.

[35] This model is contained in Arthur M. Okun, "Measuring the Impact of the 1964 Tax Reduction," in Walter W. Heller (ed.), *Perspectives on Economic Growth* (Random House, 1968).

[36] Gramlich, "Measures of the Aggregate Demand Impact," Table 2, p. 125.

[37] Ibid., Table 3, p. 126.

state weights, even the levels are not that far apart. Again for 1964:1, the range is from $40.1 billion to $50.5 billion.[38] If these two adjustments are combined—that is, first differences in $W$ are calculated from first-quarter weights—it is difficult to find any divergences among the models as large as $1 billion.[39] Of course, even that amount may be a nontrivial difference for some purposes.

## The Weighted Standardized Surplus

Even the weighted full employment surplus fails to deal with one of the difficulties with the FES that we outlined earlier: if income is far from the full employment level, the FES (and also $W$) may be misleading. We show in the appendix that the correct measure of discretionary fiscal policy in our rock-bottom model is

(6) $$\Delta F = \frac{\Delta G - c\, T_\tau \Delta\tau}{1 - c(1 - T_Y)},$$

where $T_\tau(Y, \tau)$, $T_Y(Y, \tau)$, and $c$ are all evaluated *at the initial levels of* $Y$ *and* $\tau$.

The denominator of this expression is simply the reciprocal of the multiplier. We may call the numerator the change in the "weighted standardized surplus." It is computed by deducting from the change in government purchases of goods and services the product of the marginal propensity to consume and the change in tax receipts attributable to changes in the tax code. The measure generalizes in an obvious way to accommodate a model of arbitrary complexity. It is only necessary to multiply the change in each fiscal instrument by the ratio of its own multiplier to the basic expenditure multiplier, and sum the multiplied products. This has, in fact, been done in two recent studies. In a volume prepared for the Organisation for Economic Co-operation and Development, Bent Hansen constructs a conceptual framework similar to that developed here.[40] He uses equation (6) to measure the *discretionary* effect of government stabilization policy, and the obvious measure,

$$\Delta Y - \Delta A/(1 - c),$$

---

[38] Ibid., Table A2, p. 141.

[39] Ibid., Table A3, p. 142.

[40] Bent Hansen, *Fiscal Policy in Seven Countries, 1955–1965* (Paris: Organisation for Economic Co-operation and Development, 1969).

for the *total* effect of government policy. Subtracting the former from the latter gives him a measure of the *automatic* stabilizing effect of the tax structure:

$$AUTO = \frac{c \, T_Y \, \Delta A}{1 - c(1 - T_Y)} = \frac{\Delta A}{1 - c} - \frac{\Delta A}{1 - c(1 - T_Y)}.$$

For empirical purposes, the rock-bottom model is obviously too crude. Hansen uses instead a model that is only slightly more sophisticated in that it (a) allows for two kinds of taxes (direct and indirect), (b) includes an import equation, and (c) allows for two types of government expenditure (goods and labor services).

Given measures of the discretionary and automatic effects of government policies, Hansen can construct hypothetical growth paths for each country in the absence of (a) any discretionary action ($\Delta F = 0$) and (b) the automatic stabilizers ($AUTO = 0$). Having done this, he can measure the percentage of the business cycle that was eliminated by discretionary and automatic fiscal actions. His results are summarized in Table 3. Clearly, the United States has ironed out more cyclical fluctuation than any other country. However, this does not necessarily mean that it has had the best fiscal policy, since for most of the period it was stabilizing the economy at a relatively low level of resource utilization. Also, nearly two-thirds of the accomplishment was due to the automatic stabilizers. Only Germany and the United States can claim any sizable achievements in discre-

**TABLE 3. Percentage of Business Cycle Eliminated by Discretionary and by Automatic Stabilization Policies, Selected Countries, 1955–65**

| Country | Eliminated by discretionary policy | Eliminated by automatic policy | Total percentage eliminated |
|---|---|---|---|
| Belgium | 5 | 16 | 21 |
| France[a] | −35 | 48 | 13 |
| Germany[a] | 14 | 12 | 26 |
| Italy[b] | −17 | 32 | 15 |
| Sweden | 5 | n.a. | n.a. |
| United Kingdom | −10 | −3 | −13 |
| United States | 17 | 32 | 49 |

Source: Bent Hansen, *Fiscal Policy in Seven Countries, 1955–1965* (Paris: Organisation for Economic Co-operation and Development, 1969), Table 2.6, p. 69. The figures pertain to central governments only.
n.a. Not available.
a. 1958–65.
b. 1956–65.

tionary stabilization, and such policies were actually destabilizing in France, Italy, and the United Kingdom. In England, notorious for its "stop-go" economics, even the automatic and total effects were destabilizing.

How adequate is the raw budget deficit as a proxy for the total effect of fiscal policy? While Hansen finds that this assessment varies greatly from one country to the next, for the United States the budget deficit and the *total* (not discretionary) fiscal effect have a remarkably high correlation (0.991), with the constant relating them approximately equal to the multiplier! For no other country is the agreement this good.[41] One wonders if this might be a reflection of the fact that the United States was furthest from a full employment growth path.

In an article that makes many of the points made here, Oakland constructs a rough series of quarterly changes in the weighted standardized surplus (which he calls the weighted initial surplus) from 1947 to 1966, and compares them with changes in the FES.[42] The two series generally give similar *qualitative* pictures of the impact of discretionary fiscal policy, but the *quantitative* divergence is often quite sharp. Some of this is, no doubt, due to the weighting. But the fact that the discrepancies tend to be largest in times of recession suggests that the FES tends to overstate the effect of changes in taxes when the economy is far below full employment. Table 4 compares Gramlich's series on changes in the weighted full employment surplus (based on the MIT-FRB model) with Oakland's series on changes in the weighted standardized surplus. The two columns are obviously not identical. On the other hand, they are positively correlated; in fact, adding $2 billion to $2½ billion to each estimated change in the weighted standardized surplus yields a fairly close approximation to the corresponding estimate of the change in the weighted full employment surplus. It is just barely conceivable that this systematic difference reflects the conceptual difference between the two measures. (Progression should make full employment revenues rise more rapidly than revenues standardized at a level of income below full employment.) But some of the years recorded in the table were themselves

[41] Ibid., pp. 73–81.

[42] William H. Oakland, "Budgetary Measures of Fiscal Performance," *Southern Economic Journal,* Vol. 35 (April 1969), pp. 347–58, especially Table 1. See also Saul H. Hymans and J. Philip Wernette, "The Impact of the Federal Budget on Total Spending," *Business Economics,* Vol. 5 (September 1970), pp. 29–34, where an *unweighted* standardized surplus on an annual basis is considered.

Analytical Foundations of Fiscal Policy

**TABLE 4. Change in Weighted Full Employment Surplus and Weighted Standardized Surplus, Second Quarter 1963 to Fourth Quarter 1966**

(*In billions of dollars*)

| Year and quarter | Change in weighted full employment surplus | Change in weighted standardized surplus | Difference |
|---|---|---|---|
| 1963:2 | 3.5 | 1.3 | 2.2 |
| 3 | 1.0 | −1.8 | 2.8 |
| 4 | −0.6 | −1.0 | 0.4 |
| 1964:1 | −3.0 | −5.2 | 2.2 |
| 2 | −5.1 | −6.2 | 1.1 |
| 3 | 0.6 | 0.6 | 0 |
| 4 | 2.5 | 0.7 | 1.8 |
| 1965:1 | 0.7 | −1.8 | 2.5 |
| 2 | −0.6 | −1.3 | 0.7 |
| 3 | −5.9 | −9.6 | 3.7 |
| 4 | 0.8 | −1.1 | 1.9 |
| 1966:1 | −0.4 | 1.1 | 1.5 |
| 2 | 1.1 | −4.5 | 5.6 |
| 3 | −2.3 | −6.5 | 4.2 |
| 4 | −3.0 | −4.9 | 1.9 |

Sources: For column 1, Edward M. Gramlich, "Measures of the Aggregate Demand Impact of the Federal Budget," in Wilfred Lewis, Jr. (ed.), *Budget Concepts for Economic Analysis* (Brookings Institution, 1968), Table 3, p. 126; column 2, William H. Oakland, "Budgetary Measures of Fiscal Performance," *Southern Economic Journal*, Vol. 35 (April 1969), Table 1, p 356.

not very far from full employment, so that the differences may reflect statistical technique, and not definition. The two largest discrepancies occur in the second and third quarters of 1966, which suggests that they may result from Gramlich's procedure for adjusting for changes in the price level (explained in the next section).

A measure of fiscal influence that in our terminology would be described as the change in the *unweighted* standardized surplus has been advocated by McCracken and by Hymans and Wernette. McCracken's annual time series on "the sum of the increase in outlays and the revenue cost of any changes in tax rates"[43] is given in the first column of Table 5 below. Earlier, Hymans and Wernette had suggested using "the current increase in government expenditures (net of induced changes in stabilizer elements such as unemployment insurance payments) less the increase in tax revenues (measured at current income

[43] Paul W. McCracken, "Moving Toward External and Internal Economic Balance" (paper presented to the Southwestern Economic Association Convention, San Antonio, Texas, March 31, 1972; processed), p. 3.

levels) resulting from any changes in the structure of the tax system."[44] Their time series is given in the second column of the table; it corresponds closely to McCracken's. For purposes of comparison, the last column of the table exhibits changes in the full employment surplus; during years of approximately full employment, the difference between this series and the two others is fiscal drag.

Like the FES, the unweighted standardized surplus does not depend on any particular model of the economy. While this trait is doubtless a virtue, the balanced-budget theorem undermines any fiscal measure that fails to weight appropriately the various components of the budget—that is, changes in an unweighted measure cannot be associated unambiguously with changes in economic activity. Therefore, the best procedure for the government might be to publish separately the main components of the standardized surplus— changes in expenditures, and revenue yields of changes in tax statutes —so that external users could supply their own weights.

## Price Level Problems

The literature on measuring fiscal influence has been developed within the confines of a number of important limitations that have only occasionally been explicitly acknowledged.

First, the price level has been ignored, or, at best, treated as an exogenous variable that moves independently of government policy. Several attempts to account for change in the price level have been made. We shall review them and pursue this question further in this section.[45]

Second, as a much broader problem, monetary effects in general have been omitted from the analysis. Few studies spell out a set of assumptions about monetary policy. Some seem to require that monetary policy be used to stabilize the price level. Virtually all of them also require that monetary policy stabilize interest rates. Unfortunately, it cannot normally do both. In what follows we will develop the monetary side of the question explicitly.

Third, attention has been focused on "income effects"—that is, the

[44] Hymans and Wernette, "Impact of the Federal Budget," pp. 31–32.

[45] In a critique of the FES concept, David J. Smyth correctly objects to the lack of attention to price level changes in studies using the FES. However, we hope to show that he is wrong to despair that "there seems no way out of this price-level dilemma"; p. 296 of "The Full Employment Budget Surplus: Is it a Useful Policy Guide?" *Public Policy*, Vol. 18 (Winter 1970), pp. 289–300.

**TABLE 5. Changes in Unweighted Standardized Surplus and Unweighted Full Employment Surplus, Fiscal Years 1962–73**

(In billions of dollars)

| Fiscal year | Unweighted standardized surplus | | Unweighted full employment surplus |
|---|---|---|---|
| | McCracken | Hymans-Wernette | |
| 1962 | ... | −8.7 | −4.4 |
| 1963 | ... | −5.2 | +4.6 |
| 1964 | ... | −8.6 | −7.2 |
| 1965 | ... | −4.4 | −0.8 |
| 1966 | ... | −17.9 | −4.6 |
| 1967 | ... | −16.9 | −6.9 |
| 1968 | −24.7 | −24.9 | +4.6 |
| 1969 | +11.2 | +8.1 | +18.6 |
| 1970 | −12.4 | −11.4[a] | −5.1 |
| 1971 | −22.2 | −11.7[b] | −2.2 |
| 1972 | −33.4 | ... | −11.4 |
| 1973 | −10.7[b] | ... | +0.2 |

Sources: Column 1, Paul W. McCracken, "Moving Toward External and Internal Economic Balance" (paper presented to the Southwestern Economic Association Convention, San Antonio, Texas, March 31, 1972; processed), p. 4; column 2, Saul H. Hymans and J. Philip Wernette, "The Impact of the Federal Budget on Total Spending," Business Economics, Vol. 5 (September 1970), Table 1, p. 31; column 3, 1962–71, Council of Economic Advisers, unpublished tabulations; 1972–73, from Nancy H. Teeters, "The 1973 Federal Budget " Brookings Papers on Economic Activity (1:1972), Table 3, p. 223.

[a] Estimate
[b] Projection

implications of changes in the level of aggregate demand. "Substitution effects"—that is, the implications of relative price changes that may be caused by fiscal policy—are largely ignored. With the single exception that we will explicitly treat changes in the rate of interest, we shall continue this tradition here. If there is any way to separate the macro aspects of fiscal policy (stabilization policy) from the micro aspects (allocation and distribution policies), this would seem to be it.

Gramlich appears to have been the first to grapple with the implications of inflation for measuring fiscal influence.[46] For reasons explained above, progressive tax laws set in money terms cause real tax receipts to rise with inflation. Conversely, if the government fixes its nominal expenditures, real expenditures will fall with inflation. In the search for a measure of *discretionary* fiscal policy, this pattern calls for some adjustment. For expenditures, the adjustment is easy: increase real government expenditures by the percentage rate of inflation *not* provided for by government policy. For taxes, Gramlich suggests the

[46] Gramlich, "Measures of the Aggregate Demand Impact," pp. 117–19. The remainder of this paragraph is based on these pages.

following procedure: "To calculate pre-inflation real taxes at high employment, post-inflation high employment real taxes are multiplied by the ratio of pre- to post-inflation real taxes."[47] Symbolically, if the tax function is

$$PT = f(PY),$$

and if $P_0$ and $Y_0$ denote the pre-inflation price and output levels while $P_1$ and $Y_1$ denote the corresponding post-inflation quantities, Gramlich's suggestion is to compute

$$\left[\frac{f(P_1Y^*)}{P_1}\right]\left[\frac{\frac{f(P_0Y_0)}{P_0}}{\frac{f(P_1Y_1)}{P_1}}\right].$$

This particular adjustment has no apparent rationale, except in the mythical "crude Keynesian" world where prices never rise when real output is below full employment and output never rises during inflation.[48] In such a world, moreover, the adjustment amounts simply to replacing post-inflation full employment taxes with pre-inflation full employment taxes; that is, if $Y_0 = Y_1 = Y^*$, the preceding expression simplifies to

$$T^* = \frac{f(P_0Y^*)}{P_0}.$$

As Bent Hansen has put it, the appropriate treatment of inflation depends on "whether changes in government prices and wage (salary) rates paid in connection with purchases of goods and services should be considered discretionary or automatic."[49] If the inflation is discretionary, all of its effects on the budget should be called discretionary as well, and no inflation adjustment should be made. By contrast, if the entire inflation comes "from the market," rather than from the government, a full adjustment for inflation is called for. Intermediate cases obviously call for a compromise approach. We will proceed, like Hansen, on the assumption that none of the inflation is discretionary. Hansen's treatment is to lump all of the effects of inflation with the

[47] Ibid., p. 118.

[48] See, for example, the critical comments by Warren L. Smith and Paul J. Taubman which follow Gramlich's paper in Lewis, *Budget Concepts for Economic Analysis,* pp. 129–34 and 134–38, respectively.

[49] Hansen, *Fiscal Policy,* p. 32.

automatic effect—to calculate the discretionary effects based on real quantities alone.[50] As mentioned previously, this procedure tacitly assumes some sort of classical dichotomy in the pricing system. In the absence of such a dichotomy, it is not correct.

The problem of adjusting for inflation can be considered in the context of a simple model. We take our rock-bottom model with a progressive tax function in nominal terms, and add interest-elastic investment demand and a simple monetary sector to obtain the following expressions:

(7)      $Y = C(Y - T) + I(r, Y) + G$      (income identity)

(8)      $T = \dfrac{f(PY, \tau)}{P}$      (tax function)

(9)      $\dfrac{M}{P} = L(r, Y)$      (money demanded = money supplied),

where $I$ is investment, $r$ is the interest rate, $M$ is the nominal money supply, and $L(r, Y)$ is a liquidity preference function. This is essentially the model of the first section with wealth effects omitted.

Substitution of equation (8) into equation (7) leaves two equations in the unknowns $Y, r,$ and $P$. A crude Keynesian might close the model by assuming $P$ to be exogenous; this simple model underlies most measures of fiscal impact. A crude monetarist might close the system by specifying that $Y$ must be at the full employment level, $Y^*$—which would give Patinkin's model.[51] Measuring the fiscal impact on $Y$ is simple here; it is always zero.[52] A more eclectic approach (characteristic both of Keynes and of most modern Keynesians) is to append to this model an aggregate supply equation that relates real income and the price level:

(10)                      $P = P(Y)$      $dP/dY \geq 0$.

Such a function, illustrated in Figure 1, can be rationalized on Keynesian grounds by assuming money wages to be sticky, so that employment can be raised by an inflation that lowers real wages.

[50] Ibid., pp. 28–34, especially equations (14)–(16).

[51] Don Patinkin, *Money, Interest, and Prices: An Integration of Monetary and Value Theory* (2d ed., Harper and Row, 1965).

[52] Milton Friedman has taken a similar approach in discussing the "missing equation" in his "A Theoretical Framework for Monetary Analysis," *Journal of Political Economy*, Vol. 78 (March/April 1970), pp. 193–238.

**FIGURE 1. The Aggregate Supply Schedule, $P = P(Y)$**

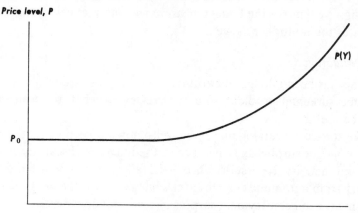

Price level, P

$P_0$

Real income, Y

Equation (10) may be substituted into (7) and (9) to arrive at a rock-bottom model with an endogenous price level:

(11)
$$Y = C\left\{Y - \frac{f[P(Y)Y, \tau]}{P(Y)}\right\} + I(r, Y) + G$$

(12)
$$M = P(Y)L(r, Y).$$

Note that if the tax function were proportional, the $P(Y)$ terms would drop out of equation (11).

In the appendix, the model consisting of equations (11) and (12) is used to show that changes in the *real* weighted standardized surplus remain a valid measure of fiscal policy when the price level is endogenous. In fact, inflation has essentially no effect on any pure budget measure. Its only important effect is on the multiplier that we use to convert budget measures like the weighted standardized surplus into measures of fiscal impact. In the simple model, inflation stabilizes (that is, reduces the multiplier) for two reasons. First, a rising price level lowers the level of real balances corresponding to any given $M$. Second, as long as the nominal tax structure is progressive, inflation raises the real tax yield at every level of real income.

This conclusion does not contradict our previous statement that a budget measure is no simpler to devise than a fiscal impact measure. If the weights for the various discretionary fiscal and monetary policy instruments are to be accurately estimated, the job will have to be done in the context of a fully specified econometric model. Such a model surely will include a monetary sector and equations to generate a price level. Any set of simultaneous-equations estimates used to assign weights for the budget measure will automatically yield estimates of the multiplier as well.

### Recapitulation

This has been a long, and at times involved, discussion of a complex measurement problem, so a brief review of what has been said may be useful.

We started by cataloguing some well-known objections to the ordinary budget surplus as a measure of the impact of fiscal policy on economic activity. Its first drawback—its failure to distinguish discretionary from automatic changes in the budget—is partially alleviated by using the full employment surplus instead; but only partially, since part of the change in the full employment surplus is automatic in a growing economy ("fiscal drag").

A second drawback, common to both the ordinary surplus and the full employment surplus, is the failure to weight the various components of the budget appropriately. Proper weighting requires some explicit or implicit model of the economy to compute, say, a weighted full employment surplus.

But such a measure has one additional failing that did not plague the ordinary deficit: it applies to a hypothetical full employment situation rather than to the actual state of the economy. Some changes in tax laws may have a revenue yield at full employment that is very different from that at actual employment; and, if this is so, the ramifications for aggregate demand will be correspondingly different. The desire to obtain a measure that both separates discretionary from automatic changes in the budget and is relevant to the current state of the economy leads naturally to the standardized surplus: the difference between the revenue yield of discretionary changes in tax and transfer programs and the change in government purchases of goods and services.

Finally, applying the appropriate weights to each component of the budget, as supplied by some model of the economy, leads to the weighted standardized surplus, our preferred measure. This measure, if computed in real terms, automatically adjusts for the effect of inflation on tax revenues in a theoretically reasonable way.

One further point must be made. Scant attention has been paid in this discussion to the practical problems involved in constructing a weighted standardized surplus, or any other measure that depends crucially upon a specific model of the economy. As later sections of this survey make clear, there are many macro models—econometric and otherwise—each giving somewhat different multipliers. Which model shall we use? Further, multipliers always have a time dimension. Should we base our fiscal impact measure on first-quarter multipliers, fourth-quarter multipliers, or what? These important questions obviously cannot be given definitive answers; we raise them merely to underscore the difficulties. Until much more knowledge is accumulated, perhaps the best procedure is to develop a number of different measures by using several models and alternative time horizons.

# Appendix: Mathematical Development of the Model

## The Full Employment Surplus

In the simple model embodied in equation (4) in the text,

$$Y = C[Y - T(Y, \tau)] + A + G,$$

the local multiplier equation is found by differentiating totally and solving for $dY$:

$$(A\text{-}1) \qquad dY = \frac{dA}{1 - C'(1 - T_Y)} + \frac{dG - C'T_\tau(Y, \tau)d\tau}{1 - C'(1 - T_Y)}.$$

This is only a small generalization of the simple multiplier formula for linear models since $C'$ is the marginal propensity to consume and $T_Y$ is the marginal propensity to tax. The second term is the correct fiscal impact measure.

Letting

$$R \equiv T(Y, \tau) - G$$

denote the actual budget surplus, the naive measure of fiscal influence would be

$$dR = T_Y dY + T_\tau d\tau - dG,$$

which is not a valid index of fiscal policy since the first term is endogenous. In any case, it is not possible to write $dY$ as a function of $dR$.

The frequently suggested alternative is the change in the full employment surplus:

$$(A\text{-}2) \qquad d(FES) = T_\tau(Y^*, \tau)d\tau - dG.$$

Comparing this with the last term in (A-1) points up both of the major weaknesses of the FES: it fails to weight the change in taxes by the marginal propensity to consume, and it computes the revenue yield of changes in tax statutes at *potential* GNP instead of at *actual* GNP. Put most succinctly, any changes in $\tau$ and $G$ that satisfy

$$dG = C' \cdot T_\tau(Y, \tau)d\tau$$

will leave $Y$ unchanged by (A-1), but will alter the FES by (A-2). Conversely, any combination of fiscal actions that satisfies

$$dG = T_\tau(Y^*, \tau)d\tau$$

will have no effect on the FES but normally will affect the GNP.

### The Concept of Fiscal Drag

When we allow for the fact that $Y^*$ grows automatically over time, the change in the FES becomes

$$d(FES) = T_\tau(Y^*, \tau)d\tau - dG + T_Y(Y^*, \tau)dY^*.$$

The first two terms duplicate equation (A-2), and the last is fiscal drag on Heller's definition.

As was stated in the text, an alternative definition of fiscal drag (adjusted fiscal drag) is obtained by first computing the discretionary change in full employment taxes needed to maintain full employment. Since $\tau$ would have to be constantly manipulated to satisfy

$$Y^* = C[Y^* - T(Y^*, \tau)] + A + G,$$

the total differentials must satisfy

$$dY^* = C'dY^* - C'T_Y dY^* - C'T_\tau d\tau + dA + dG.$$

The requisite discretionary change is obtained by solving this for $d\tau$:

(A-3)  $$T_\tau d\tau = - \frac{1 - C'(1 - T_Y)}{C'} dY^* + \frac{dA + dG}{C'}.$$

Adjusted fiscal drag is defined as the difference between Heller's definition, $T_Y dY^*$, and the total tax increase that would be needed to preserve full employment:

$$AFD \equiv T_Y dY^* - (T_\tau d\tau + T_Y dY^*),$$

where $T_\tau d\tau$ is as defined in (A-3). In brief, $AFD$ is simply the negative of (A-3).

It is clear from (A-3), then, that AFD will be positive if and only if the increase in potential GNP, $dY^*$, exceeds the increase in capacity that is required to meet the autonomous growth of demand,

$$\frac{dA + dG}{1 - C'(1 - T_Y)}.$$

If these are equal—if aggregate demand and aggregate supply grow equally —there is no fiscal drag on this definition.

When the price level may vary, if we ignore the possibility mentioned in the text that nominal spending $(PG)$ rather than real spending $(G)$ is fixed by Congress, it is natural to compute the real full employment surplus as

$$FES = \frac{f(PY^*, \tau)}{P} - G,$$

where $PT = f(PT, \tau)$ is the tax function in nominal terms. Changes in the FES will therefore be

$$d(FES) = f_1 Y^*(dP/P) - (f/P)(dP/P) + f_1 dY^* + (f_2/P) \, d\tau - dG.$$

In this expression, only the last two terms represent discretionary changes in fiscal policy; the first three are the fiscal drags (by Heller's definition) attributable to inflation and real growth:

$$FD = (f_1 Y^* - T)(dP/P) + f_1 dY^*.$$

This shows that inflation contributes to fiscal drag if and only if $f_1 PY > PT$, that is, only if the tax function is progressive.

In a like manner, we can refine our concept of adjusted fiscal drag to account for the automatic stabilizing effect of inflation. We again wish to manipulate $\tau$ to maintain

$$Y^* = c[Y^* - (1/P)f(Y^* P, \tau)] + A + G \, ;$$

that is,

$$dY^* = C'dY^* - (C'/P)f_1 Y^* dP - (C'/P)f_1 P dY^*$$
$$+ (C'/P^2)f - (C'/P)f_2 d\tau + dA + dG.$$

Or, solving for the required discretionary tax change in real terms:

$$AFD = - \frac{f_2 d\tau}{P} = \frac{1 - C'(1 - f_1)}{C'} dY^* + f_1 PY^* \frac{dP}{P} - \frac{dA + dG}{C'}.$$

The middle term—the product of the marginal propensity to tax, nominal GNP, and the rate of inflation—is the appropriate inflation adjustment mentioned in the text.

*Price Level Problems*

The model presented in the text for dealing with price level problems is as follows:

(A-4) $$Y = C \left\{ Y - \frac{f[P(Y)Y, \tau]}{P(Y)} \right\} + I(r, Y) + G$$

(A-5) $$M = P(Y)L(r, Y),$$

where, it will be recalled, $P = P(Y)$ is the aggregate supply schedule. The total differentials of (A-4)–(A-5) are:

(A-6) $\quad dY = C'\{dY - (f_1/P)[PdY + YP'(Y)dY]$
$\qquad\qquad - (f_2/P)d\tau + (f/P)(P'(Y)/P)dY\} + I_r dr + I_Y dY + dG$

(A-7) $\quad dM = P L_r dr + P L_Y dY + (M/P)P'(Y)dY.$

Solving (A-7) for $dr$, substituting the result into (A-6), and simplifying, we arrive at the following expression for the change in national income:

(A-8) $$dY = \frac{dG - \dfrac{C'}{P}f_2 d\tau + \dfrac{I_r}{L_r}\dfrac{dM}{P}}{\Delta},$$

where

$$\Delta \equiv 1 - C'(1 - f_1) + \frac{I_r L_Y}{L_r} + \frac{P'(Y)}{P}\left(C'f_1 Y - C'T + \frac{I_r}{L_r}\frac{M}{P}\right).$$

Consider first the numerator of (A-8). The first two terms are contributed by discretionary fiscal policy; they are simply the change in the real weighted standardized deficit. The third term is the effect of monetary policy. The numerator is unaffected by inflation, and therefore all budget measures are unaffected. In the denominator the first three terms constitute the reciprocal of the ordinary multiplier of the *IS-LM* model. The last term, which disappears in the crude Keynesian case, represents the automatic stabilizing effects brought about by inflation. Examining this term more closely, we note that $P'(Y) = dP/dY$, so that it may be written:

$$\frac{1}{P}\left(\frac{dP}{dY}\right)\left(C'f_1 Y - C'T + \frac{I_r}{L_r}\frac{M}{P}\right).$$

Inflation, as stated in the text, stabilizes in two ways. First, it reduces the volume of real money balances. Second, as long as the money tax structure is progressive—that is, as long as $f_1 Y > T$—it further increases the denominator, or, in other words, is stabilizing. Note that with a proportional tax function, this last effect would be absent.

## Stable Budget Proposals

The essence of modern fiscal stabilization policy is the idea that the government, by judicious manipulation of its budget, can and should offset fluctuations in private demand. This survey, for example, is predicated on such a belief. There is, however, an opposing tradition with a much longer history—the belief that the government's budgetary accounts ought to be "balanced" in some relevant sense. Writings in this tradition have run the gamut from naive diatribes about the evils of deficit spending to the more sophisticated work of the Committee for Economic Development and sometimes the Council of Economic Advisers. The common thread running through them all is that stability in the government sector is in some sense desirable per se.

At the crudest level, the desire for a steady government policy translates into a plea for an annually balanced budget. In the "bad old days," such a rule was considered a fundamental precept of sound government finance; and history records many instances of fiscal policies tailored to this notion that appear incredibly perverse from a modern viewpoint. While belief in annually balanced budgets has essentially disappeared from serious economic analysis, the idea that government deficits (but, for some reason, not surpluses) are somehow "wrong" clearly lingers in the minds of many politicians. Officials of both parties, who presumably know better, are often constrained to cater to the common shibboleths.[53]

A variation on the theme, which had an exceptionally brief life span, is the so-called "Swedish budget policy" of balancing the government accounts over the course of the business cycle rather than every year. By some more or less automatic rule, surpluses in boom years would be precisely offset by the deficits acquired in slack periods. While this concept of budget balancing had considerable appeal (perhaps as a tactical matter) in the immediate post-Keynesian years, when the balanced-budget ideology was still influential, it is almost never discussed nowadays.

A less rigid stable budget policy originated by the Committee for Economic Development apparently still influences public policy.[54] The CED suggested that an appropriate way to maintain fiscal "discipline" without destabilizing the economy would be to determine the level of government spending on its own merits, independent of the requirements of stabilization policy, and set tax rates so as to produce a balance (or a small surplus) at full employment. Apparently, the

[53] See, for example, "Statement by Secretary Connally, February 16, 1972, before the Joint Economic Committee," in *Annual Report of the Secretary of the Treasury on the State of the Finances for the Fiscal Year Ended June 30, 1972,* p. 237.

[54] Committee for Economic Development, *Taxes and the Budget: A Program for Prosperity in a Free Economy* (New York: CED, 1947).

CED had confidence that the level of private investment would gravitate naturally toward the level of private saving out of full employment income. Since a similar budget policy has been advocated by the Nixon administration (see below), its rationale is of more than historical interest.[55]

In the first place, one of the selling points of such a policy is presumably that it replaces the "rule of men" with a "rule of law"—that is, it replaces discretionary fiscal policy manipulations by more or less automatic responses. But, as Paul Samuelson pointed out long ago, this dichotomy of the discretionary versus the automatic is not rigorously defensible since any automatic mechanism "is set up by discretion, is abandoned by discretion, and is interfered with by discretion."[56] If Congress can make a rule, Congress can break it. And it is hard to imagine any rule so binding that it would prevent Congress from asking, on each occasion, whether it would not be better to violate the rule than to abide by it.

A second presumed virtue of the CED plan is that it would neutralize the influence of the government in an economy at full employment. However, as our discussion of fiscal influence in the preceding section makes clear, a full employment surplus of zero is *not* equivalent to the absence of fiscal influence. The balanced-budget theorem gives an a priori presumption that a balanced budget injects more into the spending stream (in terms of ultimate multiplier effects) than it takes out. As Heller stated: "Neutrality would require attaching a multiplier to each category of taxes and expenditures and then balancing the two sums of the multiplied products."[57] In our terminology, a policy that is neutral *at the margin* is one with an unchanged weighted standardized surplus. No such pat formula is available to define *global* neutrality. However, in terms of our rock-bottom model of income determination, there is in principle a level of government spending, $G^*$, and a set of tax parameters, $\tau^*$, such that

$$C[Y - T(Y, \tau^*)] + I(Y) + G^* = C(Y) + I(Y)$$

[55] Many of the points in the following paragraphs were made in Walter H. Heller, "CED's Stabilizing Budget Policy After Ten Years," *American Economic Review*, Vol. 47 (September 1957), pp. 634–51.

[56] Paul A. Samuelson, "Principles and Rules in Modern Fiscal Policy: A Neo-Classical Reformulation," in *Money, Trade, and Economic Growth: In Honor of John Henry Williams* (Macmillan, 1951), p. 164.

[57] "CED's Stabilizing Budget Policy," p. 638.

for any desired income level, $Y$. (Here $C$ is real spending, $T$ is real tax receipts, and $I$ is real investment.) That is, there is a budget such that the GNP with government is precisely the same as it would have been in the absence of government. Of course, the budget need not be balanced when it is neutral. In fact, the presumption is that a neutral budget would be in surplus since the balanced-budget theorem says that a balanced-budget change from a no-government situation ought to be expansionary. Moreover, one may well question the desirability of a neutral policy. Only if private saving out of full employment income would be equal to the amount firms wished to invest at this level of income does such a policy have any claim to optimality. Nor is it clear that the situation with no government at all is a sensible point of reference in the modern world.

In fact, a still deeper question is whether a balanced full employment budget is optimal even under these most favorable circumstances. From a social welfare point of view, the full employment surplus should be zero only if the aggregate of private saving at full employment could be relied upon as a guide to the socially desirable amount of saving. Then the government should refrain from altering the pool of saving, and use other means—including differential taxes and subsidies—to tailor the sum of private and public investment to this level. However, the literature points out several reasons to doubt the premise that private saving is by itself a correct index of optimal social saving: private risks and social risks may differ; perhaps society "ought to" discount the future less heavily than mortal individuals do; investment decisions of some firms may reflect managers' desires for grandeur or the distorting treatment of capital gains taxation rather than the true preferences of stockholders for current consumption.[58] Nor are government officials free of the desire for grandeur. It

[58] See for example, Stephen A. Marglin, "The Social Rate of Discount and the Optimal Rate of Investment," *Quarterly Journal of Economics,* Vol. 77 (February 1963), pp. 95–111; Robert C. Lind, "The Social Rate of Discount and the Optimal Rate of Investment: Further Comment," ibid., Vol. 78 (May 1964), pp. 336–45; Marglin, "The Opportunity Costs of Public Investment," ibid. (May 1963), pp. 274–89; Peter Diamond, "The Opportunity Costs of Public Investment: Comment," ibid., Vol. 82 (November 1968), pp. 682–88; Amartya K. Sen, "Isolation, Assurance and the Social Rate of Discount," ibid., Vol. 81 (February 1967), pp. 112–24, as well as much of the huge and ever-growing literature on the appropriate discount rate for cost-benefit analysis. See also James Tobin, "Economic Growth as an Objective of Government Policy," in American Economic Association, *Papers and Proceedings of the Seventy-sixth Annual Meeting, 1963 (American Economic Review,* Vol. 54, May 1964), pp. 1–20.

is impossible to form a precise judgment on these matters; but they at least cast doubt on glib assertions that the government ought to contribute exactly zero to the full employment saving pool.

Still another reason for holding to some sort of a balanced-budget rule is the fear that only a felt discipline from the tax side can deter legislatures from irresponsible expenditure explosions. It is possible to oppose an anti-inflationary tax increase on the ground that any tax increase will soon be followed by increased expenditures; and this will not only increase the size of the public sector, but nullify the anti-inflationary effect of the new taxes as well. This particular piece of litmus paper tests a complicated mixture of political convictions and economic principles. Clearly some truth resides in the underlying proposition; it drives home the idea that a sensible stabilization policy is not easy to carry out, whether automatic or discretionary.

Even the appealing notion that government spending ought to be set "optimally" (according, say, to the criteria set forth in the Steiner essay in this volume), and held there independently of the vagaries of the business cycle, will not stand up under rigorous examination. Suppose, for example, that a reduced willingness to invest on the part of private industry leads to a period of slack. Such a shift in the investment schedule will presumably imply a lower desired level of investment even at full employment. But such a reduction in desired investment represents both a genuine change in the relative valuation of various goods and a release of resources. Exactly the same thing can be said about a sudden drop in private consumption, or defense spending, or the balance of trade. Whenever resources are released by such an autonomous change, a rational society presumably will allocate some of them to private needs and some of them to public needs. It is unlikely that the marginal benefit from public-sector goods falls precipitously to zero at just the present level of provision. Thus the logic of choice and scarcity destroys the dogma that fiscal stabilization should restrict itself to the tax side of the ledger.[59]

In view of all this, the more eclectic position reached by the CED in its most recent statement on stabilization policy is worth summarizing.[60] Gone is the insistence that monetary policy, rather than fiscal

[59] This point was made long ago by Samuelson, "Principles and Rules," pp. 158–60.

[60] *Fiscal and Monetary Policies for Steady Economic Growth,* A Statement on National Policy by the Research and Policy Committee of the Committee for Economic Development (CED, 1969).

policy, should bear most of the stabilization burden. Instead, "Fiscal policy should be more responsive to the stabilization requirements of the economy" (pp. 17–18). Also gone is the belief in a mechanistic fiscal policy. While the CED still believes that long-run fiscal planning ought to "yield approximate balance in the over-all budget when the economy is at a high level of employment and experiencing stable prices" (p. 18), it finds that at other times "the government should offer appropriate stimulus or restraint to the economy" (p. 19). Further, and most significantly, "Taxes and expenditures cannot be left unattended and unadjusted for long periods of time. Annual review of the level of taxes and expenditures and the balance in the budget is necessary to achieve our economic objectives" (p. 19). Thus the CED also drops the principle that government expenditures should not be subject to manipulation by the stabilization authorities.[61]

This is hardly a rigid budget policy; indeed, it is hardly a policy at all. Its instructions are more or less the same as those that would be given by a fervent believer in "functional finance." About the only thing that remains of the CED's 1947 position is the belief that a full employment surplus of zero is "right" for the long haul. The CED gives only the vaguest justification for this rule: "We see no reason to believe that there will be a persistent need for government deficits to assure high employment and rapid growth. . . . Nor do we see any reasons why the government must persistently run surpluses so that the economy will be saving enough to finance the rates of growth deemed desirable" (p. 47 of the 1969 statement). It is hard to quarrel with such a position, especially if it is admitted as a corollary that *if* private saving and private investment *do not* equalize at full employment, the government should do something about it. If investment is chronically too high (despite Federal Reserve policy and everything else), then the full employment budget should run a surplus to combat inflation. Conversely, chronically low investment will imply a full employment deficit as a necessary means to achieve full employment. To say that there is nothing *in principle* to dictate a full employment surplus or deficit at any given time is one thing. To say that a long-run policy of

[61] One serious error in the CED's program remains, however—the claim that "with our current state of knowledge the best measure of the government's net effect on demand is the balance, surplus or deficit, in the over-all or 'unified' budget" (p. 51). More appropriate would be the budget in the national income accounts. See Lewis, *Budget Concepts for Economic Analysis.*

full employment balance is thus called for is quite another (and an erroneous) thing.

A stable budget policy resembling the CED program has recently been advocated by Herbert Stein,[62] the Council of Economic Advisers as a whole,[63] and the President himself. In his 1971 *Economic Report*, President Richard M. Nixon wrote that

. . . we need to abide by a principle of budget policy which permits flexibility in the budget and yet limits the inevitable tendency to wasteful and inflationary action. The useful and realistic principle of the full employment budget is that, except in emergencies, *expenditures should not exceed the revenues that the tax system would yield when the economy is operating at full employment.*[64]

Here is an expression of the principle that the full employment surplus should be no less than zero. In fact, as Eisner pointed out in his review of the council's report, the administration is prepared to diverge quite far from a balanced full employment budget—the full employment budget for calendar year 1970 was some $6.7 billion in surplus.[65] Apparently, the revealed preference of the administration is for balance in the full employment budget, except when imbalance is called for.

As Eisner notes, "One cannot avoid the suspicion that the question of fiscal discipline . . . seems to reflect certain ideological preferences as much as general economic principles."[66] What is the ideology behind such a stable-budget proposal? At the very least, it seems to make absence of change itself into a virtue of fiscal policy. In theory only a very flimsy economic case can be made for stability in the budget, on the grounds that an easily predictable environment is good for business. Perhaps a more significant case can be built on a "Pandora's Box" argument: if things are already pretty good, best leave them alone because intelligent policy can improve things only slightly, while an error can have grave consequences. Of course, this

[62] "The Rehabilitation of Fiscal Policy" (speech delivered to the National Association of Mutual Savings Banks, Minneapolis, May 26, 1969; processed).

[63] In each of its *Annual Reports* since 1970. See *Economic Report,* various years.

[64] *Economic Report, 1971,* p. 6; italics from original.

[65] Robert Eisner, "The 1971 Report of the President's Council of Economic Advisers: Inflation and Recession," *American Economic Review,* Vol. 61 (September 1971), p. 524.

[66] Ibid.

argument cuts both ways. When the economy is very far from full employment, there is much to be gained by enlightened application of the principles of compensatory finance.

But even if stability in the budget has something to recommend it, stability in the economy is surely better. The whole point of discretionary fiscal policy is the stabilization of economic activity at a satisfactory level in the face of fluctuations in private demand. If these fluctuations are small, then—and only then—can the budgetary response be small.

In practice, the policy advocated by Herbert Stein and President Nixon probably translates into a preference for slightly less activism— for less "fine tuning," if you will. However, as Arthur Okun has observed, maintaining a passive stance in the total budget is not a recipe for the quiet life; nor does it abrogate the need for discretionary fiscal policy.[67] Major destabilizing impulses often arise from within the budget—from, say, defense spending or the social security system— for reasons wholly unconnected with stabilization policy. To offset them may require prompt and strong discretionary actions. Once this is admitted, there is a still deeper point. What is the logic in the principle that instructs the stabilization authorities deliberately to offset autonomous changes in federal spending, but to make no attempt to neutralize autonomous changes in private spending?

As a variation on the stable-budget theme, a variety of proposals for "formula flexibility" have appeared from time to time in the academic literature, but apparently have never been found attractive by congressmen or Presidents.[68] Essentially, a formula flexibility plan is nothing more than a complicated rule that would supplant discretionary fiscal (or monetary) policy. For example, Congress could legislate that a temporary $A$ percent income tax surcharge would automatically be activated whenever the rate of inflation exceeded $B$ percent, and that a temporary $C$ percent tax reduction would take effect

[67] Arthur M. Okun, *The Political Economy of Prosperity* (Brookings Institution, 1970), pp. 113–14.

[68] Among the most recent studies of formula flexibility is Howard Pack, "Formula Flexibility: A Quantitative Appraisal," in Albert Ando, E. Cary Brown, and Ann F. Friedlaender (eds.), *Studies in Economic Stabilization* (Brookings Institution, 1968), pp. 5–40. Pack employs the well-known framework of A. W. Phillips for control systems to generate a variety of formulas, and simulates their effects; but he does not advocate the adoption of any such formula by the authorities.

whenever the unemployment rate rose above $D$ percent. Specify $A$, $B$, $C$, and $D$, and you have a formula for a fully automatic fiscal policy. Such a formula would probably be far less rigid than, say, the CED's stabilizing budget program. Potentially, it is also more potent as a stabilizer. However, the case for any automatic policy is, presumably, that no one knows enough to design a very helpful discretionary policy. If knowledge of the macroeconomy were really this meager, it is hard to imagine how one might go about designing a workable formula. Conversely, if knowledge is good enough to devise a successful rule, it should also be good enough to conduct an effective discretionary policy. The case for automaticity would appear, then, to be primarily political: having a fixed formula insulates macro policy from the vagaries of partisan politics. While this kind of protection has some attractive features, it is not clear that formula flexibility would accomplish it. The objections lodged above to the dichotomy between discretionary and automatic policy should be recalled here: Who makes the rule? Who decides when to abide by it and when to countermand it? Furthermore, within the framework of a political democracy, the case for taking stabilization policy out of the hands of elected politicians is an uneasy one: into whose hands shall it be placed?

Finally, before leaving this topic, we pause to ask: would a policy of "benign neglect" of the domestic economy have done better than discretionary intervention in recent years? Otto Eckstein's judgment on this is that ". . . the record of the 1960's seems to repeat the verdict of the 1950's. Discretionary policy did harm as well as good. The automatic policy developed by the Committee for Economic Development in 1947 . . . would have done better."[69] This comment by a former "fine tuner" echoes Dow's appraisal of British fiscal policy.[70] But, as Eckstein realizes, the failures of fiscal policy in the 1960s have not been primarily failures in diagnosis and prescription, nor even in forecasting, although the forecasts occasionally were far off the mark. The failures have been largely political, the most notable example being the absence of a tax increase in face of the inflationary pressure

---

[69] Otto Eckstein, "The 1961–1969 Expansion: Programs and Policies," in *American Statistical Association, Proceedings of the Business and Economic Statistics Section* (1969), pp. 327, 329.

[70] J. C. R. Dow, *The Management of the British Economy, 1945–60* (Cambridge University Press, 1964), p. 384.

that accompanied the Vietnam buildup. If the nation had had a political process capable of steadfastly executing the CED policy throughout the 1960s it would also have been capable of improving upon it.

We conclude from this brief review that no budgetary rule can be provided with a solid intellectual foundation. This will hardly be news to economists. The best that can be said for rules is that some of them may be better than incompetently managed discretionary policy if that is the only kind of discretionary policy the nation can get. But, as the previous paragraphs suggest, the institutions that produce perverse discretionary policy might equally well produce perverse rules, and follow them only spasmodically. Moreover, this argument for rules is not an argument of principle or theory at all. It is merely a judgment on the quality of actual discretionary policy.

Occasionally, proposals have been put forth to give the President authority to invoke at his own discretion a proportional surcharge or rebate on personal and corporate income taxes. In most such schemes, the size of the discretionary surcharge or rebate is limited to, say, 5 percent; the President or the Council of Economic Advisers is required to report annually to the Congress the reasons for the current rate of surcharge (even if it is zero); and the Congress has a right of veto. The intent is to give the administration the responsibility and the authority to conduct a limited discretionary stabilization policy and, at the same time, to give Congress a way to monitor discretionary actions, and to judge the consistency of tax and expenditure levels. The hope is to strike a balance between activism and passivity. No such proposal has ever seemed close to enactment.

## Monetary Factors and the Government Budget Constraint*

Thus far in our discussion of the mechanics of fiscal policy we have paid scant attention to monetary aspects. The monetary system influences the workings of fiscal stabilization policy at two distinct levels. The first is familiar even to beginning students in economics. In the simple, static *IS-LM* model with the real stocks of outside money, $M/P$, and interest-bearing government debt, $B/P$, treated as fixed in

---

* This section draws heavily on A. S. Blinder and R. M. Solow, "Does Fiscal Policy Matter?" *Journal of Public Economics*, Vol. 2 (November 1973), pp. 318–37.

**FIGURE 2. Effect of Fiscal Policy Actions on *IS-LM* Curves**

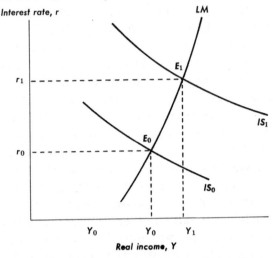

the short run,[71] any alteration in fiscal policy will run into a monetary counterforce. For example, as an increase in real government expenditures raises aggregate demand and therefore real output, it simultaneously stimulates the demand for real money balances. Therefore, since we have postulated no accommodating increase in the supply of money, upward pressure on interest rates will result. Expenditures that are interest elastic—which may include some spending by state and local governments, as well as private spending on consumer durables, residential construction, and plant and equipment—will be reduced, partially offsetting the expansionary effect of the original increase in public spending. Similarly, a deflationary fiscal policy will set off a symmetrical counterforce by lowering interest rates. As long as there are interest-elastic expenditures, the story that has no role for monetary forces systematically overstates the net effect of fiscal policy —which is to say, overestimates the multiplier.

The usual diagram for this model shows an upward-sloping *LM* curve (or liquidity preference function or velocity function) and a downward sloping *IS* curve. Discretionary increases in government spending or decreases in taxes shift the *IS* curve to the right, leading in a stable system to a new equilibrium with higher real income and interest rates (see point $E_1$ in Figure 2). If the interest rate were con-

[71] Which is not quite legitimate since changes in interest rates will induce changes in the value of the interest-bearing debt.

stant—that is, if the *LM* curve were horizontal at $r_0$—the new equilibrium income would be higher than it actually is.

All this is perfectly standard. Yet recent discussions of the "crowding out" of private expenditures by fiscal policy actions seem to amount to no more than this, coupled with a reminder that government expenditures must be financed either by taxation or by an increase in the government's monetary or nonmonetary debt.[72] (More on this later.) Everyone who has either taught or been taught the *IS-LM* apparatus knows that the multiplier is reduced from its naive value by the presence of an upward-sloping *LM* curve. To speak weightily of "crowding out" is thus mainly to assert that the *LM* curve is, if not vertical, then very steep—or, in this context, that government bonds (whatever their maturity) are very poor substitutes for money in private portfolios.[73]

These "monetary snubbing" effects will be strengthened if prices rise when real demand increases, for at least four reasons:

1. With higher prices, the real value of an unchanged nominal money stock is lower. This shifts the *LM* curve to the left, just as if the nominal money stock had declined.

2. The higher price level means a lower real value for the government debt held by the private sector, $M/P + B/P$. Any influence of wealth on consumption (or on investment, for that matter) will lower the *IS* curve.

3. Under a progressive tax system legislated in money terms, real tax receipts will rise at each level of real income, again lowering the *IS* curve.

4. In an open economy, a rising price level will depress exports and induce more imports, thus shifting the *IS* curve down.

Each of these price effects serves to reduce the size of the fiscal policy multiplier; however, none of them affects the *sign*. With this in mind, we shall proceed to ignore price level effects in the remainder of this section.

But this is not the end of the story, unless we suppose that the gov-

---

[72] See, for example, Roger W. Spencer and William P. Yohe, "The 'Crowding Out' of Private Expenditures by Fiscal Policy Actions," *Federal Reserve Bank of St. Louis, Review,* Vol. 52 (October 1970), pp. 12–24.

[73] We omit any discussion of the extent to which private wealth holders discount the future tax liabilities implied by interest-bearing government debt. That is a separate consideration, with its own literature.

ernment budget is always balanced—a supposition neither empirically accurate nor theoretically desirable. As long as there is a deficit or a surplus, the total indebtedness of the government must be increasing or decreasing; and this necessity implies the second level of monetary influence. Either the stock of high-powered money or the volume of interest-bearing debt, or both, must change; and such changes will affect the level of macroeconomic activity.

## Long-run Equilibrium with a Government Budget Constraint

As Christ and others have pointed out, whenever the government budget is not in balance the treasury and the central bank must decide how to allocate each deficit (or surplus) between the issuance (or retirement) of government bonds and increases (or decreases) in the stock of outside money.[74]

The choice falls beyond the realm of fiscal policy as we have defined it in this essay, but allocate it they must. This simple observation leads to an odd result, which has been noticed by several writers but, to our knowledge, has yet to find its way into the conventional wisdom.

Consider first the government budget restraint as it appears in the work of most authors:[75]

(13) $$dM/dt + dB/dt = P[G - T(Y)],$$

where $M$ is the nominal stock of outside money; $B$ is the nominal stock of interest-bearing debt; $P$ is the price level; $G$ is real government purchases; $T$, real tax receipts, is a function of real income, $Y$,

[74] See Carl A. Christ, "A Short-Run Aggregate-Demand Model of the Interdependence and Effects of Monetary and Fiscal Policies with Keynesian and Classical Interest Elasticities," in American Economic Association, *Papers and Proceedings of the Seventy-ninth Annual Meeting, 1966* (*American Economic Review,* Vol. 57, May 1967), pp. 434–43, or his "A Simple Macroeconomic Model with a Government Budget Restraint," *Journal of Political Economy,* Vol. 76 (January/February 1968), pp. 53–67.

[75] In addition to the above-cited papers by Christ, see William L. Silber, "Fiscal Policy in IS-LM Analysis: A Correction," *Journal of Money, Credit and Banking,* Vol. 2 (November 1970), pp. 461–72; Franco Modigliani, "Monetary Policy and Consumption: Linkages via Interest Rates and Wealth Effects in the FMP Model," in *Consumer Spending and Monetary Policy: The Linkages,* Proceedings of a Monetary Conference, 1971, Monetary Conference Series, 5 (Federal Reserve Bank of Boston, 1971), especially pp. 25–33; David J. Ott and Attiat F. Ott, "Budget Balance and Equilibrium Income," *Journal of Finance,* Vol. 20 (March 1965), pp. 71–77; and William H. Branson, "Macroeconomic Equilibrium with Portfolio Balance in Economies Open to Trade" (Princeton University, March 1973; revision in process, 1974).

and *t* is time. As we have just suggested, the condition for full long-run equilibrium is that $dM/dt = dB/dt = 0$, which implies that the budget will be balanced: $G = T(Y)$. If there are no discretionary changes in tax rates, the ultimate multiplier for an increase in government spending, whether financed by money or by bonds, follows from this equation alone, irrespective of the rest of the model:

(14) $$dY/dG = 1/T'(Y);$$

that is, in a stable system,[76] the long-run government expenditure multiplier is simply the reciprocal of the marginal propensity to tax. This happens because we have defined "equilibrium" to be a situation with a balanced budget.[77] Naturally, then, if such an equilibrium is disturbed by a maintained increase in public spending, the only possible new equilibrium is at an income level sufficient to generate enough tax revenue to balance the budget.

This, however, is a long-run proposition. Equilibrium requires constant stocks of money and bonds only in the same sense that it requires a constant stock of real capital (zero net investment). If short-run macroeconomic theory is to be developed by treating the stock of real capital as essentially constant even in the presence of positive net investment, it is at least consistent to neglect changes in the stock of real government debt even though the budget is moderately unbalanced. We are certainly not recommending equation (14) for the government spending multiplier in quarterly or annual models of fiscal policy. How seriously one takes this point depends on how rapidly the stocks change and how important one believes wealth effects to be. We emphasize the matter here because it now appears to be a central point in the monetarist critique of fiscal policy.

When we correct an oversight committed by almost all previous users of the government budget constraint,[78] a still more odd result emerges. The error has been to ignore the fact that interest payments

[76] This qualification is a deep one, which will occupy our attention in most of the remainder of this section.

[77] This definition is appropriate to a static model of the type being considered here. If we were to carry out a similar analysis for an exponentially growing economy, it would be more natural to define fiscal equilibrium as a situation in which $M/P$ and $B/P$ (and the stock of real capital) were growing at the same rate as $Y$.

[78] Exceptions are S. Murray, "Financing the Government Budget Deficit," *Journal of Money, Credit and Banking,* forthcoming; and Blinder and Solow, "Does Fiscal Policy Matter?"

on outstanding government bonds are another expenditure item in the budgetary accounts.[79] The simplest way to correct this omission is to assume that all bonds are perpetuities paying $1 per year: thus total interest charges will simply be $B$ (with $B$ denoting the *number* of bonds) and the market value of the interest-bearing debt will be $B/r$, where $r$ is the interest rate. The proper government budget constraint, therefore, is

(15) $\quad (dM/dt) + (1/r)(dB/dt) = P[G + B - T(Y + B)]$,

where interest payments are assumed to be taxable. We have included on the left-hand side only the change in the number of bonds, evaluated at the current market price, not the change in the market value of bonds outstanding, $d(B/r)/dt$.

As before, long-run equilibrium is obtained only when $dM/dt = dB/dt = 0$, that is, when the budget is balanced: $G = T(Y + B) - B$. From this condition, the steady-state fiscal multiplier follows immediately:

$$(16) \qquad \frac{dY}{dG} = \frac{1 + (1 - T')\dfrac{dB}{dG}}{T'}.$$

Again, this expression is independent of the other behavioral relations of the model, but now depends on the manner in which deficits are financed. Under a policy of strict monetary financing ($dB/dG = 0$), equation (16) reduces to equation (14), the conventional result. But the issuance of new bonds ($dB/dG > 0$) means a *greater* multiplier in the long run. This surprising result contrasts sharply with the short-run implication of Keynesian models (as summarized, say, in Figure 2) that deficit spending is more potent if accompanied by money creation. These notions are not contradictory, but to reconcile them requires delving into the long-run dynamics of a system with a government budget constraint.

### Dynamic Adjustments under Monetary Finance

We begin by tracing out the ramifications of the government budget constraint in our rock-bottom model when all deficits are fi-

---

[79] Alternatively, they can be treated as a transfer payment (negative tax), but then the interest rate must appear as an argument of $T(\cdot)$.

nanced by printing money. For expositional purposes, we simplify the model of the first section by assuming that only total wealth, and not its composition, matters for consumer spending and the demand for money, and that the price level does not change.[80] The model, then, is

(17) $\quad Y = C[Y + B - T(Y + B), M + B/r + K] + I(Y, r, K) + G$

(18) $\quad M = L(Y, r, M + B/r + K),$

where $C$ is real consumer spending, $I$ is investment, $L(\cdot)$ is the demand-for-money function, and $K$ is the (fixed) capital stock.[81] As indicated in Figure 2, for any given values of $M$, $B$, and $G$, these $IS$ and $LM$ equations will imply certain short-run equilibrium values for national income and the interest rate. However, the government budget constraint, which is now simply

$$dM/dt = G + \bar{B} - T(Y + \bar{B}),$$

points up that not every short-run $IS$-$LM$ equilibrium satisfies the long-run equilibrium condition, $dM/dt = 0$. Specifically, in the situation depicted in Figure 2, after an initial upsurge in government spending the budget will normally be in the red. More outside money will have to be issued, and this will shift the $LM$ curve outward (to $LM_2$ in Figure 3) unless the marginal propensity to demand money out of wealth exceeds unity. At the same time, the $IS$ curve will rise due to wealth effects on consumption. The new equilibrium is at $E_2$ in Figure 3. If the budget is still not balanced, a further injection of new money will be required, and the process repeats.

A steady state will be reached ultimately, with $dT = T'(Y)dY = dG$. Evidently the system is stable under monetary financing of defi-

---

[80] We have already outlined the implications of price level changes. They serve only to reduce the multiplier.

[81] Keynesian models are a bit schizophrenic in their treatment of asset stocks in the long and short run. Typically, in short-run analysis the stocks of money and bonds may change but the capital stock is fixed, while in long-run analysis all stocks may vary. It seems more consistent to define the short run as a period too short for any stock to adjust; but this would define away the possibility of monetary policy in the short run. The rationale for the conventional way of doing things is, presumably, that the stock of real capital can hardly change by more than a few percent a year, but the stock of outside money and bonds is capable of faster variation. In the present discussion, solely to facilitate understanding, we adhere to this convention. In the concluding part of this section we show how the results are modified when the capital stock is allowed to adjust simultaneously with the bond and money stocks.

**FIGURE 3. Effect of Increases in Real Government Expenditures Financed by Money on Short-run Equilibrium Values of IS-LM Curves**

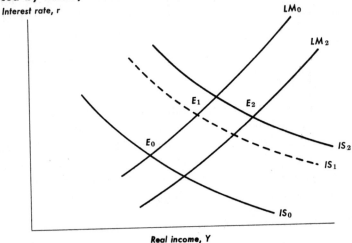

cits, since the dynamic responses are always moving the economy closer to its final equilibrium.[82]

*Dynamic Adjustments under Bond Finance*

If deficits are financed instead by floating new bonds, the relevant budget restraint becomes

$$(1/r)(dB/dt) = G + B - T(Y + B),$$

and more complicated outcomes are possible, at least in principle. Beginning with the outward shift in the *IS* curve depicted in Figure 2, suppose that bonds are issued to cover the deficit. With *M* unchanged, it is evident from equation (18) that—as long as the wealth effect on the demand for money is positive—the *LM* curve shifts upward (to $LM_2$ in Figure 4).

This mitigates the increase in income caused by the original government spending. Of course, the new bond issue also has positive wealth effects on consumption, raising the *IS* curve further, to $IS_2$ in Figure 4. In principle, then, when deficits are financed by bonds, $E_2$ may lie either to the right or to the left of $E_1$. If it lies to the left, the bond-financed increase in spending is ultimately perversely defla-

---

[82] This is hardly a rigorous demonstration. The formal proofs of this and the following propositions are given in Blinder and Solow, "Does Fiscal Policy Matter?"

**FIGURE 4. Effect of Increases in Real Government Expenditures Financed by Bonds on Short-run Equilibrium Values of IS-LM Curves**

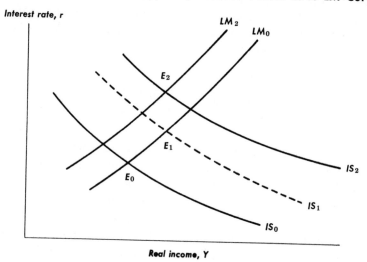

tionary, though it may take a long time for that to be apparent. Knowing which effect will dominate is vital to the analysis of fiscal policy.

There are three important cases to distinguish. First, suppose that wealth effects on consumption are trivial, so that $E_2$ falls to the left of $E_1$—that is, the net impact of an additional government bond is contractionary. Though quite contrary to the usual Keynesian story, this is, at least in principle, a possibility. But $E_2$ cannot then be a long-run equilibrium. If the budget was in deficit at $E_1$, it will exhibit an even larger deficit at $E_2$ (due to the decline in tax receipts). There will have to be another, larger, sale of bonds; and the process repeats, successively reducing national income at each step. Evidently, in this anti-Keynesian case the economy is unstable. No convergence toward a balanced-budget equilibrium occurs so long as the policy of strict bond financing is maintained.

When will this perverse case actually obtain? We have shown elsewhere that the standard *IS-LM* multiplier, $dY/dB$, will be negative if and only if

(19)
$$C_W < L_W \frac{I_r}{L_r},$$

where $C_W$ and $L_W$ denote, respectively, the wealth derivatives of the consumption and demand-for-money functions. To establish plausible values for these parameters, we start with an estimated $C_W$ of 0.053, reported by Modigliani.[83] The right-hand side of (19) can be conveniently rewritten in elasticity terms:

$$\frac{\left(\dfrac{r}{I}\dfrac{\partial I}{\partial r}\right)}{\left(\dfrac{r}{L}\dfrac{\partial L}{\partial r}\right)} \times \left(\frac{W}{L}\frac{\partial L}{\partial W}\right)\left(\frac{I}{K}\right)\left(\frac{K}{W}\right).$$

Bischoff has estimated the interest elasticity of investment as $-0.23$,[84] and Chow has estimated the interest and wealth elasticities of the demand for real balances as about $-0.64$ and $+0.64$, respectively.[85] A safely overoptimistic estimate of the growth rate of the capital stock (for the United States at least) appears to be 5 percent per annum. Then, since real capital is less than 100 percent of the total wealth of the private sector, the right-hand side of (19) is surely less than 0.0115, and (19) will almost certainly not hold in practice. There is nothing sacrosanct about this particular set of parameter values; an inventive reader can probably fabricate a set that satisfies (19). But doing so would require that the interest elasticity of investment exceed the interest elasticity of demand for money, *and* that wealth effects on demand for money outweigh wealth effects on consumption. These do not strike us as plausible suppositions.

We may feel relatively safe, then, in ruling out the possibility that additional bonds will be contractionary, other things equal. But this is not quite enough to guarantee stability. If bonds are indeed expansionary, issuing $dB$ of new interest-bearing securities will raise income by $(dY/dB)dB$, and therefore add $T'(dY/dB)dB$ to tax revenues. But, on the expenditure side of the ledger, the increased debt service (which is taxable) will cost the government $(1 - T')dB$. Only if

$$T'(dY/dB) > (1 - T')$$

—that is, only if

[83] "Monetary Policy and Consumption," p. 14.

[84] Charles W. Bischoff, "The Effect of Alternative Lag Distributions," in Gary Fromm (ed.), *Tax Incentives and Capital Spending* (Brookings Institution, 1971), pp. 61–130.

[85] Gregory C. Chow, "On the Long-Run and Short-Run Demand for Money," *Journal of Political Economy,* Vol. 74 (April 1966), Table 1, p. 119.

$$(20) \qquad\qquad (dY/dB) > \frac{1 - T'}{T'}$$

—will the budget deficit actually be closing, and thus only in this case will the system approach its new equilibrium.

Again, nothing in pure theory guarantees that (20) will hold; but we believe that a plausible argument can be made for its validity. Recall that $B$ is the volume of interest payments on the national debt, a kind of transfer payment. Thus $dY/dB$ should be about as large as a typical multiplier for transfers; a number rather larger than 1.0 is appropriate for the United States. In the simple model, $T'$ represents the combined marginal propensity to tax and reduce income-conditioned transfer payments as GNP rises. According to Modigliani,[86] this should exceed 0.5, so that (20) would hold and the model would be stable under bond financing. Only in this case is the steady-state multiplier (16) of interest.

While (20) seems plausible, we should not overlook the third possibility—that bonds are expansionary (so that $E_2$ lies to the right of $E_1$ in Figure 4), but not expansionary enough to close the budgetary gap. In this case, if the policy of strict bond financing were maintained, income would continue to rise without limit and the deficit, once opened up, would never be closed. This is a kind of super-Keynesian outcome. Note that this would be true whether the initial deficit was brought about by additional government spending, an autonomous rise in private demand, or what have you.

### Dynamic Adjustments when the Capital Stock May Vary

To this point we have followed the curious procedure of analyzing long-run macroeconomic adjustments while ignoring the fact that any net investment raises the capital stock. Fortunately for the question at hand, this omission does not lead to serious error. In fact, recognizing the feedback from $I$ to $K$ strengthens the conclusions reached in the last two subsections: the system remains stable under money finance and, in a sense to be specified shortly, the likelihood of stability under bond finance is enhanced.

The reason that adding the dynamic equation $dK/dt = I(Y, r, K)$ to our model tends to enhance its stability can be explained intuitively. Suppose that, due to some exogenous shock, investment rises. Then,

[86] "Monetary Policy and Consumption," p. 30.

in the next period, the capital stock will be higher than it otherwise would have been. Assuming that $\partial I/\partial K < 0$, this means that in the next period investment will be lower at each $(Y, r)$ combination than it would have been in the absence of the exogenous shock.

The mathematical analysis of this case, involving as it does two nonlinear differential equations, is tedious. However, the basic intuitions and results can be explained in nontechnical terms.

In the money-financing case, only two brief amendments must be made to the simple story of dynamic adjustment told above. The growing capital stock will moderate the rightward shift of the $LM$ curve through the wealth effect. The $IS$ curve is affected in two conflicting ways: an increase of $dK$ in the capital stock reduces investment spending by $I_K dK$, but increases consumption spending by $C_W dK$. It seems empirically plausible that the net effect should be contractionary—that is, that

$$(21) \qquad\qquad I_K + C_W < 0$$

—so that the $IS$ curve shifts leftward. But even if this is not true the system is stable under monetary finance.

If bonds are used to cover deficits, we again have the three possibilities. If (19) holds, so that, other things equal, the impact of new bonds is contractionary, then the economy will certainly be unstable. Economically meaningful necessary conditions for stability, however, cannot be derived easily. In particular, it remains possible that bonds are expansionary, but not sufficiently so to ensure stability. It can be shown that (20) and (21) are a pair of jointly sufficient conditions—neither of them necessary—for stability. If, as we have argued, the empirical magnitudes satisfy these inequalities, the economy will indeed approach its steady-state equilibrium under bond financing.

### Conclusions

We have seen that no simple, logical necessity dictates that the economy will behave in the very long run as Keynesians have generally assumed it will if all deficits are financed by flotation of new bonds. The usual a priori restrictions imposed on such models are sufficient to guarantee neither that the discovery of an additional government bond in the attic will increase GNP, nor that the equilibrium, once disturbed, will ever be reestablished. The existence of a nonnegligible wealth effect on consumption is sufficient to guarantee the former. The latter remains an empirical question that must be verified for each model; our sense of the standard econometric findings is that they do lead to stability under bond-financed deficits and surpluses.

One further note before leaving this topic: To their credit, the monetarists have generally acknowledged the government budget constraint and at least some of its implications. In their hands, it generally comes out: "Deficit spending carries with it either creation of new high-powered money [in which case they call it monetary policy] or new bond flotations [in which case they deny that it will be expansionary]." However, equation (15) does not take sides in doctrinal disputes. It can equally well be written:

$$dM/dt = G + B - T - (1/r)(dB/dt),$$

which we might read: "You cannot increase the high-powered money stock without either deficit spending or bond retirement." Thus the government budget restraint cuts both ways. This symmetry has only rarely been appreciated by the monetarists.[87] As we said at the outset of this survey, we have chosen to consider such actions as bond- or money-financed deficit spending as within the purview of fiscal policy, while considering swaps between $M$ and $B$ (that is, open market operations) as strictly monetary policies.

## Monetarism

The standard modern Keynesian view of the impact of discretionary fiscal policy, described in preceding sections, has come under attack from an opposing school of thought, created almost single-handedly by Milton Friedman.[88] Originally called the "new quantity theorists" or simply the "Chicago school," this group has extended

[87] David I. Fand recognizes the symmetry when he writes: "Deficits (and surpluses) are usually associated with acceleration (deceleration) in money stock growth, and it is therefore possible for Fiscalists and Monetarists to cite the same evidence to support their respective views." See his, "A Monetarist Model of the Monetary Process," *Journal of Finance,* Vol. 25 (May 1970), p. 286, note 21. We offer our opinions on monetarism in the next section.

[88] This statement is certainly unfair to important and independent scholars like Karl Brunner, Allan H. Meltzer, and David I. Fand, and no doubt to others as well. Nevertheless, it is clearly Friedman who has popularized the monetarist doctrine.

both its intellectual and geographical boundaries in recent years,[89] so that by now neither label quite fits. We might as well refer to this school as "monetarists," the name its members now seem to prefer. To give the school a name is easy; to define it is much more difficult. Economists who consider themselves monetarists have differences of opinion almost as sharp as economists who label themselves Keynesians. Further, even if we limit ourselves to the writings of Friedman, there are many different versions of monetarism. The defining characteristics of monetarism seem to differ both cross-sectionally (with nonprofessional audiences hearing the most extreme version[90]) and over time.

*What Is Monetarism?*

Knowing full well that not all monetarists will agree with our list, we shall heroically attempt to catalogue those ideas closely related to fiscal policy that seem to define monetarism.[91] Within the broad outlines of each concept, "hard" monetarists adhere to a more extreme view, while "soft" monetarists tend to be less dogmatic and, in fact, do not differ greatly from eclectic Keynesians.

1. *Money does matter.* Surely no self-respecting monetarist would deny this proposition. However, neither would a self-respecting Keynesian.[92] One gets intermediate versions of monetarism by varying

[89] For an entertaining and enlightening explanation of why the monetarist counterrevolution may have caught on, see Harry G. Johnson, "The Keynesian Revolution and the Monetarist Counter-Revolution," in American Economic Association, *Papers and Proceedings of the Eighty-third Annual Meeting, 1970* (*American Economic Review,* Vol. 61, May 1971), pp. 1–14.

[90] But see Milton Friedman, "Quantity Theory," in the *International Encyclopedia of the Social Sciences* (Macmillan, 1968), Vol. 10, pp. 432–47.

[91] This list is, therefore, not complete. Although, peculiarly enough, monetarism is largely concerned with fiscal policy, some fundamental monetarist tenets do fall in the realm of monetary theory—at least as we have dichotomized the two—and therefore will not be discussed here. For a more detailed critique of some of the more strictly monetary aspects of monetarism, see Ronald L. Teigen, "A Critical Look at Monetarist Economics," Federal Reserve Bank of St. Louis, *Review,* Vol. 54 (January 1972), pp. 10–25.

[92] It would be unfair to leave it at that. Friedman and his allies deserve credit for having restored money and monetary policy to an important place in discussions of economic policy, whether carried on by monetarists or Keynesians. It had certainly slipped from that position. David I. Fand (in "A Monetarist Model") has suggested a classification scheme running from a wing of "money only" monetarists at one end to "Radcliffe [Committee, not College!] Keynesians" at the other who seem to believe that velocity is so accommodating as to make the supply of money negligible in importance. Most macroeconomists fall nearer the center, though one could still make distinctions.

the meaning of this proposition. A true monetarist, presumably, believes that money is "almost" all that matters for the determination of money income. In the hardest version, which is typically reserved for newspapers, magazines, and congressional hearings, the statement becomes that the money supply or its rate of growth determines both nominal and real gross national product. In its softest versions, it says simply that the money supply is a principal determinant of money GNP. As Friedman himself has put it: "I regard the description of our position as 'money is all that matters for changes in *nominal* income and for *short-run* changes in real income' as an exaggeration but one that gives the right flavor of our conclusions. I regard the statement that 'money is all that matters,' period, as a basic misrepresentation of our conclusions."[93]

2. *Stable velocity function.* According to the first clear statement of the monetarist position,[94] the central tenet of the monetarist approach is that a stable demand function for money exists, with such things as interest rates and total wealth as arguments. Only very few economists would object to this assertion.[95] It is possible to read the Radcliffe Report[96] as stating the contrary; and the dominant macroeconomics of the early postwar period, extrapolating incorrectly the experience of the 1930s, did ignore the influence of monetary policy and the demand function for money in the determination of aggregate output. But the model used above, perfectly conventional as it is, contains a stable demand function for money—the upward-sloping *LM* curve. If that is the new quantity theory, it is also the old liquidity preference theory.[97] In any case, none of the typical monetarist policy

[93] "A Theoretical Framework," p. 217.

[94] Milton Friedman, "The Quantity Theory of Money—A Restatement," in Friedman (ed.), *Studies in the Quantity Theory of Money* (University of Chicago Press, 1956).

[95] The principal objection comes from those who would substitute an income variable for the wealth variable. But if wealth is measured by "permanent income" which is, in turn, a distributed lag on past measured income, this difference is quite minor. See, for example, Franco Modigliani, Robert Rasche, and J. Philip Cooper, "Central Bank Policy, the Money Supply, and the Short-Term Rate of Interest," *Journal of Money, Credit and Banking,* Vol. 2 (May 1970), especially pp. 168–69.

[96] Committee on the Working of the Monetary System, *Report,* Cmnd. 827 (London: Her Majesty's Stationery Office, 1959). The chairman of the committee was Lord Radcliffe.

[97] Some crude versions of Keynesian income analysis succeeded in submerging monetary factors by dropping wealth effects from the consumption function *and*

prescriptions follows from the notion of a stable demand function for money.

3. *Velocity is a quasi-constant.* It is a long step from assuming a stable velocity function to the notion that velocity is "almost" constant. But this is a step monetarists, in some degree, must take, since without it their reasoning leads to nothing unconventional. To see the force of this notion, consider the well-known accounting identity known as the equation of exchange:

(22)
$$MV \equiv PY,$$

where $M$ is the nominal money supply, $V$ is the income velocity of circulation, defined as

$$V \equiv \frac{PY}{M},$$

$P$ is the price level, and $Y$ is real income.

The rate-of-growth transformation of (22) tells that

(23)
$$\left(\frac{1}{M}\right)\left(\frac{dM}{dt}\right) + \left(\frac{1}{V}\right)\left(\frac{dV}{dt}\right) = \left(\frac{1}{P}\right)\left(\frac{dP}{dt}\right) + \left(\frac{1}{Y}\right)\left(\frac{dY}{dt}\right).$$

Now monetarists contend that *as an empirical matter* the changes in velocity are relatively minor compared to changes in the money supply. If this judgment is correct, then the rate of growth of the money supply "almost" fully determines the rate of growth of *nominal* income. Further, if, in the short run, prices are relatively sluggish, then $(1/M)(dM/dt)$ is the principal determinant of $(1/Y)(dY/dt)$. This is why Friedman says that "the basic differences among economists are empirical, not theoretical."[98] It has long been a fundamental tenet of Friedman's writings that—*as an empirical matter*—velocity is relatively insensitive to interest rates.[99] If this were the case, the *LM* curve would be vertical, and the money supply alone would determine aggregate income. Shifts in the *IS* curve, whether induced by fiscal policy or by anything else, would work themselves out on the interest

---

either (a) appealing to a "liquidity trap," which makes the *LM* curve horizontal, so that changes in $M$ have no effect on $r$, or (b) allowing the *LM* curve to slope upwards, but assuming that private expenditures are completely interest inelastic, so that the *IS* curve is vertical.

[98] "A Theoretical Framework," p. 234.

[99] Milton Friedman, "The Demand for Money: Some Theoretical and Empirical Results," *Journal of Political Economy*, Vol. 67 (August 1959), pp. 327–51.

rate, but would have no effect on aggregate output. From this point of view, the hard monetarist doctrine (vertical *LM*) and the crude Keynesian doctrine (horizontal *LM* or vertical *IS*) can be seen to be alternative special cases of a more general macroeconomic model, which embraces both modern Keynesianism and soft monetarism. Indeed, one model Friedman uses scarcely differs from the Hicks-Hansen version of Keynes' *General Theory*.[100]

In his recent writings Friedman has abandoned the notion that the demand for money is insensitive to interest rates. He now prefers to turn the tables in equation (23) and claim that antimonetarists—those who believe that velocity may be volatile in the short run—must believe that velocity is *highly interest elastic*.[101] Even this is not quite the case. Since, by definition,

$$\frac{1}{V}\frac{dV}{dV} = \left(\frac{r}{V}\right)\left(\frac{dV}{dr}\right)\frac{1}{r}\frac{dr}{dt},$$

*even if the interest elasticity is low*, *V* might be quite unstable in the short run, as long as the interest rate *r* moves erratically. Indeed, these are precisely the principal features of the monetary sector of the FRB-MIT-Penn model.[102]

In his most recent exchange with Tobin,[103] Friedman has laid less stress on this point, and on the oversimplified point that Keynesians tend to regard the price level as fixed or at least exogenous. Instead, he has argued that the important distinction is that monetarists expect the long-run asset-stock effects of monetary and fiscal policy to swamp the short-run income-flow effects, whereas Keynesians expect the opposite. That is why Keynesians tend first to ask if a government expenditure is tax financed or debt financed, while a monetarist lumps the two together and draws the line between them and finance through

[100] John Maynard Keynes, *The General Theory of Employment, Interest and Money* (Harcourt, Brace, 1936). See Friedman, "A Theoretical Framework," pp. 217–21; see also pp. 71–73 for our comments on this model.

[101] See "A Theoretical Framework," p. 216. Friedman, in fact, comes very close to identifying Keynesian economics with the liquidity trap and rigid wages. This is surely inaccurate, as a glance at any moderately sophisticated Keynesian writing will show. Keynes himself regarded "absolute liquidity preference" as a theoretical possibility of no particular empirical relevance. See *General Theory*, p. 207.

[102] See Modigliani and others, "Central Bank Policy."

[103] See Milton Friedman, "Comments on the Critics," *Journal of Political Economy*, Vol. 80 (September/October 1972), pp. 912–23.

the money supply. We have discussed the interesting analytical questions raised by this point in the previous section.

Finally, in many popular writings, monetarists have seemed to suggest that the *rate of growth* of the money supply determines the *level* of income. How this might occur, even if interest rates did not matter, is a mystery.[104]

4. *Fiscal policy is impotent.* Most pertinent to this survey is the notion, almost universally held among monetarists, that fiscal policy *unaccompanied by an accommodating monetary policy* is powerless to influence real output or the price level.[105]

If interest rates did not affect the quantity of money demanded, this conclusion would follow. However, most monetarists disavow the interest inelasticity of demand for money[106] but still do not believe in the efficacy of fiscal policy. How they can have it both ways is not clear, but some have purported to have "proved" this proposition econometrically.[107] We shall have more to say on this "evidence" later. Very soft versions of monetarism, which we find difficult to distinguish from eclectic Keynesianism, even drop the insistence that government spending and taxation cannot affect GNP. Fand has recently recognized that

to deny any short run stabilization effects to fiscal actions, one must be prepared to argue that surpluses (or deficits), irrespective of magnitude, have no direct effect on spending through changes in disposable income; and that they have no indirect effect through changes in desired real money balances or desired liquidity, and on velocity. But this can be true only in

---

[104] Lest the reader imagine that we are knocking down a straw man, we quote directly from a well-known monetarist paper: "The general monetarist view is that the rate of monetary expansion is the main determinant of total spending. . . ." See Leonall C. Andersen and Keith M. Carlson, "A Monetarist Model for Economic Stabilization," Federal Reserve Bank of St. Louis, *Review,* Vol. 52 (April 1970), p. 8.

[105] And if it is so accompanied, they call it monetary policy instead!

[106] Among the many references we could cite, see Allan H. Meltzer, "The Demand for Money: The Evidence from the Time Series," *Journal of Political Economy,* Vol. 71 (June 1963), pp. 219–46, and Karl Brunner and Allan H. Meltzer, "Some Further Investigations of Demand and Supply Functions for Money," *Journal of Finance,* Vol. 19 (May 1964), pp. 240–83.

[107] On pp. 52–56, we derived the condition under which bond-financed deficit spending would actually depress aggregate demand, and showed that it was quite implausible and implied instability. In any case, no monetarist has offered statistical evidence that this condition is actually met.

the exceptional case of a completely (interest) inelastic demand for money.[108]

Fand does not believe in this "exceptional case," and yet he is a respected monetarist. Here the line between the two schools is certainly blurred.

5. *Disbelief in "fine tuning."* Friedman has long been a disbeliever in discretionary policy—fiscal *or* monetary—fearing that lags will make it more likely to be destabilizing than stabilizing.[109] To say that fine tuning may be dangerous business is not the same as saying that fiscal policy is impotent. Indeed, if it is impotent, it is hard to see how poorly timed fiscal policy could do any harm! And monetarists are not the only economists who are skeptical of fine tuning. Both Walter Heller and Arthur Okun, chairmen of the Council of Economic Advisers under the activist Kennedy and Johnson administrations, have explicitly disavowed fine tuning.[110] We discuss the question of lags in fiscal policy below.

Of course, any or every discretionary act might be regarded simultaneously by Friedman as impermissible fine tuning and by Heller and Okun as a perfectly reasonable policy move. In principle, a preference for automatic as against discretionary policy could be entirely uncorrelated with the choice between monetarist and Keynesian approaches to macroeconomics. There are, in fact, some people who believe in the efficacy of fiscal policy but would prefer its use to be limited by automatic rules. Nevertheless, belief in monetarism and belief in rules are quite strongly correlated. Why that should be so is an interesting question for a sociologist of science. Lags are not enough to explain it.

## On "Testing" Single-Equation Models

Since monetarism is not primarily a theoretical doctrine, but an empirical one,[111] monetarists have been eager to demonstrate the su-

---

[108] "A Monetarist Model," p. 286.

[109] See, for example, his celebrated "A Monetary and Fiscal Framework for Economic Stability," *American Economic Review,* Vol. 38 (June 1948), pp. 245–64, or "The Supply of Money and Changes in Prices and Output," in *The Relationship of Prices to Economic Stability and Growth,* Compendium of Papers submitted by Panelists Appearing before the Joint Economic Committee, 85 Cong. 2 sess. (1958), pp. 241–56.

[110] See Okun, *Political Economy of Prosperity,* pp. 110–11.

[111] Friedman, for example, has from his earliest writings always maintained that velocity should *in theory* be an increasing function of the money rate of interest.

periority of their model in explaining the actual behavior of the economy. Since the opening salvo was fired by Friedman and David Meiselman in their study for the Commission on Money and Credit,[112] much ink has been spilled over this issue.

Friedman and Meiselman set out to compare the predictive ability of the new quantity theory, which is based on a stable velocity function, with the Keynesian "income-expenditure" theory, which is based on a stable multiplier. Not a bad idea. However, the methodology of their study is open to serious question. A stable velocity function is in no sense incompatible with a stable consumption function; both are components of the ordinary *IS-LM* model. What justification can there be for setting them up as competing hypotheses?

According to Friedman and Meiselman, the object of theory is to predict the whole system from knowledge (or external forecasts) of a small part. Further, they claim, since the quality of the data does not justify more detail, one should employ the simplest possible version of each competing theory.[113] In their words:

It is our view that the issue that divides economists is extremely basic and one that should lend itself to a common answer over a wide range of circumstances. If it does not, it means that the dichotomy posed is much too simple . . .[114]

Mindful of this last sentence, Friedman and Meiselman do enter an important caveat—which they subsequently ignore:

On the simple level at which we propose to test the two theories, [the quantity theory] might turn out to be better than [the Keynesian theory], or conversely: whereas on a more sophisticated level, when additional variables are introduced, the relative advantage of the two might be reversed.[115]

Given this statement, one wonders why they went any further. But Friedman and Meiselman proceed to compare simple correlations be-

[112] Milton Friedman and David Meiselman, "The Relative Stability of Monetary Velocity and the Investment Multiplier in the United States, 1897–1958," in E. Cary Brown and others, *Stabilization Policies,* A Series of Research Studies prepared for the Commission on Money and Credit (Prentice-Hall, 1963).

[113] Even in the late 1950s (when Friedman and Meiselman did their work) it must have been hard to consider one-equation models as very much simpler than two-equation models like the *IS-LM* system.

[114] "Relative Stability," p. 170.

[115] Ibid., p. 174.

tween "induced expenditures" and money supply on the one hand versus "autonomous expenditures" on the other over 1897–1958 and various subperiods. They find that money has a higher correlation in every subperiod except the Great Depression (the period during which Keynes wrote his *General Theory*), and conclude that this scores a point for the monetarist approach.[116]

As one might have expected, this sort of exercise gave rise to a seemingly unending discussion of the dependence of the results on the precise definitions of autonomous expenditure and the monetary variable, the time period, or some other procedural matter.[117] These critics contended that if one played the Friedman-Meiselman game fairly, the Keynesian theory appeared slightly superior to the quantity theory. Friedman and Meiselman were apparently unconvinced.[118] In our view, all of this was essentially pointless. The issue is simply not to be settled by comparing goodness of fit of one-equation models that are far too primitive to represent *any* theory adequately. In fact, we shall argue below that even existing large-scale econometric models may be incapable of resolving this dispute.

The Friedman-Meiselman single-equation approach was resurrected in 1968 by Andersen and Jordan of the St. Louis Federal Reserve Bank in a paper that has attracted a great deal of attention.[119]

[116] They also ran regressions including the price level and regressions allowing both money and autonomous expenditures to enter simultaneously (with or without the price level), and obtained essentially similar results.

[117] See for example, Albert Ando and Franco Modigliani, "The Relative Stability of Monetary Velocity and the Investment Multiplier"; Michael DePrano and Thomas Mayer, "Tests of the Relative Importance of Autonomous Expenditures and Money," and the reply and rejoinders by Friedman-Meiselman, Ando-Modigliani, and DePrano-Mayer, all in *American Economic Review*, Vol. 55 (September 1965), pp. 693–72. See also Donald D. Hester, "Keynes and the Quantity Theory: A Comment on the Friedman-Meiselman CMC Paper," *Review of Economics and Statistics*, Vol. 46 (November 1964), pp. 364–77.

[118] In "The Friedman-Meiselman CMC Paper: New Evidence on an old Controversy," *American Economic Review*, Vol. 63 (December 1973), pp. 908–17, William Poole and Elinda B. F. Kornblith test the predictive power in the post-sample period of the Friedman-Meiselman equations and those proposed by their various critics, as well as multiple regressions involving M and various definitions of autonomous spending. The Friedman-Meiselman equations do not exactly cover themselves with glory. Neither do some of the others. The best all-round performance is turned in by one of Hester's definitions of autonomous spending: gross private investment other than inventories plus government purchases plus exports; see "Keynes and the Quantity Theory."

[119] See Leonall C. Andersen and Jerry L. Jordan, "Monetary and Fiscal Actions: A Test of Their Relative Importance in Economic Stabilization," Federal Reserve Bank of St. Louis, *Review*, Vol. 50 (November 1968), pp. 11–24.

They argue that we need not specify a complete structural model of the economy to know that the reduced-form equation for income will be

(24) $$Y_t = f(G_t, T_t, M_t, Z_t),$$

where $G$ is a variable summarizing government expenditure actions, $T$ is a summary tax variable, $M$ is a variable summarizing monetary policy actions, $Z$ is a vector of "all other forces that influence total spending," and $t$ is time.[120] If $G$, $T$, and $M$ are specified properly as exogenous policy variables, this will indeed be a "true" reduced form, from which it follows that changes in income are given by:

(25) $$dY_t = a_1 dG_t + a_2 dT_t + a_3 dM_t + a_4 dZ_t + e_t,$$

where we have now added an independent stochastic error term, $e$, indicating exogenous "shocks" that affect the system but are not captured by any of the variables in the model. Now Andersen and Jordan wish to drop the last set of variables from the regression. Why? Because they cannot specify correctly a complete macro model of the economy that would tell them what to include in the vector $Z$.[121] Andersen and Jordan seem to think they can avoid this difficulty by replacing the $a_4 dZ_t$ term in equation (25) by a constant, $a_0$. They suggest interpreting the constant as the "average" value of $a_4 dZ_t$ over the period. This is simply illegitimate. If (25) is the "true" model, and they estimate instead,

(26) $$dY_t = a_0 + a_1 dG_t + a_2 dT_t + a_3 dM_t + v_t,$$

they will have misspecified the equation and so impounded $a_4 dZ_t$ into their error term:

$$v_t = e_t + a_4 dZ_t - a_0.$$

Unless $dZ_t$ is uncorrelated with $dG_t$, $dT_t$, and $dM_t$, ordinary least squares on (26) will, as is well known, yield biased and inconsistent estimates of the parameters of (25).

Let us grant them, for the sake of the argument, this orthogonality assumption, so that (26) would be a proper regression to estimate. Letting $G$ and $T$ be full employment expenditures and tax receipts,

---

120 Ibid., p. 24.

121 This inability is not to be interpreted as a criticism of Andersen and Jordan. We are not convinced that anyone is capable of doing this correctly!

respectively, and *M* the monetary base, Andersen and Jordan run equation (26) on quarterly data and find the sum of the lag coefficients on *G* and *T* to be negligible in size and of the wrong sign. They also find that most of the individual coefficients are insignificant. By contrast, the monetary base gets large and statistically significant coefficients with the correct signs.[122]

As in the case of the Friedman-Meiselman paper, it is possible to find fault with the details of the Andersen-Jordan study.[123] We prefer to ignore these subsidiary issues and concentrate instead on its conceptual basis. We shall suppose that Andersen and Jordan were perfectly correct in specifying the monetary and fiscal variables and the lag structure, and that the estimates were insensitive to the choice of a time period. We shall show that even then their results, if indeed they mean anything, would "prove" precisely the opposite of what they believe they "prove."

Since it is also used in Friedman's recent statement of the monetarist theory,[124] the standard *IS-LM* model seems eclectic enough to accommodate all shades of opinion. This model, which we have been using throughout our survey, consists of the following three equations:

(27) $$Y = C(r, Y - T) + I(r, Y) + G \qquad \text{(\textit{IS} curve)}$$

(28) $$T = T(Y, \tau) \qquad \text{(tax function)}$$

(29) $$M/P = L(r, Y) \qquad \text{(\textit{LM} curve)},$$

where *C* is real consumer spending, *I* is real investment, and *L* the liquidity preference function. For simplicity we take the price level as fixed and ignore all wealth effects. We have shown above how both of

---

[122] We are referring here to their equations (1.4) and (2.4). The other equations, which allow only one fiscal variable—*G, T,* or the full employment deficit, *G − T*—to enter the regressions, or use the money stock rather than the monetary base, are impossible to interpret.

[123] See, for example, the "Comment" by Frank De Leeuw and John Kalchbrenner and the "Reply" by Andersen and Jordan in Federal Reserve Bank of St. Louis, *Review,* Vol. 51 (April 1969), pp. 6–16, and several articles in subsequent issues of the *Review.* See also Richard G. Davis, "How Much Does Money Matter? A Look at Some Recent Evidence," Federal Reserve Bank of New York, *Monthly Review,* Vol. 51 (June 1969), pp. 119–31; and Edward M. Gramlich, "The Usefulness of Monetary and Fiscal Policy as Discretionary Stabilization Tools," *Journal of Money, Credit and Banking,* Vol. 3 (May 1971), Pt. 2, pp. 506–32. This list is far from complete; at this writing critical studies continue to appear in the journals.

[124] "A Theoretical Framework." See the following section for a detailed discussion of this paper.

these subtleties can be added, but it seems in the spirit of Andersen-Jordan to omit them. In any case, they would not alter the basic conclusions to be drawn.

Substitution of (28) into (27) reduces this to a two-equation structural model with $Y$ and $r$ as endogenous variables. If we now take the total differential of each structural equation and solve for $dY$, we obtain the equation that Andersen and Jordan, presumably, think they are estimating:

$$(30) \qquad\qquad dY = -m\,dS + m\,\frac{C_r + I_r}{PL_r}\,dM,$$

where $m$ is the multiplier

$$\left[1 - C_Y(1 - T_Y) - I_Y + \frac{C_r + I_r}{L_r}L_Y\right]^{-1},$$

and where $dS$ is what we called earlier the change in the weighted standardized surplus: $dS \equiv C_Y T_r(Y, \tau)d\tau - dG$. This equation does indeed express changes in income as a linear function of changes in a fiscal variable and changes in a monetary variable. However, Andersen and Jordan do not use the weighted standardized surplus as their fiscal measure. When they allow full employment expenditures and full employment taxes to enter the regression as separate variables, we can treat this as *equivalent* to entering the change in the weighted full employment surplus

$$dW = C_Y T_r(Y^*, \tau)d\tau - dG$$

as a single variable. But, as we pointed out above, when the economy is far from full employment, $dW$ may not be a very good proxy for $dS$. In a period that includes unemployment rates ranging from 3½ to 7 percent, this may not be a trivial matter.[125] As always, when a variable is measured with error, its coefficient will be biased toward zero. This may partially explain the extraordinarily low coefficients for fiscal policy obtained by Andersen and Jordan.[126]

---

[125] This point has been made by Robert J. Gordon in his, "Notes on Money, Income, and Gramlich, A Comment," *Journal of Money, Credit and Banking,* Vol. 3 (May 1971), Pt. 2, especially pp. 539–42. See also the paper by Hymans and Wernette, "The Impact of the Federal Budget," p. 33.

[126] In fact, E. Gerald Corrigan found that use of a fiscal variable quite similar to the unweighted standardized surplus in a "St. Louis equation" makes fiscal policy look much better. See "The Measurement and Importance of Fiscal Policy Changes," Federal Reserve Bank of New York, *Monthly Review,* Vol. 52 (June 1970), pp. 133–45.

But there is a far more fundamental problem. Suppose Andersen and Jordan actually did use $dS$ as their fiscal variable and estimated (30) by standard regression techniques.[127] In the real world, neither fiscal nor monetary policy is made in a vacuum. Suppose, based on (30), the true reduced-form equation were

$$(31) \qquad dY_t = -m\, dS_t + u\, dM_t + e_t,$$

where $m$ is the multiplier, $u$ is equal to $m(I_r + C_r)/PL_r$, and $e_t$ is a stochastic disturbance term indicating such things as exogenous shifts in the consumption, investment, and demand-for-money functions. It would then be natural to assume that both fiscal and monetary actions will be guided so as to offset the disturbance term, at least partially.

To exaggerate the point, consider two polar cases. Suppose, first, that fiscal policy perfectly offsets exogenous disturbances, without taking account of what monetary policy is doing. That is, fiscal policy sets $dS_t$ to offset $e_t$ exactly: $dS_t = (1/m)e_t$. Substituting this "reaction function" for the government into (31) gives us

$$(31') \qquad dY_t = u\, dM_t,$$

*which should hold with no error.* Verbally, if fiscal policy is planned perfectly, a regression on (31) should give a zero coefficient to fiscal policy and fit the data perfectly. Similarly, if monetary policy exactly offsets all disturbances without paying attention to the course of fiscal policy, $dM_t = -(1/u)e_t$, and (31) becomes,

$$(31'') \qquad dY_t = -m\, dS_t,$$

so that running (31) should give a perfect fit with a zero coefficient for monetary policy. There are, of course, many intermediate possibilities.[128] But the basic point should be clear. The better fiscal policy is geared to offsetting random disturbances,[129] the worse it will appear in

[127] We have already pointed out that (30) omits an entire set of exogenous variables, "autonomous expenditures" for short, and hence gives biased estimates. For the moment we ignore even this difficulty.

[128] For a full treatment of this problem, with more realistic reaction functions, see Stephen M. Goldfeld and Alan S. Blinder, "Some Implications of Endogenous Stabilization Policy," *Brookings Papers on Economic Activity* (3:1972), pp. 585–644.

[129] In the context of the grievously misspecified Andersen-Jordan equation, such behavior seems quite plausible. Though the authorities might find it difficult to anticipate a "true" random disturbance, they should be able to anticipate the Andersen-Jordan disturbance term since it includes many omitted variables that are directly measurable.

regressions to explain income; and similarly for monetary policy. In econometric terms this sounds less paradoxical: the econometrician ignores correlation of fiscal or monetary policies with the error term only at his peril.[130]

A closely related point has been made by Levis A. Kochin,[131] who formulates the stabilization problem as Friedman and Johansen do.[132] He assumes that a single imperfect instrument is used to minimize the variance of a single target variable around some desired value, and shows that, if the instrument variable is optimally managed, a regression of the target variable on the instrument variable will have a zero slope on average. This result can be generalized to the case of two instruments: if they are jointly optimally managed, a regression of the target on both instruments will have zero expectations for both coefficients. This generalized version is a pretty good representation of the St. Louis equation. As our own analysis suggests, its coefficients probably tell as much about the conduct of stabilization policy as about the effectiveness of instruments.

In summary, the Andersen-Jordan study errs for at least three reasons, any one of which is sufficient to render their results meaningless. First, by omitting all exogenous variables other than fiscal or monetary policy, they seriously misspecify the reduced-form equation for

---

[130] This point has been made before. See, for example, the comments by Rudolf R. Rhomberg and by H. T. Shapiro in *Journal of Money, Credit and Banking*, Vol. 3 (May 1971), Pt. 2, pp. 546–54. However, it appears not to have received the attention it deserves.

In this light Silber's recent results are interesting. Breaking down 1953–69 into two subperiods, Silber finds that the Eisenhower administration gives approximately the St. Louis results, but the more activist Kennedy-Johnson era shows fiscal policy to have had significant effects (with the correct signs). Were it not for the other errors in the St. Louis equation, one might interpret these results as showing (paradoxically) that fiscal policy did a better job of offsetting autonomous fluctuations in the Republican years than in the Democratic ones. However, in view of the gross misspecification of the equation, we are not inclined to draw this conclusion. See Willaim L. Silber, "The St. Louis Equation: 'Democratic' and 'Republican' Versions and Other Experiments," *Review of Economics and Statistics*, Vol. 53 (November 1971), pp. 362–67.

[131] "Judging Stabilization Policies" (paper delivered at the 1972 annual meeting of the Econometric Society; processed).

[132] "The Effects of a Full-Employment Policy on Economic Stability: A Formal Analysis," in Milton Friedman, *Essays in Positive Economics* (University of Chicago Press, 1953); also Leif Johansen, "On the Optimal Use of Forecasts in Economic Policy Decisions," *Journal of Public Economics,* Vol. 1 (April 1972), pp. 1–24.

real output. (Unfortunately, an attempt to specify a short list of other exogenous variables leads to dispute, as in the discussion of the Friedman-Meiselman paper.) Second, they use an incorrect measure of fiscal policy, which biases the coefficient toward zero. Finally, and most damaging to their position, they treat fiscal and monetary policies as exogenous when it is intuitively obvious that the authorities are in some sense reacting to movements in the macroeconomy. We conclude that the voluminous literature of single-equation "tests" of fiscal versus monetary policy, or of monetarist versus Keynesian theory, is not only inconclusive, but necessarily so.

In fact, our remarks go even deeper than this. Of the three sins of Andersen and Jordan outlined in the preceding paragraph, we may assume that serious large-scale econometric models avoid the first two as best they can. However, they do not avoid the third. Treating the fiscal and monetary policy tools, which are exogenous in the economic sense (that is, determined outside of the economic system), as exogenous in the statistical sense (that is, independent of the error term) involves a specification error that all econometric models will continue to commit until they specify and estimate a proper reaction function for the authorities.[133] We wonder (and now we are only speculating) if this observation does not go a long way toward explaining the poor policy predictions of some of these models despite impressive goodness-of-fit statistics.[134]

## Monetarist Models of the Economy

Until recently it was hard to know what a fully specified monetarist model of the aggregate economy would look like. Critics of monetarism had to construct models that they believed to be true to Fried-

---

[133] A common suggestion for the Federal Reserve's short-run reaction function during the 1950s and early 1960s is that it geared monetary policy toward stabilizing nominal interest rates. For some serious attempts at econometric estimation of a reaction function, see John H. Wood, "A Model of Federal Reserve Behavior," in George Horwich (ed.), *Monetary Process and Policy: A Symposium* (Richard D. Irwin, 1967), pp. 135–66; Kenneth E. Homa and Dwight M. Jaffee, "The Supply of Money and Common Stock Prices," *Journal of Finance,* Vol. 26 (December 1971), pp. 1045–66, especially pp. 1049–54; and Ann F. Friedlaender, "Macro Policy Goals in the Postwar Period: A Study in Revealed Preference," *Quarterly Journal of Economics,* Vol. 87 (February 1973), pp. 25–43.

[134] Goldfeld and Blinder, "Some Implications," presents some Monte Carlo experiments that suggest that biases due to reaction functions are a much more serious problem for reduced-form equations than for conventional structural models. These findings are suggestive, but not conclusive.

man's views,[135] and Friedman was always free to say that his views were being misrepresented.[136] Fortunately, this gap has recently been filled. Professor Friedman has provided a theoretical model of the determination of national income and the price level,[137] and Andersen and Carlson have published a short-run econometric forecasting model along monetarist lines.[138] By comparing these models with the theoretical and empirical models that purport to follow Keynesian doctrine, one might hope to find out what the monetarists—if they do not insist on interest-inelastic demand for money—are trying to say.

In the case of the highly aggregative theoretical models, this hope is not realized. The model Friedman presents is exactly the Hicks-Hansen *IS-LM* model that we have utilized above. As is well known, this is a "fixed-price" model—that is, it does not determine the price level. Friedman suggests that the Keynesian model is the *IS-LM* model supplemented by the specification that $P$, the price level, is an institutional datum. By contrast, he says, the new quantity theory adds the specification that $Y$, the level of real output, is determined outside the *IS-LM* framework (and hence independently of both fiscal and monetary policy) by the Walrasian general equilibrium equations.[139]

As our analysis of price level effects pointed out, the *IS-LM* model does indeed need another equation if it is to determine the aggregate price level. But this equation is not $P = P_0$, as Friedman suggests. Rather, it is the aggregate supply schedule $P = P(Y)$ depicted in our Figure 1.[140] In this framework, we can see the monetarist case and the crude Keynesian case (which Friedman unfairly takes to represent

[135] See Ando and Modigliani, "Relative Stability," and James Tobin, "Money and Income: Post Hoc Ergo Propter Hoc?" *Quarterly Journal of Economics,* Vol. 84 (May 1970), pp. 301–17.

[136] See Milton Friedman and David Meiselman, "Reply to Ando and Modigliani and to DePrano and Mayer," *American Economic Review,* Vol. 55 (September 1965), pp. 753–85; and Friedman, "Comment on Tobin," *Quarterly Journal of Economics* (May 1970), pp. 318–27.

[137] "A Theoretical Framework."

[138] "A Monetarist Model," pp. 7–25.

[139] See Friedman, "A Theoretical Framework," pp. 219–20.

[140] This aggregate supply curve comes from assuming some stickiness or money illusion in the labor market. All that is necessary is that the money wage not move quickly to clear the labor market, either for institutional reasons or, as Keynes suggested, because workers care about relative wages and cannot bargain for uniform wage changes across the board.

**FIGURE 5. A Possible Aggregate Supply Schedule, P = P(Y)**

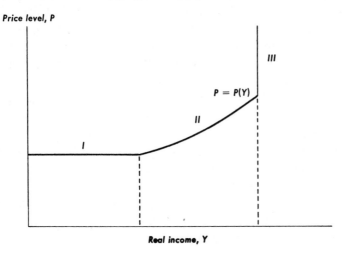

the Keynesian model) as alternate special cases of a more general, eclectic model. It is often supposed that the aggregate supply function is flat at relatively low levels of $Y$; then begins sloping upward as $Y$ passes through moderate and high levels of capacity utilization; and finally becomes vertical at full utilization of resources. Such a schedule is depicted in Figure 5, where the three ranges are labeled I, II, and III, respectively.

If the figure gives a reasonably accurate picture of the world—and eclectic Keynesians have often supposed that it does—then the crude Keynesian case appears as region I, where it is correct to view the price level as fixed. Similarly, region III, where it is correct to view real output as fixed, corresponds to the monetarist case; in the Keynesian literature this is often called "pure price inflation." The intermediate case, region II, where each increment of real output can be achieved only at some cost in terms of inflation, corresponds to the eclectic Keynesian position that underlies the Phillips curve. If Friedman is correct, as we believe he is, in directing his fire at the large number of Keynesian economists who have focused myopically on region I, then the majority of the profession is also correct to fault the monetarists for concentrating unduly on region III.

The monetarist school has yet to produce a full-blown macroeconometric model that might be compared with models constructed along more or less traditional Keynesian lines.[141] About the closest facsimile is very different from these models.[142] The Andersen-Carlson model consists of little more than the Andersen-Jordan equation for quarter-to-quarter changes in the nominal GNP, supplemented by a price equation (peculiarly formulated) that determines the change in the GNP deflator.[143] There is no further structure of any importance in the model. Although the model contains an interest rate equation, "interest rates do not function explicitly in the model as a part of a transmission mechanism running from changes in the money stock to output and prices."[144] Instead, this equation is used only to determine the distributed lag from which an "expected inflation rate" is generated from observations on past inflation rates.

The model seems open to serious question on purely econometric grounds.[145] And some of the equations have queer implications. For example, the interest rate equation has the property that if the annual rates of change of the money stock and real output are constant (and if price expectations are also given), the interest rate is determined *independent of the numerical values of these rates of change.* So it is hard for us to view this "model" as an improvement on the single-equation "reduced form" approach; indeed, that is more or less what it is.

For reasonable people to pay any attention to such a model, the existing Keynesian macroeconometric models would have to be woefully neglectful of monetary factors. While the charge of monetary naiveté can probably be leveled with some justification at the early generation of econometric models, it certainly does not apply to the latest vintage. These models, for the most part, have highly developed

[141] We are referring here to such models as those maintained by Brookings, Wharton, MIT-FRB-Penn, Michigan, Data Resources, Bureau of Economic Analysis, and others.

[142] Andersen and Carlson, "A Monetarist Model."

[143] Price level changes are predicted by price expectations and an odd measure of excess demand. Precisely, this measure is defined as $\Delta Y_t - (X_t^F - X_{t-1})$, where $Y$ is nominal GNP, $X_t^F$ is this quarter's full employment potential output, and $X_{t-1}$ is last quarter's real GNP. See ibid., p. 12. Note that $Y$ is a nominal quantity, while $X$ is a real quantity.

[144] Ibid., p. 14.

[145] To cite just two flaws, Andersen and Carlson use ordinary least squares throughout even though several equations contain contemporaneous endogenous variables on the right-hand side; and Durbin-Watson statistics as low as 0.60 appear.

monetary and financial sectors.[146] Indeed, one of them—the MIT-FRB-Penn model—was explicitly designed to elaborate the links between the real and monetary sectors.

Of course, these models do not command unlimited confidence. They differ enough among themselves so that they cannot all be right. Still, for evaluating the monetarist critique, they provide the best evidence to be had.[147]

Until very recently, it was virtually impossible to confront several of these models with the same question. While the proprietors of some models had simulated their equations in order to generate fiscal or monetary policy multipliers (or both), these simulations invariably differed in initial conditions, definition of the policy variable, or some such thing. However, this difficulty may soon be remedied by an important exercise that at this writing is being conducted by the maintainers of a number of functioning econometric models of the U.S. economy.[148] As nearly as possible, given their differing structures, each model is asked to simulate an identical policy experiment, fiscal or monetary or mixed, with the same initial conditions. Running the model with and without the indicated policy enables one to compute the quarterly and cumulative multipliers, and to compare them across models. The hope is that such an exercise will yield some consensus as to the size (and also the timing, which we discuss in the following section) of the fiscal and monetary policy multipliers. Of course, even perfect agreement could not be regarded as the definitive word; the models could all agree very well and all be very wrong. Life is hard.

Preliminary results have now been published, and some of them are reproduced in the next section. We do not attempt to reconcile the differences among the models; there is no way to do that without developing the particular structure of each model, a task far beyond the

---

[146] For a review and critique of some of these models by a Keynesian writer, see Carl F. Christ, "Econometric Models of the Financial Sector," paper delivered at the 1969 Conference on Survey of Econometric Models and published in *Journal of Money, Credit and Banking*, Vol. 3 (May 1971), Pt. 2, pp. 419–49. For a critique of these models by a monetarist, see "The Monetary Theory of Nine Recent Quarterly Econometric Models of the United States, *Comment by David I. Fand*," same journal, pp. 450–60.

[147] Though our argument above suggests that even this is relatively weak evidence.

[148] We refer here to the semiannual seminars sponsored jointly by the National Bureau of Economic Research and the National Science Foundation, held for the purpose of comparing the major U.S. macroeconometric models.

confines of this survey. Instead, in view of the challenge from the monetarists of the St. Louis Federal Reserve, it may be useful to see what the various models say about the fiscal policy experiment that the Andersen-Jordan equations conceptually conduct—the effect on *money* GNP of a sustained increment in *money* government expenditures with no accommodating monetary policy. Note that this is a different animal from the theoretical fiscal policy multipliers we have been talking about up until now—ratios of increments in *real* GNP to increments in *real* government spending. In a model with an endogenous price level, a sustained rise in nominal government purchases will very likely accelerate the rate of price inflation. This means that the implied increment in real government spending will be falling quarter by quarter. The situation is aggravated if the model includes separate price deflators for GNP and government spending, for these two price levels do not move in unison. Although it is possible to compute the implied multiplier effect of real government expenditures on real GNP, which is called for by theory, the model-to-model differences in these multipliers may tell us more about intermodel differences in the theory of the price level than about the effectiveness of fiscal policy.[149] For this reason, and because the Andersen-Jordan equations refer only to nominal quantities, we restrict our attention to the current-price multipliers.

A consensus of sorts does emerge. The models can be roughly divided into two groups: the St. Louis Fed model and all the others. The St. Louis model replicates the results of Andersen and Jordan cited above: it shows the cumulative current-price multiplier for government spending rising to a peak of around unity in the second and third quarters after the increase in government spending, and then falling back to zero and actually becoming negative by the time five quarters have elapsed. The ultimate effect of a sustained increase in nominal government purchases is a small reduction in nominal GNP. Since inflation occurs in the interim, this must translate into a substantial reduction in real output.

The other econometric models, all of them more or less Keynesian in spirit, are by no means unanimous; but they do speak with one voice in contradicting the St. Louis pattern. First-quarter impact mul-

---

[149] Some of those multipliers are given below.

tipliers range from a low of 1.1 to a high of 1.8; and by the time one year has elapsed, the cumulative multipliers vary from 1.6 to 2.8. Twelve quarters after the fiscal policy action, the cumulative multipliers vary from 1.8 to 3.0.[150] Thus these complex macroeconometric models all corroborate the back-of-the-envelope multiplier calculations of simple Keynesian analysis. A marginal propensity to consume with respect to GNP of about 0.60–0.67 implies a naive fiscal policy multiplier of from 2.5 to 3.0, which should then be scaled downward somewhat for the monetary side effects mentioned earlier. All the models save the St. Louis model are consistent with this view.

One further piece of evidence bears directly on the monetarist challenge, and again supports the eclectic Keynesian view. J. R. Moroney and J. M. Mason have recently constructed a simple linear econometric model that is comparable in size, though not in structure, to the St. Louis model.[151] Their model, which has only six stochastic equations, is just the ordinary *IS-LM* model extended to allow for an endogenous money supply. The monetary base and the rediscount rate are the Fed's exogenous policy instruments. Further, like Andersen and Carlson, they fit their model entirely in current-price terms, a procedure that we do not necessarily recommend but that facilitates comparison with the St. Louis results. Moreover, they use superior econometric techniques that should avoid some of the purely statistical problems to which we have alluded.

When they compute the cumulative multipliers from their "fundamental dynamic equation" (which explains current GNP by its own lagged values, and current and lagged values of the monetary base and the sum of government expenditures and exports), they find an impact multiplier for fiscal policy of 1.2, which rises steadily to 2.0 after four quarters and 2.7 after ten quarters. While a small model like this can hardly settle the issue, it is worth seeing that even a highly aggregative model that eschews the structural detail of the larger econometric

[150] Gary Fromm and Lawrence R. Klein, "A Comparison of Eleven Econometric Models of the United States," in American Economic Association, *Papers and Proceedings of the Eighty-fifth Annual Meeting, 1972 (American Economic Review,* Vol. 63, May 1973), Table 5, p. 391.

[151] See their "The Dynamic Impacts of Autonomous Expenditures and the Monetary Base on Aggregate Income," *Journal of Money, Credit and Banking,* Vol. 3 (November 1971), pp. 793–814.

models can give about the same results. Again the contrast with the St. Louis equations is marked.[152]

It appears to us that the various econometric models of the whole economy generally support the conventional modern Keynesian view of the operation of fiscal policy, as against the monetarist challenge.[153]

## Lags and Uncertainties in Fiscal Policy

On any view, successful operation of discretionary fiscal policy requires some dependence on forecasting. Since the accuracy of economic forecasts deteriorates as the period of forecast lengthens, the length of the lag with which fiscal policy works is important information. In general, the longer the lag, the further ahead it is necessary to forecast, and the less likely it is that policy actions will achieve their desired objective.[154]

Traditionally, the total lag in fiscal and monetary policy has been broken down into three components: the recognition lag, the policy lag, and the outside lag.[155] The first consists of the time that elapses between the need for a policy action and the realization by the authorities that such an action is in fact necessary. It exists because economic data take time to collect, process, and analyze. Now that high-speed computers are in use on a widespread basis, the recognition lag is

[152] A similar study by J. Kmenta and P. E. Smith reached similar conclusions. See their "Autonomous Expenditures versus Money Supply: An Application of Dynamic Multipliers," *Review of Economics and Statistics,* Vol. 55 (August 1973), pp. 299–307.

[153] None of these models contains an explicit government budget constraint, nor does any of them attempt to incorporate explicit reaction functions for stabilization policy. As we have shown in this and the previous section, these present complicated, but possibly important, problems, and provide an agenda for future research. All we can do now is render a verdict on the basis of the evidence already in.

[154] This statement is, perhaps, overstrong. It is now recognized that lags in economic behavior tend to be distributed lags. The first effects of a policy change may be felt very quickly, even though the ultimate effects may not be realized for some time. Thus, even if the average lag is rather long, a fairly myopic policy, playing on the immediate effects of each policy move, is in principle possible. In practice such a policy might require intolerably sharp swings in fiscal instruments to correct for the lagged impacts of previous actions. So some degree of forecasting accuracy will surely be imperative. On this last point see Robert S. Holbrook, "Optimal Economic Policy and the Problem of Instrument Instability," *American Economic Review,* Vol. 62 (March 1972), pp. 57–65.

[155] See, for example, Albert Ando, E. Cary Brown, Robert M. Solow, and John Kareken, "Lags in Fiscal and Monetary Policy," in Brown and others, *Stabilization Policies,* pp. 1–163.

probably short enough not to present a major problem. Nevertheless, it is not zero; perhaps one or two quarters will elapse between a change in the pace of macroeconomic activity and its perception. A more serious problem may be posed by inaccuracies in the preliminary national income accounts data.[156] Substantial errors in provisional estimates of gross national product and its components obviously can yield a badly distorted view of the pace of economic activity; the hazard this presents to policy makers should be clear enough.

The second lag is really not a matter of economics at all. In principle, once the need for a fiscal action is recognized, government purchases can be varied or withholding schedules altered within a matter of weeks. However, congressional action is required before many of the important fiscal instruments may be employed. The lengthy legislative battle over the Revenue and Expenditure Control Act of 1968 provides ample evidence that the policy lag may be very long indeed. Such historical episodes have given rise to frequent proposals to streamline fiscal decision making, say, by giving the President some discretion over tax rates, at least in the short run.[157] But to date the Congress has exhibited absolutely no inclination to relinquish any of its tax-levying authority; and this is pretty much a dead issue.

*Empirical Evidence on Lags in Fiscal Policy*

The bulk of economic research has naturally been directed at the one lag that is purely economic in nature—the outside lag, the period between the execution of a fiscal policy move and the time its effects on the economy are ultimately felt. The existence of a substantial outside lag has often been used to build a case against discretionary fiscal or monetary policy (more on this later); and probably no empirical issue in macroeconomics now draws more dispute than the precise lag structures in the various key macroeconomic relations. Since fiscal policy actions reverberate through the economic structure in complex ways, most notions about policy lags nowadays come from experimenting with complete macroeconometric models, such as those discussed in the preceding section. Typically, a model is run both with

[156] For a quantitative assessment of this problem, suggesting that the errors are sizable, see Rosanne Cole, *Errors in Provisional Estimates of Gross National Product* (Columbia University Press for the National Bureau of Economic Research, 1969).

[157] See for example, *Money and Credit: Their Influence on Jobs, Prices and Growth*, The Report of the Commission on Money and Credit (Prentice-Hall, 1961), pp. 136–37.

and without the policy move being analyzed, and the difference between the two solutions, quarter by quarter, is taken as an estimate of
the size and timing of the effects of the policy. In the real world, mere
discussion of a policy change can precipitate important effects—as
when debate over increasing an excise tax generates anticipatory purchases—but no formal system of equations can be expected to account
for such phenomena.[158] Moreover, the pervasive autocorrelation in
most economic time series makes timing relationships notoriously
difficult to pin down econometrically. But, despite these shortcomings,
the models again offer the best evidence on lag structures to be had;
so it is worth surveying briefly what they have to say.

The National Bureau of Economic Research–National Science
Foundation seminars on comparison of econometric models, whose
results we found useful in evaluating the monetarist challenge in the
preceding section, again provides a fruitful point of departure.[159]
As was explained there, the main fiscal policy action analyzed by
these models was a sustained increment in nominal government
spending. The models also traced the effects of higher government
spending and an increase in personal income taxes, each with an accommodating monetary response to stabilize short-term interest rates.
But these are mixed fiscal-monetary policy experiments, and the time
pattern of their effects tells very little about the response of the
economy to pure fiscal policy.

Figure 6 shows the cumulative multipliers from several of the
models. In each case, the graph indicates the total change in nominal
GNP from a sustained $1 billion increment in nominal government
purchases. The reader is again reminded that the increment in real
government expenditure is generally declining over time as a result of
inflation, so these are not the government spending multipliers of
pure theory.

Although the lag structures obviously differ, all the models save
that of the St. Louis Federal Reserve clearly show a substantial short-
run impact for fiscal policy. The Wharton model, for example, shows
a four-quarter multiplier of 1.8, which builds to about 2.4 after three

---

[158] The FRB-MIT-Penn model deals with this problem by recording some
changes in policy instruments—for example, the investment tax credit—before the
fact. While this may be a useful way to keep an econometric model "on track,"
the procedure is rather ad hoc, to say the least.

[159] See Fromm and Klein, "Comparison of Eleven Econometric Models."

**FIGURE 6.** Quarterly Cumulative Impact of Sustained Increment in Nominal Nondefense Government Spending, Selected Econometric Models of the United States

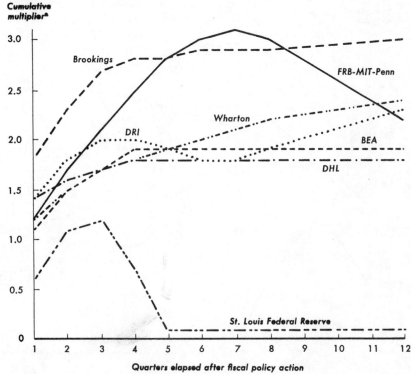

Cumulative
multiplier*

*Quarters elapsed after fiscal policy action*

Source: Gary Fromm and Lawrence R. Klein, "A Comparison of Eleven Econometric Models of the United States, n American Economic Association, *Papers and Proceedings of the Eighty-fifth Annual Meeting, 1972* (*American Economic Review*, Vol. 63, May 1973), Table 5, p. 391.

a. Cumulative multipliers = $\Delta GNP/\Delta G$ (current dollars), where G is government spending. The periods for which the multipliers are calculated generally cover a ten-year span. Some of the models use $1 billion increments, some $5 billion increments. Multipliers for quarters 9, 10, and 11 are not available, and have been interpolated linearly.

years. According to the FRB-MIT-Penn model, the multiplier actually peaks at about 3.1 after seven quarters, and has declined to just over 2 by the end of three years. In the Bureau of Economic Analysis (BEA) and Michigan (DHL-III) models, the four-quarter multipliers are identical to the twelve-quarter multipliers; and in the Brookings and Data Resources (DRI) models they are very close. In short, the models suggest that at least 75 percent, and probably much more, of the ultimate effect is felt within the first year after the initiation of the policy.[160]

[160] The actual simulation results for several of the models show no tendency to converge to a steady-state multiplier. The decision to cut off consideration of the results after twelve quarters was an arbitrary one.

**FIGURE 7. Quarterly Cumulative Impact of Sustained Increment in Real Nondefense Government Spending, Selected Econometric Models of the United States**

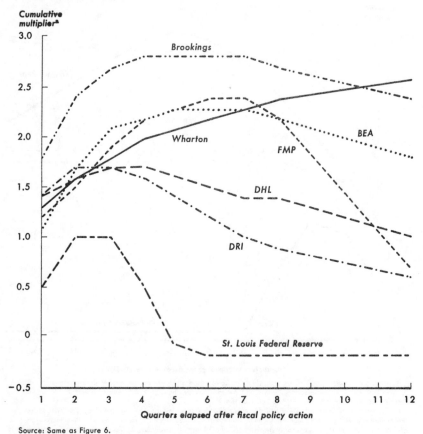

Source: Same as Figure 6.
a. See note a, Figure 6. Multipliers are calculated analogously, using data n 1958 dollars.

The St. Louis model is the iconoclast. Its computed multiplier peaks at just over unity in the second and third quarters after the policy change, and reaches its steady-state value of 0.1 by the fifth quarter.

While in our view the manner in which the multiplier experiments were conducted makes the nominal multipliers more meaningful, it is also possible to deflate both GNP and government expenditures in each quarter and compute the ratio of the cumulative increment in real GNP to the cumulative increment in real government spending (which is falling steadily due to inflation). Such computations, the results of which are displayed in Figure 7, give us something akin to—but hardly identical with—the real government expenditure multipliers of pure theory. The time paths turn out to be similar to those of Figure 6, except for a more pronounced tendency for the cumulative multipliers to decline in later quarters owing to the well-known contractionary effects of a rising price level.

These results generally confirm the few previously published simulation experiments with econometric models. For example, Fromm and Taubman, reporting extensively on simulations with the Brookings model using a variety of policy instruments, find a real government expenditure multiplier of 2.9 after ten quarters.[161] About two-thirds of the ultimate effect has already appeared after two quarters, and the first-quarter impact multiplier is 1.4.[162] De Leeuw and Gramlich find weaker, but also rather fast-acting, fiscal effects by simulating an early version of the FRB-MIT model. Their maximum real multiplier of 1.8 is reached after five quarters, but more than 90 percent of this is in hand by the second quarter after the policy change. After the fourth quarter, monetary side effects and inflation reduce the multiplier steadily to just 1.0 by the end of four years.[163] Simulations run by Evans using one version of the Wharton model imply that essentially all of the effects of an increase in government purchases are felt within the first quarter. His impact multiplier of 1.98 scarcely differs from the twelve-quarter multiplier of 2.07.[164] Finally, the Moroney-Mason model discussed in the previous section displays an impact multiplier of 1.2, a fourth-quarter multiplier of 2.1, and a steady-state multiplier of about 2.7 (all in current-price terms).[165]

These models seem to agree that a government able to see six to nine months ahead—not necessarily with complete accuracy, but well enough to know whether stimulus or restraint will be needed, and whether the dosage should be large or small—can make intelligent fiscal policy. Of course, it can also make mistakes, but that is hardly news.

[161] Gary Fromm and Paul Taubman, *Policy Simulations with an Econometric Model* (Brookings Institution, 1968).

[162] Ibid., Table 2.5, p. 48.

[163] Frank de Leeuw and Edward M. Gramlich, "The Channels of Monetary Policy," *Federal Reserve Bulletin*, Vol. 55 (June 1969), Table 4, p. 489.

[164] Michael K. Evans, *Macroeconomic Activity: Theory, Forecasting, and Control; An Econometric Approach* (Harper and Row, 1969), Table 20.3, p. 567. Evans in fact computes a forty-quarter multiplier (essentially the steady-state outcome) of 1.93.

[165] Moroney and Mason, "Dynamic Impacts of Autonomous Expenditures."

## Lags and the Workability of Discretionary Policy

The need for forecasting and the weakness of forecasts are sometimes made the basis of a pessimistic view of the practical possibility
of a stabilizing fiscal policy. Norman Ture, for example, mentions
three "basic premises" of what he calls the "new" view of fiscal policy:

1. In the absence of an active compensatory tax policy, the economy
   would be highly unstable and would experience intolerable swings in
   the rate of employment and periodic inflationary outbursts.
2. Potential deviations of the economy from the trend of steady, non-
   inflationary growth can be detected sufficiently in advance of their actual occurrence to allow the offsetting, stabilizing tax changes to be
   made on a timely basis . . .
3. Moderate temporary changes in income taxes induce quick, significant,
   and systematic, hence predictable, responses in the spending of households and businesses.[166]

Ture proceeds to deny the truth of each of these "basic premises."
Healthy skepticism, by definition, is a good thing. Surely some of the
claims about the delicacy and deftness with which stabilizing fiscal
policy can be managed have been excessive; the catch-phrase "fine
tuning" suggests what we have in mind. But such claims do not usually
appear in the professional literature. They are more often made in
advocacy of specific fiscal policy actions, and can perhaps be excused
on the ground that, in the American system of government, one must
claim to be able to do everything in order to be permitted to do anything. Nevertheless, we conclude that the skepticism of Burns, Ture,
and others is itself excessive. They make a case against fine tuning and
interpret it as a case against discretionary fiscal policy altogether.

The first of Ture's "basic premises" reflects the view that the object of stabilization policy is to iron out a persistent and violent business cycle: "intolerable swings in the rate of employment." This view
leads to the notion that the primary guide to policy needs is the direction of movement of the major economic indicators. In recent years

[166] Norman B. Ture, "Priorities in Tax Policy for the Next Decade," Tax Foundation, *Tax Review,* Vol. 29 (January 1968), pp. 1–2. Also see Ture, "The New Economics: Stabilizing Tax Policy," Selected Papers 25 (University of Chicago, Graduate School of Business, 1967; processed). Similar ideas are expressed less directly by
Arthur F. Burns at several points in his *The Business Cycle in a Changing World*
(Columbia University Press for the National Bureau of Economic Research, 1969),
especially pp. 284–85, 290–95, 310–11.

this view has been generally replaced by another: that in the absence
of an active stabilization policy the economy would sometimes exhibit
a persistent tendency for slack—that is, for excess capacity and unemployment—and sometimes a persistent tendency for demand to out-
run productive capacity. These "gaps" may be large or small, depending on the strength of private demand, the volume of government expenditures, and the revenue-raising capacity of the tax system. There
are some cumulative tendencies that make it harder to eliminate a gap
the longer it has persisted, but one would hardly call the economy
"highly unstable." The primary object of discretionary fiscal policy is
to close such a gap when one appears, or at least to narrow it.

This view of fiscal policy does not of course reduce it to a merely
qualitative or directional exercise. The size of a fiscal stimulus or restraint should be proportioned to the size of the existing or expected
gap, so numerical estimates of the effects of policy moves, such as
those discussed earlier, are still required. Furthermore, the need for
forecasting remains, as Ture's second premise correctly suggests. It is
necessary to know whether a gap will still exist when the effects of a
policy move are actually felt. Nevertheless, two consequences follow
from this view of the fiscal policy problem that considerably weaken
the argument of Burns and Ture.

In the first place, if the fiscal policy problem is more like steering a
wayward but moderately stable vehicle in the right direction, and less
like walking a tightrope, then groping toward the target is a feasible
policy and minor errors of judgment are not catastrophic.

In the second place, much of the evidence on the unreliability of
forecasts is evidence of an inability to predict algebraic changes in
time series, particularly the incidence of turning points. But, on our
view of the problem, the main requirement is for an answer to the
much simpler question: in the absence of any discretionary change in
policy, will output and employment much exceed or fall much short of
capacity so many quarters ahead?[167] No attempt has been made to test
that ability systematically, so we cannot make any strong statement
one way or the other. But since the task is easier than precise forecasting, the results of any such test would very likely be more optimistic than the results of Zarnowitz and others frequently cited as a

---

[167] This is recognized by Ture, "New Economics," p. 9; but earlier (p. 5) he
talks entirely in terms of cyclical turning points.

source of pessimism.[168] The combination of the difficulty of forecasting and the intrinsic lag between the time the need for a policy move is recognized and the time its actual effects are felt, does undoubtedly make fine tuning a chancy and difficult, perhaps impossible, job. But it does not make impossible the achievement of substantial stabilization effects through discretionary fiscal policy. At least that is our conclusion from both recent history and the recent literature on the determinants of private expenditures.

An important distinction must be made between fine tuning and what might be called "continuous adaptation." Reliance on fine tuning implies a great deal of optimism, a belief that stabilization policy can be pursued accurately enough to keep the economy always within a hair's breadth of full employment (or some other target). It presupposes the ability to forecast accurately both the course of private spending under present policy and the marginal effects of changes in policy. Even if one is not that optimistic, we still believe that it is better to make many small fiscal (and monetary) policy moves than a few large ones. For example, moving tax rates up and down by small amounts with each annual budget, in whatever direction seems appropriate in the light of current knowledge and forecasts, is better than waiting until growing excesses or deficiencies in aggregate demand call unmistakably for a major shift in the degree of fiscal stimulus. (Perhaps this system could be established best by giving the President some limited authority to alter tax rates.) The main reason for a policy of continuous adaptation is the nonlinearity of economic behavior: it is more than twice as hard to make a smooth correction in a boom or slump once it has gone twice as far. Moreover, the democratic process is likely to make big changes in fiscal policy the occasion for other changes in taxes and expenditures unrelated to economic stabilization. The outcome is likely to be unsatisfactory from both points of view. Finally, occasional big changes in tax rates and the volume of spending are more unsettling to private decision making than a steady stream of small changes, none big enough to disturb the private calculus.[169] Thus, except for responses to big exogenous

[168] Victor Zarnowitz, *An Appraisal of Short-Term Economic Forecasts,* Occasional Paper No. 104 (Columbia University Press for the National Bureau of Economic Research, 1967), pp. 4–8.

[169] This is essentially the typical argument for the superiority of floating over fixed exchange rates.

shocks, the need for major reversals in fiscal policy ought to be read as a signal of past error.

Another point has to be made, though its detailed discussion does not belong here. Regardless of the economics of the problem, fiscal policy can be paralyzed by political events.[170] One could certainly argue that this was the case between 1966 and 1970—that stabilizing fiscal policy fell victim to sharp differences of opinion within the Congress and within the country on quite different matters: the war in Vietnam, problems of race and poverty, even law and order. This possibility is sometimes made the basis of the argument that some discretionary power over tax rates ought to be lodged in the President. On balance, that is probably so. But it is naive to believe that a President could afford to act on purely technical grounds at a time of deep political division, or that at such a time Congress would be prepared to see much of its leverage taken away.

## The Predictability of Fiscal Policy Effects

There has been, and there continues to be, gradual progress in understanding of the qualitative nature and quantitative dimensions of different fiscal policy instruments. Generally speaking, the instruments that are analyzed are changes in government purchases of goods and services, in the rules governing transfer payments, in the definitions of the base for various taxes, and in tax rates. The effects of primary importance are usually taken to be changes in the volume and composition of national output, the level of employment, and the rate of change of prices. Predicting the impact of any fiscal policy tool involves two conceptually distinct steps. Except in the case of government purchases, which are themselves a component of aggregate demand, the first step is generally to analyze the effects of any policy action on the proximate determinants of some component of private spending. For example, it is obviously vital to know how any proposed change in the personal income tax statutes will affect disposable income. The second step is to study the relations between each component of private demand and its proximate determinants. This second step is usually more difficult, as exemplified by the unending debate over the determinants of business fixed investment. But the

---

[170] See the discussion by Joseph A. Pechman in "Fiscal Policy: Performance and Prospects" (paper prepared for delivery to the Midwest Economic Association, April 1968; processed). The point is also made by critics of fiscal policy.

first step may also involve some knotty problems; analyzing the incidence of the corporate income tax is perhaps the clearest example.

The ability to predict the consequences of fiscal policy actions thus depends primarily on progress in quantitative macroeconomics. Therefore, virtually every bit of new theoretical or empirical knowledge about the macroeconomy has some bearing on the nature and predictability of fiscal policy. As more precise econometric knowledge of the key functional relationships has accumulated, quantitative understanding of fiscal policy has been sharpened. And, with fairly reliable answers to some of the cruder questions firmly established, analytical and practical interest has turned to the much more subtle and tricky questions of the timing of responses to policy actions. Here the difficulties are enormous, and very little is settled.

An attempt to survey all the available quantitative knowledge on the determinants of the components of aggregate demand is obviously beyond the scope of this paper. Instead, we shall content ourselves with an abbreviated look at the main qualitative channels through which the key fiscal policy instruments are believed to work, with an emphasis on those areas where major uncertainties still exist.

Not much needs to be said about government spending. Federal outlays on goods and services are a direct contributor to aggregate demand on the "first round"; after that the multiplier process begins and, as even our rock-bottom model of earlier sections shows, the numerical value of the multiplier depends on all the important functional relationships in the model. We have already seen that the major econometric models differ somewhat on the exact value of the multiplier. But the significance of these differences should perhaps not be exaggerated; a fiscal policy planner will not often be led astray if he uses a multiplier of 2 in his back-of-the-envelope calculations. The main issues of econometric debate for the near future appear to be over timing. Which type of government purchase exhibits the fastest impact on aggregate spending? Which component of federal spending can be altered most expeditiously in accord with stabilization requirements?

For the most part, countercyclical variations in government transfer programs (to the extent that they are applied at all) are aimed at influencing consumer expenditures by altering disposable income. The macroeconomic theory of consumption is, perhaps, the area in which the widest consensus has evolved. Most economists nowadays subscribe to the notion that consumption is a fairly constant fraction of some concept of long-run income. In the "permanent income" variant, originated by Friedman,[171] long-run income is taken to be a distributed lag on past measured income. If this lag is assumed to have the geometric form, as it often is, the theory leads to predicting consumption as a linear function of current income and lagged consumption. In the "life cycle" variant of Modigliani, Brumberg, and Ando,[172] consumption is deduced to be a linear function of current *labor* income (which serves as a proxy for lifetime labor income) and lagged net worth (which serves as a proxy for lifetime property income). The two theories generate essentially the same predictions, although any two empirical studies will differ over the precise timing. An increase (decrease) in transfer payments will at first have a relatively minor impact on consumption since the short-run marginal propensity to consume (MPC) is rather low; however, if the increase (decrease) is maintained, consumption spending will eventually rise (decline) by nearly as much as the change in disposable income since the long-run marginal propensity to consume is equal to the long-run average propensity to consume, which is almost unity. The main issue here is whether temporary and permanent variations in disposable income are treated differently by consumers. We will discuss this question in some detail in our analysis of the 1968 income tax surcharge below. One further econometric issue is whether the propensity to consume out of transfer payments differs from the propensity to consume ordinary income. Although the received doctrine on the subject is that they are not very different, some recent work by Taylor calls this conclusion into question.[173]

The economic issues surrounding the effectiveness of changes in the personal income tax as a stabilizing device are basically the same. Personal tax payments are losses of disposable income, which should affect consumer spending in the same way as any other decline in in-

[171] Milton Friedman, *A Theory of the Consumption Function* (Princeton University Press for the National Bureau of Economic Research, 1957).

[172] See Franco Modigliani and Richard Brumberg, "Utility Analysis and the Consumption Function: An Interpretation of Cross-Section Data," in Kenneth K. Kurihara (ed.), *Post Keynesian Economics* (Rutgers University Press, 1954); and Albert Ando and Franco Modigliani, " 'The Life Cycle' Hypothesis of Saving: Aggregate Implications and Tests," *American Economic Review,* Vol. 53 (March 1963), pp. 55–84.

[173] Lester D. Taylor, "Saving out of Different Types of Income," *Brookings Papers on Economic Activity* (2:1971), pp. 383–407.

come. As indicated above, the main outlines of this channel of fiscal policy are well established and the remaining empirical questions are on fine points. For example, should we measure disposable income in the way the Commerce Department does—net of tax *payments*—or should we deduct taxes when the *liability* accrues? Two studies of the impact of the 1964 tax reduction illustrate that the answer may influence our view of the speed with which fiscal policy works. They also illustrate the grave econometric problems involved in estimating timing relations.

Both Okun and Ando and Brown utilize a "permanent income" consumption function that predicts quarterly expenditures of consumers as a linear function of current disposable income and last quarter's consumption.[174] Okun estimates his consumption function in current-price terms, using the official concept of disposable income (which deducts tax payments), and finds a short-run MPC of 0.37, and an eventual long-run MPC of 0.95. By the fourth quarter after any tax cut, consumption is already up 82 cents for each $1 of reduced taxes. Ando and Brown work with taxes on a liability basis, but do their estimation in constant-dollar terms, so it is hard to make a clean comparison. Worse yet, they present two radically different consumption functions, one estimated by ordinary least squares and the other by a method due to Liviatan which is intended to eliminate the bias present in least squares regressions when the lagged dependent variable appears as an independent variable and the disturbances are serially correlated.[175] The least squares estimate resembles Okun's in the long run (their long-run MPC is 0.94), but implies a rather slower response of consumption to a tax cut—the short-run MPC is only 0.21, and the first-year effect is only 59 cents of additional consumption for each $1 of tax reduction. But the estimates based on the Liviatan procedure imply a much faster response. According to these estimates, which are a priori preferable on statistical grounds, a $1 tax reduction leads to 76 cents of increased consumption in the same quarter, and has had virtually its full effect (93 cents) after one year. Since discretionary changes in personal income tax liabilities can be made very quickly,

[174] See Okun, "Measuring the Impact of the 1964 Tax Reduction," pp. 25–49; and Albert Ando and E. Cary Brown, "Personal Income Taxes and Consumption Following the 1964 Tax Reduction," in *Studies in Economic Stabilization,* pp. 117–37.

[175] Nissan Liviatan, "Consistent Estimation of Distributed Lags," *International Economic Review,* Vol. 4 (January 1963), pp. 44–52.

this estimate is very optimistic about the speed with which fiscal policy can operate on aggregate consumer expenditure.

But how is one to choose between this optimistic estimate on the liability basis and the much more sluggish consumption functions produced by Ando and Brown on the liability basis and by Okun on the Commerce Department cash-payment basis? Even at this late date one hesitates to base high policy on refined matters of least squares bias. Ando and Brown find that their more fast-acting consumption function tracks the post-1964 behavior better than their other one; but this is merely another way of saying that consumers responded very quickly to the 1964 tax reduction. Presumably a much slower-acting consumption function would have done a superior job of tracking behavior after the 1968 tax surcharge. It appears, then, that empirical study of the consumption function—at least as to timing questions— is not yet exhausted.

Much more controversy surrounds the workings of the less direct instruments of fiscal policy, such as the corporation income tax and the investment tax credit. Agreement on the nature of these channels of fiscal policy obviously awaits some consensus on the determinants of business investment; and the empirical and theoretical divergences among economists in this area are only too well known.

While popularity is not the same as accuracy, some variant of the "neoclassical" theory of investment, pioneered by Jorgenson and several collaborators,[176] is certainly encountered most frequently in econometric work. On this view, the desired stock of real capital is a function of nominal output and the nominal user cost of capital. The latter is, very roughly, the product of the price of capital goods times the sum of the depreciation rate and a weighted average of the after-tax costs of debt and equity funds, suitably adjusted to account for the tax system. In Jorgenson's work, which employs a Cobb-Douglas production function, the desired capital stock is constrained to be homogeneous of degree one in output and degree minus one in user cost.

---

[176] See Dale W. Jorgenson, "Capital Theory and Investment Behavior," in American Economic Association, *Papers and Proceedings of the Seventy-fifth Annual Meeting, 1962* (*American Economic Review,* Vol. 53, May 1963), pp. 247–59; Robert E. Hall and Dale W. Jorgenson, "Tax Policy and Investment Behavior," *American Economic Review,* Vol. 57 (June 1967), pp. 391–414; and Jorgenson's summary of the literature, "Econometric Studies of Investment Behavior; A Survey," *Journal of Economic Literature,* Vol. 9 (December 1971), pp. 1111–47.

Other, more general, specifications drop this restriction.[177] Net investment is assumed to be a distributed lag function of changes in the desired capital stock and replacements are assumed proportional to the existing stock. A one-time change in the desired stock, therefore, sets in motion a train of investment responses. On this theory, changes in tax provisions (such as the rate of corporate profits tax or investment tax credit) have their initial impact on the prices of capital goods relative to other things. An increase in the rate of tax credit, for example, obviously enhances the profitability of fixed investment by lowering the user cost. Oddly enough, an increase in the corporation income tax rate has an ambiguous effect. It clearly reduces the flow of future returns from any capital investment, but it may simultaneously reduce the after-tax discount rate.[178] Other complex fiscal weapons, such as changes in depreciation regulations, can also be analyzed by studying their effects on the user cost of capital.

Of course, the determinants of business investment are not to be decided upon by a popularity poll of econometricians. Several investigators have found some measure of liquidity to be a useful explanatory variable. They argue, for example, that past profits serve as an indicator of future profitability; or that firms have rather rigid dividend requirements and will invest any earnings above these requirements.[179] The usefulness of a liquidity variable can even be rationalized along more or less neoclassical lines. Since floating a new issue of debt or equity involves nonnegligible transactions costs, internal financing (through earnings retention) is cheaper than external financing. Thus the user cost of capital will be lower the greater the proportion of total financing that is accounted for by internal funds. Liquidity theories of investment give the most scope to the corporate income tax as a fiscal policy tool, since it influences retained earnings immediately and directly. Such theories attach rather less importance to tools like the investment tax credit that play on relative price effects.

[177] See, for example, Bischoff, "Effect of Alternative Lag Distributions."

[178] See Robert E. Hall and Dale W. Jorgenson, "Application of the Theory of Optimum Capital Accumulation," in Fromm, *Tax Incentives and Capital Spending*, especially pp. 17–18.

[179] See, for example, Edwin Kuh, "Theory and Institutions in the Study of Investment Behavior," in American Economic Association, *Papers and Proceedings of the Seventy-fifth Annual Meeting, 1962 (American Economic Review*, Vol. 53, May 1963), pp. 260–68.

A third major school of thought sees investment expenditures as determined largely by the accelerator—that is, as being proportional to changes in output—at least in the long run. Eisner, one of the most influential proponents of this view, has advocated a permanent income theory of investment analogous to the permanent income theory of consumption.[180] In this model, the desired stock of capital is proportional to long-run expected sales, and the latter is a distributed lag on past actual sales. Note that, if the relative price of capital goods and rates of interest are roughly constant in the long run, the neoclassical model also has this implication. But the policy implications of these two views of investment differ radically. According to the accelerator theory, the best way to spur investment spending is to increase aggregate demand, presumably through higher government spending or lower personal taxes or both.

If the controversy over the proximate determinants of investment is substantial, the controversy over the precise timing of the investment response to fiscal policy is monumental. This is due not so much to weaknesses in the imaginations of the investigators as to the unsolved—and perhaps unsolvable—problems of estimating timing relationships. It seems clear from the literature, both theoretical and econometric, that the response must involve a distributed lag of some length and possibly some complexity. But, no matter how sophisticated the estimation technique, the hard fact remains that most economic time series look very much like lagged values of themselves.

One might have hoped that the succession of investment incentives in recent years would have produced what economists are always looking for—a "controlled experiment." After all, we have seen accelerated depreciation (1954), relaxed depreciation guidelines (1962), the investment tax credit (1962), repeal of the Long amendment, which had required firms to deduct the amount of the credit from the depreciation base (1964), reduction of the tax rate on corporate profits (1964), suspension of the investment tax credit (October 1966), and its later resumption (originally scheduled for December 1967, but actually occurring in March 1967). Perhaps it is an indication of the vanity of such hopes that no consensus has yet emerged on the quan-

---

[180] See, for example, Robert Eisner, "Investment: Fact and Fancy," ibid., pp. 237–46; or his, "A Permanent Income Theory for Investment: Some Empirical Explorations," *American Economic Review,* Vol. 57 (June 1967), pp. 363–90.

titative effectiveness of such fiscal devices in controlling plant and equipment purchases.[181]

It is impossible to summarize the disagreements briefly. Here are just a few examples. Hall and Jorgenson estimate the aggregate volume of investment spending (in 1954 dollars) induced by all investment incentives from 1954 to 1963 inclusive to be $4.5 billion of equipment and $2.2 billion of structures. Coen, arguing that the elasticity of substitution between labor and capital is more like 0.2 or 0.4 than the 1.0 assumed by Hall and Jorgenson, claims that the figure ought to be $1.4 billion for equipment and $1.2 billion for structures (both in 1954 dollars). In addition, Coen has a rather different model of his own, but its estimates of the effects of investment incentives are not exactly comparable to those of Hall and Jorgenson.

Charles Bischoff has estimated some of these fiscal policy effects on equipment spending only, using a model related to that of Hall and Jorgenson but far from identical to it. Hall and Jorgenson estimate the effect of the 1964 cut in the corporate tax rate to have been a *reduction* of equipment purchases of $403 million in 1965 and $398 million in 1966 (both in 1965 prices). Bischoff attributes increases of $52 million and $166 million, respectively, in the two years. Hall and Jorgenson credit the repeal of the Long amendment with $1.3 billion, $1.4 billion, and $1.1 billion of equipment purchases (in 1965 prices) in 1964, 1965, and 1966. Bischoff finds a negligible stimulus in 1964, $940 million in 1965, and $2.04 billion in 1966. Hall and Jorgenson credit the 1962 depreciation guidelines with the stimulation of roughly a billion dollars of equipment purchases in each year from 1962 to 1966; the Bischoff figures show no effect in 1962, $52 million in 1963, and then $374 million, $561 million, and $613 million in the next three years (1965 dollars).

In brief, fixed investment is today the subject of extensive research and considerable disagreement. As with consumption, most (but not all) of the debate is over the link between investment spending and its

----

[181] The reader can get some of the flavor of the discussion in Fromm, *Tax Incentives and Capital Spending*, a symposium volume published by the Brookings Institution in 1971 (cited in note 84 above). See also, "Tax Policy and Investment Behavior: Comment," by Robert M. Coen; "Comment" on the same paper by Robert Eisner, and "Tax Policy and Investment Behavior: Reply and Further Results," by Robert E. Hall and Dale W. Jorgenson, all in *American Economic Review,* Vol. 59 (June 1969), pp. 370–401; and "Further Comment," by Eisner in the same journal, Vol. 60 (September 1970), pp. 746–52.

proximate determinants rather than the link between the latter and the fiscal policy tools. At least for the present, attempts to control the volume of investment by tax incentives ought to be regarded as cases of "multiplier uncertainty" (see the following paragraphs). There is every reason to believe that our understanding of the investment process will improve; and, as it does, so will the capacity of governments to discriminate more finely in allocating the burden of stabilization policy between investment and consumption. It seems likely, however, that the intrinsic irreducible variability, or "noise," is proportionately greater in investment than in consumption. This, of course, is what one would expect from an activity so closely attuned to expectations about future sales, future prices, and future profits. There may well be serious limits to the degree of fineness with which fiscal policy planners can deliberately act upon private investment.

## Multiplier Uncertainty and Fiscal Activism

What are the theoretical implications for the conduct of discretionary policy of the uncertainty that attaches to many fiscal policy instruments, and to the course of the macroeconomy in general? Should policy makers simply ignore these uncertainties and proceed as if their best guesses were in fact certainties? Should they abandon all discretionary actions and rely instead on the inherent stability of the economic system, as modified by the automatic stabilizers? Or does the existence of uncertainty suggest modification of the decisions that would be taken under certainty, without going all the way to abandonment of discretionary policy?

To answer these questions, as Brainard has pointed out, we must distinguish carefully between two kinds of uncertainty—uncertainty about policy multipliers, and all other kinds of uncertainty.[182] This can best be illustrated by use of a simple "reduced form" model of the determination of GNP. Assume that GNP, the only target of policy, can be expressed as a linear function of $k$ policy instruments, $F_i$; $m$ exogenous variables that are beyond the control of the authorities, $X_j$; and a stochastic disturbance, $u$:

$$(32) \qquad Y = a_1F_1 + \cdots + a_kF_k + b_1X_1 + \cdots + b_mX_m + u.$$

[182] William Brainard, "Uncertainty and the Effectiveness of Policy," in American Economic Association, *Papers and Proceedings of the Seventy-ninth Annual Meeting, 1966* (*American Economic Review*, Vol. 57, May 1967), pp. 411–25. The following paragraphs draw freely on this analysis.

The Andersen-Jordan equation discussed above is a special case of this formulation, in which $k = 2$ and $m = 0$. The kinds of uncertainty that *can* legitimately be ignored by policy makers, in the sense that they should simply form expectations of these uncertain variables and then proceed as if these expectations were certainties, include uncertainty over the values that the exogenous variables will assume in future periods (the $X$s), imprecise knowledge of the coefficients of the exogenous variables (the $b$s), and lack of knowledge of the future values of the stochastic disturbance ($u$). Henri Theil and others have shown that, if these are the only types of uncertainty that plague the policy maker, he should formulate his policy *one period ahead* just as if he were living in a world of certainty where $X$, $b$, and $u$ were all sure to take on their expected values.[183]

But Brainard has pointed out that things are not so simple when there is uncertainty surrounding the policy multipliers (the $a$s). In fact (though this cannot be rigorously established for the many-instrument case), there is a general presumption that the greater the uncertainty over the multiplier, the more conservatively the policy instrument should be used. To see this in the case of a single policy instrument ($k = 1$), let us follow Brainard in assuming that the authorities attempt to minimize the expected squared deviation of $Y$ from its target value, $(Y - Y^*)^2$, subject to equation (32) with $k$ set equal to unity and the symbol $X$ used as a shorthand notation for the random variable: $b_1 X_1 + \ldots + b_m X_m + u$. Thus, it is desired to minimize

$$E(Y - Y^*)^2 = E(aF + X - Y^*)^2.$$

Taking the first derivative with respect to the policy instrument, $F$, and setting the result equal to zero, yields the policy rule

$$F = \frac{\bar{a} Y^* - E(aX)}{E(a^2)},$$

which can be rewritten as

$$F = \frac{\bar{a}(Y^* - \bar{X}) - \mathrm{cov}(a, X)}{(\bar{a})^2 + \sigma_a^2},$$

where $\mathrm{cov}(a, X)$ is the covariance between the policy multiplier and $X$,

[183] See several of Theil's published works, such as *Economic Forecasts and Policy* (2d ed., Amsterdam: North-Holland, 1961), or *Optimal Decision Rules for Government and Industry* (Rand McNally, 1964). This conclusion also requires a quadratic welfare function.

and $\sigma_a^2$ is the variance of the policy multiplier. Note that only in the special case where $a$ is known with certainty will the policy rule call for bringing the expected value of $Y$ all the way to its target value: $F = (Y^* - \bar{X})/\bar{a}$. If the covariance between $a$ and $X$ is negligible, the indicated fiscal policy is more conservative than this in the sense that the authorities attempt to close only part of the gap. In particular,

$$(33) \qquad F = \frac{(Y^* - \bar{X})/\bar{a}}{1 + v^2},$$

where $v$ is the coefficient of variation of the policy multiplier. Clearly this implies a smaller policy response the greater the uncertainty over the multiplier. For example, if our econometric estimate of $a$ (the marginal impact of $F$ on GNP) is about 2.0 with a standard error of about 1.0, then $v$ is $\frac{1}{2}$, and the change in $F$ should be about 20 percent *less* than the change that would fully close the gap in the certainty case. This is a relatively small allowance for a substantial degree of uncertainty. Of course, if $a$ and $X$ have a strong negative covariance, we can no longer be sure that fiscal policy should be more conservative in an uncertain world than in a certain world. The reason is that in such a case, if our estimate of the fiscal multiplier is too low, it is very likely that our estimate of $X$ will simultaneously be too high, and vice versa. So errors in estimating the multiplier tend to compensate for errors in forecasting $X$.

In a multi-instrument context, things are more complicated because covariances among the various policy multipliers must also be considered. As a concrete example, suppose the greatest amount of uncertainty is over the interest elasticity of the demand for money. *IS-LM* reasoning says that if this elasticity turns out to be lower than expected, the multiplier for fiscal policy will be lower *and* the multiplier for monetary policy will be higher than expected. So less uncertainty will surround the impact of a fiscal-plus-monetary policy package than will surround either pure policy taken separately. Even when the covariance of two policy multipliers is positive, diversification will still normally yield gains.

The principal lesson from this analysis appears to be that in the presence of uncertainty over fiscal policy multipliers, it will generally be advisable to employ as many fiscal instruments as are available, and to employ most of them more conservatively than in a certain world. The present analysis is also relevant to our earlier discussion of the two views of the principal goal of stabilization policy: the "old view" (as exemplified by Ture and Burns) of lessening the severity of persistent business cycles, versus the "new view" of closing persistent gaps (positive or negative) between actual and potential output. In the old view, the divergence between the GNP level expected in the absence of discretionary policy ($X$) and the target level ($Y^*$) is small relative to the uncertainty over the fiscal multiplier, so equation (33) calls for only very mild policy responses. By contrast, the new view admits multiplier uncertainty, but holds that it is often rather small as compared with the gaps between actual and desired GNP. In such a case, equation (33) would call for an activist fiscal policy, though not necessarily for fine tuning (which we may characterize as small stabilization moves undertaken when $X$ is not very far from $Y^*$).[184]

### Fiscal Policy as an Anti-inflationary Device

Most of our discussion thus far has focused on the effects of any fiscal policy move on aggregate demand and employment. But the twin goals of stabilization policy are usually taken to be the simultaneous avoidance of high levels of unemployment and high rates of inflation. Our rationale for paying such scant attention to inflation is as follows. The impact of fiscal policy on aggregate demand is relatively straightforward and immediate. A large body of received knowledge exists that can be brought to bear on the subject. But once we seek to determine how any increment in aggregate demand is apportioned between increases in real output and increases in prices, we must enter a second branch of macroeconomic theory—the theory of inflation. Here the state of the art is much less settled, and to attempt to summarize it would be both perilous and beyond the scope of this survey. We have made no such attempt, and will make none. Nevertheless, there are some simple remarks that can be made, but most commonly are not, about the effects of fiscal policy actions, especially tax increases, on aggregate supply.

The basic remark is so obvious that it is almost embarrassing that it does not appear in textbook expositions of the analytics of fiscal policy. It is simply this: most taxes are, in the short or long run, incorporated into business costs, and therefore (at least partially)

---

[184] For further discussion of these and related issues, see Arthur M. Okun, "Fiscal-Monetary Activism: Some Analytical Issues," *Brookings Papers on Economic Activity* (1:1972), pp. 123–63.

passed on to the consumers in the form of higher prices. Therefore, if the contractionary fiscal medicine administered to cure an inflation takes the form of higher taxes, it may well have the desired deflationary impact on aggregate demand, but also an unintended cost-push inflationary impact on aggregate supply. The net result is, in many cases, unclear on purely theoretical grounds.[185]

In comparing these two opposing effects, an ambiguity arises that can be eliminated only by a more detailed model of the dynamics of inflation than we can take time to develop. An inflationary gap sets off a chain or process of *price increases;* whereas the passing on of a tax increase changes the *equilibrium price level.* If the inflationary process would go off to infinity, then any one-time, tax-induced increase in the price level is ultimately negligible. But if (say, in the absence of monetary accommodation) the inflation would eventually burn itself out and prices would converge to a new, and higher, level, then that new equilibrium will be higher than it would have been in the absence of a tax increase. If the Congress pays attention to the real value of the tax change, however, the true process is still more complicated. In that case a tax increase that contributes to higher prices might lead to further tax increases (to recoup the real revenue loss) which would then become part of the dynamic inflationary process.

The clearest example of an inflationary tax hike is probably an increase in excise taxes. Any such increase represents a decline in consumers' real income; but this is only one, if an important, impact. Unless demand for the product is completely inelastic, the primary effect is to redirect consumers' dollars away from the taxed good *by raising its price.* The inflationary tendency could hardly be more obvious. Further, to the extent that the unspent dollars flow into the markets for other consumer goods rather than into savings, their prices will be pushed upward as well.

A similar argument can be made with respect to the corporate income tax. This tax can be viewed as a selective excise tax on the use of capital, but not labor, as a factor of production. Unless there is no

---

[185] This has been noticed by Thomas Wilson, who estimated that about half of the inflation in Canada over 1964–71 was directly attributable to tax increases of various sorts. See T. A. Wilson, "Taxes and Inflation," in Canadian Tax Foundation, *1972 Conference Report,* Proceedings of the Twenty-fourth Tax Conference (1973), pp. 174–84.

forward shifting at all, part of this tax will be paid by the consumers of the output of the corporate sector when they are confronted by higher prices. When this notion is combined with the uncertain effect of the corporation tax on investment spending, it begins to look like a very strange anti-inflation device indeed.

It has recently been recognized that an analogous argument applies to increases in the personal income tax as a tool to curb inflation.[186] This can be seen by extending our rock-bottom model just a little bit to include wage determination in a labor market. Let there be an aggregate demand function for labor:

$$N^d = N^d(w), \quad \frac{dN^d}{dw} < 0,$$

where $w$ is the before-tax real wage and $N^d$ is the quantity of labor demanded; and let there be an aggregate supply of labor function:

$$N^s = N^s[w(1 - \tau)], \quad \frac{dN^s}{d[w(1 - \tau)]} > 0,$$

where $\tau$ is the rate of income taxation.[187] From the market-clearing equation, $N^d(w) = N^s[w(1 - t)]$, it is easy to show that any increase in the income tax rate will push wages upward. In most reasonable macro models, such a wage push will lead, ceteris paribus, to a higher equilibrium price level. So an increase in the income tax will simultaneously reduce aggregate demand (by lowering the *IS* curve) and restrict aggregate supply (by inducing workers to demand a higher pretax wage). It will unambiguously lower output, but its effect on the price level is indeterminate a priori. For our rock-bottom model, it can be shown that the necessary and sufficient condition for a rise in the income tax rate, $\tau$, to reduce the equilibrium price level is

[186] See the comments (to a paper by Eisner) by Bent Hansen and John H. Hotson, *American Economic Review,* Vol. 61 (June 1971), pp. 444–51; and Robert Eisner, "What Went Wrong?" *Journal of Political Economy,* Vol. 79 (May/June 1971), pp. 629–41. See also Alan S. Blinder, "Can Income Tax Increases be Inflationary? An Expository Note," *National Tax Journal,* Vol. 26 (June 1973), pp. 295–301, upon which much of the following is based.

[187] This differs from the usual presentation of the full Keynesian model by ignoring any money illusion in the labor supply function. It is proven in ibid., Appendix, pp. 299–301, that this phenomenon is irrelevant for the question at hand; that is, the same results hold whether or not there is money illusion or wage rigidity in the labor market.

$$m > \frac{\dfrac{\alpha}{1 - \tau}}{\dfrac{1 - \tau}{e_s} - \dfrac{1}{e_d}},$$

where $m$ is the income tax multiplier, $\alpha$ is labor's share in national output, and $e_s$ and $e_d$ are, respectively, the supply and demand elasticities for labor.

The actual dynamics of the inflationary process are far more complicated than our rock-bottom model indicates. The logical extension of the preceding analysis to a dynamic Phillips curve context calls for the inclusion of the rate of change of the personal tax rate as a determinant of the rate of change of money wages. R. J. Gordon has done approximately this in a recent Phillips curve study, and found that each 1 percent rise in the personal tax rate results in about a ⅙ percent rise in money wage rates in the short run. In the long run the effect is much greater since higher rates of change of money wages result in higher rates of inflation which in turn feed back (through expectations) into still faster rates of increase of money wages. Erik Lundberg pointed out long ago that if the tax system is progressive, and if prices respond rather fully to increased wage costs, it may take a very large wage increase to compensate for an autonomous price increase.[188]

We conclude then that tax raising may not be the best way to curb inflation. The same deflationary aggregate demand effect, without the accompanying inflationary aggregate supply effect, can always be achieved by expenditure reductions instead. For the sake of symmetry, we should also note that tight money as a cure for inflation runs into analogous objections. Restrictive monetary policies generally imply high interest rates, and interest payments are a significant component of costs to many firms.[189]

---

[188] Robert J. Gordon, "Inflation in Recession and Recovery," *Brookings Papers on Economic Activity* (1:1971), pp. 105–58. Gordon actually does something slightly different since his tax variable is not $\tau$ itself but rather $1/(1 - \tau)$, where $\tau$ is the average personal tax rate. A similar tax variable is used by Otto Eckstein and Roger Brinner, *The Inflation Process in the United States,* A Study Prepared for the Use of the Joint Economic Committee, 92 Cong. 2 sess. (1972); Erik Lundberg, *Business Cycles and Economic Policy* (tr., Harvard University Press, 1957).

[189] This problem may be of limited practical importance since only the interest rate on new debt, not that on existing contractual obligations, will be affected.

## Conclusion: The Economics of Fiscal Policy in 1968–70

The "New Economics"—a bad name for the general ideas we have been describing and espousing—became a household word after the success of the Revenue Act of 1964. "Success" in this context means that a major fiscal policy action, designed to move the economy to higher employment levels, was undertaken, and lo! employment expanded along just about the path that economists had predicted.[190] By contrast, the Revenue and Expenditure Control Act of 1968—essentially a 10 percent surcharge on personal and corporate income taxes and a proposed $6 billion cutback on expenditures—was intended to eliminate an inflationary gap and restrain a rising price level. It did not do so; at least, prices rose faster in 1969–70 than they did in 1968. The promises that accompanied this latter piece of legislation were not fulfilled, and this outcome has been widely interpreted outside the profession as a failure of the New Economics, which has now become just a bad name.

Inside the profession, the monetarists have argued that the experience of 1968–70 merely illustrates the impotence of fiscal policy, and thus verifies their doctrine. Robert Eisner, surely no monetarist, has gone even further and argues that these events illustrate the impotence of *both* fiscal and monetary policy in relieving the inflationary pressure generated by the Vietnam war. This perhaps overstates his conclusion, since Eisner presumably believes that abandonment of the war and reduction of military (or civilian) expenditures would have been effective. It is only the tax side of fiscal policy that Eisner sees as ineffectual. His general point seems to be that an inflationary gap opened by excessive public spending can be closed only by reducing government spending, not by taxation or monetary policy.[191] If valid, this reasoning would seem to apply to inflation caused by an upward shift in any spending schedule—public or private, and therefore would cast severe doubt on the ability to manage the economy. Other economists have, at the very least, revised downward their estimates of the ability to fine tune the economy through stabilization policy.

[190] This episode is well documented by a leading participant, Walter Heller, in *New Dimensions of Political Economy,* especially Chap. 2.

[191] See his two articles, "Fiscal and Monetary Policy Reconsidered," *American Economic Review,* Vol. 59 (December 1969), pp. 897–905, and "What Went Wrong?"

We cannot conclude this survey without offering an eclectic interpretation of the 1968–70 episode and its implications for the theory of fiscal policy.

There is an important preliminary point. The reasoning that prescribes a tax increase as an antidote for continuing inflation has two distinct steps. The first step claims that fiscal (or monetary) contraction will lead to a reduction in aggregate spending. The second step claims that the fall in aggregate spending will relieve the inflationary pressure. The medicine will fail to work if either of these steps fails. Most of this survey, like most of the work on fiscal stabilization policy, has been concerned with the first step—the link from the government budget to aggregate demand. If it were found that the tax surcharge of 1968 changed aggregate demand in precisely the predicted amount, but nevertheless failed to curb inflation, then most of the analytical underpinnings of fiscal policy that we have been discussing would be completely vindicated. Much less is known about the second link— from aggregate demand to inflation. Aside from our brief comments on the inflationary-deflationary effect of the income tax in the preceding section, we have had little to say about this. Most of the recent work on the Phillips curve can be interpreted as an investigation of this important question. Research on inflation theory is proceeding rapidly and few areas of consensus have evolved; we make no attempt to survey the literature here.[192]

### The Impact of Fiscal Policy

To assess the evidence generated by the 1968 experience, then, we must begin with a measure of the fiscal impact of the tax increase. As we pointed out above, the best measure would be the change in the weighted standardized surplus. In fact, no time series for a weighted standardized surplus over the 1968–70 period exists. But since the economy was very close to full employment in 1968 and 1969, a weighted full employment surplus (FES) is almost as good.[193] Unfortunately, we lack even this. As an imperfect substitute, we have computed a crude weighted FES based on FRB-MIT-Penn model

[192] Many of the interesting questions surrounding the step from curbing demand to curbing inflation are outlined in Eisner's stimulating paper, "What Went Wrong?"

[193] The unemployment rate averaged 3.6 percent in 1968 and 3.5 percent in 1969. The full employment surplus is conventionally calculated at 4 percent unemployment.

**TABLE 6. Quarterly Changes in Unweighted and Weighted Full Employment Surpluses, 1968–70**
(In billions of dollars)

| Year and quarter | Change in unweighted full employment surplus | Change in weighted full employment surplus |
|---|---|---|
| 1968:2 | −1.7 | −3.1 |
| 3 | 6.3 | 2.3 |
| 4 | 2.4 | 0.7 |
| 1969:1 | 11.0 | 4.6 |
| 2 | 4.4 | 3.1 |
| 3 | −2.9 | −3.2 |
| 4 | 0.9 | −1.0 |
| 1970:1 | −0.9 | −1.1 |
| 2 | −8.2 | −9.1 |

Source: Data for actual FES are from Nancy H. Teeters, "Budgetary Outlook at Mid-Year 1970," *Brookings Papers on Economic Activity* (2:1970), Table 1, p. 304. This source also provided the raw data from which the weighted full employment surplus was calculated; the weighting procedure is discussed in text note 194.

weights as given by Gramlich.[194] This series is given in Table 6, where it is juxtaposed against the ordinary FES. The most salient point made by this table is that using an unweighted FES drastically overstates the swing in fiscal impact. The ordinary FES indicates a substantial movement toward restraint by any standard—from a $13.5 billion *deficit* in the full employment budget in 1968:2 to a $10.5 billion surplus in 1969:2.[195] When we apply weights—recall that the contraction came largely in the form of tax hikes—the swing toward restraint looks considerably smaller; it amounts to under $11 billion over the same four quarters.

In any case, according to theory the 1968 fiscal package should have contracted the level of economic activity—not necessarily in absolute terms but relative to what would have occurred without the revenue act. But by how much? As we have pointed out earlier, to give an answer to that question requires a complete model of the economy, and then the answer is subject to all the uncertainties of the

[194] As a reasonable compromise between first-quarter weights and steady-state weights, we employ the one-year weights, that is, the sum of the first four quarters. Gramlich's level of disaggregation is rather coarse; with government spending weighted as unity, he assigns weights of 0.657 to personal taxes and 0.135 to corporate taxes (based on the FRB-MIT-Penn model). See Edward Gramlich, "Reply," in Lewis, *Budget Concepts for Economic Analysis*, p. 140.

[195] A combination of tax reductions and expenditure increases resulted in an expansionary reversal in the first half of 1970.

model. Furthermore, even given an estimate of the expected impact on gross national product, one cannot check simply by seeing whether GNP fell by the expected amount. Instead, the estimated path of GNP has to be compared with still another estimate—the hypothetical path of GNP in the absence of the fiscal policy change. Even keeping score in this ball game is a difficult matter.

Nevertheless, one must conclude that the response of the economy to fiscal policy from the second half of 1968 until 1970 was less than had been anticipated. Arthur Okun, who was chairman of the Council of Economic Advisers when the surtax was enacted, has suggested by how much, in his view, the outcome fell short of official expectations:

It was hoped and expected that this legislative victory would usher in a period of gradual disinflation. . . . A real growth rate of about 2 percent between mid-1968 and mid-1969 was expected to push the unemployment rate up slightly above 4 percent from its 3½ percent level of the time. . . .

Actual developments did not follow the flight plan. The slowdown was not nearly so pronounced as had been anticipated. Still, economic activity did change pace. If GNP had advanced as rapidly in the five quarters after the enactment of the fiscal program as it had in the preceding two quarters, it would have been $965 billion rather than the $942 billion actually reached in the third quarter of 1969. The moderation in the growth rate of real output was more marked—from 6½ percent in the first half of 1968 to 3½ percent in the second half and 2½ percent in the first half of 1969.[196]

## The Effect on Consumption

The 1968 *Economic Report* forecast that, with reasonably prompt enactment of the surcharge,[197] money GNP for 1968 would be about $846 billion. In fact it was about $20 billion higher.[198] Even recognizing that some political wishful thinking probably influenced the official forecast, this is a rather large discrepancy. The largest part of the underestimate of GNP was accounted for by consumption expenditures, which were underpredicted by $11 billion as the saving rate tumbled from 7.4 percent in 1967 to 6.7 percent in 1968. (The Council

---

196 Okun, *Political Economy of Prosperity*, pp. 91–92.

197 Although enactment was postponed until late June, the surcharge was made retroactive to April 1 for individuals and January 1 for corporations. Earlier enactment would no doubt have done better, but probably only slightly better.

198 *Economic Report, 1970*, p. 177.

of Economic Advisers predicted slightly under 7.1 percent for 1968.) This is an important error in view of the fundamental role that the consumption function plays in eclectic Keynesian theory. While the Council's forecast for 1969 in the January 1969 *Economic Report* was much more accurate, it is interesting to note that virtually the entire GNP error is accounted for by a $6.7 billion underestimate of consumption spending.[199]

Some economists—in particular, Eisner[200]—have argued that temporary changes in income tax rates are likely to be weak or useless for stabilization purposes, because consumption spending is geared to permanent income or some other variant of long-run disposable income.[201] In this view, the 10 percent surcharge was foredoomed to failure.

The precise extent to which the marginal propensity to consume out of temporary increases in disposable income falls short of the marginal propensity to consume out of permanent changes is still a matter of econometric debate. The findings of Katona and Mueller suggest that transitory increases in income have a much smaller immediate effect on consumer spending than do sustainable increases. There is evidence, however, that many transitory windfalls are eventually either spent on major purchases or in compensation for transitory reductions in income, or frittered away. In any of these cases, they add to consumer spending.[202] It is not always clear that consumers can distinguish between permanent and temporary changes in disposable income. However, if the MPC out of temporary increases and decreases is very low, and if temporary changes in tax rates are perceived as such, the multiplier effects of such changes are bound to be negligible. Specifically, suppose the marginal propensity to consume out of temporary changes in disposable income is $\beta$, a small number, and that the MPC for permanent changes is $c$, a larger

[199] This is not to say that all other components of GNP were predicted accurately, but only that there were countervailing errors.

[200] See his two articles cited in notes 186 and 191 above. See also the comments on his 1969 article by Bent Hansen, John H. Hotson, Barbara Henneberry and James G. Witte, and Keith M. Carlson, and Eisner's reply in *American Economic Review*, Vol. 61 (June 1971), pp. 444–61.

[201] It is possible to question whether taxpayers ever regard tax increases as temporary. But if they ever do, the 1968 surcharge was presumably such a case because it was so explicitly temporary.

[202] George Katona and Eva Mueller, *Consumer Response to Income Increases* (Brookings Institution, 1968), especially pp. 105–06.

number. Then even a temporary tax change would give rise to some first-round change in consumption spending; and the rest of the multiplier chain would proceed according to the *permanent* MPC, because consumers could hardly be expected to realize the temporary nature of the secondary and tertiary changes in disposable income. It is easily seen that the multiplier for a discretionary tax increase is[203]

$$(-\beta)/[1 - c(1 - \tau)],$$

where $1 - \tau$ is the fraction of a change in GNP that becomes a change in disposable income. Eisner suggests that $\beta$ is about 0.1,[204] in which case the temporary tax multiplier would be only $\frac{1}{4}$ even if $c(1 - \tau)$, the permanent marginal propensity to consume with respect to GNP, were as high as 0.6. It is certainly reasonable to expect $\beta$ to be less than $c$, but Eisner's figure of 0.1 seems unreasonably small, especially since a portion of consumer expenditures as measured in the national accounts (durables) is really part of saving rather than consumption.

Okun has investigated this question in the following way. The consumption equations (usually somewhat disaggregated) of four major econometric models are fed the actual data they need in order to grind out estimates of consumption spending from the third quarter of 1968 through the third quarter of 1970.[205] Each model then proceeds to generate a sequence of consumption forecasts on each of two polar assumptions: (a) that the reduction in disposable income on account of the surcharge is treated like any other change in disposable income ("full effect"); and (b) that it is ignored by consumers—that is, that the additional tax payments should be added back to get an appropriate measure of disposable income ("zero effect"). The two sequences of consumption forecasts for each model can then be compared to the real-world outcome, to see which of the extreme assumptions comes closer to the truth. It would perhaps make more sense to test some intermediate hypothesis like "half effect" or "three-quarters effect." Since most of the models contain only minor nonlinearities, the ap-

---

[203] One way is to observe that the multiplier chain per dollar of tax increase is

$$- \beta - c(1 - \tau) \beta - c^2 (1 - \tau)^2 \beta - \cdots.$$

[204] Eisner, "Fiscal and Monetary Policy Reconsidered," p. 900.

[205] Arthur M. Okun, "The Personal Tax Surcharge and Consumer Demand, 1968–70," *Brookings Papers on Economic Activity* (1:1971), pp. 167–211. Where lagged consumption is an argument in an equation, the equation's earlier forecast is fed back.

**TABLE 7. Root Mean-Squared Errors in Predicting Total Consumption under Various Hypotheses, Four Models**

(*In billions of 1958 dollars*)

| | Model | | | |
|---|---|---|---|---|
| Hypothesis | Data Resources | Michigan | Office of Business Economics | Wharton |
| Full effect | 2.1 | 3.3 | 2.5 | 2.5 |
| Half effect | 1.5 | 2.8 | 1.5 | 3.4 |
| Zero effect | 2.2 | 3.3 | 1.8 | 4.7 |

Source: Computed for the period 1968:3 through 1970:3 from data in Arthur M. Okun, "The Personal Tax Surcharge and Consumer Demand," *Brookings Papers on Economic Activity* (1:1971), Table 2, pp. 188–89.

propriate linear combinations of the zero-effect and full-effect results are fair approximations for this purpose. We do this in Table 7.

Okun's results are interesting, though not always easy to interpret. For nondurable goods and services, the full-effect predictions are perceptibly better than the zero-effect ones. For durable goods except automobiles, there is little to choose between them, though three of the four models make the full-effect hypothesis marginally more accurate than the zero-effect one. For automobiles, zero effect is plainly closer to the mark. In fact even it underpredicts automobile purchases substantially: from the middle of 1968 to the end of 1969 auto purchases were unusually high not only relative to measured disposable income but also relative to disposable income *plus* the surcharge! Actually, this circumstance is not entirely favorable to the zero-effect hypothesis. If there was in fact a substantial exogenous—or at least unexplained—burst of demand for cars, then this, rather than the permanent income hypothesis, may explain the strength of consumption after the surcharge. In that case, the moral to be drawn would be not that fiscal policy is impotent, but simply that all stabilization policy is difficult when the strength of private demand shifts unpredictably.

However, this disaggregated interpretation of consumption behavior may not be the appropriate one for comparing the zero-effect and full-effect hypotheses. If there was indeed exogenous strength in automobile demand, consumers may have financed their purchases partly from saving and partly by diverting expenditures from other consumption goods. In that case, had it not been for the high volume of auto spending, other consumption spending would have been higher; this reasoning favors the zero-effect hypothesis. When total consumption expenditure, rather than the three components, is considered, the two hypotheses come out about equally well. This observation suggests a "half-effect" hypothesis as a compromise; and, indeed, it appears to be somewhat better for predicting total consumption than either of the polar extremes, as Table 7 reveals.

The 1968–70 history of consumer spending thus does not appear to provide conclusive evidence of the powerlessness of fiscal policy as a stabilization tool. One reason why consumption rose so strongly after the surcharge is that an upsurge of demand, especially for automobiles, probably was in the works anyway. It was not foreseen, and the restraint on disposable income was too weak to yield the desired result. Another reason is that *temporary* income tax changes should certainly be discounted somewhat to allow for permanent income effects. The size of this discount is not clear, but 50 percent seems a reasonable guess of the effectiveness of temporary across-the-board tax changes relative to permanent ones.[206] Eisner's guess that the MPC out of temporary fluctuations in disposable income is 0.1 seems to be wide of the mark.

## The Effect on Investment

Consumption spending was not the only component of GNP to surprise the designers of fiscal policy in 1968. Inventory investment was seriously underestimated, presumably out of fear of the remaining overhang of inventories after the rapid accumulation in 1965–67, and perhaps also due to the general overestimate of the contractionary effect of the surcharge. Also, the strength of business fixed investment was substantially underestimated in 1969.[207] That plant and equipment spending is difficult to predict accurately is hardly news. A fundamental question for countercyclical policy arises only if there is

[206] For example, when Okun freely estimates (that is, without constraints and adjustments) the fraction of the income loss from the surcharge that was treated as permanent by consumers, his percentages for the four models are 53, 47, 34, and 133. The last percentage, which is wildly inconsistent with the others, is for the Wharton model, which has the odd property of actually *over*estimating consumption spending even assuming the surcharge had full effect. See "Personal Tax Surcharge," p. 190.

[207] The Council of Economic Advisers forecast an increase of about $7 billion or $8 billion in 1969; the expansion was actually $10.6 billion. For a discussion of some possible reasons for this, see Okun, *Political Economy of Prosperity*, pp. 94–95.

some reason to expect investment to move perversely against stabilization efforts.[208]

Eisner has proposed such a reason.[209] Suppose, as seems plausible, that investment spending is fundamentally guided by expected long-run profitability. Then an explicitly temporary increase in corporate income tax rates will affect the *timing* of investment much more than the *volume*. As Eisner notes, the installation of new plant and equipment carries with it many ancillary expenses that are immediately tax deductible, though closely associated with the act of investment. In addition, under favorable tax provisions, much of the depreciation can be taken in the first few years of the life of the project. Astute corporations may therefore respond to a temporary tax increase by advancing planned expenditures, so that the installation costs and depreciation can be charged against the higher tax rates, while the returns on the investment are not reaped until the lower tax rates are back in effect. This is, in principle, a possibility. Its importance depends on the magnitude of the ancillary expenses and early depreciation write-offs; they must be large enough to more than offset the reduction in the earliest part of the stream of after-tax quasi-rents. The most important item here is very likely to be the first year or so of depreciation allowances. For example, use of double-declining-balance accounting with a five-year lifetime can generate a first-year depreciation allowance of 40 percent of the purchase price. To write that off under a 10 percent surcharge "saves" 4 percent of the cost of the capital asset, which, if not tremendous, is surely not negligible. At the very least, this weakening of fiscal policy control over investment spending is a hidden cost of such devices as accelerated depreciation and artificially short depreciation lives.

The same arguments that weaken the case for the stabilization potential of temporary variations in the corporate income tax suggest that temporary variations in taxes and subsidies like the investment credit may be very useful. The timing effects of variations in the investment tax credit reinforce the policy—that is, a temporary suspension or reduction of the credit provides a powerful motive to postpone investment until the credit is restored. A similar line of reasoning suggests that more attention might be paid to the possibility of temporary

---

[208] However, a serious practical question arises even if the response of investment is in the right direction but is very small.

[209] "Fiscal and Monetary Policy Reconsidered," p. 900, note 7.

consumption taxes.[210] These would have strongly favorable timing effects,[211] though some care would have to be devoted to selecting the base if the tax were not to be highly regressive.

*Errors in the Government Sector*

Another source—unexpected and often overlooked—of the failure of the surcharge to live up to its advertising was the official underestimate of government purchases. The size of the surcharge was predicated on an increase in federal expenditures of $6 billion in 1968. In fact, even after Congress inserted an expenditure limitation in the act, federal spending rose $8.8 billion for the year. This may not have been so surprising; at the time, many observers believed the expenditure control provisions to be no more than window dressing. Perhaps more important was the substantial underestimate of the rise in state and local government purchases. The *Economic Report* forecast an increase of $8 billion to $9 billion; in fact, the rise was $11.3 billion.[212] For total government purchases, the underestimate in 1968 comes to about $5.6 billion. One way to appreciate the true order of magnitude of this error is to set it against the fact that the personal tax part of the surcharge was designed to raise $8 billion at the 1968 level of GNP. The underprediction of government purchases thus directly offsets 70 percent of the surcharge on personal income taxes. Further, if one applies appropriate multiplier weights, as in the calculation of a

[210] Although probably every teacher of macroeconomics has at one time or another discussed the use of temporary taxes that seek to exploit intertemporal substitution effects for stabilization purposes, there is remarkably little literature on the subject. A fleeting reference to *temporary* consumption taxes as a stabilizer appears in E. Cary Brown, "Analysis of Consumption Taxes in Terms of the Theory of Income Determination," *American Economic Review*, Vol. 40 (March 1950), especially p. 76. James Tobin advocated the use of some such device, probably a variable tax credit on net investment, in his Janeway Lectures at Princeton University (forthcoming from Princeton University Press). William H. Branson discussed the likely effectiveness of a variety of temporary taxes and, based on the belief that businesses are more sensitive to the subtleties of intertemporal pricing than consumers, concluded that the best bet might be a temporary tax (subsidy) on some long-lived investment goods. See his "The Use of Variable Tax Rates for Stabilization Purposes," in Richard A. Musgrave (ed.), *Broad-Based Taxes: New Options and Sources* (Johns Hopkins University Press for the Committee for Economic Development, 1973).

[211] Prior discussion of such taxes has a perverse timing effect. Thus, to be an effective stabilization tool, they would probably have to be discretionary within statutory limits.

[212] The *Economic Report* for each year, 1963–68, managed to underestimate the year's rise in state and local spending.

weighted budget surplus, the error on the spending side offsets even more of the income tax increase, and may even make the net fiscal impact expansionary.

### Monetary Factors: The Theory Illustrated (Painfully)

Finally, we must say something about the monetary policy that preceded and accompanied the tax increase. The relevant question is not merely whether overall stabilization policy was well coordinated— which it was not—but whether the size of the fiscal dose adequately took into account the lagged effects of earlier monetary expansion. In our view, it did not. We suspect that, if the lagged and contemporaneous effects of monetary and fiscal policy were fully accounted for, the impact of fiscal-cum-monetary policy would be judged only mildly contractionary, or perhaps even expansionary, during most of the surcharge period.

The period of tight money associated with the "credit crunch" ended in January 1967. As an indication of what happened next, unborrowed reserves of member banks increased more than $1.7 billion in the second half of 1967, stayed level in the first half of 1968, and rose some $1.5 billion in the second half of 1968. The result was an expansion of the money supply (narrowly defined) at a 7.3 percent annual rate over the January 1967–January 1969 period, the fastest sustained rate of monetary growth for any period since 1946.[213]

To convert this history into an estimate of the impact of monetary policy on GNP requires a sequence of current and lagged money multipliers from an econometric model. We have done some rough computations using the money multipliers from the versions of the FRB-MIT and Brookings models that were published at that time.[214] The two models give quantitatively different but qualitatively similar results. They both assert that the impact of monetary policy on GNP was expansionary from the middle of 1968 until the end of 1969, especially in the last quarter of 1968 and the first half of 1969. (These

[213] The data on unborrowed reserves are from *Economic Report, 1969* and *1970,* pp. 289 and 241, respectively, and are not seasonally adjusted. The money stock data are from "Money Supply and Time Deposits, 1914–69," Federal Reserve Bank of St. Louis, *Review,* Vol. 52 (March 1970), Table II, p. 7, and are seasonally adjusted.

[214] For the FRB-MIT model, see two papers by Frank de Leeuw and Edward Gramlich, "The Federal Reserve-MIT Econometric Model," *Federal Reserve Bulletin,* Vol. 54 (January 1968), pp. 11–40, and "The Channels of Monetary Policy." For the Brookings model, see Fromm and Taubman, *Policy Simulations.*

**TABLE 8. Net Impact on Money GNP of Fiscal and Monetary Policies, Two Models, 1968–69**
(In billions of dollars)

| Model | 1968:3 | 1968:4 | 1969:1 | 1969:2 | 1969:3 | 1969:4 |
|---|---|---|---|---|---|---|
| FRB-MIT 1968[a] | 3.8 | 2.4 | 2.5 | −4.3 | −16.2 | −13.7 |
| FRB-MIT 1969[b] | 7.8 | 10.9 | 13.1 | 8.6 | −0.7 | 3.4 |
| Brookings | −2.1 | −3.4 | −1.2 | 0.9 | −8.1 | −5.4 |

Source: FRB-MIT and Brookings econometric models.
[a] Computed using tax multipliers of the 1968 version.
[b] Computed using tax multipliers of the 1969 version.

estimates include the cumulated lagged effects of earlier changes in unborrowed reserves.[215]) As for orders of magnitude, the FRB-MIT model suggests a contribution to GNP averaging about $16 billion in the last quarter of 1968 and the first half of 1969; the estimates from the Brookings model run about half that.[216]

These models also provide estimates of the deflationary effect of the personal income tax surcharge. Here too they differ. The Brookings model attributes to the surcharge a negative contribution to GNP of about $9 billion, at annual rates, in the fourth quarter of 1968 and the first half of 1969. The FRB-MIT model gives two answers, depending on the set of tax multipliers used: one version gives an average deflationary impact of just under $16 billion in those three quarters, while the other version puts it at about $5 billion.

Combining the monetary and fiscal impacts for each model produces the story outlined in Table 8. The three models give rather different assessments of countercyclical policy. According to the 1968 FRB-MIT model, monetary expansion was just about strong enough to counter the substantial influence of the surcharge and provide a mild stimulus to the economy during 1968:3–1969:1. Starting with 1969:2, contractionary policy began to take hold, becoming quite potent in the last half of 1969. The 1969 FRB-MIT model is less sanguine about the effectiveness of tax increases. As a result, it shows a strongly expansionary net impact of countercyclical policy for the first four quarters after the surtax. Only in 1969:3, according to this model, was

215 For approximation purposes, we allowed lags only up to six quarters. Some models profess much longer lags than this.
216 This should not necessarily be interpreted as evidence that the Fed was managing monetary policy incompetently. It has been argued that the monetary expansion was in response to the surcharge, which the Fed thought would pass the Congress much sooner than it did.

any contraction felt; and even this was short-lived. The Brookings model ascribes less potency to *both* fiscal and monetary policy, but tells a story that is not qualitatively different from the 1968 FRB-MIT model. According to the Brookings multipliers, the surcharge was able to overwhelm the monetary expansion during 1968:3–1969:1, but only by a relatively small margin. Only in the last half of 1969 did it apply a significant brake to the economy.[217]

If the three models yield any consensus, it is this: The deflationary impact of the surcharge was either weaker, or only marginally stronger, than the inflationary influence of past monetary policy. The models agree that if any significant contractionary influence was felt, it was only in the latter half of 1969. It is somewhat encouraging (to the model builders at least!) to observe that these predictions come quite close to what most observers believe happened in the post-surtax period.

*The Lessons of 1968*

In summary, our reading of the 1968–69 episode does not suggest the need for any fundamental revision of the eclectic theory of income determination presented here, despite the disappointing results of the 1968 act. But the analysis does indicate that the size[218] of the deflationary dose was definitely inadequate to the need for at least four reasons:

1. There appears to have been an exogenous strengthening of consumer demand, especially for automobiles, roughly coincident with the enactment of the surtax. This development underscores the difficulty of fine tuning, but in no way casts doubt on the analytical underpinnings of fiscal policy with which this survey has been concerned.

2. The effectiveness of the personal and corporate income tax surcharges on consumption and investment was insufficiently discounted for the explicitly temporary nature of the actions, a point that was apparently ignored in the pre-1968 literature.[219]

---

[217] The preceding calculations were based on data taken from various *Economic Reports*, which have since been revised.

[218] The timing was also certainly off; but that has to be accounted one of the lesser disasters of the Vietnam War.

[219] But see Albert Ando and E. Cary Brown, "Personal Income Taxes and Consumption Following the 1964 Tax Reduction," in Ando and others, *Studies in Economic Stabilization*, especially p. 137.

3. Both federal and state and local government expenditures on goods and services were seriously underestimated. If the published forecasts represent what those in government actually believed, then much (and perhaps all) of the deflationary impact of the tax increase was dissipated in canceling out the unexpected surge in government purchases.

4. There was a hangover of expansionary monetary policy dating back to the reversal of monetary policy after the credit crunch, and not reversed by any tightening in 1968. Fiscal restraint probably did not allow adequately for the need to offset the lagged effects of this monetary expansion. But this *reinforces* rather than *undermines* the received doctrine on monetary factors as we outlined it above.

In addition, one should perhaps give some weight to the difficulty of legislating very large tax increases at any time, but especially in a frenetic political climate such as prevailed in 1968. If this political difficulty is real, it operates against the success of deflationary stabilization policy. But it is a problem of politics and not economics, and in no way casts doubt on the analytical foundations of fiscal policy.

We conclude that the experience of 1968–69 should be sobering but not stunning. Fine tuning is difficult—perhaps even impossible—given our present state of knowledge. Any stabilization move so subtle as to seek to alter the unemployment rate by a single point or less runs the risk of being nullified by unpredictable (or at least unpredicted) shifts in the strength of private (or public) demand. This is cause for care in advertising, but not for paralysis.

# The Incidence and Economic
# Effects of Taxation

GEORGE F. BREAK

# The Incidence and Economic Effects of Taxation

TAX SHIFTING AND INCIDENCE, long topics of rather esoteric concern
to fiscal economists, have with mushrooming public expenditures and
rising taxpayer resistance begun to attract the interest they deserve
from tax policy makers. Fortunately this is a propitious time for a
focusing of such interest. During the past twenty years scholars working in this field have produced an impressive body of literature which
should provide a useful basis for future policy decisions. They have
developed a consistent general equilibrium theoretical framework to
serve as a basic analytical tool. They have compiled a substantial body
of empirical data to evaluate the effects of tax policy. And their findings have begun to uproot some old orthodoxies and to direct new attention to other ideas once considered too far-out and implausible to
be taken seriously.

It is with the policy maker in mind, therefore, that the highly technical economic literature of recent years is here summarized and appraised. The starting point is the general theoretical framework for
incidence analysis. Attention then is focused on ways in which this
can be extended and refined to produce useful evaluations of specific
taxes. This analytical process is first applied to the corporate profits

tax and the general property tax, the two levies that lend themselves most readily to such evaluation and also happen to evoke the widest diversity of opinion among economists. Much of the discussion of these taxes can readily be applied to others. Some special aspects of tax incidence, however, are illustrated by the federal payroll tax for social insurance and by the general sales and individual income taxes. These are therefore considered separately. The first of these has been the outstanding growth tax of the postwar period; the others need further exposure to the incidence controversy.

Modern incidence theory makes a basic distinction between tax incidence on the sources-of-income side of household budgets and incidence on the uses-of-income side. Of fundamental importance is how the burdens of different taxes are distributed vertically, according to family income. Table 1 shows the major sources from which families at different income levels derive their incomes and the distribution of these sources along the income scale. By revealing some extremely sharp contrasts between rich and poor in the important matter

**TABLE 1. Percentage Shares of Aggregate Money Income, by Type, Received by Each Tenth of Households, Ranked by Income, 1962**

| Income rank (tenths of total households) | Total income | Wages and salaries | Business income[a] | Property income Total[b] | Dividends from publicly traded stock | Interest income | Pensions and annuities |
|---|---|---|---|---|---|---|---|
| Lowest | 1 | 0 | −1 | 1 | 1 | 3 | 11 |
| Second | 3 | 1 | 1 | 3 | 1 | 6 | 19 |
| Third | 4 | 3 | 3 | 4 | 2 | 6 | 16 |
| Fourth | 6 | 5 | 4 | 4 | 2 | 6 | 17 |
| Fifth | 7 | 8 | 6 | 4 | 2 | 5 | 4 |
| Sixth | 9 | 10 | 7 | 6 | 7 | 6 | 9 |
| Seventh | 11 | 13 | 7 | 4 | 3 | 6 | 5 |
| Eighth | 13 | 15 | 10 | 7 | 1 | 12 | 6 |
| Ninth | 16 | 18 | 13 | 12 | 14 | 12 | 4 |
| Highest | 30 | 27 | 49 | 53 | 68 | 39 | 8 |

Source: Dorothy S. Projector, Gertrude S. Weiss, and Erling T. Thoresen, "Composition of Income as Shown by the Survey of Financial Characteristics of Consumers," in Lee Soltow (ed.), Six Papers on the Size Distribution of Wealth and Income, Studies in Income and Wealth, Vol. 33 (Columbia University Press for National Bureau of Economic Research, 1969), pp. 128, 133, 139. Percentages do not total 100 because of rounding.

[a] Includes income from unincorporated businesses, farms, and closely held corporations managed by income recipient.

[b] Includes interest income, dividends from publicly traded and from closely held corporations, rents and royalties and income from trusts and estates.

of where family income comes from, these data point up how very different the burden pattern of a tax on wages and salaries is, for example, from one of equal yield on business or property income. The high concentration in the upper income groups of dividends paid on publicly traded corporate shares, furthermore, would indicate that if the incidence of the corporate profits tax on the sources side is confined to corporate shareholders, as some maintain, its vertical burden distribution is clearly more progressive than it is if those burdens are spread broadly to all recipients of business and property income, as others contend.

On the uses-of-income side of household budgets there is wide agreement that, relative to income, any tax burdens that may be said to fall on consumers in general are regressive, as Table 2 shows. In addition to these burdens, which are most evident in the case of broad-based retail sales or value added taxes, there is a widespread and complex set of burdens generated by all taxes that fall on consumers of particular goods and services. Though the general nature of these excise tax effects, as they have been called, is well established, surprisingly little is known either about their relative importance (or unimportance) in the total tax burden picture or about which ones may be said to be progressive and which regressive in relation to family taxpaying abilities. More analyses of these excise tax effects are clearly needed. That the results might run counter to generally accepted beliefs is nicely illustrated by two recent empirical studies showing that the exemption of clothing, and particularly of children's

**TABLE 2. Distribution of U.S. Household Income and Consumption Expenditures, by Income Class, 1960**

(In percentage of totals)

| Family money income | Money income | Consumption expenditures |
|---|---|---|
| Under $2,000 | 2 | 4.6 |
| $ 2,000–2,999 | 4 | 7.6 |
| 3,000–3,999 | 5 | 8.8 |
| 4,000–4,999 | 8 | 16.1 |
| 5,000–7,499 | 28 | 38.9 |
| 7,500–9,999 | 20 | 11.7 |
| 10,000 and over | 33 | 12.3 |
| Total | 100 | 100.0 |

Source: W. Irwin Gillespie, "Effect of Public Expenditures on the Distribution of Income," in Richard A. Musgrave ed.), *Essays in Fiscal Federalism* (Brookings Institution, 1965), pp. 170–71.

clothing, from the retail sales tax base tends to make that tax more, rather than less, regressive.[1]

The distinguishing mark of a good theoretical incidence model is its ability to reveal the basic tax burden picture without simplifying things so much that important details are lost in the process. How well the models so far devised perform these tasks can best be determined by means of empirical analyses of their major assumptions. These matters and other important economic effects of taxation are the concluding topics of this discussion. Attention is given to the effects of taxation on the work-leisure and consumption-saving choices, the impact of tax policy on the level and structure of business investment, and the "welfare" effects of taxation on the allocation of resources. A summary assessment focuses on the influence of taxation on economic growth.

# INCIDENCE OF TAXATION

THOUGH EXTREMELY esoteric and abstruse to the layman, incidence theories have had an important impact on everyday ideas about the burdens of different tax levies. Unfortunately, practical men of affairs are currently operating with tax theories which, oversimplified even in their day, have by now been largely discredited by experts. Notable examples are the widely held views that sales taxes and business property taxes are borne by consumers and impose few if any burdens on producers, that the corporate tax burden is split between consumers and shareholders, and that the incidence of residential property taxes falls entirely on current homeowners and tenants. Modern incidence theories support none of these propositions. It seems appropriate, therefore, to assess the state of current thinking in this important fiscal area.

In the extensive and productive discussion of tax incidence theory among economists during the last two decades, three milestones stand out. In the early 1950s Earl R. Rolph, drawing on the neglected work

[1] Jeffrey M. Schaefer, "Clothing Exemptions and Sales Tax Regressivity," *American Economic Review*, Vol. 59 (September 1969), pp. 596–99; and David G. Davies, "Clothing Exemptions and Sales Tax Regressivity: Note," ibid., Vol. 61 (March 1971), pp. 187–89.

of Harry Gunnison Brown, mounted a sharp attack on orthodox theories of excise tax incidence, stimulating major reactions from other fiscal economists.[2] During the same decade Richard A. Musgrave made numerous theoretical contributions which have evoked less controversy and therefore less comment than the output of some of his competitors, but have undoubtedly added more to the professional literature on tax incidence than has the work of any other single economist. His concept of incidence as the changes brought about by a given public finance instrument in the distribution of real income available for private use is a natural starting point for any discussion of the topic. Finally, in the early 1960s Arnold C. Harberger, inspired by general equilibrium theories of international trade, including a neglected fiscal analysis by James E. Meade, presented a general model of the incidence of the corporation profits tax. His work has been fruitfully extended and elaborated on by Charles E. McLure, Jr., and Peter M. Mieszkowski.[3]

---

[2] Harry Gunnison Brown, "The Incidence of a General Output or a General Sales Tax," and "The Incidence of a General Output or a General Sales Tax: A Correction," *Journal of Political Economy,* Vol. 47 (April and June 1939), pp. 254–62, 418–20, reprinted in *Readings in the Economics of Taxation* (Irwin for American Economic Association, 1959), pp. 330–39; Earl R. Rolph, "A Proposed Revision of Excise-Tax Theory," *Journal of Political Economy,* Vol. 60 (April 1952), pp. 102–17, "A Theory of Excise Subsidies," *American Economic Review,* Vol. 42 (September 1952), pp. 515–27, and *The Theory of Fiscal Economics* (University of California Press, 1954), pp. 123–71; Richard A. Musgrave, "On Incidence," *Journal of Political Economy,* Vol. 61 (August 1953), pp. 306–23, and *The Theory of Public Finance: A Study in Public Economy* (McGraw-Hill, 1959), Chaps. 10, 15, 16; John F. Due, "Toward a General Theory of Sales Tax Incidence," *Quarterly Journal of Economics,* Vol. 67 (May 1953), pp. 253–66, "Sales Taxation and the Consumer," *American Economic Review,* Vol. 53 (December 1963), pp. 1078–84, and *Government Finance: Economics of the Public Sector* (4th ed., Irwin, 1968), pp. 194–236; and James M. Buchanan, *Fiscal Theory and Political Economy: Selected Essays* (University of North Carolina Press, 1960), pp. 125–50.

[3] J. E. Meade, *The Theory of International Economic Policy,* Vol. 2, *Trade and Welfare: Mathematical Supplement* (Oxford University Press, 1955), pp. 34–46; Arnold C. Harberger, "The Incidence of the Corporation Income Tax," *Journal of Political Economy,* Vol. 70 (June 1962), pp. 215–40; Charles E. McLure, Jr., "The Theory of Tax Incidence with Imperfect Factor Mobility," *Finanzarchiv,* Vol. 30 (Tübingen: 1971), pp. 27–48, "The Inter-regional Incidence of General Regional Taxes," *Public Finance,* Vol. 24 (1969), pp. 457–83, "Taxation, Substitution, and Industrial Location," *Journal of Political Economy,* Vol. 78 (January/February 1970), pp. 112–32, and "Tax Incidence, Macroeconomic Policy, and Absolute Prices," *Quarterly Journal of Economics,* Vol. 84 (May 1970), pp. 254–67; Peter M. Mieszkowski, "On the Theory of Tax Incidence," *Journal of Political Economy,*

These scholars have clarified the meaning of tax incidence and hence the assumptions that can and should be made in its analysis. They also have identified some of the structural parameters of the economic system that are essential to accurate empirical estimation of tax burden distributions. The advances have not, of course, been accomplished without major disagreements, some of them still unresolved.

## Basic Conceptual Framework

The incidence of a tax—its impact on the distribution of private real incomes—is the result of a myriad of interacting effects. Each and every effect cannot, and indeed should not, be analyzed. Only the important ones are worth the cost and effort of detailed study. Choosing the proper scope of an incidence analysis, however, is as much an art as a science, for no systematic body of data gives the size and probability of occurrence of each tax effect. At one extreme is the traditional partial equilibrium analysis, often an important first analytical step, but seldom an acceptable final one.[4] At the other extreme is the comprehensive, but incomprehensible, general equilibrium analysis, incorporating every conceivable effect in its many-equation models of the economy and consequently generating results whose significance, or reliability, is almost impossible to determine. Somewhere between these limits lies the ideal incidence model that is manageable yet neglects nothing of major importance. The Harberger model, in one or more of its variants, may prove to be that happy analytical choice.

Not the least of Musgrave's many contributions is his careful distinction between incidence effects on the sources-of-income side of household economic accounts and those on the uses-of-income side.[5] Obvious as these two sets of effects may be—altering on the sources side the prices of the factor services that people sell for wages, interest, profits, and rents, and on the uses side the prices of the con-

Vol. 75 (June 1967), pp. 250–62, and "Tax Incidence Theory: The Effects of Taxes on the Distribution of Income," *Journal of Economic Literature*, Vol. 7 (December 1969), pp. 1103–24. This last paper contains a detailed bibliography of tax incidence theory.

[4] For a careful statement of the conditions under which partial equilibrium analysis may be satisfactorily used to ascertain the incidence of a given tax, see Carl S. Shoup, *Public Finance* (Aldine, 1969), pp. 9–10.

[5] Musgrave, *The Theory of Public Finance*, pp. 211–21.

sumer goods and services they buy—most incidence analyses deal with effects on one side only. Sales tax analysis typically concentrates on the uses side, analyses of other broad-based taxes on the sources side.[6] If such asymmetry is defensible, it is presumably because of the importance of the tax effects included in the analysis and the unimportance, or nonexistence, of those excluded.

A good example of the controversial nature of this issue is provided by the long-continued debate between Rolph and most of the rest of the profession concerning the incidence of sales and excise taxes. The essence of Rolph's general equilibrium analysis is that incidence on the uses side is made up of both burdens, suffered by consumers of taxed products, and benefits, enjoyed by consumers of nontaxed products, and that this mixture of offsetting effects is unlikely to produce a significant net impact on the welfare of the average consumer. This leads him to concentrate on the sources-of-income side of the picture.[7] The counterargument emphasizes the uses side, the hallmark of partial equilibrium analysis. This simply ignores, as unimportant, all effects resulting from the shift of resources out of the taxed industry into productive activity elsewhere.[8] Early in the debate the two sides were in almost complete disagreement, Rolph placing the incidence of sales taxes on factor owners and his critics placing it on consumers.

As general equilibrium analyses of tax incidence have gained the ascendancy, the area of disagreement has narrowed somewhat. The consensus now appears to be that an excise tax on a limited number of commodities will generate both consumer burdens and consumer benefits. This is no small change in point of view. No longer can the established proposition that consumption of particular products tends to decline as a percentage of income as family income in-

[6] John A. Brittain, *The Payroll Tax for Social Security* (Brookings Institution, 1972), pp. 52–53.

[7] Rolph so emphasized the income side that he seemed to many to neglect the uses side altogether. See, for example, Musgrave, *The Theory of Public Finance*, p. 228.

[8] It is well established that partial equilibrium analysis of excise taxes produces a mixture of both consumer and producer burdens according to the nature of the demand and supply curves that characterize the output of the taxed commodity. Nevertheless, full forward shifting to consumers appears to be the common assumption, and as Shoup has noted, this may be a close enough approximation, in the limited context of the analysis, as long as the tax rate is moderate and the taxed industry is growing. *Public Finance*, p. 275.

creases be used to demonstrate regressivity in the vertical pattern of excise tax burdens. Instead, consumption of taxed products must be shown to decline more rapidly than consumption of nontaxed products.[9] This progress toward consensus at the theoretical level is regrettably not yet reflected in empirical analyses, where sales and excise taxes are still allocated in the traditional fashion.[10] Nor are the theoretical arguments completely settled; sharp disagreements about the incidence of general retail sales taxes still exist.

Another major contribution by Musgrave is his delineation of three alternative concepts of tax incidence: specific, differential, and balanced-budget incidence. This conceptual clarification appears to have led to wide agreement on the desirability of dealing separately with the distributional effects of taxation on the one hand and of inflation, deflation, and changes in the level of involuntary unemployment on the other. All so-called macroeffects are thus excluded from incidence analysis which, it is argued, should be based on the assumption that the level of aggregate demand is constant. Stated differently, tax incidence deals primarily, though not exclusively, with changes in relative, not absolute, prices.[11] The Rolphian concept of specific incidence is the least satisfactory of the alternatives by this test since it deals with the distributional effects of a given tax change in isolation, not allowing for changes in expenditures, transfers, or other taxes to help counteract the effects of the given tax change on aggregate demand. For this reason, a specific tax incidence approach is not widely used in the profession.

The concept of differential tax incidence deals with the distributional effects brought about by substituting one tax for another of equal yield to the government. Though the role of macroeffects is minimized in this approach, other difficulties remain. Strictly speaking, it is impossible to specify a unique differential incidence pattern

[9] See Richard A. Musgrave and Peggy B. Musgrave, *Public Finance in Theory and Practice* (McGraw-Hill, 1973), p. 429; and Melvyn B. Krauss and Harry G. Johnson, "The Theory of Tax Incidence: A Diagrammatic Analysis," *Economica*, N.S., Vol. 39 (November 1972), p. 373.

[10] For a recent study see Musgrave and Musgrave, *Public Finance in Theory and Practice*, pp. 366–77. For a critical review of earlier studies see Carl S. Shoup, "Quantitative Research in Taxation and Government Expenditure," in *Public Expenditures and Taxation*, Fiftieth Anniversary Colloquium IV (Columbia University Press for National Bureau of Economic Research, 1972), pp. 3–15.

[11] See McLure, "Tax Incidence, Macroeconomic Policy, and Absolute Prices."

for any particular tax. One can speak only of how the incidence of tax A differs from that of tax B or tax C. In this framework, in other words, there is no way of describing the incidence of any tax except by comparing it with the incidence patterns of other taxes. Such comparisons achieve realism at the cost of generality. Probably the most useful approach, though not ideal either, is to compare each tax with an equiyield set of perfectly neutral levies, designed to have no impact either on economic decision making or on the distribution of income and wealth. The problem is that perfect tax neutrality is generally conceded to be unattainable in practice. By this approach, then, incidence is defined with reference to purely hypothetical alternatives. Though such tax comparisons seem perfectly sensible to some, others are clearly bothered by the lack of realism. Their only alternatives, however, are either to abandon differential incidence altogether or to accept the existence of multiple incidence patterns for each and every tax.

A second set of difficulties arises from what may be called the side effects of redistributional tax policies. When one is attempting to determine the differential incidence of two taxes of equal money yield to the government, for example, what should be done if one has a greater impact on aggregate private demand than the other, or if one raises the prices of government purchases more than does the other?[12] Such questions reflect the basic dilemma of incidence analysis: the need to deal with all the complex interrelationships of modern economic systems, and the practical impossibility of doing so. Carl Shoup has proposed a goal-oriented solution:

To take a more complex case, . . . if there are eight goals to be achieved, by the public finance system, eight public finance instruments will normally be required, with a unique set of eight rates or values. If the value for one of these goals is to be changed, as when the distribution of disposable income is to be made less unequal, while the values of each of the other seven goals are to be unchanged, the values of all eight of the public finance instruments must normally be changed. All eight are changed, just to alter one of the goal values (and to keep the other goal values unchanged). The new distribution of disposable income is necessarily the "incidence" of changes in eight public finance instruments.[13]

---

[12] See Musgrave, *The Theory of Public Finance*, pp. 215–17.
[13] Shoup, *Public Finance*, p. 14.

While Shoup's solution focuses sharply on the distributional goal, it deals only with alternative packages of fiscal instruments. Tax incidence in the pure sense is impossible to isolate, the closest means of simulating it being a package containing one tax instrument that is so dominant that all the nontax instruments present are of only minor importance. The more common solution, an instrument-oriented one, is to define incidence so as to include the total set of distributional effects resulting from a given tax change, including those generated indirectly by the impact of the tax on other public finance goals, such as economic growth and balance of payments equilibrium. The result, of course, is a network of effects much too large and complex to handle, and each analyst must then practice the difficult art of selecting from all possible effects those that are too fundamental to be ignored.

The balanced budget approach to incidence theory, as defined by Musgrave, has the important, and for present purposes fatal, disadvantage of combining tax and expenditure effects and hence of rendering impossible any useful conclusions concerning tax incidence per se, except under exceedingly special circumstances. Only for a government restricted to one tax, and required to balance its budget by suitable variations in that one source of revenue, could it be argued that an increase in that tax must be accompanied by an equal increase in expenditures; and even then, there would be a different incidence pattern for each of the individual expenditure programs that the government might choose to undertake. A unique pattern for each tax could, of course, be obtained by assuming, as is often done by users of the Harberger model of tax incidence, both that the government spends its additional funds at the margin in exactly the same way as the taxpayers would have spent them if the tax increase had not been enacted, and that the new public benefits in no way affect decisions in the private sector (that is, the new government services are neither substitutes for nor complements to private goods and services). These highly artificial assumptions indicate vividly the difficulties involved in using a balanced budget model to study tax incidence alone.

One problem inherent in this approach to tax incidence is the deeply ingrained popular belief that taxes impose real burdens on people. Only the balanced-budget incidence model, with its shift of resources from the private to the public sector, is consistent with this viewpoint. In the specific and differential incidence models, in contrast, there is no aggregate net private burden, apart from excess burdens.[14] Instead, there is a redistribution of claims to a fixed potential amount of private output and this does appear to be what in the simplest and purest sense should be meant by tax incidence. Aggregate real private burdens are imposed by governmental use of resources (government expenditures) and taxation is not a prerequisite for such use.[15]

What, then, is the relative usefulness of the three concepts of tax incidence? Each is, of course, useful in its own special way—that is, to answer the particular policy questions posed below:

| *Policy question* | *Appropriate incidence pattern* |
|---|---|
| What are the distributional effects of: | |
| —increasing taxes to combat inflation? | Specific tax incidence |
| —financing government expenditures by tax A rather than tax B? | Differential tax incidence |
| —raising taxes to finance transfer payments? | Differential tax incidence[16] |
| —raising taxes to expand government purchases of goods and services? | Balanced budget incidence |

More fundamentally, however, one should choose the concept that deals most directly, and most simply, with the distributional effects of taxation that are the essence of incidence analysis. The one that does this is the differential incidence concept.

## The Harberger Relative-Prices Model

The discussion so far has dealt only with the assumptions that it is necessary to make in order to define an unambiguous concept of tax incidence. The next step is to establish the assumptions governing the derivation of a useful, first-approximation estimate of the incidence of different taxes. The original Harberger model included seven assumptions, made for the sake of convenience, that raise

[14] The excess burdens and benefits of taxation are discussed on pp. 221–30.

[15] A national government, of course, has the greatest number of alternatives for financing its expenditures, but even state and local governments can rely in part on their unused borrowing powers.

[16] Though nominally a balanced budget operation, this policy is simply a combination of positive and negative taxes (or negative and positive transfers) and hence represents a special case of differential tax incidence.

serious questions about its usefulness even as a first approximation or that require extended treatment in the derivation of second, and higher-order, approximation effects. The seven assumptions, some of which were relaxed in subsequent work with the model by McLure and Mieszkowski, are:

• *Fixed aggregate factor supplies;* eliminates need to consider the work-leisure choice, the effects of taxation on saving, investment, and growth, and any interactions between the supply of labor and the supply of capital.

• *Perfect factor mobility;* ignores impediments to the movement of labor and capital among industries, with the result that net-of-tax rates of return are equalized for each factor in all of its alternative uses; thus the model can be applied only to tax incidence in the long run.

• *Perfect competition in factor and product markets;* especially questionable in analysis of the incidence of the corporation income tax.

• *Closed economic system;* though not unduly restrictive for the analysis of U.S. federal taxation, it is clearly inappropriate for dealing with state and local taxes or with national taxes in a country with a relatively large foreign trade sector.

• *Linear homogeneous production functions;* increases in both labor and capital inputs are assumed to produce equal percentage increases in output; economies of scale, which the corporate form of enterprise is particularly well adapted to realize, are thereby ruled out.

• *Homogeneous marginal consumption propensities;* makes marginal propensities to consume goods the same for all spending units, even though their average propensities may differ; eliminates the impact of income redistribution on the allocation of resources in the private sector.

• *No fixed-money assets;* considers only relative price changes, ignoring the possibility that absolute changes are also important. For laborers and equity capital owners it is clearly irrelevant whether a given tax raises product prices and keeps factor prices unchanged or lowers factor prices while keeping product prices constant; for pensioners and bondholders, however, there is a world of difference between the two sets of tax effects.

This list of restrictive assumptions is formidable and may well create doubt about the practical value of the whole set of Harberger-McLure-Mieszkowski (HMM) models. The usefulness of abstract models, however, must be judged by the realism of both their assumptions and their results. As McLure puts it: "This model is used without apologies, since the conclusions derived here may hold, at least qualitatively, in a more realistic description of an economy. Even these have seldom been recognized or demonstrated rigorously in the public finance literature."[17]

Though only a two-product, two-factor, eleven-equation abstraction from economic reality, the basic HMM model effectively illuminates several important features of tax incidence theory.[18] The essential complexity of the subject, even in its simplest form, is evident from a glance at any of the publications dealing with the HMM model. Even though the model includes nine possible taxes, only four need be analyzed in order to derive the complete incidence picture, as the basic tax matrix for the model shown:

$$\begin{array}{ccccc}
T_{XY} & \equiv T_{LK} & = T_L & + T_K \\
\| & & \| & \| \\
T_X & & = T_{XL} & + T_{XK} \\
+ & & + & + \\
T_Y & & = T_{YL} & + T_{YK},
\end{array}$$

where $X$ and $Y$ stand for the two consumer goods included in the model and $L$ and $K$ for the two factors of production, labor and capital. The first proposition, which now seems generally agreed upon, is that given the assumption of the HMM model that the capital stock is constant (net saving equals zero), a tax on gross output or sales, $T_{XY}$, is equivalent to a tax on gross incomes, $T_{LK}$, each being borne in proportion to consumption or income which, by assumption, are identical.[19] Given this identity, knowledge of the incidence of a single commodity tax, say, $T_X$, makes it possible to derive the incidence of the other commodity tax, $T_Y$. Similarly, knowledge of the incidence of one of the factor taxes, say, $T_L$ on labor income, is sufficient to determine the incidence of the other factor tax, $T_K$. Finally,

[17] "Tax Incidence, Macroeconomic Policy, and Absolute Prices," p. 255.

[18] Charles E. McLure, Jr., "General Equilibrium Incidence Analysis: The Harberger Model After Ten Years," Discussion Paper 37 (Rice University, Program of Development Studies, Fall 1972; processed).

[19] Musgrave, *The Theory of Public Finance*, Chap. 15; and Mieszkowski, "On the Theory of Tax Incidence," pp. 250–52, 260–62, and "Tax Incidence Theory: The Effects of Taxes on the Distribution of Income," pp. 1104–06.

since a tax on each factor used in producing a commodity is equivalent to an equal-rate tax on the commodity in question, as shown in the second and third rows in the matrix, and since a tax on one factor in each of its uses is equivalent to a general tax on the factor in question, as shown in the second and third columns of the matrix, knowledge of only one of the remaining "partial-partial" taxes is needed to complete the incidence analysis. For example, after determination of the incidence of $T_{XK}$, a tax on capital used in the production of $X$ (which may be interpreted as a corporation income tax if $X$ is defined to be the corporate and $Y$ the noncorporate sector of the economy), the incidence of $T_{XL}$ and $T_{YK}$ may be derived directly, and these two results may then be used to obtain $T_{YL}$.[20] For a complete picture of tax incidence in the HMM model, then, it is necessary to study in detail only a tax on one commodity, a tax on one factor, and a tax on the use of one factor in the production of one commodity.

The most important accomplishment of the HMM model is the identification of the structural parameters that determine the direction and amount of the relative price changes brought about by taxation. It is not that the significance of these parameters was unknown before Harberger's 1962 article, but rather that the interrelationships among them had never been systematically and precisely specified in a general theoretical formulation that could be used to distinguish incidence effects that theory alone can establish unambiguously from those that can only be determined by empirical estimation.[21] The key structural parameters are:

* the average and marginal propensities to consume different consumer goods and services,
* the relative price elasticities of demand for different consumer goods and services,
* the substitutability of different factors in the production of different goods and services,

[20] McLure, "The Theory of Tax Incidence with Imperfect Factor Mobility," pp. 28–29.

[21] Brown, Musgrave, and Rolph had all discussed these parameters in their contributions to the general equilibrium theory of tax incidence (see note 2 above). See also Paul Wells, "A General Equilibrium Analysis of Excise Taxes," *American Economic Review*, Vol. 45 (June 1955), pp. 345–59; and Harry G. Johnson, "General Equilibrium Analysis of Excise Taxes: Comment," ibid., Vol. 46 (March 1956), pp. 151–56.

- the relative intensities of use of different factors in the production of different goods and services, and
- the mobilities of the different factors of production and, in the analysis of the incidence of local government taxes, of households and shoppers.

The nature of the general incidence propositions that may be derived from an extended HMM model that allows for factor immobilities may be illustrated by taking in turn each of the three kinds of partial taxes distinguished in it. McLure has shown that a general tax on one factor in both industries ($T_L$ or $T_K$) is borne entirely by the taxed factor, regardless of the mobility of either factor, and that a tax on production in one industry ($T_X$ or $T_Y$) causes the price of the mobile factor to fall while the price of the immobile factor rises in the untaxed industry and falls in the taxed industry.[22] A tax on one factor in one use ($T_{XL}$, for example), on the other hand, exerts opposing, and hence indeterminate, effects on factor prices when both factors are perfectly mobile, though it does have an unambiguous effect on product prices, raising those in the taxed industry relative to those elsewhere.[23]

The HMM model has two significant weaknesses. Because it is written and analyzed in terms of differentials and implicitly assumes the absence of any preexisting taxes, the model can, strictly speaking, be applied only to the analysis of the imposition of infinitesimally small taxes in a zero-tax world. Of course, no one wants to use the model that way, and indeed no one ever has. Though many have risked the uncertain jump from the abstract model to the real world, few have systematically studied the potential losses from dealing with infinitesimal, rather than discrete, changes. Conspicuous among the few are Krauss, Johnson, McLure, Shoven, and Whalley, all of whom stress the need for special caution in using the differential (linear) version of the HMM model to draw conclusions

---

[22] "The Theory of Tax Incidence with Imperfect Factor Mobility," pp. 37–40.

[23] For discussion of applications of the basic Harberger model see McLure, "General Equilibrium Incidence Analysis." For a diagrammatic presentation of the model see Charles E. McLure, Jr., "A Diagrammatic Exposition of General Equilibrium Tax and Expenditure Incidence Analysis with One Immobile Factor," Discussion Paper 31 (Rice University, Program of Development Studies, Fall 1972; processed).

about large-scale tax changes.[24] Very little has been done to deal explicitly with the possible differences in incidence patterns created by a specific tax change in a zero-tax world and in a world with existing taxes, but a beginning has been made by Feldstein.[25] One problem is that tax changes in a nonzero-tax world are likely to create significant excess burdens, and fiscal economists are not agreed on whether these should be incorporated into incidence analysis or handled separately as additional economic effects.

Another major weakness of the HMM model is its inability to handle tax effects on saving, investment, and economic growth. That task, however, is the specific goal of dynamic incidence studies.

## Dynamic Incidence

Its name alone would indicate that "dynamic incidence" has every advantage over the undramatic, traditional "static incidence" methodology as a means of analyzing the effects of taxation on the distribution of real income. Yet this has so far not been the case, and only major changes in the nature of dynamic incidence analysis can make it so.

In an early clarification of the basic issues Douglas Dosser proposed that "dynamic incidence" be used to refer to the effects of tax and other public finance instruments on the rates of change of individual and group real incomes. He stressed the importance to incidence patterns of that particular time at which they are examined,

[24] Melvyn Krauss, "Differential Tax Incidence: Large versus Small Tax Changes," *Journal of Political Economy*, Vol. 80 (January/February 1972), pp. 193–97; Krauss and Johnson, "The Theory of Tax Incidence"; McLure, "A Diagrammatic Exposition," pp. 30–35; and John B. Shoven and John Whalley, "A General Equilibrium Calculation of the Effects of Differential Taxation of Income from Capital in the U.S.," *Journal of Public Economics*, Vol. 1 (November 1972), pp. 281–321. Krauss shows that for finite tax changes capitalists might prefer a partial tax on profits in one sector to a partial commodity tax in the same sector, whereas for infinitesimal changes, the reverse would unambiguously be true. McLure uses his diagrammatic analysis to present a qualitative exposition of the changes implied by the shift from linear to curvilinear functions in the HMM model.

[25] Martin S. Feldstein, "Tax Incidence in a Growing Economy with Variable Factor Supply," and "Incidence of a Capital Income Tax in a Growing Economy with Variable Savings Rates," Discussion Papers 263 and 300 (Harvard University, Institute of Economic Research, December 1972 and June 1973; processed).

and he suggested that a tax system be designed to redistribute income in the desired direction not only immediately after it was established but in all succeeding years as well.[26] Neither the proposed concept of dynamic incidence nor the idea of tax systems with built-in redistributive powers seemed to have much policy appeal, however.[27]

A. Mitchell Polinsky in exploring dynamic tax effects has recently raised important questions for both theorists and practitioners.[28] He notes that in addition to the traditionally studied direct redistributional effects on current annual incomes, taxation affects both the amount and the timing of lifetime incomes. By stressing potential differences between the effects on annual and lifetime incomes, including the dramatic possibility that a given fiscal system could be progressive in relation to the former but regressive in relation to the latter, Polinsky makes a strong case for the expansion of traditional incidence analysis to include redistributional effects on lifetime incomes. In another analysis he argues that imperfect capital markets bias lifetime consumption choices by preventing attainment early in life of the amounts preferred on the basis of a given expected lifetime income, and he then derives the theoretical optimal tax structure that would eliminate these intertemporal distortions.[29] Though the solutions he prefers lack practical appeal, the second-best policies he suggests, such as lifetime income averaging for tax purposes, deserve further study.

Marian Krzyzaniak and Martin Feldstein have been major participants in an ambitious study of tax incidence in growth models—

[26] "Tax Incidence and Growth," *Economic Journal*, Vol. 71 (September 1961), pp. 572–91.

[27] A. R. Prest, "Observations on Dynamic Incidence," *Economic Journal*, Vol. 73 (September 1963), pp. 535–46. See the comments by A. D. Bain in the same issue, pp. 533–35, and the response by Dosser, pp. 547–53.

[28] "A Note on the Measurement of Incidence," *Public Finance Quarterly*, Vol. 1 (April 1973), pp. 219–30, and "Imperfect Capital Markets, Intertemporal Redistribution, and Progressive Taxation," in Harold M. Hochman and George E. Peterson (eds.), *Redistribution Through Public Choice* (Columbia University Press, 1974).

[29] Compare Lester C. Thurow, "The Optimum Lifetime Distribution of Consumption Expenditures," *American Economic Review*, Vol. 59 (June 1969), pp. 324–30, and discussion by Kan Hua Young, Brian Motley, Samuel A. Morley, and Thurow, ibid., Vol. 60 (September 1970), pp. 736–45, and by Thurow, ibid., Vol. 61 (March 1971), pp. 248–49.

that is, in economic systems characterized by varying degrees of sensitivity of saving, investment, and labor supply to tax changes.[30] This exceedingly complex subject permits few a priori conclusions.[31] While dynamic incidence models appear to be as hyperopic as static models are myopic, growth modeling will undoubtedly continue to play an important role in tax incidence analysis.

Perhaps the most striking result of the Krzyzaniak analyses of profits tax incidence is his finding that the total, or "global," burden is significantly greater for a tax that reduces the rate of private investment than for one that does not. The extra burden of the former is simply the lower future level of private real incomes resulting from any present curtailment of private investment. That profits taxation will in fact reduce investment is guaranteed in the Krzyzaniak two-sector neoclassical growth model by the assumptions that private investment is determined solely by the supply of private saving and that private propensities to save are higher from profit, than from wage and salary, incomes. Using a saving propensity of 0.50 for profit income but of only 0.05 for nonprofit income, for example, Krzyzaniak estimates that a 20 percent profits tax would impose a global tax burden of $2.33 for every $1.00 of revenue raised and that 50 percent of the burden would fall on corporate investors, 40 percent on workers, and 10 percent on noncorporate investors.[32] This means that the extra burden of a profits tax, which

[30] Marian Krzyzaniak, "Effects of Profits Taxes: Deduced from Neoclassical Growth Models," in Marian Krzyzaniak (ed.), *Effects of Corporation Income Tax* (Wayne State University Press, 1966), pp. 17–106; "The Long-run Burden of a General Tax on Profits in a Neoclassical World," *Public Finance*, Vol. 22 (1967), pp. 472–91; "The Burden of a Differential Tax on Profits in a Neoclassical World," ibid., Vol. 23 (1968), pp. 447–73; "Factor Substitution and the General Tax on Profits," ibid., Vol. 25 (1970), pp. 489–514; "Some Sensitivity Analyses of the Long-Run Incidence of a General Tax on Profits" (Rice University, Program in Applied Mathematics and Systems Theory, 1969; processed); and "The Differential Incidence of Taxes on Profits and on Factor Incomes," *Finanzarchiv*, Vol. 30 (Tübingen: 1972), pp. 464–88. Martin Feldstein, "Tax Incidence in a Growing Economy" and "Incidence of a Capital Income Tax." See also Kazuo Sato, "Taxation and Neo-Classical Growth," *Public Finance*, Vol. 22 (1967), pp. 346–70.

[31] See, for example, Musgrave, *The Theory of Public Finance*, pp. 372–74.

[32] "The Burden of a Differential Tax on Profits," pp. 464, 471. Krzyzaniak obtains a static aggregate real burden of taxation equal to the yield of the tax by using a balanced-budget incidence model and assuming that government expenditures are a complete waste.

is a deadweight loss to society, is placed at the very considerable level of 133 percent of the revenue to be raised from that source.

To stop at this hyperopic view of the situation, of course, is to ignore the fact that in a full employment economy, less consumption later because of less investment now also means more consumption now. The potential burdens and benefits of tax-induced intertemporal redistributions of aggregate consumption are therefore pertinent. Under certain social discount rates, Krzyzaniak's excess global burden could, in fact, be an extra benefit, though he argues that it is not likely to be so.[33] The issue must be regarded as far from settled, particularly in the light of the Polinsky and Thurow analyses of optimal lifetime consumption patterns.

Dynamic incidence models need to consider not only the long-run equilibrium solution but also the time paths by which that solution is approached, for in most growth models the rate of adjustment to final equilibrium is exceedingly slow. Though a promising beginning has been made for dynamic models by Feldstein,[34] little has been done to apply a time-path approach to static equilibrium tax analysis. The general sales tax, for example, may have a different incidence pattern depending on whether it shifts its burdens smoothly through product and factor price changes at a given level of aggregate employment, or first depresses the level of employment and brings about the required price changes only slowly and imperfectly.

## Summary

Simple and clear-cut as they seem to the average taxpayer, the burdens of taxation are in fact elusive phenomena. Pursuit of them requires a skillful blending of high technical competence and sound pragmatic judgment. In spite of great difficulties, progress has been made during the past two decades, and in particular a sounder theoretical base has been built. The construction of that base has been the work of many economists—some public finance specialists and some not, some using partial equilibrium, some general equi-

---

[33] See "The Differential Incidence of Taxes," pp. 473–82.

[34] See "Tax Incidence in a Growing Economy" and "Incidence of a Capital Income Tax."

librium, and others dynamic incidence analyses. Though the resulting framework still has rough edges and unfinished segments, its application to specific taxes has already provided much of importance for fiscal practitioners to ponder.


# INCIDENCE OF SPECIFIC TAXES


THE INTRICACIES of the shifting and incidence of taxation can best be understood by applying the general theoretical models to a detailed analysis of specific taxes. Because of their inherent complexities and the controversial nature of their incidence patterns, the corporate profits tax and the general property tax are instructive for this purpose. The less controversial federal payroll tax for social insurance deserves attention also because its very rapid growth during the postwar period—it now ranks second in the nation's total tax structure by a considerable margin—raises important policy issues whose resolution requires firm knowledge about the distribution of its burdens. Finally, some of the neglected aspects of the incidence of general sales and individual income taxes deserve comment.


## The Corporation Income Tax

The range of professional opinion about the incidence of the corporation income tax is vast. In his 1962 study Harberger assumed the short-run incidence to be on shareholders and then, using plausible empirical values for the key structural parameters in his theoretical model, demonstrated that the long-run incidence falls on owners of capital in general.[35] A year later, in their pioneering econometric analysis of tax incidence, Krzyzaniak and Musgrave presented evidence that has been widely interpreted to support 100 percent, or even greater, forward shifting of manufacturing corporate tax burdens to consumers in the short run. Shoup has stressed, however, that their 100 percent figure does not represent pure

[35] "The Incidence of the Corporation Income Tax," pp. 215–40.

tax shifting but is contaminated to an unknown extent by balanced budget incidence.[36] In the years since it was published the Krzyzaniak-Musgrave model has been widely criticized by other economists, strongly defended by its authors, and applied to four foreign economies, but most important of all, it has been successful in stimulating the development and testing of more sophisticated econometric tax incidence models.[37] Unfortunately, very few of the points of controversy have been resolved in the process. Three studies of short-run shifting by U.S. manufacturing corporations, for example, support the no-shifting hypothesis, while a fourth defends the opposite hypothesis of 100 percent shifting.[38]

It is, of course, exceedingly difficult to isolate empirically the effects of tax changes on corporate profits, for the effects of some of the other profit determinants are highly correlated with the tax changes. As both the Musgraves and Shoup have suggested,[39] the most promising future research may lie in the area of micro studies of pricing policies of individual companies rather than in the further development of macro econometric models.[40] For the present, however, the theoretical case for each of the conflicting views concern-

---

[36] Marian Krzyzaniak and Richard A. Musgrave, *The Shifting of the Corporation Income Tax: An Empirical Study of Its Short-Run Effect Upon the Rate of Return* (Johns Hopkins Press, 1963), and Shoup, "Quantitative Research," pp. 19–20.

[37] For a summary of the controversy, leading to the conclusion that no definitive results have yet been reached, see Musgrave and Musgrave, *Public Finance in Theory and Practice*, pp. 409–10. For an evaluation of the foreign applications see Jeffrey Davis, "The Krzyzaniak and Musgrave Model—Some Further Comments," *Kyklos*, Vol. 26, Fasc. 2 (1973), pp. 387–94.

[38] Robert J. Gordon, "The Incidence of the Corporation Income Tax in U.S. Manufacturing, 1925–62," *American Economic Review*, Vol. 57 (September 1967), pp. 731–58, and the discussion by Krzyzaniak and Musgrave and by Gordon, ibid., Vol. 58 (December 1968), pp. 1358–60, 1360–67; Joan L. Turek, "Short-Run Shifting of the Corporate Income Tax in Manufacturing, 1935–1965," *Yale Economic Essays*, Vol. 10 (Spring 1970), pp. 127–48; William H. Oakland, "Corporate Earnings and Tax Shifting in U.S. Manufacturing, 1930–1968," *Review of Economics and Statistics*, Vol. 54 (August 1972), pp. 235–44; and Richard Dusansky, "The Short-Run Shifting of the Corporation Income-Tax in the United States," *Oxford Economic Papers*, Vol. 24 (November 1972), pp. 357–71.

[39] *Public Finance in Theory and Practice*, p. 410, and "Quantitative Research," pp. 59–60.

[40] A micro study by William R. Moffat indicates the presence of some degree of short-run shifting of the corporate tax. See "Taxes in the Price Equation: Textiles and Rubber," *Review of Economics and Statistics*, Vol. 52 (August 1970), pp. 253–61.

ing corporate tax incidence is best presented in the framework of the Harberger and Harberger-McLure-Mieszkowski models.

## The Harberger Model

The corporation income tax may be symbolized in the Harberger model as $T_{XK}$, a tax on the use of one factor, capital, in the production of one commodity, in this case the entire output of the corporate sector. The crucial feature of the model is the existence of competitive markets and highly mobile factors of production, so that the net-of-tax, net-of-risk rate of return on capital is equalized, in equilibrium, in all of its uses. Imposed within this environment, a corporate income tax upsets the equilibrium and induces a flow of capital from the less profitable corporate to the more profitable noncorporate sector until rates of return are again equal. In the process, several changes occur. Noncorporate output expands at the expense of corporate, and corporate product prices rise relative to noncorporate. Finally, workers shift from corporate to noncorporate employment, the net impact on their wage rates depending on production functions in the two sectors. It is not difficult to identify the conditions most favorable to the shifting of corporate tax burdens to workers: a corporate sector that is highly labor intensive relative to the noncorporate sector, and elasticities of substitution between capital and labor that are not high in either sector. Under such circumstances the corporate profits tax would force the corporate sector to release labor in substantially larger amounts than the noncorporate sector could absorb at pretax wage rates. Given strictly limited substitutability of labor for capital in noncorporate production functions, wage rates would then have to fall significantly and would continue to do so until unincorporated enterprises had reemployed all of the released workers.

Less obvious than these qualitative results, however, is the interesting proposition, demonstrated by Harberger, that if the two elasticities of substitution between labor and capital in the two sectors are equal both to each other and to the elasticity of substitution in consumption between the two sector outputs, capital bears the full burden of the corporate income tax. Be this as it may, the incidence of the corporation income tax remains an empirical question, and Harberger proceeds to show that for plausible values of the key parameters there is a strong presumption that on the sources side the burdens of this tax rest on capital owners in general.[41] If, for example, the corporate and noncorporate sectors were equal in size and if the pretax rate of return on capital employed in enterprises of average risk were 10 percent, a 50 percent corporate income tax would reduce net-of-tax returns on corporate capital temporarily to 5 percent; but the subsequent reallocation of resources would, in Harberger's view, establish some intermediate net return in both sectors in the long run. If the equilibrium rate of return in the untaxed sector were 7.5 percent, for example, the gross-of-tax rate of return in the taxed sector would be 15 percent and the net-of-tax rate of return 7.5 percent. This view that capitalists in general bear the burdens of a tax levied only on corporate capital does not appear to command wide acceptance in the profession. For the most part, critics have concentrated on the effects of relaxing Harberger's assumptions of highly competitive markets and highly mobile factors of production. Questions have also been raised about the impact of the corporate tax on private investment and the changes that this might bring about in relative income shares.

## Noncompetitive Market Models

Among the weaknesses of noncompetitive pricing models are their great variety and their frequent failure to arrive at any decisive results. As Rolph has observed:

In order to arrive at definitive conclusions, all theories of tax shifting need a pricing system that is determinant [*sic*] as opposed to one that is capricious or random. . . . Actual price systems in Western countries exhibit capricious elements arising from market power. . . . Systematic tax theory, like the economic theory of which it is a part, assumes the orderly features of price systems and fails to the extent that the actual world lacks these characteristics. Economists differ widely in their outlook on the degree of orderliness exhibited in contemporary societies; some find that the economic world neatly illustrates the properties of a perfectly competitive pricing system, and, at the opposite pole, others find no system to explain and as a consequence deprecate economic theory.[42]

---

[41] Harberger did not deal in detail with incidence on the uses side.

[42] Earl R. Rolph, "Taxation: General," in David L. Sills (ed.), *International Encyclopedia of the Social Sciences* (Macmillan and Free Press, 1968), Vol. 15, p. 526.

Neither of those poles needs detailed discussion here, but between them is a middle ground of determinate noncompetitive theories that does.[43]

A common feature of one set of theories, dealing with the behavior of large economic organizations possessing considerable discretionary pricing power, is the proposition that corporate prices are frequently not set at their maximum-profit levels. Corporations with some degree of monopoly power in their product markets can keep their selling prices relatively low, and those with monopsonistic powers in factor markets can exercise restraint by setting input prices, particularly wage rates, higher than profit considerations alone might dictate.

DEFENSIVE PRICING. Corporations may fail to maximize short-run profits for fear that higher profits would attract either entry by other enterprises or unwelcome attention from antitrust prosecutors. Faced with higher taxes, therefore, corporations in this situation would simply increase prices sufficiently to maintain their net-of-tax profit levels. This conclusion, however, seems to underestimate the risks involved in such behavior. If the danger of entry is a function of relative profit rates, defensive corporations must allow their profits to be reduced by the tax to the same extent that those of other enterprises are reduced.[44] The potential reactions of the antitrust authorities would also have to be taken into account by any corporation contemplating a price increase to restore pretax profit rates. Excess profits could conceivably be calculated from (1) gross-of-tax profit margins, the basic test used in the first phases of the federal price-control program initiated in the summer of 1971; (2) net-of-tax profit rates in a given industry relative to those elsewhere, particularly in industries subject to similar risks; or (3) net-

---

[43] See also Musgrave, *The Theory of Public Finance*, pp. 278–87.

[44] If corporate tax rates alone were raised, restoration by the defensive corporations of their pretax profit rates would not increase the risk of entry from the noncorporate sector. It would, however, make their industry more attractive to other corporations. On the other hand, if corporate and personal income tax rates were raised together, as is more likely, defensive corporations would acquire few new price-raising abilities. Sergio Bruno, in "Corporation Income Tax, Oligopolistic Markets and Immediate Tax Shifting: A Suggested Theoretical Approach," *Public Finance*, Vol. 25 (1970), pp. 363–78, concludes that a separate corporate tax will increase entry-preventing prices, thus permitting a forward shifting of tax burdens in the short run. This result, however, is based on the highly restrictive assumption that normal profit rates are not lowered by the tax.

of-tax profit rates in each industry without reference to rates elsewhere. Only under the third test, the weakest theoretically, would the price-raising, profit-maintaining corporation escape adverse antitrust attention.

FAIR PRICING. If corporate managers have in mind some concept of a just price or of some maximum socially acceptable profit margin, a higher corporate tax rate would induce upward adjustments in these as long as ample margins of unused profit-making powers existed before the tax change. As Musgrave has noted, a corporate tax rise could induce price increases in a sellers' market, when unused profit margins would be relatively large, but fail to do so in a buyers' market, when they would be small or nonexistent.[45]

How prevalent something like the medieval idea of a just price may be in the modern world is highly conjectural. With consumer attention increasingly focused on business products and policies, however, its existence cannot be rejected out of hand. Restraint in corporate product pricing, which sets the stage for short-run forward shifting of the corporate tax, may also exist simply because the world is an uncertain place in which to carry out business operations.

UNCERTAINTY. Suppose that several corporations, operating in a relatively concentrated industry, were convinced individually that a price rise would increase everyone's profits but each feared that the others would not follow its price lead. In that situation a corporate profits tax might have "a precipitant effect,"[46] leading to an immediate price increase because the tax would remove each rival's fear of being left alone on the higher-price limb. This theory, however, is no more certain a means of forecasting economic effects than are the corporation manager's intuitions about his competitors' intentions. Will a corporate tax increase induce a price increase, and will it be one that otherwise would not have occurred? In the absence of the tax rise, might not a wage increase, or a chance meeting of business executives at a conference, precipitate a similar price rise? These are some of the crucial questions to which there appear currently to be no answers.

[45] *The Theory of Public Finance*, p. 281.

[46] Leif Johansen, *Public Economics* (Rand McNally, 1965), p. 286. Musgrave saw the tax as a signal to businessmen that prices could be raised "with impunity" in oligopolistic markets. *The Theory of Public Finance*, pp. 281–82.

CONSTRAINED SALES MAXIMIZATION BEHAVIOR. Baumol's much-discussed theory holds that corporate managers, particularly when they have only a relatively small ownership interest in their own enterprises, act not to maximize profits but to increase the size of the business as much as possible without reducing profits below some minimum acceptable level.[47] Under these circumstances, as Michael E. Levy demonstrates, the effect of a higher corporate tax rate may well be higher corporate prices but unimpaired net-of-tax profits, at least in the short run.[48] Whether such corporate behavior is widespread is debatable, particularly since the tax laws, through their encouragement of stock options, have greatly stimulated top executives to acquire shares in their own corporations. A leading expert on corporate compensation, Wilbur G. Lewellen, in a study of 950 senior executives, covering the period 1940 to 1963, found the "over-all picture is one of a man who enjoys a $600,000 aggregate annual income, $500,000 of which originates from equity or equity-like sources. This does not, on its face, seem to be a situation leading executives to neglect the interests of shareholders in formulating operating policies."[49]

MARK-UP PRICING. Under special circumstances mark-up pricing, presumably a widespread mode of behavior in the business world, makes the short-run forward shifting of the corporation income tax plausible. Corporations, the theory goes, frequently set prices by adding a mark-up margin to average total costs computed at some average, or normal, level of output. If corporate taxes are included in total costs, or alternatively, if the firm seeks to maintain a target ratio of net-of-tax profits to sales, the stage is set for the appearance of price increases whenever corporate tax rates are raised. Whether this happens depends, however, on the restraint previously shown by corporate managers. If prices were already at, or close to, maximum-profit levels, tax-induced increases are unlikely to be made or, if made, unlikely to be long maintained.

[47] William J. Baumol, *Business Behavior, Value and Growth* (rev. ed., Harcourt, Brace and World, 1967), Chaps. 6–8.
[48] "Professor Baumol's Oligopolistic Model and the Corporation Income Tax," *Public Finance*, Vol. 16 (1961), pp. 366–72.
[49] "Managerial Incomes and Stockholder Returns," in National Bureau of Economic Research, *New Challenges for Economic Research*, 49th Annual Report (1969), pp. 98–99. See also his "Management and Ownership in the Large Firm," *Journal of Finance*, Vol. 24 (May 1969), pp. 299–322, and the discussion by Richard S. Bower, ibid., pp. 339–41.

How prevalent submaximal-profit prices are is a matter of professional disagreement. While relatively little attention has been paid in the public finance literature to the possibility of tax-induced reductions in monopsonistically set wage rates, great stress has been placed on the probability of widespread tax-induced increases in administratively set product prices.[50] If tax-induced changes were universally successful enough to maintain net-of-tax corporate rates of return, the long-run Harberger shifting mechanism from the supply side would not come into operation at all. Such a result, however, seems highly unlikely. While submaximal-profit pricing may occasionally occur in markets conducive to its operation, strong competitive pressures would preclude its occurrence in many situations. Moreover, as Shoup has emphasized, differences in capital structure and turnover rates make it harder for some firms than for others to recoup the corporate tax through an increase in product prices. Thus forward shifting is unlikely to be complete even in markets most conducive to its occurrence.[51]

One well-established feature of corporate tax incidence is the general proposition that a tax on the profits of a maximizing monopolist will induce neither short-run product price increases nor a long-run shift of resources to the untaxed sector as long as after-tax monopoly profit rates remain above the levels prevailing elsewhere. Shifting might occur if a strong labor union shared the monopoly profits with the corporations in question, so that an increase in profit taxes would force a reduction in negotiated wage rates. Otherwise, a tax on monopoly profits will be borne entirely by the shareholders of the monopoly corporations.[52]

A second, rather startling, possibility concerning corporate tax incidence in noncompetitive markets has been developed by Rudolph G. Penner. In his model, corporate managers, being uncertain

[50] It is a long-established doctrine that similar increases in competitively determined prices would occur to the extent that the corporate tax falls on such short-run costs as the imputed normal return to equity capital invested in inventories. See E. Cary Brown, "The Corporate Income Tax in the Short Run," *National Tax Journal*, Vol. 7 (September 1954), pp. 240–41.

[51] Carl Shoup, "Incidence of the Corporation Income Tax: Capital Structure and Turnover Rates," *National Tax Journal*, Vol. 1 (March 1948), pp. 12–17, reprinted in *Readings in the Economics of Taxation*, pp. 322–29.

[52] Such tax burdens will presumably be substantially capitalized, so that in one sense the burden falls entirely on those owning corporate stock at the time the tax increases were announced, and not on subsequent purchasers. In another sense, however, as Harvey Brazer argues, the burden may be said to rest on those current share-

about the future prices they will receive for their products, base their decisions on a subjective probability distribution of such prices and seek to maximize a utility function incorporating the firm's wealth position over the relevant planning period.[53] Penner shows that if they have diminishing marginal utilities, managers will set prices above maximum-profit levels and will frequently, though not invariably, react to the corporate tax by reducing prices and expanding output! While the Penner model yields few definite results, his approach has considerable intellectual appeal and may, with further development, provide a useful basis for the empirical estimation of corporate tax shifting and incidence parameters.

Imperfectly competitive economic markets introduce a great number of complexities and uncertainties into tax incidence analysis. Nevertheless, the long-run Harberger shifting mechanism, originating from the supply side from tax-created differentials in net rates of return and analyzed in detail in the HMM model, is an indispensable part of incidence analysis. Moreover, to the extent that it does not operate because of short-run tax-induced increases in corporate product prices, a similar resource-shifting mechanism, originating from the demand side as a direct result of the higher relative price for corporate output, can be expected to replace it.[54] Addition of the effects of this demand-originating reallocation on factor prices, which the Harberger model was not set up to analyze, would be a worthy enterprise for incidence model builders. It would presumably serve mainly to generalize the results of the HMM model to many noncompetitive market situations.

## Imperfect Factor Mobility

Factor immobilities tend to impede the shifting of tax burdens. If the mobility of capital between the corporate and noncorporate

---

holders who would gain from the reduction of the present corporate tax rate, their gain being the capitalized value of all future expected tax reductions resulting from the tax rate drop.

[53] "Uncertainty and the Short-run Shifting of the Corporation Tax," *Oxford Economic Papers*, Vol. 19 (March 1967), pp. 99–110.

[54] Since a constant level of aggregate private demand is a key assumption of differential tax incidence analysis, any price elasticity of demand for corporate output greater than zero will lead to a shift of resources to the noncorporate sector with all of the potential effects on product and factor prices analyzed in the HMM model.

sectors is high, corporate taxes not shifted to labor will be borne by capitalists in general rather than shareholders, as predicted by the Harberger model; if it is low, those burdens will remain on corporate shareholders.[55] Similarly, to the extent that the corporate tax reduces the relative size of the corporate sector—either because investment shifts out of that sector or because large corporations raise product prices along with their tax rates—workers with talents that are specialized to corporate management or to types of production unique to corporate enterprise will suffer income losses because of the corporate tax.

Controversy about the mobility of corporate capital is well illustrated in an argument between Dan Throop Smith and Jacob Stockfisch over the capitalization of the corporation income tax.[56] Stockfisch took the position that investment funds were highly mobile, that a separate corporate profits tax would consequently be shifted to capitalists in general, in the fashion of the Harberger model, and that this shifting would reduce the rate of return on capital generally and hence prevent any capitalization of the corporate tax. In the case of a 50 percent corporate tax imposed when rates of return are 10 percent throughout equal-sized corporate and noncorporate sectors, a share yielding $10 a year indefinitely would be worth $100 before the corporate tax was imposed and $50 immediately thereafter while the capitalization rate remained at 10 percent. As capital was reallocated, however, the capitalization rate would fall, and in final equilibrium the corporate share would earn, say, $15 a year before taxes ($7.50 a year net of taxes) and would again be worth $100 on the open market, since the new capitalization rate would be only 7.5 percent.

Smith objected to these conclusions: "The suggestion that investors shift from corporate to noncorporate forms implies a fluidity which is especially unlikely. Security holders may shift from one

---

[55] McLure, in "The Theory of Tax Incidence with Imperfect Factor Mobility," concludes that "a factor tax levied upon one use of an immobile factor is borne entirely by the owners of that factor in the taxed use" (p. 37). Were corporate capital for some reason completely unable to shift out of that sector, in other words, all corporate tax burdens not shifted to labor would rest on corporate shareholders.

[56] Dan Throop Smith, "Corporate Taxation and Common Stock Financing," *National Tax Journal*, Vol. 6 (September 1953), pp. 209–25; J. A. Stockfisch, "Common Stock Financing and Tax Capitalization," ibid., Vol. 7 (June 1954), pp. 182–86; and Smith's "Rejoinder," ibid., pp. 186–88.

form of security to another (which might mean from corporate stock to corporate bonds), but a shift from corporate stock to diversified participation in partnerships or noncorporate ventures would be extreme and improbable indeed."[57]

Since this exchange there has been a considerable development of special mutual funds and other financial intermediaries concentrating on the financing of unincorporated enterprises, no doubt increasing the fluidity of capital markets. How closely they now approach the perfection assumed by Stockfisch and Harberger is a question on which qualified experts are likely to disagree for some time to come.

Even if portfolio investments could be shifted freely from one type of enterprise to another, direct investment might be subject to important impediments. In response to a separate corporate tax, real investment might be shifted out of the corporate sector in a number of ways:

• Corporations that otherwise would have expanded by borrowing or by issuing equity capital might fail to do so. This would reduce the competition for portfolio investment funds and, with a high degree of mobility in those markets, help redirect them toward unincorporated enterprises.

• Substitution of the corporate tax for some other equal-yield levy would automatically shift a certain amount of funding for real investment from corporations to other businesses by changing the distribution of retained earnings in the economy. Suppose a general 25 percent tax on all capital income, which would produce the following situation in corporate and noncorporate sectors of equal size using 60 percent payouts:

|  | Corporate sector | Noncorporate sector |
|---|---|---|
| Gross-of-tax profits | $200 | $200 |
| Tax | 50 | 50 |
| Net-of-tax profits | 150 | 150 |
| Distributed profits | 90 | 90 |
| Retained profits | 60 | 60 |

If a 50 percent corporate profits tax were now substituted for the

[57] "Rejoinder," p. 187.

general capital income tax, the situation at impact would change to:

|  | Corporate sector | Noncorporate sector |
|---|---|---|
| Gross-of-tax profits | $200 | $200 |
| Tax | 100 | 0 |
| Net-of-tax profits | 100 | 200 |
| Distributed profits | 60 | 120 |
| Retained profits | 40 | 80 |

In this case there would be no difficulty in reallocating real investment between the two sectors to the extent of the change in retained profits.

• If these two mechanisms failed to eliminate the intersectoral differential in after-tax profit rates, the sole remaining option would be for corporations to increase dividends so that their shareholders could take advantage of the superior profit prospects in unincorporated enterprises. The federal income tax structure itself, however, is a major barrier to the operation of this shift mechanism. Because dividends are taxed on distribution to the stockholders and capital gains at a later date and substantially lower rates (if indeed at all), a corporate manager will think twice before shifting funds from the corporate to the noncorporate sector via the higher dividend route. In John A. Brittain's comprehensive empirical study of corporate dividend policies,[58] for example, the level of personal income tax rates was found to have an important, inverse effect on dividend payout ratios, suggesting that corporate profit retention is an important tax shelter device, which would permit further corporate expansion even when rates of return were higher in the noncorporate sector.

In summary, then, barriers to the free movement of both portfolio and direct investment do exist, and by existing they imply that some corporate tax burdens remain on stockholders and are not shifted to capitalists in general.

## Corporate Efficiency Profits

Still another barrier to corporate tax shifting to other capitalists would be a higher profit rate of corporations over unincorporated

[58] *Corporate Dividend Policy* (Brookings Institution, 1966).

enterprises arising from greater efficiency of operation. The premier advantage of the corporation, of course, is its ability to raise large amounts of capital, and there is evidence that, other things equal, large firms tend to have higher average profit rates than small firms.[59] Suppose that in pretax equilibrium the rate of return were 12 percent for large corporations, but only 9 percent for unincorporated businesses generally.[60] Imposition of any separate corporation tax up to 25 percent would keep net-of-tax profit rates in large corporations at least equal to those available elsewhere and hence would provide no incentive for a shift of investment from corporations to other businesses. The burdens of such a tax, therefore, would tend to remain on shareholders.

## Saving and Investment

One of the major potential weaknesses of the HMM model is its assumption of a constant capital stock, normally thought to be only a short-run phenomenon, in the analysis of the long-run incidence of different taxes. This apparent inconsistency can be justified either if saving and investment are not in fact very sensitive to the tax changes considered, or if the effects of tax-induced changes in saving and investment do not materialize quickly. While such a defense of the HMM model cannot be rejected on the basis of currently available evidence, it is sufficiently questionable to make incidence analyses that drop the constant capital stock assumption attractive. This requires a shift from static general equilibrium to dynamic growth models.

These models assume that changes in saving are automatically translated into changes in investment; a tax change therefore can affect the consumption-investment allocation of private sector resources either by changing the net rate of return on saving or by redistributing income between high and low savers. Two of the key incidence parameters, then, are the interest elasticity of saving and the set of marginal propensities to save at different income levels

[59] Marshall Hall and Leonard Weiss, "Firm Size and Profitability," *Review of Economics and Statistics*, Vol. 49 (August 1967), pp. 319–31; and Matityahu Marcus, "Profitability and Size of Firm: Some Further Evidence," ibid., Vol. 51 (February 1969), pp. 104–07.

[60] These rates are close to the rates found by Hall and Weiss for large and small corporations respectively.

(frequently represented in growth models by a higher propensity to save from capital than from labor income).[61] The potential importance of these parameters may be brought into focus by considering the differential incidence of general profits and payroll taxes, the chief question of interest being the extent to which a shift from the latter to the former would fail to shift all of the burdens from workers to capitalists. Using a one-sector, neoclassical, Cobb-Douglas growth model in which wages account for two-thirds of total income, Feldstein, for example, has derived the following estimates:[62]

| Interest elasticity of saving | Ratio of propensity to save from capital income to propensity to save from labor income | Proportion of differential burden of profits tax borne by labor in long run |
|---|---|---|
| 0.00 | 1.0 | 0.00 |
| 0.00 | 2.0 | 0.25 |
| 0.00 | 1.5 | 0.14 |
| 0.33 | 1.0 | 0.25 |
| 0.25 | 1.0 | 0.20 |
| 0.33 | 2.0 | 0.47 |
| 0.25 | 1.5 | 0.35 |

The share of the differential tax burden borne by labor varies directly with the values of the key parameters; the combined effect of unequal saving propensities and nonzero saving elasticities is not simply an additive one. In addition, Feldstein shows that the labor share varies inversely with the elasticity of substitution between capital and labor in production, other things equal, except when saving is completely insensitive to changes in interest rates and capitalist propensities to save are equal to those of workers.

Though these answers are not directly applicable to a partial profits tax, such as that on corporate income, they suggest that the assumption of a constant capital stock is unrealistic if saving is not completely interest inelastic or if saving propensities differ significantly according to family income level. Unfortunately, empirical evidence on the interest elasticity of saving is rare, and that on dif-

[61] A third is the elasticity of substitution between capital and labor in production.
[62] "Incidence of a Capital Income Tax," pp. 12–13.

ferential saving propensities, though not rare, is interpreted differently by supporters of different theories of consumer behavior.

Colin Wright's estimates of the income-compensated interest elasticity of saving for the periods 1897–1949 and 1929–58 appear to be the only estimates of the pure substitution effect, which he places in a minimum range of 0.18 to 0.27.[63] Even if nonzero interest elasticities are confirmed by future empirical studies and permanent-income theorists concede significant income-related differentials in saving propensities, the HMM model can still be defended. If the long-run incidence effects of tax-induced variations in saving and investment do not materialize quickly, the HMM results will apply without substantial modification for a considerable length of time after a tax change has been made. Many dynamic incidence models suggest this outcome.[64]

If the convenient neoclassical assumption that savings are always invested is dropped, an equal-yield substitution of one tax for another can no longer be assumed to maintain the same aggregate private demand. The incidence theorist then has two alternatives. He can hold to the traditional assumption of constant private demand by presuming any tax-induced departures from constancy to be counteracted by the use of suitable nontax fiscal instruments. For any tax substitution involving significant macro effects his analysis would then deal not with tax incidence but with the incidence of the entire package of fiscal instruments used. Or he can assume variations in the tax instrument only, drop the assumption of constant aggregate private demand, and incorporate into tax incidence both macro and distributional effects. Regardless of which choice is made, a major shift of emphasis must also occur, from the effects of taxation on saving to those on investment.

[63] "Some Evidence on the Interest Elasticity of Consumption," *American Economic Review*, Vol. 57 (September 1967), pp. 850–55, and "Saving and the Rate of Interest," in Arnold C. Harberger and Martin J. Bailey (eds.), *The Taxation of Income from Capital* (Brookings Institution, 1969), pp. 275–300. Wright's estimates are minimum estimates because of their recognized failure to exclude the income effect of a change in interest rates completely.

[64] See the papers by Marian Krzyzaniak cited above in note 30; Feldstein, "Tax Incidence in a Growing Economy"; and Ryuzo Sato, "Fiscal Policy in a Neo-Classical Growth Model: An Analysis of Time Required for Equilibrating Adjustment," *Review of Economic Studies*, Vol. 30 (February 1963), pp. 16–23.

## The Shoven and Whalley Algorithmic Approach

A promising new approach to the empirical estimation of tax incidence patterns, based on a procedure developed by Herbert E. Scarf for calculating general equilibrium prices in a competitive economy, has recently been made by Shoven and Whalley.[65] Unlike the HMM model, their solution requires no linearity assumptions; it can deal with more than two sectors and two factors of production and handle more than one distortion at a time. Aggregate factor supplies need not be held constant, and household groups may be distinguished both by their taste for consumer goods and by their ownership of different productive factors. Using the same data as Harberger, Shoven and Whalley derive a wide variety of quantitative estimates of incidence on the sources side of the picture.[66] While some show the possibility of significant corporate tax burdens on labor incomes (if the elasticities of substitution between labor and capital are relatively low in both the corporate and noncorporate sectors), in most of the cases capital is estimated to bear at least the full burden of the corporate tax.

The Scarf–Shoven-Whalley approach to tax incidence estimation cannot yet be regarded as the source of hard-and-fast answers. It does, however, appear to be a highly promising addition to the tool boxes of fiscal economists and should bode well for the future.

## Conclusion

The wide divergences in opinion about the incidence of the corporation income tax are not likely to be resolved soon. The true corporate tax incidence pattern probably contains a mixture, in unknown proportions, of all of the plausible group burdens—those on corporate shareholders, on receivers of noncorporate property incomes, on workers in corporate and noncorporate businesses, and on consumers of corporate output. These uncertainties must be resolved before any realistic appraisal of the equity and economic efficiency of the U.S. tax system can be made. Both the average pro-

---

[65] "A General Equilibrium Calculation."

[66] They do hypothesize, however, that high-income households are likely to have stronger tastes for corporate output than low-income households, making corporate tax incidence on the uses side progressive. Ibid., p. 304.

gressiveness of federal taxes and the fairness of their distribution over different kinds of income depend critically on whether the corporate profits tax is borne mainly by shareholders and other capitalists or by consumers and workers. How badly federal taxes distort the allocation of resources depends on whether the Harberger long-run shifting mechanism is a major or minor effect of the corporate tax. And whether federal government use of value added, rather than corporate profits, taxation would improve the U.S. balance of payments depends largely on the extent to which corporate tax burdens rest on consumers.[67] On the other hand, the present uncertainty has obvious noneconomic attractions: politicians may be able to sell a corporate tax increase simultaneously to workers and consumers who think it would mainly burden capitalists and to capitalists and businessmen who think it would mainly burden consumers.

The promising areas for future research concerning the burdens of the corporate profits tax include: the uses-of-income side of the incidence picture; the disaggregation and further elaboration of dynamic growth models of tax incidence; detailed study of the alternative adjustment paths by which final incidence patterns, both short run and long run, are reached and of how the nature of the adjustment path affects the final incidence pattern; attention to discrete rather than infinitesimal tax changes and to the interactions between new and existing taxes; and micro studies of the specific pricing policies and behavior of individual corporations operating under different market structures. There is much to do. The one consolation is that the corporate profits tax will probably stay for the doing of it.

## General Property Taxation

Traditional theories of property tax incidence, relatively undisturbed until quite recently, hold that a tax on unimproved land, an

[67] See Richard A. Musgrave, "Effects of Business Taxes upon International Commodity Flows," in Krzyzaniak, *Effects of Corporation Income Tax*, pp. 118–35; Robert Z. Aliber and Herbert Stein, "The Price of U.S. Exports and the Mix of U.S. Direct and Indirect Taxes," *American Economic Review*, Vol. 54 (September 1964), pp. 703–10; and Maurice D. Weinrobe, "Corporate Taxes and the United States Balance of Trade," *National Tax Journal*, Vol. 24 (March 1971), pp. 79–86.

immobile factor of production in fixed supply, is borne by the land-owner; taxes on all other types of business property are shifted forward to consumers; and taxes on residential structures and furniture are either borne by owner-occupants or shifted forward to tenants. These widely held views have fueled popular criticism of the property tax as a highly regressive levy imposing excessive burdens on those least able to bear them. The tax is still the mainstay of independent local government finance in this country, and with budgets rising steeply it has come under increasing attack from disgruntled taxpayers. Numerous straws in the wind indicate, however, that established doctrine concerning the property tax is in for some searching reappraisal.

As early as 1924, Harry Gunnison Brown argued that the burdens of either a partial or a general tax on capital, provided it did not decrease the total volume of capital in existence, would not be shifted forward to consumers but would fall on capital owners in general. Alternatively, if the tax did lower the rate of capital formation, some of its burdens would be shifted, though to workers and landowners rather than to consumers.[68] In spite of the limited impact these nonconformist views had for many years, discontent with existing doctrine is rising and there are signs of a shift of emphasis in property tax analysis from consumer to capitalist burdens. Buchanan has emphasized both the slowness with which housing tax burdens are likely to be shifted to renters and the proposition that the property tax does reduce the rate of return on capital investment generally.[69] Richman's analysis of the incidence of urban taxes "differs sharply with the traditional conclusion that a tax on real estate improvements is shifted forward to the occupier. It argues that the tax on improvements is borne by the landowner except for minor effects of the tax on the intensive development of a parcel."[70] In an important extension of the HMM model, Mieszkowski concludes that property tax incidence involves some hard-to-

[68] Harry Gunnison Brown, *The Economics of Taxation* (Holt, 1924), pp. 178–96.

[69] James M. Buchanan, *The Public Finances: An Introductory Textbook* (3rd ed., Irwin, 1970), p. 411.

[70] Raymond L. Richman, "The Incidence of Urban Real Estate Taxes Under Conditions of Static and Dynamic Equilibrium," *Land Economics*, Vol. 43 (May 1967), p. 179.

**TABLE 3. Effective Property Tax Rates under Alternative Incidence Assumptions, by Income Class, 1966**

(In percentage of income)

| Adjusted family income[a] | Tax on property income in general | Land portion of tax on landowners; remainder on consumers |
|---|---|---|
| Under $3,000 | 2.5 | 6.5 |
| $  3,000–5,000 | 2.7 | 4.8 |
| 5,000–10,000 | 2.0 | 3.6 |
| 10,000–15,000 | 1.7 | 3.2 |
| 15,000–20,000 | 2.0 | 3.2 |
| 20,000–25,000 | 2.6 | 3.1 |
| 25,000–30,000 | 3.7 | 3.1 |
| 30,000–50,000 | 4.5 | 3.0 |
| 50,000–100,000 | 6.2 | 2.8 |
| 100,000–500,000 | 8.2 | 2.4 |
| 500,000–1,000,000 | 9.6 | 1.7 |
| Over $1,000,000 | 10.1 | 0.8 |

Source: Joseph A. Pechman and Benjamin A. Okner, *Who Bears the Tax Burden?* (Brookings Institution, 1974), p. 59. The rates are computed from the Brookings MERGE file of 72,000 family units.
[a] Includes wages, interest, dividends, rents and royalties, accrued capital gains, interest on state-local bonds, government transfer payments, and a large number of nonmonetary income sources.

determine blending of consumer, capitalist, labor, and landowner burdens.[71]

Exactly what that blending of burdens may be is one of the most important unresolved issues in fiscal economics. In 1972 property taxes provided 12.5 percent of all government taxes and 35 percent of state and local taxes.[72] How regressive or progressive the vertical distribution of the burdens is depends on where the incidence of the tax mainly lies, and in particular on the division of burdens between consumers and capitalists. As Table 3 shows, if all property taxes other than those on land were shifted to consumers, the effective tax rate would decline steadily from 6.5 percent in the lowest income class to 0.8 percent in the highest. If all property taxes, on the other hand, fell on property income, the effective rate at the bottom of the income scale would be only 2.5 percent and at the top 10.1 percent.

Determining the incidence of the property tax, then, is a high-

[71] Peter Mieszkowski, "The Property Tax: An Excise Tax or a Profits Tax?" *Journal of Public Economics*, Vol. 1 (April 1972), pp. 73–96.

[72] *Survey of Current Business*, Vol. 53 (July 1973), pp. 30–31. Total tax revenues include social security contributions.

priority fiscal goal. The exceedingly complex analysis required has several new features:

• Investment in taxable property typically includes land, which is distinguished by its high inelasticity of supply. Landowner tax burdens are consequently an important possibility, and to deal with them the two-factor HMM model must be extended to cover at least three factors of production.

• The two roles played by the owner-occupant of residential property should be sharply distinguished. As owner he is a capitalist interested in the net-of-tax rate of return obtainable on his home, relative to the rates on other investments. As occupant he is a tenant concerned about the quality of the housing services he receives, reflected in the imputed gross rental value of his premises. Property taxes affect rates of return on housing investment directly, but their impact on gross rental values is indirect and highly complex.

• Housing rentals reflect much more than the value of the services of the house itself. In particular, they reflect the value of all those local government services that are enjoyed only by residents of the community in question and typically are financed by property taxes. These benefit aspects of property taxation must be given explicit attention in incidence analysis.

• Property taxes are imposed, particularly in urban areas of this country, by local jurisdictions operating side by side with other governments that are pursuing their own independent tax policies. The standard assumption in incidence analysis of a closed economic system must therefore be dropped and close attention given to tax effects on interregional trade and on industrial, commercial, and residential location decisions.[73]

## Incidence from the National Point of View

Though the property tax is levied by independent local governments, it does have a nationwide scope, or virtually so, and it does finance much the same kind of local public services in all parts of the country. Some of the larger dimensions of property taxation are best seen from a national perspective, as are the factors common to

---

[73] The HMM incidence model has been extended to deal with these matters by McLure, "The Inter-Regional Incidence of General Regional Taxes," and "Taxation, Substitution, and Industrial Location."

all communities that have caused the long-continued rise in property tax rates.

From a national point of view, as Mieszkowski has stressed, it is natural to analyze property tax incidence first as though dealing with a nationwide proportional tax on all property, levied at the average tax rate for the country as a whole, and then in terms of state and local tax rate differentials above and below that average rate. The HMM model may be applied directly to a nationwide tax imposed on all property at the same rate; it is readily shown not to be shiftable, and hence to rest on capital income generally. That is true as long as aggregate saving and investment are not affected by the tax; if they are affected, the shifting possibilities are like those derived for the corporate income tax in dynamic incidence models.

The property tax, of course, is not a uniform levy on all industries and sectors of the economy. Rosenberg estimated for 1953–59 that average property tax rates on capital income were relatively low for manufacturing (6.7 percent) and wholesale trade (7.3 percent) and relatively high for transportation (17.5 percent) and nonfarm residential dwellings (26.7 percent); the nationwide average rate was 14.2 percent.[74] These tax rate differentials will set in motion the usual excise-type effects including higher prices and lower outputs in the relatively heavily taxed industries, as well as changes in factor prices resulting from tax-induced shifts of resources between labor-intensive and capital-intensive industries.

Quantitative estimation of these interindustry excise tax effects remains a distant fiscal goal. Nor is that all. The unneutralities of the property tax and of all the other major taxes in the country need to be integrated. The total U.S. tax system may be better than or worse than its separate parts, depending on whether the unneutralities offset or reinforce one another. In spite of its relatively high property tax burdens, owner-occupied housing appears to be very much undertaxed when compared to other kinds of personal consumption or investment.[75] The relative position of rental housing is

[74] Leonard Gerson Rosenberg, "Taxation of Income from Capital, by Industry Group," in Harberger and Bailey, *The Taxation of Income from Capital*, pp. 174–77. See also Dick Netzer, *Economics of the Property Tax* (Brookings Institution, 1966), Chap. 2.

[75] See Henry Aaron, "Income Taxes and Housing," *American Economic Review*, Vol. 60 (December 1970), pp. 789–806 (Brookings Reprint 193); Musgrave and Musgrave, *Public Finance in Theory and Practice*, pp. 333–35; and Richard Netzer,

a matter of dispute, quite apart from the unresolved issue of the tenant-landlord division of property tax burdens.[76] For all these reasons the nationwide aspects of property taxation are far from satisfactorily determined.

## Incidence of Interstate and Interlocal Property Tax Differentials

Analysis of the incidence of interregional property tax rate differentials introduces three major new elements: the importance of the benefit aspects of taxation; the high taxpayer mobilities and business competitive forces characterizing the open economic systems in which state and local governments operate; and the significance of tax exporting and importing.

BENEFIT ASPECTS. As Alfred Marshall long ago emphasized, it is important to distinguish sharply between property taxes that yield compensating benefits to the taxpayer and those that do not.[77] Whereas onerous tax rate differentials, as Marshall called those that conferred no compensating benefits, will be a negative element in the locational decisions of all households and business enterprises, beneficial tax rate differentials will repel only those whose tastes for the benefits in question are not sufficiently strong to justify paying the extra tax. Beneficial tax differentials will not be shifted to the extent that onerous differentials are, but will tend to remain on the taxpayer-beneficiaries, thus contributing to both fiscal equity and economic efficiency goals.[78] Local governments, for example,

---

"Housing Taxation and Housing Policy," in Adela Adam Nevitt (ed.), *The Economic Problems of Housing* (Macmillan and St. Martin's, 1967), pp. 123–36 (Brookings Reprint 136).

[76] Compare, for example, Aaron, "Income Taxes and Housing," pp. 801–02, and Emil M. Sunley, Jr., "Tax Advantages of Homeownership Versus Renting: A Cause of Suburban Migration?" in National Tax Association, *Proceedings of the Sixty-Third Annual Conference on Taxation* (1971), pp. 380–92. An important element in the debate is the extent to which tax depreciation exceeds economic depreciation, and the extent to which the resulting tax savings under the federal income tax are passed on to tenants. For estimates that economic depreciation is considerably less accelerated than even straight-line depreciation, see Paul Taubman and Robert Rasche, "Subsidies, Tax Law, and Real Estate Investment," in *The Economics of Federal Subsidy Programs*, Pt. 3, *Tax Subsidies*, A Compendium of Papers Submitted to the Joint Economic Committee, 92 Cong. 2 sess. (1972), p. 351.

[77] *Principles of Economics* (8th ed., Macmillan, 1920), App. G, p. 794.

[78] The classic analysis of these aspects of local finance is Charles M. Tiebout, "A Pure Theory of Local Expenditures," *Journal of Political Economy*, Vol. 64 (October 1956), pp. 416–24.

could help to optimize business locational choices by keeping local business taxes closely in line with the value of the free services they provide to business firms. Whether the property tax is the best available choice for this purpose is not at issue here. The economic dimensions of that choice are as controversial[79] as are those concerning the use of property taxes to finance local schools.[80]

What is important is the proper treatment of beneficial property taxes in incidence analysis. When the levying government, such as a school district, has no other source of local revenue, a balanced budget approach, involving the allocation of both benefits and burdens to different income groups, may be of interest. The applicability of this approach is strictly limited, however. Most local governments have access to more than one tax source, and those that don't could be given it. The differential incidence approach is the appropriate method of analysis in all such cases. One version of it, which is of considerable policy interest, would investigate the distributional effects of substituting various kinds of local income taxes for existing property taxes.[81] Another, under which all interregional property tax differentials are onerous by definition, compares the present complex set of local property taxes with a nationwide uniform property tax for financing the same local government services.

INTERLOCAL MOBILITIES AND COMPETITION. In incidence literature, especially that dealing with long-run tax shifting, capital is usually assumed to be perfectly mobile among the different regions of a country. Thus onerous property tax differentials will raise the before-tax price of capital to relatively high-tax areas and lower that price to low-tax areas. Onerous property tax differentials, in other

---

[79] Harvey E. Brazer, for example, proposes that a state-coordinated local value added tax be substituted for business property taxes in "The Value of Industrial Property as a Subject of Taxation," *Canadian Public Administration*, Vol. 4 (June 1961), pp. 137–47.

[80] See Robin Barlow, "Efficiency Aspects of Local School Finance," *Journal of Political Economy*, Vol. 78 (September/October 1970), pp. 1028–40; and the individual papers by Noel M. Edelson, Yoram Barzel, Theodore Bergstrom, Timothy Hogan, and Robert Shelton, and Robin Barlow, prepared for the Symposium on Efficiency Aspects of Local School Finance, ibid., Vol. 81 (January/February 1973), pp. 158–202.

[81] See, for example, R. Stafford Smith, *Local Income Taxes: Economic Effects and Equity* (University of California, Berkeley, Institute of Governmental Studies, 1972).

words, will be shifted to other groups, and the problem is to try to trace the direction of these shifts. Although incidence models cannot yet provide the disaggregation required for the most useful results, the main factors necessary to a full analysis are apparent.[82]

To begin with, factor and consumer mobilities and competitive forces will both vary significantly, depending on whether the onerous property tax differentials exist between urban areas or within a single area, and whether the areas are rapidly growing or static and declining. Consider first the case of tax differentials between urban areas.

The ability of a given business enterprise to shift onerous property tax differentials forward in the short run will depend on whether it is engaged principally in export production or home production (that is, whether its output is sold outside or inside the taxing jurisdiction). Those in export production can be categorized as either dominant or nondominant firms in the national industry. Those in home production can be distinguished by whether they are protected from or subject to import competition and whether they operate within an oligopolistic or a competitive home market. Clearly, exporting firms that are dominant in the national industry and home producers that are protected from both outside and inside competition will be better able than others to raise product prices.

The ability of business to shift onerous property tax differentials to labor will depend on the structure of local labor markets and the mobility of workers both into and out of the market. In static or declining tax jurisdictions the restraining force would be a high outmobility in response to low local wage rates, particularly among younger, better educated, and higher income workers. In a growing high-tax jurisdiction an important restraining force would be the sensitivity of potential immigrant workers to higher tax burdens on owner-occupied housing and higher consumer prices induced by relatively high property taxes. If this forced new and expanding firms to pay higher wage rates, location or expansion in the taxing jurisdiction would be unattractive unless land prices were low

---

[82] See McLure's comprehensive theoretical analysis using the HMM model in "The Inter-regional Incidence of General Regional Taxes," and his considerably more disaggregated empirical analysis in "The Interstate Exporting of State and Local Taxes: Estimates for 1962," *National Tax Journal*, Vol. 20 (March 1967), pp. 49–77 (Brookings Reprint 132).

enough to make after-tax profit rates there comparable to those in lower-tax areas. Wage rate reductions would also be relatively difficult in urban areas whose labor markets were dominated by unions that bargain nationally, rather than locally, with employers (unless the high-tax area itself dominated the national labor market).

These complexities, as well as the standard parameters of the HMM model, which are as relevant here as in the analysis of national tax incidence, make it clear that few quantitative generalizations can be drawn concerning the incidence of interurban property tax differentials. The incidence is likely to differ from area to area, and only extensive micro research can hope to unravel many of the closely intertwined mysteries of this aspect of property tax incidence.

Such need not be the case, however, for many intraurban property tax differentials. If these differentials affect a relatively small part of a large metropolitan area, landowners are likely to bear their burdens because workers, tenants, and consumers to whom they might otherwise be shifted are too mobile to provide a lasting target.[83] Such tax burdens, moreover, will tend to be capitalized and to be borne fully by those who owned the land at the time the tax differentials came into existence.[84]

[83] Larry L. Orr, relying on high tenant mobilities and an insensitivity of the housing stock to rent differentials even over fairly long time periods, concludes in "The Incidence of Differential Property Taxes on Urban Housing," *National Tax Journal*, Vol. 21 (September 1968), pp. 253–62, that intraurban property tax differentials are borne by landlords rather than by tenants. His empirical evidence has been disputed; see comment by J. D. Heinberg and W. E. Oates and response by Orr, ibid., Vol. 23 (March 1970), pp. 92–98, 99–101; and Robert M. Coen and Brian J. Powell, "Theory and Measurement of the Incidence of Differential Property Taxes on Rental Housing," Orr, "The Incidence of Differential Property Taxes on Urban Housing: Reply," and Heinberg and Oates, "The Incidence of Differential Property Taxes on Rental Housing: An Addendum," ibid., Vol. 25 (June 1972), pp. 211–16, 217–20, 221–22.

[84] See Wallace E. Oates, "The Effects of Property Taxes and Local Public Spending on Property Values: An Empirical Study of Tax Capitalization and the Tiebout Hypothesis," *Journal of Political Economy*, Vol. 77 (November/December 1969), pp. 957–71, reprinted in Oates, *Fiscal Federalism* (Harcourt Brace Jovanovich, 1972), and his reply to a criticism by Henry O. Pollakowski and presentation of further results in *Journal of Political Economy*, Vol. 81 (July/August 1973), pp. 1004–08; R. Stafford Smith, "Property Tax Capitalization in San Francisco," *National Tax Journal*, Vol. 23 (June 1970), pp. 177–93; and John H. Wicks, Robert A. Little, and Ralph A. Beck, "A Note on Capitalization of Property Tax Changes,"

TAX EXPORTING AND IMPORTING. The shifting of tax burdens from the residents of one state or local jurisdiction to those of another is of special interest both in the theory of local government behavior and in the design of an efficient and equitable system of fiscal federalism. In his pioneering study, McLure found interstate tax exporting rates that varied in 1962 between 17 percent and 38 percent of state-local taxes in the short run and between 15 percent and 35 percent in the long run.[85] While much of the normative significance of tax burden exporting depends on whether it is or is not accompanied by comparable exports of expenditure benefits, its effects on state and local tax capacities and tax effort are direct, unequivocal, and complex enough to render those much-used concepts highly ambiguous.[86] If the burden that a local tax dollar imposes on local residents varies both with the type of tax used and with the economic characteristics of the governmental unit imposing it, allocation of federal grant moneys based partly on tax effort measures that take no account of burden exporting, as exemplified in the general revenue sharing program of 1972,[87] must be regarded as a dubious contribution to fiscal equity.

Some kinds of tax effort, in short, are more equal than others. It is extremely difficult to rank them realistically. The problem of deriving a weighted index of fiscal effort sufficiently reliable to be incorporated into the allocation formulas of intergovernmental grants-in-aid is much more intransigent. This is particularly true at the local governmental level, for the major source of local funds is

---

ibid., Vol. 21 (September 1968), pp. 263–65. Darwin W. Daicoff found that property tax capitalization is difficult to measure empirically unless the model used is carefully specified to control for tax-financed local government benefits and to distinguish interregional tax differentials from the average, nationwide level of property tax rates; "Capitalization of the Property Tax," in Harvey E. Brazer (ed.), *Essays in State and Local Finance* (University of Michigan, Institute of Public Administration, 1967), pp. 46–73.

[85] "Interstate Exporting of State and Local Taxes," p. 63.

[86] For a detailed analysis of alternative measures see Advisory Commission on Intergovernmental Relations, *Measures of State and Local Fiscal Capacity and Tax Effort* (ACIR, 1962), and *Measuring the Fiscal Capacity and Effort of State and Local Areas* (Government Printing Office, 1971).

[87] The State and Local Fiscal Assistance Act of 1972, signed by the President on October 20, 1972, appropriated $30.2 billion to be distributed as unrestricted grants to states, counties, and cities during the five calendar years 1972 through 1976.

the property tax, whose exportability cannot be determined until the question of its incidence is settled.[88]

*Conclusions*

The present state of knowledge about the incidence of the general property tax is like that of an audience at the end of the second act of a complex mystery drama. The degree of uncertainty about the final outcome is probably greater than it was at the end of the first act, but at least some of the seeming certainties of the first act have been dispelled. Since the denouement in this fiscal drama is not likely to be near at hand, it is important to identify as clearly as possible the probable roles being played by the major participants and the significance of those roles for current tax policy.

Property tax burdens on landowners are probably considerably greater than has commonly been supposed. The continuing strong appeal of land value taxation to disciples of Henry George and many others makes this an important issue.[89] From their point of view, presumably, the more heavily the property tax bears on landowners, the higher should it be rated on grounds of equity and efficiency, and the less need is there to replace it with a tax on site values. Those who are less convinced that land is the ideal tax base would prefer to judge the property tax on broader grounds. Nevertheless, to the extent that interregional property tax differentials are borne by landowners, rather than by workers or consumers, a progressive element is imparted to property tax incidence.

An important, though surprising, uncertainty in the debate about landowner burdens is the size of the relative share of land in total property values. If it is small, the opportunities for shifting property taxes on improvements to landowners would be correspondingly restricted. According to Mieszkowski, for example, landowners are unlikely to bear more than 40 percent of the total inter-

---

[88] In fiscal 1970 property taxes provided 64 percent of all local government general revenue from local sources, compared to 66 percent in 1967 and 69 percent in 1957. ACIR, *State-Local Finances: Significant Features and Suggested Legislation* (1972 ed., Government Printing Office), p. 16.

[89] For an analysis of site value taxation, together with other alternatives to the present property tax, see James Heilbrun, *Real Estate Taxes and Urban Housing* (Columbia University Press, 1966); Netzer, *Economics of the Property Tax*, Chap. 8; and Peter M. Mieszkowski, "A Critical Appraisal of Land Value Taxation" (May 1970; processed).

regional property tax differentials on structures primarily because land rents in most cities are less than 5 percent of total income and only about 16.7 percent of nonwage income.[90] These averages for the economy as a whole, however, do not necessarily reflect actual property tax laws and practice. In California, for example, where a careful attempt is made to assess land separately from the improvements on it, land assessments were 37 percent of total taxable property assessments for fiscal 1973.[91] Ratios are even higher for some other parts of the country.[92] If land is one-third or more of the property tax base, its relative inelasticity of supply[93] makes it a prime candidate to bear a significant portion of interregional property tax differentials—close to 60 percent by Mieszkowski's relatively conservative estimate.[94] In addition, landowners must bear their share of the average nationwide property tax burden.

Property tax burdens on consumers, in contrast, are probably less important than commonly supposed. They are a function only of interregional and intraurban tax differentials and not of the total property tax rate; the excise tax effects generated by those tax differentials contain labor and landlord burdens which reduce the pressures making for consumer burdens; and such national consumer burdens as do exist fall not on consumers in general but only on those with relatively strong tastes for the output of the industries that are more heavily taxed than others.[95]

[90] "The Property Tax," pp. 89–90.

[91] California State Board of Equalization, *Annual Report, 1971–72*, Table 5, p. A-5. If the California tax were levied on real property only, land would have been 42.7 percent of the total base.

[92] M. Mason Gaffney, "The Property Tax Is a Progressive Tax," in National Tax Association, *Proceedings of the Sixty-Fourth Annual Conference on Taxation* (1972), p. 418.

[93] Though the total supply of land is fixed, individual parcels can sometimes be shifted from high- to low-tax uses and in the process would avoid some of the differential property tax imposed directly on them. The opportunities for such reallocations, however, are strictly limited. Uniform assessment of land on the basis of its highest and best use would preclude such shifts, and in its absence they would be discouraged by difficult-to-change zoning laws or by the presence of buildings that are costly to demolish.

[94] Computed as the sum of land's direct share (0.33) plus 40 percent of the tax on improvements ($0.4 \times 0.67 = 0.268$).

[95] Rough empirical estimates, showing differential property tax burdens on the uses side to be mildly regressive, are given in Henry Aaron, "New Views of Property Tax Incidence" (paper prepared for delivery at the 1973 annual meeting of the American Economic Association; processed).

Particularly prominent in the consumer group are residential tenants, who occupy property that constitutes nearly 10 percent nationally of the total tax base.[96] The traditional assumption that this group bears the full property tax burden on rental residential property appears to overestimate tenant burdens significantly.[97] This means that the property tax is less regressive, or more progressive, than is generally supposed, as the following ratios of effective property tax rates at selected income levels to those at the lowest income level show:[98]

|  | Effective property tax ratio | |
|  | --- | --- |
| Family income | Tenants | Capitalists |
| $ 4,000–5,700 | 1.00 | 1.00 |
| 12,500–17,500 | 0.62 | 0.75 |
| 35,000–92,000 | 0.85 | 1.23 |
| 92,000 and over | 1.09 | 1.61 |

In addition, the case for extending property tax relief to renters simply because it is being given to homeowners is a weak one. The burdens on renters are not commensurable with those on owners, and property tax rebates to renters are to a large extent outright subsidies.[99] Nor does the role of the property tax as an efficient benefits-received local levy have much validity, unless, of course, tenants continue to believe they pay property taxes even when they do not.

Unlike tenants, homeowner-occupants bear property taxes on both the uses and the sources side. Since they own a large share of

[96] Musgrave and Musgrave, *Public Finance in Theory and Practice,* p. 418.

[97] The argument is that the average nationwide property tax burden is not borne by tenants or any other consumers, that relatively heavy property taxes on rental housing are offset, perhaps to a considerable degree, by relatively light income tax burdens on landlords resulting from excessive depreciation allowances, and that if urban housing markets are reasonably competitive, tenants are protected from the burden of intraurban tax differentials by their high mobility. On the other hand, if landlords in a given area act collusively to set rentals below maximum-profit levels, or if they are forced to do so by rent control laws, higher property taxes on them are likely to be shifted to tenants. The less landlords exploit the greedy monopoly role sometimes assigned to them, the more able they will be to shift property tax burdens to their tenants.

[98] Ibid., p. 370; data are for 1968; business property taxes are assumed to rest on capitalists, nonrental residential property taxes on owner-occupants, and rental residential property taxes on tenants or on capitalists.

[99] In 1973 all fifty states had some form of property tax relief for the elderly; seventeen provided relief to renters as well as owner-occupants. See the ACIR's *Information Bulletin,* No. 73-6 (July 13, 1973).

the total taxable property in the country,[100] the nature of their burdens is important. While the total amount is not in serious dispute, it being assumed that in one role or the other they bear the full burden of what they pay to the government, the vertical distribution definitely is. Homeowner property tax burdens have conventionally been regarded as uniformly regressive over all income levels, the only disagreement being over how steep that regressivity was.[101] Of late, however, considerable doubt has been thrown on the conventional position. The challengers find the empirical evidence usually presented to show regressivity to be inadequate. They point to several gaps in the evidence pertaining to ability to pay. Typical of most distributions of residential property taxes by family income class is the failure to include in the total income base the very income presumed to be the source, and support, of the tax payments —namely, the imputed rental income enjoyed by occupants who own their own homes. Another flaw is the use of annual incomes as a base instead of the permanent, or lifetime, incomes on which home buyers are presumed to found their expenditures.[102] The evidence fails, moreover, to give adequate attention to such special kinds of housing as mobile homes and vacation homes, which are rapidly increasing in importance. Since mobile homes are frequently undertaxed compared to immobile homes and since their ownership is concentrated in the lower income groups, their frequent omission from the property tax distribution tends to give it a regressivity bias. So does the typical practice of making the statistical distribution in terms of homes (assuming one to a family) instead of families, since an increasing number of families, particularly in the upper income ranges, own more than one home.

The traditional views on property tax incidence are also criticized on the grounds that owner-occupants are more likely to bear

[100] According to the Musgraves, 30 percent; *Public Finance in Theory and Practice,* p. 418.

[101] See Netzer, *Economics of the Property Tax,* pp. 45–66.

[102] For a discussion of the significance of current versus permanent income see ibid., pp. 62–66. While the income elasticity of demand for housing is presumed to be greater for permanent than for current income, it need not be as great as unity and hence may still imply regressive tax burdens. See Frank de Leeuw, "The Demand for Housing: A Review of Cross-Section Evidence," *Review of Economics and Statistics,* Vol. 53 (February 1971), pp. 1–10, and the comment by Sherman J. Maisel, James B. Burnham, and John S. Austin, ibid. (November 1971), pp. 410–13.

their property tax burdens as investors than as consumers. A large part of that burden is simply their share of the generally progressive portion of the total property tax burden imposed on capitalists in general.

The critics call attention to the fact that investors in homes are highly subsidized by the total tax system, and that much of the property tax they do pay may be regarded as a benefits-received levy, not subject to such ability-to-pay considerations as regressivity or progressivity. While pity for the harassed homeowner may be appropriate for many reasons, excessive or inequitable tax burdens do not appear to be among them, except possibly at the lowest income levels. All states have now enacted property tax relief programs for the elderly poor, and several have extended these to all age groups.

Much is still to be learned about the incidence of property tax burdens. But for the moment at least, the tax does not appear to be quite the regressive fiscal villain it is sometimes made out to be.

## Payroll Taxes

As the most rapidly growing source of federal government revenues during the postwar period,[103] payroll taxes have drawn the attention of both the public and the experts. A major uncertainty in the discussions, often not recognized by the participants, has been the incidence of the portion of the tax paid by employers. Is it simply what it says it is, as many workers may believe, or do employers shift it to some other group, as most economists have concluded? And if it is shifted, do the burdens fall mainly on consumers in the form of higher prices or on workers in the form of lower money wage rates? On this last point the experts are sharply divided. Toward the resolution of these questions, on which a number of the major policy issues surrounding the future financing of social insurance in this country depend, both static and dynamic incidence models have contributions to make.

### Static Models

Under the conditions hypothesized in the HMM model, a perfectly general payroll tax, $T_L$, is borne entirely by the taxed factor,

---

[103] From 12 percent of federal tax receipts in 1947, contributions for social insurance (as payroll taxes are called in the national income accounts) rose to 28 percent in 1972.

regardless of the mobility or immobility of either factor. Given the competitive market assumptions and the comparative equilibrium focus of the model, this is true for both the employee and the employer shares of the payroll tax. Public finance specialists generally agree that, except for frictions and institutional imperfections, the economic effects of a tax are the same regardless of which side of the market it happens to be imposed on.[104]

Present federal payroll taxes, however, are not perfectly general in their application to the labor force; moreover, such nonmarket activities as household work, recreation, and other leisure time pursuits are excluded.[105] In the HMM context, then, the relevant tax is that imposed on the use of one factor in one sector, $T_{XL}$. Though strictly speaking the incidence of such a levy cannot be determined a priori,[106] John Brittain has made a strong argument that labor bears the entire payroll tax.[107]

The essence of Brittain's case is his careful distinction between those effects that are too important to be omitted and those that merely add relatively minor refinements. Excluding the latter is not only convenient; it is essential if a clear picture of the basic incidence pattern is to be obtained. It is in this way that Brittain reaches his unequivocal conclusion that a payroll tax levied on employers will be fully shifted to workers. Two aspects of Brittain's classification scheme seem sufficiently controversial and important to merit discussion.[108]

[104] See Brittain, *The Payroll Tax for Social Security*, p. 57.

[105] In 1971 U.S. payroll taxes for social security applied to 90 percent of all wages and salaries, the major exceptions being railroad and government employees, who had their own retirement plans. Unemployment insurance coverage, on the other hand, is considerably less general.

[106] See McLure, "The Theory of Tax Incidence with Imperfect Factor Mobility," pp. 37–41. Michael J. Boskin has applied the Harberger model to a general payroll tax on all labor income by interpreting its two sectors as covering (taxed) market output and (untaxed) household production in "The Incidence of the Payroll Tax: An Alternative Approach," Memorandum No. 136 (Stanford University, Center for Research in Economic Growth, September 1972; processed). By incorporating alternative plausible values for the key parameters into a sensitivity analysis of the model, he concludes that labor is likely to bear the full burden of the payroll tax. He extends this approach to the entire tax system in "Efficiency and Equity Aspects of the Differential Tax Treatment of Market and Household Economic Activity," Memorandum No. 149 (Stanford University, Center for Research in Economic Growth, August 1973; processed).

[107] *The Payroll Tax for Social Security*, Chap. 2.

[108] Other simplifications include the assumption that payroll tax incidence on the uses side is distributionally neutral, and neglect of the price and resource realloca-

Brittain uses real factor shares as his measure of incidence rather than the more conventional, and much more disaggregated, real household incomes. This obviates the need to consider the mechanism by which tax burdens are shifted and to distinguish between backward shifting, via lower money wage rates, and forward shifting, via higher consumer goods prices. The choice is not one of convenience but of principle. Drawing on Shoup's skepticism about the very meaning of incidence when it is applied to broad-based taxes and on McLure's separation of incidence on the uses side from the effects of macroeconomic policies on the general price level,[109] Brittain argues that it is analytically impossible to distinguish the general price level effects of taxation from those of accompanying macroeconomic policies and that such a separation is of only secondary interest in the factor shares approach to tax incidence.[110]

One result of his relatively narrowed focus is the consignment to a minor status of payroll tax burdens on fixed-income recipients. Disparate as this group is, all of its components—owners of long-term bonds, welfare recipients, retired persons living on fixed-money annuities and social security—are united by one common characteristic. They all stand to lose more from the forward shifting of payroll tax burdens than from backward shifting. The significance of the losses depends not only on the relative importance of the fixed-income group when the tax increases under consideration are made, but also on how quickly various components of that group escape from their fixed-income status. Long-term bonds do eventually mature and may be replaced with higher-yielding securities. Welfare and social security beneficiaries may sooner or later have their money payments raised in line with price-level increases. Given these uncertainties, Brittain's choice of a two-group, rather than a three-group, model is not unreasonable. Nevertheless, his conclusion that full forward tax shifting by employers is equivalent to full tax incidence on labor would have to be modified if future empirical research shows the fixed-income group to be of more than very short-run importance.

A second problem concerns the application in the present in-

---

tion effects resulting from the taxation of only one factor of production, or from the lower effective tax rates imposed on high-priced labor services than on low-priced services (because of the ceiling on taxable earnings).

[109] Both of these conceptual issues are discussed on pages 124–26.

[110] *The Payroll Tax for Social Security*, pp. 44–46, 49–59.

stance of the widely accepted proposition that "nothing can be said about the effect of a tax per se on the absolute price level."[111] To leave the matter there is not simply restrictive, as Brittain acknowledges, but also unnecessary. If it is reasonable to assume, as he does, that the use of higher payroll taxes to finance higher social insurance benefits will not change the level of aggregate private demand, surely it could also be concluded that payroll taxation will not impose general consumer burdens. Incidence on the uses side would then be confined to those specific product price increases and decreases that Brittain quite properly assigns to his second-order-of-importance category. Acceptance of this argument resolves the uncertain choice between forward and backward shifting in favor of the latter and offers the further advantage of validating all of Brittain's findings concerning the payroll tax even if the fixed-income group were shown to be important enough to be included in the incidence analysis.

Suppose, however, that the assumption of constant aggregate demand is questionable. Higher employer payroll taxes might induce widespread increases in administered product prices, and either consumers or the government might then provide the monetary expansion required to keep aggregate employment levels constant. In that situation the standard approach, which assumes constant aggregate demand, runs a real risk of confining the whole tax incidence question to a second order of importance. The alternative is to consider explicitly the probabilities that a balanced increase in payroll taxes and in benefit payments would induce a monetary expansion, and hence an increase in the general price level, that otherwise would not have occurred. If that probability were judged to be high, measures of payroll tax incidence could be defined, quite reasonably, to include the general price level increases so induced. Whether tax incidence analysis could be usefully extended in this manner remains to be determined. Tax variables are being incorporated in wage-price models, and Robert J. Gordon has been able to conclude from his studies that "the average annual rate of inflation was 0.45 percent faster in 1966–69 than it would have been if 1965 tax rates [for both federal personal and social security taxes] had remained in effect."[112]

[111] Ibid., pp. 54–55.
[112] "Wage-Price Controls and the Shifting Phillips Curve," in *Brookings Papers on Economic Activity* (2:1972), p. 416.

Another debatable aspect of Brittain's payroll tax incidence model is his assumption that tax-induced changes in labor supplies may be regarded as minor effects. This assumption enables the analysis to be extended from competitive to noncompetitive markets without changing the general conclusion that labor bears the full burden of the tax; it also avoids the complexities and ambiguities that result from tax-induced changes in the aggregate level of employment.[113] Nevertheless, its validity is questionable, particularly with regard to such labor force groups as married women, teenagers, and older men.

Feldstein has addressed this problem in a study that begins with a static, one-product, two-factor, competitive, general equilibrium model that explicitly allows for variable factor supplies and distinguishes between the effects of imposing a new payroll tax and raising the rates of an existing one.[114] A major finding is that the key determinants of final incidence patterns are not simply each factor's price elasticity of supply, but rather the ratios of these elasticities to the elasticity of substitution of the two factors in production. For both new and existing tax changes, labor's relative share of the payroll tax burden is shown to be a decreasing function of the ratio of its own supply elasticity to the elasticity of substitution and an increasing function of the comparable ratio for capital (both supply elasticities are assumed to be nonnegative). In a simplified numerical version of the model using a Cobb-Douglas production function, when capital is in completely inelastic supply, a supply elasticity of 0.33 for labor implies that labor bears 90 percent of the total tax burden, and a supply elasticity of 1.33 implies that it bears only 70 percent. On the other hand, supply elasticities of 1.33 for both factors imply a tax burden share for labor of 82 percent, and if labor is in completely inelastic supply it bears the full tax burden regardless of the supply elasticity of capital.

A variable, tax-sensitive labor supply, then, implies some ability of labor to shift part of its own share of the U.S. payroll tax to capital and to avoid bearing the full burden of the employer share of that tax. Whether these possibilities represent a major, or only a minor, qualification to Brittain's finding of full labor incidence re-

---

[113] *The Payroll Tax for Social Security*, pp. 36–44.
[114] "Tax Incidence in a Growing Economy."

mains to be seen. Perhaps more important, however, in view of the significance attached to it by many tax specialists, is the potential impact on payroll tax incidence of a variable capital supply. Investigation of these possibilities requires the use of growth models, one of the less developed areas of fiscal economics.

## Dynamic Models

The long-run, steady-state incidence of a payroll tax in a growing economy is investigated by Feldstein by converting his simple static model into dynamic terms. Though his analysis is very general, and must be interpreted in that light, his model does establish the surprising proposition that the long-run incidence of the payroll tax is independent of labor supply elasticities. It indicates also that the economy's rate of adjustment to its long-run, steady-state equilibrium may be so slow as to throw considerable doubt on the practical significance of dynamic incidence analysis. Feldstein's numerical application of the model, for example, shows that twenty years would be required for half of the adjustment to be completed from the initial pretax situation to the final equilibrium. It may be, then, that dynamic incidence models are of only limited policy interest and that future research can best concentrate on the nature and speed of the adjustment process by which the economy moves to a new dynamic steady-state equilibrium whenever a given tax change disturbs the old equilibrium.

## Empirical Studies

Broadly speaking, theoretical analysis of payroll tax incidence leads to firmer and less controversial conclusions than the analysis of either corporate or property tax incidence. Nevertheless, it is desirable to have systematic empirical verification, or rejection, of the major a priori hypotheses. A good beginning toward this goal is provided by two recent studies, each employing a different approach.

The first, by John Brittain, involving application of estimating equations derived from a constant elasticity of substitution production function to data for sixty-four countries in the 1957–59 period, led to the conclusion that labor is likely to bear the full burden of the payroll tax.[115] A similar application to U.S. time series data for

[115] *The Payroll Tax for Social Security*, Chap. 3.

1947–65, however, yielded far less definite results. The hypothesis of full shifting of the employer's share of the tax was, however, generally favored over the alternative hypothesis of no shifting. In this country the tax variable has apparently not fluctuated enough to provide a solid statistical basis for distinguishing between the two hypotheses.

This, too, was one of the findings of a study in which Wayne Vroman applied a money-wage estimating equation to time series data for the United States and fourteen other countries for 1954–69.[116] While the results lacked statistical precision, they did not provide strong support for the complete backward shifting hypothesis. At best those for the United States indicated partial backward shifting when the tax variable was lagged two quarters in the estimating equation. These findings do not necessarily contradict Brittain's hypothesis of full shifting of the employer payroll tax since the possibility of forward shifting was not investigated in Vroman's study.

## Conclusions

If the burdens of the employers' share of the payroll tax were not shifted, that part of the tax would be a progressive part of the U.S. tax system and would represent a significant addition to the burdens on capital income imposed by the corporate profits and general property taxes. Professional support for this point of view, however, is conspicuously absent. If the aggregate supply of labor is insensitive to wage rate changes, economists typically conclude that an employers' payroll tax will be completely shifted, and even for implausibly high labor supply elasticities the unshifted portion is unlikely to exceed 20–25 percent.

There is, however, considerable disagreement as to whether the burdens of the shifted portion of the tax fall mainly on workers or on consumers. Significant as this difference of opinion is for some of the policy issues pertaining to the financing of social insurance, for others it appears to make very little difference. The payroll tax, as currently constructed, is a regressive levy in either case, though it

[116] "Employer Payroll Taxes and Money Wages: Two Tests of Backward Shifting," in *Proceedings of the Sixty-Fourth Annual Conference on Taxation*, pp. 660–82.

would be slightly more so if it were shifted mainly to consumers.[117] Nor would Brittain's estimates of the prospective lifetime rates of return likely to be realized by contributors to social security be changed much if some portion of the cost were paid by consumers since covered workers themselves constitute a major portion of the nation's consumers.[118] On the other hand, the ability of the federal government to control inflation during a period of rising payroll tax rates would be greater in the case of backward shifting of those burdens than it would be in the case of forward shifting. Finally, whereas substantial forward shifting would imply corresponding impairment of the worldwide competitive position of countries relying heavily on employer payroll levies, substantial backward shifting would not.

## General Sales and Income Taxes

Prominent among the relative certainties of incidence theory are the propositions that the individual income tax is borne by the legal taxpayers and that the general sales tax is shifted to consumers. Helpful as these rare examples of expert agreement have been in many ways, they have had the unfortunate effect of diverting attention from other important aspects of these two taxes.

### General Consumer Burdens of Broad-Based Sales Taxes

The conventional view of general sales taxes is that they burden consumers by inducing sellers to raise prices by the amount of the sales tax collected by the government on each item sold. Economists, however, have long stressed the fact that this is only the beginning, rather than the end, of the adjustment process that determines the final incidence of the sales tax. More recently, theorists have

[117] The Musgraves' estimates indicate that the average rate of a payroll tax borne completely by labor would be 5.6 percent at the $4,000–$5,700 level of family income and 7.4 percent at the $12,500–$17,500 level, compared to rates of 6.8 percent and 7.1 percent at the same two income levels for a tax whose employee portion was borne by labor and whose employer portion was borne by consumers. See *Public Finance in Theory and Practice*, p. 370.

[118] Brittain's estimates of the average real rate of return, based on the assumptions that labor bears the full burden of the payroll tax and that future benefits will grow as fast as do real earnings, range from 2.8 percent to 6.3 percent; see *The Payroll Tax for Social Security*, Chap. 6.

stressed the proposition that tax incidence has to do only with *relative* price changes and that changes in *absolute* prices should be attributed to other government policies.[119] When one equal-yield tax is substituted for another, in other words, the private money supply, the level of aggregate private demand, and the general price level may all be assumed to remain constant, to a first approximation, for purposes of differential incidence analysis.

What then can be said about the consumer burdens of sales taxes? The essence of these burdens, as Musgrave in particular has emphasized,[120] is that on the uses-of-income side of the budget consumers must be judged worse off relative to savers when a sales tax is compared with an equal-yield income tax. Whereas under the sales tax the terms of trade between future and present consumption are simply a function of the rate of return, $r$, that can be earned on savings, the terms of trade under an income tax are a function of the net-of-tax rate of return, $r(1-t)$, where $t$ is the income tax rate. This is an unequivocal differential consumer burden of sales taxes; moreover it is independent of the extent to which the prices of taxed products rise in absolute terms. It does, however, depend on the assumption that the rate of return, $r$, is not affected by the substitution of the sales tax for an income tax. Since an important effect of that substitution is presumably to shift resources from consumption to investment,[121] the rate of return should be lower under the sales tax, and this will clearly affect the quantitative importance of its general consumer burdens. In addition, the shift of resources into private investment may affect particular factor rates of pay enough to make incidence on the sources side important, and the rise in capital formation will accelerate the economy's rate of economic growth and generate, sooner or later, all the tax effects discussed in dynamic incidence models. Very little attention has been given to any of these issues concerning the differential incidence of general sales taxes.[122]

[119] See especially McLure, "Tax Incidence, Macroeconomic Policy, and Absolute Prices."

[120] Musgrave, *The Theory of Public Finance*, pp. 379–82.

[121] This means that the incidence of sales taxation cannot be analyzed in the framework of the static Harberger model which assumes a constant capital stock but must be dealt with by means of dynamic incidence or growth models.

[122] For a concise qualitative discussion of all the complex and highly interrelated effects see John Bossons, "The Economic and Redistributive Effects of a Value-

## Excise Tax Effects of Broad-Based Sales Taxes

Though discussion of the incidence and effects of general sales taxes occupies an important part of public finance literature, there has never been, and probably never will be, such a tax. McLure has estimated that whereas even a sales tax with strictly limited exemptions would cover only 75 percent of personal consumption expenditures as defined for national income account purposes, a tax that allowed many of the exemptions with strong political appeal would cover barely 47 percent of total consumption expenditures.[123] It is clear that analyses of so-called general sales taxes are likely to be seriously incomplete unless they explicitly consider the nature of the changes in relative consumer prices brought about by those taxes and deal with the differential incidence, if any, of those changes on households at different income levels.[124] This, too, remains largely a research task for the future.

## Local Sales Taxes

A maverick in the general sales tax family is a tax that is levied in only one part of a metropolitan area or at different rates in different parts of the area. The incidence of such differential levies has its own special features, brought about by the high mobility within urban areas of both workers and consumers. The resulting tax burdens, therefore, are likely to settle mainly on local businessmen and landowners, and since the pattern of those burdens is unlikely to resemble what would be regarded as a rational structure of local profits and land taxation, the local sales tax must be regarded mainly as a tool for areawide local taxation.[125] This is not to say

Added Tax," *Proceedings of the Sixty-Fourth Annual Conference on Taxation*, pp. 255–60.

[123] Charles E. McLure, Jr., "Economic Effects of Taxing Value Added," in Richard A. Musgrave (ed.), *Broad-Based Taxes: New Options and Sources* (Johns Hopkins University Press, 1973), p. 165; he excluded from the limited-exemption tax base such items as housing rentals, domestic and private education services, the nonpriced services of banks and other financial institutions, foreign travel, food produced and consumed on farms. To derive the narrower tax base he further excluded medical services, the cost of home-prepared meals, household utility expenses, and legal and burial services.

[124] Since a general sales tax should make capital goods relatively cheaper, these excise tax effects would include relatively lower prices for consumer goods produced under relatively capital-intensive methods.

[125] For empirical analyses of these local sales tax effects see John L. Mikesell, "Central Cities and Sales Tax Rate Differentials: The Border City Problem,"

that intraurban sales tax rate differentials must be ruled completely out; but presumably beyond some point, not yet determined empirically, they would generate more adverse than helpful fiscal and economic effects.

### Income Taxation in a Wage-Push World

In the postwar period workers in many countries have become increasingly aware of the burdens of payroll and income taxes. Their heightened sensitivity has resulted on the one hand from the rapid growth of payroll taxes, and on the other from inflation, which has pushed taxpayers farther and farther up the graduated income tax rate scale.[126] A potential result of these changes in attitude is that unionized workers will choose to bargain with employers not just in terms of real wage rates but in terms of real wages *net of income and payroll taxes*.[127] Such a development, if it became widespread, would have serious economic implications. Increases in income and payroll tax rates might themselves cause inflation,[128] and the income position of nonunionized labor might be worsened still further in comparison with unionized workers.[129] Long-accepted views concerning the incidence of income taxes and the employee share of payroll levies would clearly have to be changed as well.

---

*National Tax Journal*, Vol. 23 (June 1970), pp. 206–13; and Henry M. Levin, "An Analysis of the Economic Effects of the New York City Sales Tax," in *Financing Government in New York City*, Final Research Report to the Temporary Commission on City Finances, City of New York (New York University, Graduate School of Public Administration, 1966) (Brookings Reprint 127).

[126] An interesting empirical study of this phenomenon is Charles J. Goetz and Warren E. Weber, "Intertemporal Changes in Real Federal Income Tax Rates, 1954–70," *National Tax Journal*, Vol. 24 (March 1971), pp. 51–63.

[127] That this has already happened in other countries is indicated by such studies as Assar Lindbeck, "Theories and Problems in Swedish Economic Policy in the Post-War Period," *American Economic Review*, Vol. 58, Pt. 2 (*Supplement*) (June 1968), pp. 1–87; and Dudley Jackson, H. A. Turner, and Frank Wilkinson, *Do Trade Unions Cause Inflation?* (London: Cambridge University Press, 1972).

[128] For a theoretical analysis see Thomas F. Dernburg, "Direct Taxation, Wage Retaliation, and the Control of Inflation" (International Monetary Fund, Nov. 19, 1973; processed). For empirical analyses see particularly Robert J. Gordon, "Inflation in Recession and Recovery," *Brookings Papers on Economic Activity* (1:1971), pp. 105–58, and "Wage-Price Controls and the Shifting Phillips Curve," ibid. (2:1972), pp. 385–421.

[129] See Harry G. Johnson and Peter Mieszkowski, "The Effects of Unionization on the Distribution of Income: A General Equilibrium Approach," *Quarterly Journal of Economics*, Vol. 84 (November 1970), pp. 539–61.

*Income Tax Shifting in Noncompetitive Markets*

Though the wage-push exception to the general conclusion that individual income taxes are not shifted has arisen only quite recently, the possibility of forward shifting of some income tax burdens by business executives, doctors, lawyers, and others who operate in oligopolistic markets has been recognized for some time. The possible interaction of such forward shifting with the work-leisure effects of taxation should not be neglected. If doctors, for example, are able to raise their fees in response to income tax increases, they should not also be subject to work disincentives because of the tax rise; on the other hand, if they reduce their services instead of raising their fees, and if they do this to a greater extent than do other workers, a relative increase in the price of medical services should still occur. In any case, since workers presumably are unable to shift the full amount of their income tax burdens to others, analyses of the effects of income taxation on work incentives usually employ a no-shifting assumption.

# TAXATION AND ECONOMIC CHOICE

TURNING FROM considerations of interpersonal equity and tax shifting and incidence to questions of economic efficiency means moving into an area in which empirical research has been more plentiful but disagreements among the experts no less prevalent or sharp. The problem of economic efficiency involves a vast array of individual choices—between work and leisure, consumption and saving, one kind of consumption goods or financial assets and another. It also includes the baffling maze of business decisions—whether to invest in new plant and equipment, to pay out dividends, to finance expansion by the issue of new debt or equity capital, to allocate resources to this or that activity. Complex as these problems are, however, analysis within this area is greatly aided by some well-established and sophisticated products of economic theory. The many uncertainties about the effects of taxation on economic choice arise mainly over the magnitudes of the agreed-upon determinants of those effects.

The traditional approach to economically efficient tax policy takes for granted the efficient operation of unregulated economic markets on a broad scale. As the President's Council of Economic Advisers put it in 1971: "Competition in the free market will normally lead to the optimal use of . . . resources."[130] Given this belief, the basic canon of efficient taxation is neutrality. If tax-free markets are normally optimal, in other words, taxes should be set so as not to interfere with the operation of those markets.

The opposing view is much less optimistic about the efficiency of untrammeled markets. Seeing pervasive imperfections and externalities, its adherents seek tax policies geared deliberately to mitigate imperfections and encourage desirable nonmarket effects. While it is undoubtedly true that general-revenue taxation generates beneficial as well as adverse allocational effects, the policy importance of these helpful side effects remains to be demonstrated. The more successfully externalities can be handled by nontax fiscal instruments or by special earmarked taxes, in other words, the more realistically can general-revenue tax instruments be judged by the classical test of neutrality. For the present the issue must be regarded as unresolved.

## The Work-Leisure Choice

The modern theory of the work-leisure choice is based on the opposing substitution and income effects of a given wage rate or tax rate change. When the wage rate is reduced (tax rate increased), the reward for an additional unit of labor and the price of an additional unit of leisure are both lowered, and on this account the worker will tend to substitute leisure for work. At the same time, a lower wage rate (higher tax rate) means a lower income from a given amount of labor, and with lower incomes people normally will wish to have fewer units of leisure. A wage rate decrease (tax rate increase) therefore normally induces a substitution effect unfavorable to work effort and an income effect favorable to it, the net outcome depending on the relative strengths of the two effects.[131] For

[130] *Economic Report of the President, Together with the Annual Report of the Council of Economic Advisers, February 1971*, p. 107.

[131] By opening directly with the substitution and income effects, the discussion leaps over the well-established theory of a utility-maximizing worker subject to a

many tax policies it would be sufficient to estimate directly the net result of the two opposing effects; for others separate empirical estimation is required. A negative income tax, for example, would raise both the level of income and the marginal tax rate for many low-income families, thus generating income and substitution effects in the same direction, and full assessment of their importance would require separate quantitative determination of each of them. The whole broad question of economic efficiency, being a function of relative prices, also depends crucially on the substitution effects of taxation.

The basic economic theory of worker behavior usually assumes that each person is always "on" his own individual supply curve of labor, having been able to adjust his hours of work precisely to maximize his utility at the real wage rate offered him. In reality, numerous institutional restrictions preclude such fine adjustments. When the 1966 Survey of Consumer Finances interviewers "asked people whether they would like to work more hours a week, more than a third said yes, and among the uneducated and unskilled, more than half said that they would like more work."[132] As long as such aspirations for additional income prevail, the income effect of larger subsidies to the poor which, if operative, would make for less work effort on their part, can safely be assumed to be zero.

The interrelationships among work-leisure choices in the family are equally complex. A wife's decision to enter the labor force and the number of hours of work per week she prefers tend to be a function both of her husband's wage rate and of his desire for leisure; his labor force choices in turn are related to his wife's earning power and career aspirations. Full estimation of the effects of taxation on family labor supplies must take these cross effects into account, as well as those relevant to the behavior of teen-age children.

---

budget constraint; see, for example, Gershon Cooper, "Taxation and Incentive in Mobilization," *Quarterly Journal of Economics*, Vol. 66 (February 1952), pp. 43–66; reprinted in *Readings in the Economics of Taxation*, pp. 470–92. See also Gary S. Becker, "A Theory of the Allocation of Time," *Economic Journal*, Vol. 75 (September 1965), pp. 493–517; and John D. Owen, *The Price of Leisure* (Universitaire Pers Rotterdam, 1969, and Montreal: McGill-Queen's University Press, 1970).

[132] James N. Morgan, "The Supply of Effort, the Measurement of Well-Being, and the Dynamics of Improvement," in American Economic Association, *Papers and Proceedings of the Eightieth Annual Meeting, 1967* (*American Economic Review*, Vol. 58, May 1968), p. 31.

*Empirical Studies: Survey Research*

Sample surveys of the effects of taxation on work effort seek, by means of personal interviews, to identify the working behavior and motivations of selected groups of people. While they have a unique contribution to make to empirical analysis, they provide only partial answers to the basic problem.

The special significance and subtleties of the evidence uncovered by survey research are illustrated by four completed studies and two currently under way. In 1964 in a large interview survey financed by the National Science Foundation and the National Committee on Government Finance of the Brookings Institution, the working and investment habits of a nationwide probability sample of 957 individuals with annual incomes of $10,000 or more were studied.[133] This study is unique in its breadth and hence in the general significance of its findings.

As a part of a series of studies for the National Bureau of Economic Research dealing with the effects of taxation on economic growth, Daniel M. Holland in 1965–66 conducted intensive interviews with 122 U.S. business executives that probed more deeply into working behavior and motivations than any other sample survey.[134] His tape recordings of the interviews provided not only a more reliable basis for his own interpretations of the evidence but also an unprecedented opportunity for other researchers to compare their own assessments of the significance of the different tax effects with his.

In an unusual follow-up of an empirical study, Donald B. Fields in 1969 interviewed 285 English solicitors and accountants, using a random sample design and questionnaire form similiar to those employed by George F. Break in his 1956 study of 306 individuals chosen from those two groups of self-employed professionals.[135] The

[133] Robin Barlow, Harvey E. Brazer, and James N. Morgan, *Economic Behavior of the Affluent* (Brookings Institution, 1966).

[134] Daniel M. Holland, "The Effect of Taxation on Effort: Some Results for Business Executives," National Tax Association, *Proceedings of the Sixty-Second Annual Conference on Taxation* (1970), pp. 428–517.

[135] George F. Break, "Income Taxes and Incentives to Work: An Empirical Study," *American Economic Review*, Vol. 47 (September 1957), pp. 529–49; Donald B. Fields and W. T. Stanbury, "Incentives, Disincentives and the Income Tax: Further Empirical Evidence," *Public Finance*, Vol. 25 (1970), pp. 381–415, and "Income Taxes and Incentives to Work: Some Additional Empirical Evidence," *American Economic Review*, Vol. 61 (June 1971), pp. 435–43.

Fields-Stanbury study provides a number of significant thirteen-year comparisons with the Break study as well as new evidence concerning the effects of high taxation on professional behavior.

A controlled experiment, financed by the Office of Economic Opportunity (OEO), designed to identify the economic factors affecting human behavior and to explore means of eradicating poverty from American society has been under way since 1968. The first data, on selected urban areas in New Jersey and Pennsylvania and two rural areas in Iowa and North Carolina, have already yielded some evidence on the work incentives of the poor.[136]

In 1973 over 2,000 weekly paid workers in Great Britain were asked, in interviews averaging one and a quarter hours, about their work attitudes and behavior, then about their income, spending, and leisure activities, and finally about their attitudes toward taxation. Both a complex evaluation of the answers for internal consistency and detailed comparisons of attitudes and reported behavior with independent evidence about actual behavior are under way.[137] This study may provide a good test for the skepticism of those who have long doubted the usefulness of any data that rely on people's identification of their own motivations.

These empirical studies are interesting primarily for their estimates of the overall incidence and significance of tax incentives and disincentives. In the 1964 study of high-income individuals, 12 percent reported they worked less hard because of taxes, but half of the replies were judged to be suspect because the respondents either had no opportunities to work more or were already working sixty or more hours a week.[138] The 1956 and 1969 studies of English solicitors and accountants reported that 13 percent and 19 percent,

---

[136] Harold W. Watts, "Graduated Work Incentives: An Experiment in Negative Taxation," American Economic Association, *Papers and Proceedings of the Eighty-first Annual Meeting, 1968* (*American Economic Review*, Vol. 59, May 1969), pp. 463–72, and "The Graduated Work Incentive Experiments: Current Progress," *Papers and Proceedings of the Eighty-third Annual Meeting, 1970* (*American Economic Review*, Vol. 61, May 1971), pp. 15–21. See also Mordecai Kurz and Robert G. Spiegelman, "The Seattle Experiment: The Combined Effect of Income Maintenance and Manpower Investments," and Terence F. Kelly and Leslie Singer, "The Gary Income Maintenance Experiment: Plans and Progress," ibid., pp. 22–29, 30–38.

[137] C. V. Brown and E. Levin, "First Report on a National Survey of the Alleged Disincentive Effects of Personal Income Taxation" (University of Stirling, July 1973; processed).

[138] Barlow, Brazer, and Morgan, *Economic Behavior of the Affluent*, p. 141.

respectively, felt a "definite tax disincentive" to work.[139] The difference between the ratios in these comparable studies was found to be statistically significant at the 3 percent level. The increase in tax disincentives during that thirteen-year period in England might be attributed to either the long-continued high levels of income taxation or declines in the nonmonetary satisfactions received from work (as Fields found), or both. These two surveys, like the Barlow-Brazer-Morgan study, found an inverse relationship between work effort and the level of marginal income tax rates, and both noted the appearance of statistically significant disincentive-over-incentive differentials among respondents subject to the highest tax rates.[140]

For the connoisseur of subtle and complex work effects, Holland's 1965–66 study of U.S. business executives is the most interesting.[141] It employed an innovative line of questioning aimed at achieving greater economic realism at the risk of some loss of respondent credibility. Executives were asked about the hypothetical impact on their work habits of replacing the federal individual income tax with an equal-yield levy on each person's potential earnings at average levels of work effort. Such a tax would, of course, impose a zero marginal tax rate on everyone, and any executive who assumed that under the new tax he would have the same total liability as now but no tax on additional earnings would be reporting a pure substitution effect in its most dramatic terms. As it turned out, however, many of the respondents, believing that they were currently working much harder than the average, automatically

---

[139] Break, "Income Taxes and Incentives to Work," p. 541, and Fields and Stanbury, "Income Taxes and Incentives to Work: Some Additional Empirical Evidence," p. 437. The Break study makes a distinction between *questionable* and *definite* tax disincentives. The first category includes all respondents for whom taxation was one of many relatively unimportant influences and also those who indicated that it could under hypothetical future circumstances affect their propensities to work. Respondents classified as subject to *definite* disincentives ranged from those who had frequently turned down work because of high taxes to those for whom taxes were only one of several important factors that had once or twice prompted them to refuse work.

[140] Similar evidence is provided by a 1968 survey of 369 professional and nonprofessional hourly-rated workers in the Kitchener-Waterloo metropolitan area in Canada; A. Chatterjee and J. Robinson, "Effects of Personal Income Tax on Work Effort: A Sample Survey," *Canadian Tax Journal*, Vol. 17 (May/June 1969), pp. 211–20.

[141] See the similar study by Thomas H. Sanders, *Effects of Taxation: On Executives* (Harvard University, Graduate School of Business Administration, 1951).

assumed that their own tax liabilities would be *lower* under the new levy. Any alteration in work habits reported by them would consequently be a result of the conventional income and substitution effects, operating in opposing directions. While 15 percent of the respondents reported definite tax disincentives in terms of their primary jobs,[142] 26 percent reported disincentives in terms of consulting and outside business ventures. The difference in sensitivity to taxation in the two areas is not surprising, but Holland's detailed analysis indicated that the disincentive effect on outside work was "vague, ambiguous and equivocal and not likely to release floodgates of energy."[143]

While survey research is ideally suited to the qualitative analysis of complex human motivations and is quite capable of providing reliable quantitative confirmation of the unimportance of tax-induced work incentives and disincentives for particular groups of people, its usefulness becomes more questionable as the percentage of people reporting tax effects increases. Partly this results from the difficulty of obtaining reliable information about actual hours worked, and partly it is because the behavior of different workers at one point in time need not be the same as their behavior over time. Problems of the first kind are minimized in the Brown-Levin study of British weekly paid workers by the use of independent sources of data; problems of the second kind are avoided in the OEO graduated work experiments by focusing directly on behavioral responses to changing economic conditions.

Neither study has yet uncovered any evidence of serious work disincentives. Indeed, the Brown-Levin survey found that those reporting some kind of tax effect, both men and women, were in fact working longer hours on the average than were those judged to be unaffected by taxation.[144] Analysis of nearly 700 husband-and-wife

---

[142] As a measure of the substitution effect alone this estimate has an unknown amount of downward bias, but as a measure of the net impact of taxation on work effort its bias is in the opposite direction.

[143] "The Effect of Taxation on Effort," p. 464.

[144] Brown and Levin, "First Report." Among men, incentive reactions were twice as frequent as disincentive ones (14 percent and 7 percent of respondents, respectively), and this whole group was found to be working an average of four hours a week more than the remainder of the sample. Women, on the other hand, reacted less frequently to taxation and in the opposite direction (1 percent reporting incentive effects and 3 percent disincentive ones). Nonetheless, this small tax-sensitive group

families that remained in the New Jersey-Pennsylvania OEO sample
for the duration of the three-year experiment shows some statistically
significant, but small, decreases in work effort by white and Spanish-
speaking husbands and large relative reductions in labor force participation rates by white wives, but not by black or Spanish-speaking
ones.[145] While much more analysis of graduated work incentive experimental data remains to be done and generalization of the findings
to a national negative income tax program is risky in any case, it can
be said that one important source of working behavior information
places a low probability on any mass withdrawal of labor services in
response to unrestricted income subsidies for the working poor. The
burden of proof has thus been shifted to those who would argue otherwise.

*Empirical Studies: Econometric Analyses*

Quantitative estimation of the shape of the supply curve of labor
has long been a major interest of empirically minded economists.

---

worked an average of over five hours a week longer than all other women in the
sample. This was because those reporting tax disincentives still worked slightly more
than those not affected by taxation, while those reporting an incentive effect worked
an average of thirteen hours a week more. Similar behavior on the part of disincentive-prone respondents was observed in the Break and Fields-Stanbury studies.
   [145] Institute for Research on Poverty, "Final Report of the Graduated Work
Incentive Experiment in New Jersey and Pennsylvania" (University of Wisconsin,
December 1973; processed); and U.S. Department of Health, Education, and Welfare, "Summary Report: New Jersey Graduated Work Incentive Experiment" (HEW,
Office of Assistant Secretary for Planning and Evaluation, December 1973; processed). For a summary of these results see Harold W. Watts and Glen G. Cain,
"Basic Labor Supply Response Findings from the Urban Experiment (New Jersey–
Pennsylvania)" (paper delivered at the 1973 annual meeting of the American Economic Association; processed). The results are also discussed in several papers
in *Journal of Human Resources*, Vol. 9 (Spring 1974). Labor supply responses
varied in a complex fashion among the different subsidy plans offered and with such
family characteristics as health, size, potential earning power, and earnings variability. The estimated working hour reduction in response to a plan providing a basic
benefit equal to a poverty line family income and a 50 percent implicit tax rate, for
example, was 7 percent on the average for white, and 9 percent for Spanish-speaking,
husbands; HEW, "Summary Report," pp. 29–30. Under the same subsidy plan white
wives were estimated to reduce their labor force participation rate by 8 percentage
points on the average, or by 50 percent of their presubsidy rate; ibid., p. 34. As an
indicator of labor force behavior under a full-scale negative income tax program,
this estimate has an unknown amount of upward bias. Truncation of the OEO
sample by family income resulted in an underrepresentation of wives with steady,
full-time jobs, and there is an a priori presumption that secondary family workers
would react more strongly to a temporary subsidy plan than to a permanent one.

Since the pioneering study of Paul H. Douglas published in 1934, numerous estimates have been made of the relation between wage rates and both labor force participation and hours of work.[146] Until quite recently, however, all of these studies were plagued in varying degrees by the well-known problems of precomputer econometric analyses: their forced reliance on data for broad population groups precluded measurement of some of the most interesting potential variations in work effort, such as those related to age, or race, or family composition and size; their neglect of labor demand relations raised serious questions about the accuracy of their estimates of labor supply parameters; and perhaps most serious of all, the available data frequently failed to satisfy theoretical economic specifications, or if they did, were subject to large errors of measurement. Wage rates were usually averages for broad geographical areas or population groups rather than specific values for individual families and were typically measured in money terms rather than being adjusted for both price and tax differentials. Moreover, official estimates of labor force participation rates failed to distinguish between the firmly committed worker and the casual seeker of additional income, and census data for hours worked were normally based on experience during a single week which may not have been typical of the entire year.

Though aggregation, simultaneous-equation, specification, and errors-in-variables biases are all extremely difficult to eradicate, progress has been made, and in the process, additional aspects of the work-leisure choice have been revealed. Using disaggregated data from the one-in-a-thousand sample of the 1960 census, Kosters focused on families likely to be especially sensitive to tax-induced work incentives and disincentives—those headed by males aged fifty through sixty-four—and, in an effort to supply information requisite to the evaluation of many tax-policy problems, derived separate estimates of the substitution and income effects of tax rate changes.[147] These important steps forward were not sufficient, however, to pro-

[146] *The Theory of Wages* (Macmillan). This and other studies are summarized in George F. Break, "Income Taxes, Wage Rates, and the Incentive to Supply Labor Services," *National Tax Journal*, Vol. 6 (December 1953), pp. 350–51. Subsequent studies are summarized in Glen G. Cain and Harold W. Watts (eds.), *Income Maintenance and Labor Supply: Econometric Studies* (Rand McNally for Markham, 1973), pp. 6–13.

[147] Marvin Kosters, "Effects of an Income Tax on Labor Supply," in Harberger and Bailey, *Taxation of Income from Capital*, pp. 301–24.

duce a completely plausible set of empirical estimates. The substitution effect, in particular, turned out to have the wrong sign more frequently than not, suggesting either that a true supply curve of labor was not obtained, or that the combination of a zero substitution effect and a negative income effect produced a backward-bending curve.[148]

Recent quantitative analyses of work incentives have concentrated on the potential effects of a negative income tax (NIT) on work effort. Though all agree that such a tax would probably produce some reduction in the supply of labor by its low-income beneficiaries, the range of their quantitative estimates is too large to be useful to the policy maker.[149] Nor do those who foresee significant reactions agree that their source would be the substitution effect alone, the income effect alone, or both. A study by Kalachek and Raines for the President's Commission on Income Maintenance Programs[150] produced some of the highest estimates of both effects. Based on a carefully designed theoretical model that paid particular attention to the interrelatedness of household work-leisure decision making, and using data from a very large sample of low- and medium-income families drawn in 1966,[151] the analysis fitted separate regressions for men and women and tested the significance of a large number of independent variables, including age, race, and various measures of transitory income. Particularly high income and substitution effects were found for the labor force participation decision, but hours worked were also

---

[148] Further empirical evidence supporting the backward-bending supply curve of labor is found in John D. Owen's time series study (covering 1900–61) of the behavior of nonstudent male employees in the private, nonagricultural sector of the U.S. economy; "The Demand for Leisure," *Journal of Political Economy*, Vol. 79 (January/February 1971), pp. 56–76.

[149] Cain and Watts, *Income Maintenance and Labor Supply*, pp. 339–40. The range in question is from almost no reduction in supply to one of 46 percent.

[150] Edward D. Kalachek and Fredric Q. Raines, "Labor Supply of Lower Income Workers," in President's Commission on Income Maintenance Programs, *Technical Studies* (1970), pp. 159–81.

[151] The sample, consisting of some 19,000 families and 3,800 unrelated individuals, was chosen from a larger group of people interviewed in the February and March 1966 Current Population Surveys of the U.S. Bureau of the Census; the sample excludes those whose total income exceeded twice the Social Security Administration's low-cost budget income level ($3,800 for single individuals and $8,200 for a family of four). Though focused on the group of policy interest, such truncated samples involve special econometric problems. See Cain and Watts, *Income Maintenance and Labor Supply*, pp. 340–48.

found sufficiently sensitive to changes in rates of pay to suggest the likelihood of serious NIT work disincentives in that respect too.

A rather different picture of labor supply functions is given in an analysis by Boskin of a subsample of the 1967 Survey of Economic Opportunity.[152] He estimated separate labor supply functions for individuals classified by sex, by race (white and black only), by age (teenage, prime-age, and elderly), and by family status (single, married, head of household, and dependent relatives). His equations, estimated separately for labor force participation and hours worked per year and for two different income models, provide a wealth of empirical information about working behavior derived by modern econometric techniques. Among the most important findings were small positive substitution effects for prime-age and elderly husbands of both races and for white prime-age wives, no influence of income changes on decisions to participate in the labor force, but some strong negative income effects on hours worked. Applied to different NIT plans, these coefficients produced disturbingly large work disincentive reactions.[153]

Thus far, cross-section econometric analyses of the labor supply have failed to produce consistent estimates of the relative importance either of the income and substitution effects of taxation, or of the participation and hours-worked behavioral decisions, or of

[152] Michael J. Boskin, "The Effects of Taxes on the Supply of Labor: With Special Reference to Income Maintenance Programs," in *Proceedings of the Sixty-Fourth Annual Conference on Taxation*, pp. 684–98; and Boskin, "The Economics of Labor Supply," in Cain and Watts, *Income Maintenance and Labor Supply*, pp. 163–81. The Survey of Economic Opportunity was an augmented version of the U.S. Census Bureau's Current Population Survey designed to obtain economic data for poor and nonwhite families by oversampling nonwhite areas of the country. Nearly 26,500 families were interviewed, and slightly over 10,500 of them were in the special nonwhite segment of the sample. The Survey of Economic Opportunity contains unusually varied and detailed measures of labor force and economic behavior. See David H. Greenberg, "Problems of Model Specification and Measurement: The Labor Supply Function" (RAND Corporation, December 1972; processed), pp. 63–68.

[153] In one case the predicted labor supply reduction was 14 percent for black prime-age husbands and 46 percent for white prime-age husbands, two of the largest groups in the total labor force. Boskin, "Effects of Taxes on the Supply of Labor," p. 692. Discussing these results in *Proceedings of the Sixty-Fourth Annual Conference on Taxation*, p. 734, Elizabeth L. David noted the sharp contrast with the very similar black and white family labor supply reactions found by Sandra S. Christensen in "Income Maintenance and the Labor Supply" (Ph.D. thesis, University of Wisconsin, 1972).

the total labor supply reactions of different demographic and social groups.[154] In addition, there is the basic, unproved assumption that observed interpersonal differences in behavior at a given time can be used successfully to predict the reactions of the same groups over time. Only longitudinal studies, such as the OEO work incentive experiments or econometric analyses of survey data from panels of respondents,[155] can hope to resolve these uncertainties.

### Work Effort: Composition Effects

At least in a qualitative sense, the effects of taxation on the composition of work effort are well established. In 1949 Richard Goode published the basic analytics of the problem,[156] and subsequent empirical studies have added only a few quantitative refinements to his general picture. While it does appear that career choices are only marginally affected by expected lifetime after-tax earnings differentials,[157] differences in the tax treatment of different kinds of income may lead to occupational shifts among adult workers. In Holland's study of business executives' behavior, five

[154] Much of the observed variety in parameter estimates results from different model specifications and other methodological choices; see Cain and Watts, *Income Maintenance and Labor Supply*, pp. 12 and 361–62; and Irwin Garfinkel, "On Estimating the Labor-Supply Effects of a Negative Income Tax," in ibid., pp. 205–64. A major aim of future research will be a substantial narrowing of the range of useful parameter estimates; compare Cain and Watts, pp. 362–67, and Greenberg, "Problems of Model Specification," p. 69.

[155] A pioneering example is Belton M. Fleisher, Donald O. Parsons, and Richard D. Porter, "Asset Adjustments and Labor Supply of Older Workers," in Cain and Watts, *Income Maintenance and Labor Supply*, pp. 279–327. Their data come from a 1966–71 study, directed by Herbert S. Parnes of Ohio State University's Center for Human Resource Research, of the labor-market behavior of men aged 45 to 59 years.

[156] "The Income Tax and the Supply of Labor," *Journal of Political Economy*, Vol. 57 (October 1949), pp. 428–37, reprinted in *Readings in the Economics of Taxation*, pp. 456–69.

[157] A study of medical school graduates found no impact of income differentials on the choice between general practice and specialty practice, and though earnings differentials did appear to affect the choice among different specialties, the estimated impact of those differentials was small; see Frank A. Sloan, "Lifetime Earnings and Physicians' Choice of Specialty," *Industrial and Labor Relations Review*, Vol. 24 (October 1970), pp. 47–56. Among a small group of Stanford University undergraduates little evidence was found of any impact of expected income tax differentials on career choice; Herbert G. Grubel and David R. Edwards, "Personal Income Taxation and Choice of Professions," *Quarterly Journal of Economics*, Vol. 78 (February 1964), pp. 158–63.

engineers and scientists had been induced, at least in part, by the relatively favorable treatment of capital gains under the federal income tax to shift from university and consulting work to the management of their own companies. This tax effect, while by no means unexpected, is of special interest for its potential impact on economic growth. The consensus of these five executives was that the result of such work shifts is "an acceleration in the pace of the community's technology. More new ideas, techniques and products are generated and brought to fruition than would otherwise be the case."[158] If this is true, economic change, for better or for worse, is now being encouraged by the tax system and would be affected by the enactment of any of the major reforms proposed for the tax treatment of capital gains and losses.[159]

## The Consumption-Saving Choice

Important as the effects of taxation are on a family's work-leisure choices, their impact on the allocation of a household's income is no less significant. How much is budgeted for consumption, how much for saving, and specifically what kinds of consumption expenditures are made and what kinds of financial assets are chosen for investment portfolios—all these decisions are the product to some degree of government tax policy.

### Aggregate Consumption and Saving Effects

The substitution of one tax for another with equal yield can affect the level of consumption expenditures in two different ways. By changing the terms of trade between present and future consumption, or between present consumption and indefinite accumulation, the tax change may either stimulate or discourage current expenditures on consumer goods and services. Empirical estimates of this pure substitution effect are sufficiently rare, and those that exist sufficiently

---

[158] "The Effect of Taxation on Effort," p. 490.

[159] For a brief discussion of the issues see Joseph A. Pechman, *Federal Tax Policy* (rev. ed., Brookings Institution, 1971), pp. 96–99. A detailed analysis is given in Richard Goode, *The Individual Income Tax* (Brookings Institution, 1964), pp. 184–221, and in Martin David, *Alternative Approaches to Capital Gains Taxation* (Brookings Institution, 1968).

small, to justify its classification, for most purposes, in the second-order-of-importance category.[160] Whether the same can be said about income effects is less certain. These would arise whenever marginal propensities to consume are not the same at all levels of family income and would mean that any tax-induced vertical redistribution of income would change consumption expenditures accordingly.

Exactly how much the marginal propensity to consume varies from one level of family income to another, if indeed it varies at all, has long been a matter of dispute among economists. Basically it is an empirical question, and the main sources of information give conflicting answers: cross-section data on household income and consumption patterns strongly suggest a declining marginal propensity as income rises; time series data on aggregate income and consumption suggest a constant marginal propensity. A recent econometric study reconciles this apparent inconsistency and in the process derives estimates of both short-run and long-run marginal propensities to consume.[161] Table 4 illustrates the use of these data to estimate the impact on aggregate consumption of substituting a progressive income tax for an equal-yield proportional one. Whereas families with incomes under $2,000 a year, for example, would have their disposable incomes increased by 1.4 percent of the government revenue involved in the tax shift, families with incomes of $10,000 and over would have their incomes reduced by 24.3 percent. The long-run effects on each group's consumption expenditures (the change in disposable income multiplied by their marginal propensity to consume) are shown in the last column of the table. Compared to an equal-yield proportional income tax, the progressive-rate federal individual income tax in 1960 stimulated long-run consumption expenditures by 5.14 percent of the revenue raised in that year ($42 billion).

It is tempting to conclude from this that the long-run reduction in aggregate saving would also be 5.14 percent of the tax revenue. The impact on saving, however, cannot be determined separately from the impact on investment, since the two are always equal ex

---

[160] See Wright, "Some Evidence on the Interest Elasticity of Consumption," and "Saving and the Rate of Interest."

[161] Ralph D. Husby, "A Nonlinear Consumption Function Estimated from Time-Series and Cross-Section Data," *Review of Economics and Statistics*, Vol. 53 (February 1971), pp. 76–79.

**TABLE 4. Differential Effect of Proportional and Progressive Income Taxes on Aggregate Consumption**

| Family income | Distribution of proportional income tax burdens (percent of total)[a] | Distribution of equal-yield progressive income tax burdens (percent of total)[a] | Excess of proportional over progressive tax shares | Long-run marginal propensity to consume[b] | Percent change in consumption due to substitution of progressive for proportional tax |
|---|---|---|---|---|---|
| Under $2,000 | 2 | 0.6 | +1.4 | 0.83 | +1.16 |
| $2,000–3,000 | 4 | 1.7 | +2.3 | 0.81 | +1.86 |
| 3,000–4,000 | 5 | 3.1 | +1.9 | 0.79 | +1.50 |
| 4,000–5,000 | 8 | 4.7 | +3.3 | 0.77 | +2.54 |
| 5,000–7,500 | 28 | 17.4 | +10.6 | 0.74 | +7.84 |
| 7,500–10,000 | 20 | 15.2 | +4.8 | 0.70 | +3.36 |
| 10,000 and over | 33 | 57.3 | −24.3 | 0.54 | −13.12 |
| Total | 100 | 100.0 | 0.0 | — | +5.14 |

a Distributive-share estimates for 1960 from Gillespie, "Effect of Public Expenditures on the Distribution of Income," pp. 133, 162. The equal-yield progressive tax used here is the federal individual income tax.
b Estimates derived from cross-section data for 1960–71 by Ralph D. Husby, "A Nonlinear Consumpton Function Estimated from Time-Series and Cross-Section Data," *Review of Economics and Statistics*, Vol. 53 (February 1971), p. 78. Estimate for families with incomes of $10,000 and over is the mean of Husby's estimates for families with $10,000–$15,000 (0.64) and for families with $15,000 and over (0.45).

post; and the knowledge that a $10 billion shift from proportional to progressive income taxation would increase consumption by $514 million does not help much in predicting the ultimate impact on investment. Many other factors affect the level of investment, and only joint analysis of the operation of all will determine the change in investment, to which the ex post change in saving must be equal. In the derivation of these final estimates, however, a useful first approximation may involve the assumption that the level of aggregate personal income remains constant. In this case a tax-induced increase of $514 million in consumption does imply a reduction in saving of the same amount, and this estimate can serve as a useful input for analyses of that part of the total impact of the tax change on investment that operates through financial market variables.

Table 5 gives a basic set of such first-approximation estimates of the differential impact of taxation on aggregate personal saving, all using a proportional income levy as the tax of reference. Compared to such a tax, an equal-yield flat-rate tax on total consumption expenditures, for example, would raise saving by 2.1 percent of the tax yield in the short run and by 5.4 percent in the long run. A proportional tax on dividends, on the other hand, would reduce saving by 8–12 percent of the tax yield in the long run. Goode's 1950 estimate of the differential impact on saving of the federal individual income tax was 5 percent, virtually identical to the long-run estimate in Table 5, but his estimate for a flat-rate consumption tax was only 1 percent.[162] While Musgrave's estimates for 1957 (using the distribution of savings for 1950) of the absolute impact of the tax structure on saving are not directly comparable with those in Table 5, they can be used to show the impact on saving of substituting an equal-yield federal individual income tax for a general sales tax. Musgrave estimates the substitution would reduce saving by 13 percent.[163] Goode's estimated reduction in saving is 6 percent, whereas the method used in Table 5 produces an estimated 10.5 percent reduction.

The two major taxes not shown directly in Table 5 are the corporate profits and general property taxes. The great uncertainty about the incidence of their burdens makes the effects of these taxes extremely hard to estimate. If their burdens are shifted forward to consumers in general, their long-run impact on saving (as compared with the comprehensive proportional income tax used in Table 5) could be an increase amounting to as much as 5 percent of the tax yield. If the burdens are borne by recipients of capital income, on the other hand, they could produce a savings decrease of equal size. An even larger long-run decrease, between 8 percent and 12 percent, would be generated by whatever reduction in dividends was brought about by the corporate profits tax.

An unshifted corporate tax would also reduce corporate retained profits;[164] while this has a direct effect on corporate saving,

---

[162] *The Individual Income Tax*, p. 67.

[163] Richard A. Musgrave, "Effects of Tax Policy on Private Capital Formation," in *Fiscal and Debt Management Policies*, A Series of Research Studies Prepared for the Commission on Money and Credit (Prentice-Hall, 1963), pp. 58–67. Also see Goode, *The Individual Income Tax*, pp. 332–40.

[164] The short-run impact of an unshifted corporate income tax will be mainly on retained profits rather than on dividends, but as payments of the latter adjust downward to the firm's target payout ratio, the relative impact will become larger on

**TABLE 5. Basic Estimators of the Differential Impact of Taxation on Aggregate Saving**

| Tax | Impact on saving of substituting tax for equal-yield proportional income levy (percent of tax yield) | |
| --- | --- | --- |
| | Short run | Long run |
| Federal individual income tax | −1.9 | −5.1 |
| State and local individual income taxes | −1.2 | −3.1 |
| Proportional tax on total consumption expenditures | +2.1 | +5.4 |
| Proportional tax on wages and salaries | +1.0 | +2.7 |
| Proportional tax on capital income | −1.9 | −5.2 |
| Proportional tax on dividends | | |
| Method 1 | −2.8 | −7.7 |
| Method 2[a] | −4.0 | −12.0 |

Source: Derived by method used in Table 4; distributive-share estimates for 1960 from Gillespie, "Effect of Public Expenditures on the Distribution of Income"; marginal propensities to consume from Husby, "A Nonlinear Consumption Function."

[a] Distributive-share estimate from Projector, Weiss, and Thoresen, "Composition of Income," pp. 128, 139.

its impact on personal, and hence on total, saving is highly controversial. At issue is the extent to which household consumption can be expected to react either directly to the tax-induced fall in retained corporate profits or indirectly to the capital losses on corporate shares that would result from that profit decline. According to many neo-Keynesian models of consumption behavior there would be no reaction at all, with the result that the tax impact on corporate and on total saving would be exactly the same. According to Fisherian and Ando-Modigliani models, however, household consumption expenditures would react negatively to the decline in corporate source income, with the result that personal saving would rise so as to offset at least part of the tax-induced fall in corporate saving.[165]

The quantitative impact of corporate profits taxation on total private saving may be estimated by contrasting its impact under two

dividends than on retained profits. For empirical estimates of magnitudes involved see Brittain, *Corporate Dividend Policy*; and Thomas A. Wilson, "Implications of the Carter Corporate Reforms for Corporate Savings Behaviour," Working Paper Series 6803 (University of Toronto, Institute for the Quantitative Analysis of Social and Economic Policy, 1968; processed).

[165] For a discussion of these alternative models of consumption behavior and of their significance for tax policy see Martin Feldstein and George Fane, "Taxes, Corporate Dividend Policy and Personal Savings: The British Postwar Experience," *Review of Economics and Statistics*, Vol. 55 (November 1973), pp. 399–411.

different assumptions. The first assumption is that retained corporate profits, or the capital gains to which they give rise on corporate common stock, stimulate household consumption as much as would an equal increase in dividends. The second holds that neither retained corporate profits nor capital gains have any effect on aggregate consumption demand. In the first case the impact of the corporate tax on private saving would be the same regardless of its relative incidence on dividends and retained earnings as long as these two forms of income were distributed in the same way among households. While there are good theoretical reasons for expecting low payout corporate securities to be more concentrated in the upper income groups than low payout shares, empirical evidence suggests the differences are not great.[166] If this is so, the last two lines of Table 5 provide the differential saving impact estimates required by the first set of assumptions. In the second case there would be no personal saving offset to the corporate dissaving induced by the corporate tax, and hence total saving would be even more adversely affected. If short-run and long-run corporate propensities to save are, say, 0.70 and 0.30, respectively,[167] the corporate tax differential saving estimates would be raised from the 4–12 percent range given in the last line of Table 5 to a 19–29 percent range.[168]

[166] This may be seen by comparing the Census Bureau–Federal Reserve distributive share data for dividends on publicly traded stock given in Dorothy S. Projector, Gertrude S. Weiss, and Erling T. Thoresen, "Composition of Income as Shown by the Survey of Financial Characteristics of Consumers," in Lee Soltow (ed.), *Six Papers on the Size Distribution of Wealth and Income,* Studies in Income and Wealth, Vol. 33 (Columbia University Press for National Bureau of Economic Research, 1969), p. 139, with similar data for total holdings of such stock given in Dorothy S. Projector and Gertrude S. Weiss, *Survey of Financial Characteristics of Consumers* (Board of Governors of the Federal Reserve System, 1966), p. 136.

[167] These propensities appear plausible on the basis of empirical evidence in Brittain, *Corporate Dividend Policy,* and Wilson, "Implications of the Carter Corporate Reforms."

[168] If capital gains have no impact on consumption, the differential saving impact of substituting a capital gains tax for an equal-yield tax on total income, calculated in the same way as the earlier estimates, would be −0.26 and −0.67 in the short and long runs, respectively, and hence the required corporate tax saving estimates would be:

$$\text{short run: } \Delta S/T = -(0.7 \times 0.26 + 0.3 \times 0.04) = -0.194;$$
$$\text{long run: } \Delta S/T = -(0.3 \times 0.67 + 0.7 \times 0.12) = -0.285,$$

where $T$ is the tax revenue involved.

The issue, then, is an important one, and fortunately, two recent econometric analyses provide some valuable evidence concerning the effects of capital gains on aggregate consumption demand. Using U.S. data for the 1948–64 period, Kul B. Bhatia found that both accrued and realized capital gains had some influence on consumption and that realized gains, which had the greater influence, were less powerful but faster acting stimulants to consumption than equal amounts of ordinary income.[169] In a study covering 1929–41 and 1948–66, Feldstein found that capital gains generated by retained corporate profits had a significant impact on consumption that in the long run was approximately two-thirds of the impact of ordinary disposable income.[170] Both studies emphasize that it is not sufficient simply to estimate the effect of a given tax policy on corporate saving, as has often been done. It is the net impact on total saving that matters, and changes in corporate saving tend to generate offsetting changes in personal saving. In the present instance this means that the long-run differential saving impact of an unshifted corporate profits tax must be placed somewhere between 12 percent and 29 percent of the tax yield. For example, if Feldstein's estimate of the relative magnitudes of the long-run marginal propensities to consume from ordinary income and from capital gains generated by retained corporate profits are used, the long-run differential saving estimate would be 0.15.

## Consumption: Composition Effects

In principle, taxation affects the structure of aggregate consumption in two different ways. Any tax-induced change in total income or total expenditures is likely to change consumer expenditures on different goods and services differently. And any tax-induced change in relative consumer prices should shift household purchases from the more to the less expensive goods and services.

Estimation of the relevant consumption parameters has long been a strong interest of econometricians. Houthakker and Taylor, in a recent application of a dynamic demand model to national in-

---

[169] "Capital Gains and the Aggregate Consumption Function," *American Economic Review*, Vol. 62 (December 1972), pp. 866–79.

[170] Martin S. Feldstein, "Tax Incentives, Corporate Saving, and Capital Accumulation in the United States," *Journal of Public Economics*, Vol. 2 (April 1973), pp. 159–71.

come accounts data for eighty-one categories of personal consumption expenditures, found that total expenditure (and presumably, therefore, total income) is the most important factor explaining the pattern of U.S. consumption. Prices, in contrast, were found to be much less important, appearing in only forty-four of the eighty-one equations and bordering on statistical insignificance in many of those.[171] Taxation, it appears, is much more likely to affect the structure of U.S. consumption through its impact on household spending powers than through its effects on relative product prices. Among the items found by Houthakker and Taylor to have high expenditure elasticities, and consequently to be particularly sensitive to changes in family tax burdens, were housing services; medical services; foreign and airline travel; cosmetics and drug preparations; radios, television sets, records, and musical instruments; toys; motion picture admissions; and sport and recreation equipment and services. Few kinds of consumption, on the other hand, appeared from their calculations to be highly sensitive to tax-induced changes in relative product prices. The notable exceptions were foreign travel, intercity bus and railway transportation, household china and glassware products, radio and television repair services, motion pictures, and sport and recreation equipment. Their data strongly suggest that excise taxation is not likely to have much impact on specific consumption expenditures from the uses-of-income side of household budgets.

### Saving: Composition Effects

Knowledge of differential tax effects on aggregate saving provides important insights into the strength of the financial incentives or disincentives that a given tax change will provide for business investment. Equally if not more important is information about the effects of taxation on the kinds of assets in which savers choose to invest—particularly about investors' decisions to hold assets expected to generate long-term capital gains, and their choices among assets of varying degrees of risk. This latter kind of choice has been a favorite subject of economic theorists who, in spite of the highly abstract nature of their analyses, have provided useful policy guidelines for the design of optimal tax systems.

[171] H. S. Houthakker and Lester D. Taylor, *Consumer Demand in the United States: Analyses and Projections* (2nd ed., Harvard University Press, 1970), pp. 164–65.

The holding of assets expected to appreciate in value is attractive to taxpayers both because of the preferential tax rate applied to long-term capital gains under the federal individual income tax and because of the postponement of actual tax payments as long as the investor continues to hold the assets. In the limit, of course, income tax can be avoided completely on all appreciating assets held until the death of the investor. Thus corporate shareholders, and particularly those in the highest income groups, have an incentive to hold low payout stocks. With a proportional corporate profits tax and exact reflection of retained earnings in higher stock prices,[172] the relation between the total tax rate on corporate source income, $t^*$, and the corporate payout ratio, $p$, as Bailey has shown,[173] is

$$dt^*/dp = (t - g)(1 - c),$$

where $t$ is the shareholder's marginal personal income tax rate, $g$ the present value of the shareholder's expected tax rate on capital gains if and when realized, and $c$ the tax rate on corporate profits. Since both terms of this expression are unambiguously positive,[174] average shareholder tax rates vary directly with stock payout ratios, and since the absolute gap between $t$ and $g$ increases as the shareholder's taxable income increases, high-income portfolio investors have a stronger tax incentive to seek low payout stocks than do lower income investors.[175]

Tax differentials are not the only factor affecting investor choices between capital gains and dividends. Both stock market volatility and well-established corporate policies to stabilize dividend flows make capital gains relatively unattractive to safety- and liquidity-conscious investors.[176] While investors seeking high current disposable income from their stocks could in principle obtain it from either dividends or capital gains, the latter involve higher transac-

---

[172] This assumes investment of retained earnings at a net-of-corporate-tax rate of return equal to the rate obtainable elsewhere on projects of equivalent risk.

[173] See Martin J. Bailey, "Capital Gains and Income Taxation," in Harberger and Bailey, *The Taxation of Income from Capital*, p. 27.

[174] Bailey, using data for the ratio of realized to accrued capital gains for the 1926–61 period, estimates $g$ at less than 10 percent, whereas marginal personal income tax rates for 1954–63 ranged from 20 percent to 91 percent; ibid., pp. 15–26.

[175] See Edwin J. Elton and Martin J. Gruber, "Marginal Stockholder Tax Rates and the Clientele Effect," *Review of Economics and Statistics*, Vol. 52 (February 1970), pp. 68–74.

[176] See Brittain, *Corporate Dividend Policy*.

tion costs and may also require more time and effort for portfolio management. Barlow, Brazer, and Morgan in their study of the behavior of high-income Americans found widespread stockholder desires to avoid making decisions about the composition of their portfolios.[177]

An important nontax factor is the prevalence or absence of what the Canadian Royal Commission on Taxation called "goodwill gains"—those corporate stock gains not arising from the normal reinvestment of retained earnings, but from such factors as the widespread availability of above-average profit opportunities, improved management techniques and capabilities, and an expected general reduction in the riskiness of corporate operations.[178] During the stock market boom after World War II, when Standard and Poor's five-hundred stock price index was rising at nearly 10 percent a year, investors had little doubt that stock prices in general would rise at least as fast as corporate profits were retained and reinvested, and hence they had little reason to regard low payout stocks with suspicion. That twenty-year boom, however, may have come to an end in late 1965.[179] If this changed situation persists and if it produces a widespread tendency for retained earnings to be less than fully reflected in higher corporate stock prices, holders of low payout stocks will in effect be subjected to a special management-imposed tax that will counter the special tax favors bestowed by the federal individual income tax.

Finally, there is the possibility that the U.S. stock market is changing from a highly competitive structure with many buyers and sellers to an oligopolistic market dominated by a relatively small number of large financial institutions. As the market becomes more and more affected by the opinions of institutional money managers, and less and less by the actual profit performance of individual companies, the ordinary investor is likely to view capital gain prospects

---

[177] *Economic Behavior of the Affluent*, p. 39.

[178] The definition of goodwill gains and losses, then, is

$$G_g = G - RE,$$

where $G_g$ is goodwill gains or losses, $G$ total capital gains or losses, and $RE$ retained earnings, all measured per share. See *Report of the Royal Commission on Taxation* (Ottawa: Queen's Printer, 1967), Vol. 4, pp. 40, 97.

[179] Between the end of 1965 and late 1973 Standard and Poor's five-hundred stock price index barely increased at all.

with increased uncertainty, compared to dividend and interest income opportunities. Speculative as these developments still are, they have been cited by financial experts as a major reason for the disappearance of the small investor from the stock market since the mid-1960s.[180]

Nevertheless, capital gains remain a tax-favored form of income, subject at worst to relatively low personal tax rates and at best to no tax rate at all.[181] Presumably a major justification for this kind of nonneutral tax structure is the fear that full taxation of all gains would unduly impair investor incentives to hold risky assets. These fears, insofar as they are not simply a convenient rationalization for less progressive income taxation in general, are probably more illusory than real.

Significant investor information and transaction costs, together with high uncertainty about the outcomes of alternative choices, make for both conservatism and sluggishness in investor behavior. As a result, specific tax changes may have no effect at all, because they fail to move investors beyond the threshold at which portfolio adjustments are called for, or their effects may be so widely diffused over future time periods as to be relatively unimportant in any one of them. Unfortunately, there appears to be no solid empirical evidence that would enable tax policy makers to distinguish between tax changes that would or would not materially affect portfolio investment choices.

A long series of theoretical analyses of the effects of taxation on investor behavior, largely ignoring institutional and frictional effects, points to a wide variety of plausible circumstances under which income taxation would increase rather than reduce private risk taking. Domar and Musgrave, in a classic paper stimulated by an equally classic paper by Lerner,[182] demonstrated both that a proportional income tax with full loss offsets would stimulate risk

---

[180] See "The Small Investor," *Wall Street Journal*, May 7, 1973.

[181] The Tax Reform Act of 1969 did increase the relative tax burdens on capital gain income somewhat, and further changes of a similar nature have been prominent in recent discussions of federal income tax reform.

[182] Evsey D. Domar and Richard A. Musgrave, "Proportional Income Taxation and Risk-Taking," *Quarterly Journal of Economics*, Vol. 58 (May 1944), pp. 388–422, reprinted in *Readings in the Economics of Taxation*, pp. 493–524; and Abba P. Lerner, "Functional Finance and the Federal Debt," *Social Research*, Vol. 10 (February 1943), pp. 38–51.

taking and that though the effects of a progressive, full-loss-offset income tax were more ambiguous, they might well be in the same direction. Suppose that an investor with $100 to invest can choose between a safe asset with a given return and a risky one that he expects to yield him $10 more a year, and that this extra $10 is just sufficient to induce him to pick the risky asset. He would clearly not do so, however, if he were subject to a 10 percent income tax with no loss offsets, since he would still be risking the entire $100 while his potential reward, cut to $9, would not be enough to induce him to take the risk. If, on the other hand, the 10 percent tax allowed for full loss offset, the investor would receive a $10 cash rebate from the government if his investment failed, so that in effect he would be risking only $90 of his own funds. Since the after-tax reward for doing so would be $9, his rate of return for risk taking would remain at the no-tax level of 10 percent, and he would buy the risky asset. The investor, however, might well think beyond this no-tax effect on risk taking. Since his disposable income would be less under the 10 percent full-loss-offset tax than under, say, an equal-yield sales tax, he might feel the need to recoup some of this income loss. He could do so, on the average, by shifting funds from safe to risky assets—thus demonstrating a tax-induced increase in risk taking.[183]

Such conclusions, derived from abstract models, cannot, of course, be applied directly to the real world, and their generality has also been challenged by more recent analysts of investor decision making under conditions of uncertainty.[184] Some of the criticisms of the Domar-Musgrave results, however, appear to have more theoretical than practical significance. The risk-stimulating effects of a full-loss-offset, proportional income tax, for example, have been shown to be critically affected, under certain circumstances, by the absence of a safe asset with a zero return and no risk. While

[183] These two reactions are examples of the substitution and income effects, respectively, in the basic theory of taxation and economic choice.

[184] See, especially, J. E. Stiglitz, "The Effects of Income, Wealth, and Capital Gains Taxation on Risk-Taking," *Quarterly Journal of Economics*, Vol. 83 (May 1969), pp. 263–83; and Martin S. Feldstein, "The Effects of Taxation on Risk Taking," *Journal of Political Economy*, Vol. 77 (September/October 1969), pp. 755–64. For a summary of the literature see Marc J. Roberts, "Portfolio Models and the Impact of Taxation on Investment: A Reconsideration," Discussion Paper 213 (Harvard University, Institute of Economic Research, November 1971; processed).

bank demand deposits are not inherently such an asset, they could be converted into one by means of effective governmental insurance and either purchasing power adjustment guaranties or government stabilization policies that would keep inflation under sufficient control to make portfolio investors in effect ignore the possibility of future changes in the general price level.[185]

Theoretical analyses of portfolio investment also suffer from other weaknesses. One is their failure to agree on the appropriate goal for rational behavior.[186] Another is the relatively narrow, partial equilibrium framework within which they analyze the whole problem of choice.[187] Much remains to be done. While the output of economic analysis in this area may appear to be meager, it has established the importance of the tax treatment of business and portfolio losses as a means of altering investor attitudes toward risk. As Roberts has concluded, at least a slight burden of proof rests on those who argue that federal income tax reform would unduly discourage risk taking.[188]

## Business Investment Choices

The effects of taxation on the level and structure of business investment have been a subject of spirited debate in recent years. From a seemingly innocent revival of interest during the early

[185] That this might have been the case in this country in the 1950s is suggested by William E. Gibson's study, "Interest Rates and Inflationary Expectations: New Evidence," *American Economic Review*, Vol. 62 (December 1972), pp. 854–65.

[186] Although the investor's goal should ideally be the maximization of future expected utility, simpler rules may be more realistic—to select the portfolio that either minimizes the probability of a loss greater than some maximum acceptable amount, or maximizes the average expected return while keeping the cumulative probability of unacceptably large losses sufficiently small. See George L. S. Shackle, *Expectation in Economics* (Cambridge University Press, 1949); A. D. Roy, "Safety First and the Holding of Assets," *Econometrica*, Vol. 20 (July 1952), pp. 431–49; Karl W. Roskamp, "Proportional Income Taxation and Risk-Taking: The Case of the 'Safety First' Investor," *Public Finance*, Vol. 22 (1967), pp. 333–41; and William J. Baumol, "An Expected Gain—Confidence Limit Criterion for Portfolio Selection," *Management Science*, Vol. 10 (October 1963), pp. 174–82.

[187] See Feldstein, "Effects of Taxation on Risk Taking," pp. 761–63; Roberts, "Portfolio Models," pp. 80–93; and Aiko N. Shibata, "Effects of Taxation on Risk-Taking," in American Economic Association, *Papers and Proceedings of the Eighty-first Annual Meeting, 1968*, pp. 553–61.

[188] "Portfolio Models," p. 94.

1960s in the neoclassical theory of optimal capital accumulation—
stimulated by the elegant reformulations of that theory by Dale
Jorgenson[189]—the academic conflict soon grew to include leading
economic theorists and econometricians, as well as a distinguished
group of young economists, bent on the elucidation and empirical
testing of alternative theories of business investment behavior. A
Brookings conference in November 1967 revealed very strong disagreements about the effects of tax incentives on investment,[190] and
during the next three years the debate continued in two of the leading economic journals.[191] Though the controversy has thus far failed
to provide policy makers with hard, quantitative answers, definite
progress has been made in clarifying the basic issues.[192]

[189] Dale W. Jorgenson, "Capital Theory and Investment Behavior," American
Economic Association, *Papers and Proceedings of the Seventy-fifth Annual Meeting,
1962 (American Economic Review,* Vol. 53, May 1963), pp. 247–59; "Anticipations
and Investment Behavior," in James S. Duesenberry and others (eds.), *The Brookings
Quarterly Econometric Model of the United States* (Rand McNally, 1965), pp. 35–
92; and Jorgenson, "The Theory of Investment Behavior," in Robert Ferber (ed.),
*Determinants of Investment Behavior,* A Conference of the Universities-National
Bureau Committee for Economic Research (Columbia University Press for National
Bureau of Economic Research, 1967), pp. 129–55.

[190] Gary Fromm (ed.), *Tax Incentives and Capital Spending* (Brookings Institution, 1971).

[191] In the *American Economic Review:* Robert E. Hall and Dale W. Jorgenson,
"Tax Policy and Investment Behavior," Vol. 57 (June 1967), pp. 391–414; Robert
M. Coen, "Effects of Tax Policy on Investment in Manufacturing," Vol. 58 (May
1968), pp. 200–11; Coen, "Tax Policy and Investment Behavior: Comment," Vol.
59 (June 1969), pp. 370–79; Robert Eisner, "Tax Policy and Investment Behavior:
Comment," Vol. 59 (June 1969), pp. 379–88; Hall and Jorgenson, "Tax Policy and
Investment Behavior: Reply and Further Results," Vol. 59 (June 1969), pp. 388–
401; Laurits R. Christensen, "Tax Policy and Investment Expenditures in a Model of
General Equilibrium," Vol. 60 (May 1970), pp. 18–22, and discussions by Arnold
C. Harberger and Vernon L. Smith, pp. 28–30; and Eisner, "Tax Policy and Invest-
ment Behavior: Further Comment," Vol. 60 (September 1970), pp. 746–52. In the
*Review of Economics and Statistics:* Jorgenson and James A. Stephenson, "The Time
Structure of Investment Behavior in United States Manufacturing, 1947–1960,"
Vol. 49 (February 1967), pp. 16–27; Eisner and M. I. Nadiri, "Investment Behavior
and Neo-Classical Theory," Vol. 50 (August 1968), pp. 369–82; Jorgenson and
Stephenson, "Issues in the Development of the Neoclassical Theory of Investment
Behavior," Vol. 51 (August 1969), pp. 346–53; Charles W. Bischoff, "Hypothesis
Testing and the Demand for Capital Goods," Vol. 51 (August 1969), pp. 354–68;
and Eisner and Nadiri, "Neoclassical Theory of Investment Behavior: A Comment,"
Vol. 52 (May 1970), pp. 216–22.

[192] For a survey of the literature see Dale W. Jorgenson, "Econometric Studies of
Investment Behavior: A Survey," *Journal of Economic Literature,* Vol. 9 (Decem-

*The Neoclassical Theory of Investment*

The essence of the neoclassical theory of investment is that relative prices do matter, and that by changing those prices tax policy can have an important effect on the level and structure of business investment expenditures. Opposing theories, while not denying the influence of relative prices, assign greater importance to such factors as recent changes in output or sales, future profit expectations, and the liquidity position of business firms. There is wide agreement that the factors determining the amount of investment to be put into replacing worn out or obsolete plant and equipment and the amount to be put into increasing the size of the capital stock are likely to be different. There is also wide agreement that changes in what businessmen regard as the optimal stock of capital assets, which provide the motivation for all new investment, give rise to investment expenditures only with a lag, and that the length and variability of this lag is a matter of great importance for stabilization policy. There is serious disagreement, however, over the determinants of the size and composition of the desired stock of capital assets, and hence over the extent to which tax policy is capable of changing the nature of that desired stock.

In the Jorgenson formulation of the neoclassical theory of investment the crucial determinant of the desired stock of capital is the rental price of capital services. For the maximizing firm[193] it is given by the expression:

$$c = q(r + d) - \dot{q},$$

where $c = $ the rental price of capital asset services; $r = $ the rate of discount, or rate of return on capital assets, taken, for simplicity, to be uniform throughout the economy; $d = $ the rate of depreciation of capital assets, that is, the rate at which they must be replaced if the capital stock is to be kept intact; and $q = $ the average price of capital

---

ber 1971), pp. 1111–47. This, too, has stimulated a large number of reactions, as the editor of the journal, Mark Perlman, indicated; ibid., Vol. 11 (March 1973), p. 56.

[193] The basic assumption is that each firm seeks to maximize its current market value. For a discussion of the relation of this goal to the more familiar one of maximizing profits see Dale W. Jorgenson and Calvin D. Siebert, "Optimal Capital Accumulation and Corporate Investment Behavior," *Journal of Political Economy*, Vol. 76 (November/December 1968), pp. 1123–51.

assets and $\dot{q}$ the rate of change in that price index (frequently taken to be zero).

Since most firms own rather than rent their capital assets, this rental price is basically an implicit, or shadow, price constructed in order to permit parallel analytical treatment of capital and labor inputs, the services of each being viewed as demanded by the firm in different amounts at different prices. In addition, the influence of tax factors is readily incorporated in the expression for the rental price of capital services. Assuming static price expectations so that $\dot{q}$ equals zero, as does the basic Jorgenson model:

$$c = q[r(1 - u) + d]\frac{(1 - k - uz)}{1 - u},$$

where $u =$ the rate imposed on business profits by a proportional income tax, $k =$ the rate of tax credit allowed on all new investment, and $z =$ the present value of the depreciation deduction allowed for tax purposes on one dollar of new investment, computed by discounting all future depreciation deductions at the rate $r(1 - u)$.

Employing a Cobb-Douglas production function, with its controversial assumption that the elasticity of substitution between labor and capital is equal to unity, Jorgenson then shows that for the maximizing, competitive firm the desired stock of capital assets, $K^*$, will simply be a function of the level of output and the price of that output relative to the rental price of capital:

$$K^* = a\left(\frac{p}{c}\right)Q,$$

where the price of output is $p$, the quantity $Q$, and the elasticity with respect to capital $a$.

Since the firm's reaction to an increase in its desired stock of capital must first be to plan the new investment project, then to secure the necessary funds, then to let the contracts and place the orders, and finally to make the expenditures for the desired new structures or equipment, new investment is taken to be a distributed lag function of past changes in the desired stock of capital assets. Replacement investment, on the other hand, is assumed simply to be proportional to the capital stock and equal to its economic depreciation. The final equation in the basic Jorgenson model, then, is:

$$I_t = \sum_{s=0}^{\infty} w_s \Delta K^*_{t-s} + dK_t,$$

where $I_t$ = gross investment in period $t$; $w_s$ = the proportion of the change in desired capital in period $t - s$ that results in investment expenditures in period $t$; $\Delta K^*_{t-s}$ = the change in desired capital in period $t - s$; and $dK_t$ = replacement investment in period $t$.

When the parameters of the basic Jorgenson model are estimated empirically, the effects on gross investment of such tax policies as accelerated depreciation and investment credits turn out to be substantial.[194] To policy makers, always eager to find effective ways of influencing the behavior of the economy, the attractiveness of such findings is obvious. Their usefulness for that purpose, however, is subject to important qualifications. Replacement investment is not analyzed in economic terms but is assumed to be proportional to the capital stock, and expansion investment is dealt with in a partial, rather than a general, equilibrium framework. Both the rental price of capital services and the present value of future depreciation deductions are determined by the net-of-tax rate of interest, $r(1-u)$, rather than by the gross-of-tax rate, $r$; this restricts the applicability of the model considerably. The elasticity of substitution between labor and capital is not estimated in the model but is simply assumed, on the basis of independent evidence, to be equal to unity; this assigns a questionably high value to the price elasticity of demand for capital assets.

### General Equilibrium Effects

Prominent among the simplifying features of the Hall-Jorgenson tax policy model is the assumption of constant aggregate output. This means that the large, tax-induced increases in business investment predicted by the analysis must result from commensurate reallocations of resources whose product price effects appear to have been less than fully accounted for. Firms operating in a concentrated industry, for example, are not likely to react to investment tax incentives by basing their plans on a lower rental price of capital services *at a given level of output*. Rather, they will expect higher investment on their part to lead to more industry output, salable only at relatively lower product prices, and in the Jorgenson model

[194] See Roger Gordon and Dale W. Jorgenson, "Investment Incentives in the 1971 Tax Bill," *Business Economics*, Vol. 7 (May 1972), pp. 7–13; or any of the articles cited above in note 191.

lower output prices, ceteris paribus, reduce the desired level of the capital stock. In a competitive industry, on the other hand, firms may well act initially on the basis of the lower rental price of capital only, but when the resultant expansion of output depresses the price of industry output, their desired level of capital assets will fall back toward its pretax level.[195]

Perhaps the most important omission from the Hall-Jorgenson analysis is explicit consideration of the potential effects on investment of the fiscal means used to finance tax incentives. If the revenue lost by the use of such devices is recovered by raising tax rates, the way in which the flow of personal saving changes will depend on the particular tax chosen; and the change, in turn, is likely to affect business investment incentives. Similarly important effects would be generated if the revenue lost by the use of investment tax incentives were balanced by government debt issue or were recovered by reductions in specific government expenditures. Christensen has shown, with a relatively simple general equilibrium macroeconomic model, that the behavior of business investment may vary substantially under alternative financing schemes.[196] The closely related question of the monetary policies that the Board of Governors of the Federal Reserve System might have pursued in the absence of the investment tax incentives has been investigated by Harberger. He has shown how the indirect investment effects generated by alternative monetary policies could either offset or augment the direct investment effects of the tax incentives.[197] Taubman and Wales, in their general equilibrium analysis of the long-run steady-state effects of investment subsidies, have demonstrated that the form of the saving function is an important determinant of the impact of tax incentives on business investment.[198]

Like the Harberger-McLure-Mieszkowski incidence model, the Hall-Jorgenson investment model makes some debatable choices between causal variables of primary and secondary importance. Their analysis does focus sharply on the direct effects of tax incentives on

[195] Compare Coen, "Tax Policy and Investment Behavior: Comment," p. 378.

[196] "Tax Policy and Investment Expenditures."

[197] Arnold C. Harberger, "Discussion," in Fromm, *Tax Incentives,* pp. 264–68.

[198] Paul Taubman and Terence J. Wales, "Impact of Investment Subsidies in a Neoclassical Growth Model," *Review of Economics and Statistics,* Vol. 51 (August 1969), pp. 287–97.

business investment, but for many policy applications it should be extended to include more variables and more indirect effects.[199]

## Interest Rate Effects

One of the most startling but least discussed findings of the Hall-Jorgenson analysis is that the 1964 reduction in the corporate profits tax rate from 52 percent to 48 percent, taken by itself, *decreased* net investment by small amounts in each of the four sectors studied.[200] The authors stressed that their analysis ignored the effects on investment of any increase in aggregate output that the 1964 tax cuts induced. Even so, it is a remarkable finding that deserves careful discussion.

The basic question at issue is: "When is a tax not a tax as far as investment incentives are concerned?"[201] Since the answer depends on the impact of the tax on rates of return, it is useful to examine separately the two polar cases of a partial income tax that leaves rates of return in the untaxed sector completely unchanged, and a perfectly general income tax that reduces rates of return proportionately everywhere.

Take, first, the partial tax. In the absence of any tax, the implicit rental price of capital asset prices (assuming static price expectations for capital asset prices) may be written:

$$c_o = q(r + d).$$

If a proportional income tax is imposed in a sector of the economy that is so small that rates of return are not depressed elsewhere as resources shift out of the taxed sector, the rental price of capital in that sector will be:

$$c_t = q(r + d)\frac{(1 - uz)}{(1 - u)}.$$

---

[199] See Gordon and Jorgenson, "Investment Incentives in the 1971 Tax Bill," and Jorgenson, "Economic Impact of Investment Incentives," in *Long-Term Implications of Current Tax and Spending Proposals*, Joint Economic Committee, 92 Cong. 1 sess. (1971), pp. 176–92.

[200] "Tax Policy and Investment Behavior: Reply and Further Results," pp. 397–98; and Robert E. Hall and Dale W. Jorgenson, "Application of the Theory of Optimum Capital Accumulation," in Fromm, *Tax Incentives*, p. 53.

[201] See Melvin White and Anne White, "Tax Neutrality of Instantaneous Versus Economic Depreciation," in Richard M. Bird and John G. Head (eds.), *Modern Fiscal Issues: Essays in Honor of Carl S. Shoup* (University of Toronto Press, 1972), pp. 105–16.

Since $z$, the present value of future depreciation deductions on one dollar of new current investment, is necessarily less than one at all positive discount rates, $c_t$ is greater than $c_o$, signifying the presence of investment disincentives in the taxed sector. In the limit, if the tax law were to permit the immediate deduction of all new capital expenditures, the rental price of all such services would be:

$$c_t = q(r + d) = c_o,$$

when $z$ equals one. With instant depreciation, in other words, there would be no tax at all as far as investment incentives were concerned.[202]

Consider, now, the perfectly general income tax. Since investors, by assumption, have no opportunities to invest free of its burdens, the relevant discount rate for their calculations is the interest rate net of tax, and the rental price of capital services will be:

$$c_t = q[r(1 - u) + d]\frac{(1 - uz)}{(1 - u)}.$$

Suppose, further, that tax depreciation is based, as it should be, on the decline in market value of depreciable assets throughout their productive lives. As Hall and Jorgenson have shown,[203] when tax depreciation equals economic depreciation:

$$z' = \frac{d}{r(1 - u) + d},$$

$$c_t' = \frac{q}{(1 - u)}[r(1 - u) + d]\left[1 - \frac{ud}{r(1 - u) + d}\right]$$

$$= q(r + d) = c_o.$$

What this says is that the perfectly defined, perfectly general proportional income tax would be perfectly neutral in its impact on investment because, rates of return on all economic activities being lowered proportionately everywhere, investors would have no reason or opportunity to alter their behavior in response to its enact-

---

[202] See E. Cary Brown, "Business-Income Taxation and Investment Incentives," in *Income, Employment and Public Policy: Essays in Honor of Alvin H. Hansen* (Norton, 1948); reprinted in *Readings in the Economics of Taxation*, pp. 525–37.
[203] "Application of the Theory of Optimum Capital Accumulation," p. 17.

ment.[204] It follows immediately from this general proposition that a general income tax that allows only decelerated depreciation deductions, relative to those appropriate under economic depreciation, will tend to discourage business investment, the more so the higher the tax rate imposed. Conversely, any general income tax that allows accelerated depreciation deductions will stimulate business investment, the more so the higher its tax rate.

Hall and Jorgenson relied on this last proposition in their empirical estimation of the effects on investment of the tax cuts of 1964. Based on the assumption of the constancy of the gross-of-tax interest rate, and the assertion that in 1964 tax depreciation in this country was in excess of economic depreciation, their conclusion that the 1964 tax rate reductions discouraged business investment is theoretically sound. Its applicability to the real world, however, is something else again. Their calculations appear to have been based only on the reduction in the rate of the corporate income tax, which is a partial investment levy with respect to both the noncorporate sector in this country and corporate investment in the rest of the world. It seems highly unlikely that a decrease in the U.S. corporate tax rate would leave the gross-of-tax interest rate unchanged; and to the extent that it did not, some stimulus to corporate investment would be provided. Broadening the interpretation of the Hall-Jorgenson conclusion by applying it to the reductions under both the corporate and individual income taxes helps little. Even if those rate reductions were strictly proportional in the two sectors of this economy—and there is no demonstration that this was indeed the case—foreign corporate investment, carried out through subsidiaries, was granted no tax reduction as long as the proceeds were reinvested abroad. Particularly for multinational U.S. corporations, then, the 1964 tax rate reductions appear more as potential stimulants to new domestic investment than as the reverse. The reductions may also have affected investment indirectly by altering the economic determinants of the consumption-saving choice.

In sum, the interest rate effects of investment tax incentives are

[204] See Paul A. Samuelson, "Tax Deductibility of Economic Depreciation to Insure Invariant Valuations," *Journal of Political Economy*, Vol. 72 (December 1964), pp. 604–06. Note also the assumption that aggregate saving and investment are unaffected by changes in the rate of return.

important and must be estimated quantitatively before the investment incentives themselves can be fully evaluated. By holding those
effects constant, the Hall-Jorgenson analysis, and many others,
leaves investment policy makers a good way short of the answers
they seek to their problems.

### Factor Elasticities of Substitution

By choosing relative prices as an important determinant of business purchases of new capital assets, the neoclassical theory of investment focuses attention directly on the nature of production
functions, and particularly on the extent to which labor can be substituted for capital, and vice versa, when the relative prices of those
two factors change. In the theoretical disagreements over this question, the major competitor of the neoclassical proposition that
capital and labor can be substituted for each other with ease is the
"putty-clay" hypothesis. It states that whereas factor proportions are
variable before new capital assets are designed and produced, they
tend to be fixed within narrow limits once the capital assets have
been placed in operation. Production functions involving new capital assets, in other words, are highly malleable, like putty, but those
involving old capital assets are rigid, like hard-baked clay. This
implies that new business investment will respond both less rapidly
and less strongly to a change in relative factor prices than to a
change in aggregate output. Neoclassical theories, in contrast, tend
to place these two determinants on a par.[205]

On the empirical side, controversy has centered on alternative
means of deriving accurate estimates of the size of the crucial
structural parameter—the elasticity of substitution between labor
and capital. Whereas the cross-section approach favored by Hall
and Jorgenson has frequently produced evidence consistent with
their hypothesis that the elasticity of substitution is equal to unity,
the time series equations used by Coen, Eisner, Nadiri, and others
all produce estimated values significantly less than unity.[206] When

[205] For a concise, nontechnical exposition of these relations see Charles W.
Bischoff, "Business Investment in the 1970s: A Comparison of Models," *Brookings
Papers on Economic Activity* (1:1971), pp. 51–54.

[206] See articles cited above in note 191, as well as Robert E. Lucas, Jr., "Labor-
Capital Substitution in U.S. Manufacturing," in Harberger and Bailey, *The Taxation
of Income from Capital*, pp. 223–74; and B. D. Boatwright and J. R. Eaton, "The

two alternative methods of estimating elasticities of factor substitution from cross-section data were applied to 1957 U.S. two-digit manufacturing industries, one method accepted the hypothesis that the elasticity was equal to unity while the other rejected it.[207] The evidence, then, is highly mixed. Unfortunately, the effectiveness of investment tax credits will remain uncertain until this particular empirical issue is resolved.

## Replacement Investment

Although it is the dominant component of gross business capital formation in this country, replacement investment has received much less attention from economists than has expansion investment. Jorgenson and others, assuming replacement investment to be a constant proportion of the capital stock, have implied that it is governed by technological rather than economic forces. In their models the role of replacement investment is purely passive.

Several recent studies, however, have attacked the proportionality assumption and presented empirical evidence that purchases of durable business assets to maintain existing output capacity are responsive to some of the same economic factors as are those undertaken to expand capacity. Feldstein and Foot and Eisner find replacement investment to be positively related to measures of cash flow and capacity utilization, and Feldstein and Rothschild stress its sensitivity to changes in interest rates and in tax rates, credits, and depreciation allowances.[208] Such tax changes, they show, may affect replacement investment either by altering the optimal capital-output ratio or by changing the optimal durability of new machines, which in turn alters the ratio of replacement investment to the capital

---

Estimation of Investment Functions for Manufacturing Industry in the United Kingdom," *Economica*, N.S., Vol. 39 (November 1972), pp. 403–18.

[207] Phoebus J. Dhrymes and Paul Zarembka, "Elasticities of Substitution for Two-Digit Manufacturing Industries: A Correction," *Review of Economics and Statistics*, Vol. 52 (February 1970), pp. 115–17.

[208] Martin S. Feldstein and David K. Foot, "The Other Half of Gross Investment: Replacement and Modernization Expenditures," *Review of Economics and Statistics*, Vol. 53 (February 1971), pp. 49–58; Robert Eisner, "Components of Capital Expenditures: Replacement and Modernization Versus Expansion," ibid., Vol. 54 (August 1972), pp. 297–305; and Martin S. Feldstein and Michael Rothschild, "Towards an Economic Theory of Replacement Investment," Discussion Paper 249 (Harvard University, Institute of Economic Research, August 1972; processed).

stock. These two tax effects may reinforce or offset each other: when an investment tax credit is introduced, for example, replacement investment in the long run should be stimulated to a greater degree than is expansion investment, and when tax depreciation is shifted from straight-line to sum-of-the-years-digits, expansion investment should receive the greater stimulus.

There is disagreement, however, over some of the short-run effects of taxation on the two types of investment. Feldstein and his associates present both theoretical and empirical evidence that expansion and replacement investment tend to be inversely related to each other;[209] Eisner's studies indicate that the two types of investment tend to fluctuate together. The issue, clearly, is an important one for tax policy makers, particularly those concerned with stabilization rather than growth effects. Should the Feldstein hypothesis be confirmed, the potential short-run impact of tax policy on gross business investment would have to be taken to be significantly less than its predicted impact on expansion investment. Another important policy question is whether either of the two types of investment could be varied independently of the other, should the government view such a structural change as desirable. Modernization of the existing capital stock, for example, might be accorded a higher social priority than its expansion. While this question cannot now be answered with confidence, the Eisner studies suggest that policies designed to raise business liquidity might well have the desired effect.

In any case the Jorgenson model at best goes only part of the way toward explaining the effects of taxation on total business investment, and at worst—as some of its critics have suggested—may even be an unsatisfactory explanation of the behavior of expansion investment because its parameter estimates are based on an unrealistic treatment of replacement investment.

## Alternative Investment Models

While a definitive investment model has yet to be developed, the crucial question for policy makers is what can be learned from the models in existence. The current state of the art of constructing such

[209] They argue that the two types of investment compete with each other for scarce funds and management resources and that of the two, replacement investment is likely to be the less costly to postpone. Empirical evidence in support of this hypothesis is given in Feldstein and Foot, "The Other Half of Gross Investment."

models is like the earliest preseason games in professional football. Opportunity is provided for head-to-head contests between alternative investment functions, but the results are tantalizingly ambiguous.

In one test, Dale W. Jorgenson, Jerald Hunter, and M. Ishaq Nadiri fitted four different models, selected to represent the main alternative theories of investment, to the same quarterly 1949–64 data for fifteen manufacturing industries from the regular investment survey of the Office of Business Economics and the Securities and Exchange Commission.[210] The models were the Jorgenson-Stephenson model, which stresses the importance of the rental price of capital asset services; the Eisner model, which minimizes the role of financial factors and stresses the importance of changes in business sales and profits (the so-called flexible accelerator); the Anderson model,[211] which includes a variety of financial factors such as internal cash flow, interest rates, long-term debt capacity, and accrued tax liabilities; and the Meyer-Glauber model,[212] which also stresses financial factors by including internal cash flow, interest rates, and the rate of change of common stock prices. When tested for their ability to explain the behavior of business investment during the period of study, the Jorgenson-Stephenson model ranked first, the Eisner second, the Meyer-Glauber third, and the Anderson fourth. When tested for the absence of structural change from 1949–60 to 1961–64, the Eisner model ranked first and the Jorgenson-Stephenson second, while the other two held the same positions as in the explanatory test.

In another systematic test, Bischoff fitted five models to quarterly data for 1953–68.[213] He used the standard neoclassical model of Jorgenson and his associates, the flexible accelerator model of Eisner, a straight cash flow model, a model based on the proposition (stressed by James Tobin and others) that corporate managers invest in order to maximize the market value of their firms, and the

[210] "A Comparison of Alternative Econometric Models of Quarterly Investment Behavior," and "The Predictive Performance of Econometric Models of Quarterly Investment Behavior," *Econometrica*, Vol. 38 (March 1970), pp. 187–212, 213–24.

[211] W. H. Locke Anderson, *Corporate Finance and Fixed Investment: An Econometric Study* (Harvard University, Graduate School of Business Administration, Division of Research, 1964).

[212] John R. Meyer and Robert R. Glauber, *Investment Decisions, Economic Forecasting, and Public Policy* (Harvard University, Graduate School of Business Administration, Division of Research, 1964).

[213] "Business Investment in the 1970s."

Federal Reserve Board–Massachusetts Institute of Technology–Pennsylvania econometric model (FMP model) on which he had worked and which incorporates the putty-clay hypothesis. All five models performed reasonably well, and fairly similarly, during the period to which they were fitted, but when they were used to predict investment in 1969–70, both the cash flow and the corporate market value equations showed large errors. Bischoff preferred the FMP model, and the flexible accelerator was his second choice.

A much less systematic test of investment models was made at the 1967 Brookings conference.[214] The authors fitted their own functions to their own selected data, and two specialists evaluated the models. Arnold C. Harberger, who refused to take sides, concluded simply that "the quality of the work presented here is very high, but the analyses leave unfinished and unclear the picture of the quantitative effects of the tax incentives that have been examined."[215] Franklin M. Fisher, clearly agreeing with Harberger's general assessment, ranked the studies according to their lack of vulnerability to criticism: he preferred the investment sectors of either the FMP model, presented by Charles Bischoff, or the Wharton model, presented by Lawrence Klein and Paul Taubman, and found the standard neoclassical model of Hall and Jorgenson and the cash flow adjustment model of Robert Coen more open to criticism.[216]

Despite the inconclusiveness of the test results, these models offer clues about the relative qualities of the different components and combinations. Not only does the growth of aggregate output appear to be a basic determinant of new business investment but it probably outranks tax policy in quantitative importance. Governments that fail to keep their economies growing, in other words, are not likely to be able to make up for the investment lost on that account by the use of tax incentives. In addition, to the extent that factor proportions are more variable ex ante than they are ex post (as Bischoff's tests of the putty-clay hypothesis suggest), a rapidly growing economy provides more opportunity for investment tax incentives to alter production functions than does a static economy.

[214] Fromm, *Tax Incentives.*
[215] Ibid., p. 268.
[216] Ibid., p. 255.

From a theoretical point of view the Jorgenson method of incorporating different tax incentives in the formula for the rental price of capital services is attractive, and as generalized in Bischoff's model, it appears highly promising as a means of quantifying the direct effects of taxation on investment. One of Bischoff's most intriguing findings is that while "the investment tax credit adopted in 1962 has probably directly stimulated more investment spending than the policy has cost the government in taxes. . . . In this model, the data [on expenditures for producers' durable equipment in the United States from 1947 through 1966] give no support to the hypothesis that accelerated depreciation has any effect at all on investment!"[217]

Though such a sharp difference in the performance of the two investment stimulants may not show up in future studies, confirmation of the relative superiority of the investment credit would be welcomed by those who have long preferred it as a regulator. Depreciation at rates faster than economic depreciation distorts profit statements in ways that few outsiders can successfully adjust for,[218] whereas investment credits cause no such distortion. The amount of the subsidy granted business under tax credits is readily computed and reported; under accelerated depreciation it is obscured, so that neither the public nor the Congress can ascertain the effects.

An investment credit is a flexible tax instrument that can be implemented, eliminated, or changed at relatively low administrative and compliance costs. Depreciation policy is not. Empirical analysis of use of the credit for stabilization purposes in this country in 1966–67 indicates that it has had a significant impact on investment expenditures.[219]

The benefits of accelerated depreciation may be significantly less

[217] Charles W. Bischoff, "The Effect of Alternative Lag Distributions," in Fromm, *Tax Incentives*, pp. 123–25.

[218] The government could, of course, require companies to adjust their profits to an economic depreciation basis before reporting them. This requirement, however, would add materially to the compliance costs involved in the use of accelerated depreciation as an investment stimulant, and these are probably already greater than those associated with the use of investment credits.

[219] See the estimates of Hall and Jorgenson in "Application of the Theory of Optimum Capital Accumulation," pp. 56–59, and Lawrence R. Klein and Paul Taubman in "Estimating Effects within a Complete Econometric Model," in Fromm, *Tax Incentives*, pp. 233–35.

visible to businessmen than those of a tax credit, as the relatively
slow rate of adoption of the accelerated depreciation allowances
first made available in 1954 implies.[220] The more widespread this
general response is, the greater the overestimate of the effectiveness
of tax depreciation allowances in models of the Hall-Jorgenson type
that assume full impact of any tax incentive on the rental price of
capital.[221] This is but one example of the risks that current investment models run by incorporating tax effects in other determining
variables, such as rates of return and rental prices of capital, rather
than dealing directly with the tax policies themselves.[222]

One potential determinant of business investment that is directly, and significantly, affected by all tax policies is internal cash
flow.[223] At this point, however, neither the nature nor the importance
of the role of cash flow is entirely clear. Jorgenson rejects it as a
separate and independent determinant of the desired capital
stock.[224] Coen has suggested that cash flow does not determine the
size of the optimal stock of capital assets but does directly affect the
speed with which business firms adjust, through new investment, to
changes in their desired stock of capital.[225] The extent to which
other economic policies affect the importance of cash flow as a factor in investment decisions must also be considered. The question
arises from the fact that financial markets and tax laws are imperfect. In the ideal economy, businessmen would have no reason to
consider the size of their internal cash flows when making their investment plans. Hence anything government does to improve the
operation of capital markets presumably weakens the cash flow
impact of tax policy on investment expenditures.

[220] See Norman B. Ture, *Accelerated Depreciation in the United States, 1954–60*
(Columbia University Press for National Bureau of Economic Research, 1967).
   [221] However, Bischoff explicitly allowed for the slow adoption of 1954 accelerated depreciation allowances in his generalization of the Hall-Jorgenson model.
"The Effect of Alternative Lag Distributions," pp. 85–86.
   [222] See remarks of Franklin Fisher, in a Fromm, *Tax Incentives*, pp. 243–47.
   [223] Cash flow is defined as the sum of depreciation allowances and profits net of
taxes, and possibly also net of dividends. For an analysis that explicitly considers
investment behavior and dividend policies jointly see Phoebus J. Dhrymes and
Mordecai Kurz, "Investment, Dividend, and External Finance Behavior of Firms," in
Ferber, *Determinants of Investment Behavior*.
   [224] "Econometric Studies of Investment Behavior," pp. 1133–34.
   [225] Robert M. Coen, "The Effect of Cash Flow on the Speed of Adjustment," in
Fromm, *Tax Incentives*, pp. 131–96.

## Summary and Conclusions

When all other conditions are favorable, or can be rendered so by policy actions, tax incentives do appear to be capable of stimulating business investment. How great the response is likely to be in the long run and how quickly it will develop in the short run are unsettled questions. Governments should not restrain their use of tax incentives and disincentives on that account, however. Only the amount, not the direction, of the effects is in doubt, and the use of such policy instruments may well be preferable to no action at all. Moreover, systematic experimentation with alternative tax measures offers the most promising means of reducing uncertainties about the strength of business investment reactions to tax changes.

The potential stimulus of investment tax incentives will be aborted if the demand for funds is allowed to drive interest rates up and if the aggregate supply of saving is highly interest inelastic. Successful use of the incentives to change the composition of full employment output therefore would require both relatively easy monetary policies and higher tax burdens with a primary impact on private consumption rather than saving. In the basic Jorgenson model, which produces results highly favorable to investment tax incentives, a crucial assumption is that the gross-of-tax rate of return is held constant.

When one investment tax incentive package is replaced by another, it is likely to be difficult to predict the net outcome without the help of an econometric investment model capable of dealing with the major feedbacks and interactions. That it may also be seriously misleading is suggested by the conflicting interpretations put on the 1970 British tax shift from a system of cash grants to one of accelerated depreciation allowances. Whereas this change was regarded as a stimulus to business investment by the chancellor of the exchequer, an econometric analysis by Boatwright and Eaton predicted exactly the opposite result.[226]

Replacement investment, which has frequently been more important than expansion investment in the United States in recent years, has also been shown to be sensitive to economic forces and hence to certain kinds of tax incentives and disincentives. By such

---

[226] "Estimation of Investment Functions," pp. 415–16.

means it appears that the government could expand both kinds of business investment together in the long run. It is not clear whether this could also be done in the short run, or whether a short-run stimulus to the one kind of investment must necessarily be dissipated by an accompanying counterreaction from the other kind of investment.

Important as the broad distinction between replacement and expansion investment is to economists, policy makers are likely to be more interested in different tax effects on incentives to invest in particular kinds of assets, such as commercial or industrial buildings, business equipment, or housing facilities, or in assets with different expected useful lives. The basic Jorgenson model, it appears, is readily adapted to the answering of such questions, qualitatively if not quantitatively. An analysis of the 1971 depreciation revisions indicated they were approximately even-handed in their effects on assets with different useful lives, and a study of the Tax Reform Act of 1969 and the Revenue Act of 1971 found the first stimulated residential investment and discouraged investment in business equipment while the second had precisely the opposite effect.[227]

When the direct effects of particular policy instruments are uncertain, public decisions about their use are likely to rest primarily on their prominent indirect effects—in the case of investment tax incentives, on the distribution of income and wealth. Because of the concentration of both high savers and profit receivers in the upper income groups, stimulating business investment by means of tax incentives is not likely to appeal to anyone who regards the current distribution of income as excessively unequal. For such people, clearly, the onus is on tax incentives to prove themselves sufficiently effective in stimulating investment to overbalance their adverse distributional effects. Those not disturbed by income inequalities, on the other hand, are likely to be much more favorably inclined toward investment tax incentives. Basically, the choice is between price incentives whose distributional effects sustain or intensify in-

[227] Emil M. Sunley, Jr., "The 1971 Depreciation Revision: Measures of Effectiveness," *National Tax Journal*, Vol. 24 (March 1971), pp. 19–30; Henry Aaron, Frank S. Russek, Jr., and Neil M. Singer, "Tax Reform and the Composition of Investment," ibid., Vol. 25 (March 1972), pp. 1–13, and "Tax Changes and Composition of Fixed Investment: An Aggregative Simulation," *Review of Economics and Statistics*, Vol. 54 (November 1972), pp. 343–56.

equalities, and the aggregate output (income) incentives that could be provided to business investment by running the economy at higher capacity and lower unemployment levels than have heretofore been thought advisable. While lower unemployment levels clearly would reduce income inequalities, output incentives would presumably involve the distributional (and other) costs either of more rapid inflation or of widespread wage-price controls or both. Even more basically, the choice is between a high growth and a low growth economy and the qualities of life characterizing them.

## Resource Allocation Choices

Although the allocation effects of taxation are intimately associated with the shifting and incidence process, they deserve separate treatment. The distinction between the two sets of tax effects may be seen most clearly by supposing the enactment of a set of Pigovian taxes and transfers, the former on activities with external social costs and the latter on activities generating external social benefits.[228] If the system were self-financing, there would be neither a monetary transfer to the government nor any public use of resources (abstracting from the minimal necessary administrative costs of the program) and hence no tax burdens. There would, however, presumably be an improvement in the allocation of resources in the private sector. More generally, a combined tax-expenditure operation would shift resources from the private to the public sector, imposing direct burdens, to be identified as the incidence of the program, and (unless a very special tax instrument were used) would alter the allocation of the resources remaining in the private sector, creating either additional burdens or welfare benefits.

### Theory

At the heart of the complex discussion of the excess burdens of taxation[229] is a single proposition: since demand and supply prices measure, respectively, the pleasures enjoyed by people from actual consumption and the benefits they could have received had the re-

---

[228] See A. C. Pigou, *The Economics of Welfare* (4th ed., Macmillan, 1932), Pt. 2.

[229] For a concise summary of the issues see Shoup, *Public Finance*, pp. 28–31. A detailed theoretical analysis is given in Musgrave, *The Theory of Public Finance*, pp. 140–59.

sources been allocated differently, the level of economic welfare would be highest when there were no gaps between those demand and supply prices. The absence of gaps means that the pleasure obtained by consuming the last unit of any one good is exactly equal to the pleasure that could have been obtained by devoting the same resources to the production of additional units of any other good. Conversely, the presence of gaps means that economic welfare may be increased by shifting resources from inferior to superior uses.

In an ideal, first-best economic world there would be no distortions of demand-supply price relationships. Thus the elimination of distortions as rapidly as possible would seem to be the appropriate grand strategy for public policy makers. But that is probably impossible. Certain economic distortions are ineradicable, and in such a second-best economic world the elimination of distortions that are responsive to policy actions is not necessarily the best possible strategy.[230] Rather, it may be preferable to try to equalize the incidence of economic distortions in some relevant sense. This complex problem has been a preoccupation of welfare economists in recent years.[231]

The change in economic welfare induced by the application of a specific tax instrument to any given economic activity may, in broad general terms, be said to be measured by the sum of the distortions thereby imposed on that activity and the changes brought about in any preexisting distortions in all other economic activities.[232] A use-

---

[230] See the systematic treatment of these issues by R. G. Lipsey and Kelvin Lancaster in "The General Theory of Second Best," *Review of Economic Studies*, Vol. 24 (1956), pp. 11–32; a much earlier analysis in a similar vein is F. P. Ramsey, "A Contribution to the Theory of Taxation," *Economic Journal*, Vol. 37 (March 1927), pp. 47–61.

[231] See the discussion of "the mystery of the mislaid maxim" by William J. Baumol and David F. Bradford in "Optimal Departures from Marginal Cost Pricing," *American Economic Review*, Vol. 60 (June 1970), pp. 265–83. The proposition in question, which the authors suggest is at variance with the beliefs of many economists, is that "generally, prices which deviate in a systematic manner from marginal costs will be required for an optimal allocation of resources, even in the absence of externalities" (ibid., p. 265). For a general theoretical treatment of the whole subject see Jagdish N. Bhagwati, "The Generalized Theory of Distortions and Welfare," in Bhagwati and others (eds.), *Trade, Balance of Payments and Growth: Papers in International Economics in Honor of Charles P. Kindleberger* (Amsterdam: North-Holland, 1971), pp. 69–90.

[232] See Arnold C. Harberger, "Three Basic Postulates for Applied Welfare Economics: An Interpretative Essay," *Journal of Economic Literature*, Vol. 9 (September 1971), especially pp. 789–91.

ful, and relatively simple, example to consider is Harberger's analysis of the imposition of a corporate income tax in a world of no economic distortions.[233] Assume that the aggregate supply of capital assets is fixed and that competitive forces bring about equality in the net rates of return in all uses of capital, and consider the following schedules of the marginal productivity of capital for the corporate and noncorporate sectors of the economy:

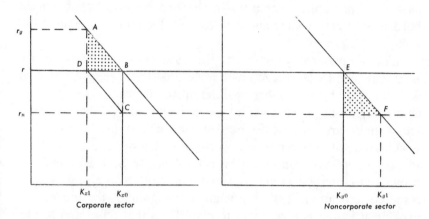

In the absence of any tax, the equilibrium rate of return to capital in the two sectors is $r$. When a tax is imposed on corporate profits, the shifting mechanism is set in motion, and when long-run equilibrium is reached, the quantity of capital used in the corporate sector will have fallen from $K_{x0}$ to $K_{x1}$, and in the noncorporate sector it will have risen by an equal amount, from $K_{y0}$ to $K_{y1}$. The gross-of-tax rate of return will then be $r_g$ in the corporate sector, and the net-of-tax rate of return will be $r_n$ in both sectors. During the entire reallocation process the economy will be shifting capital from higher and higher to lower and lower yielding uses, and in equilibrium the total loss of economic welfare will equal the sum of the triangles ABD and EFG, which is equal to the area ABCD or one-half of the product of the tax rate $(r_g - r_n)$ and the change in the use of capital in the taxed sector $(K_{x0} - K_{x1})$.[234]

---

[233] Harberger, "The Incidence of the Corporation Income Tax," and Arnold C. Harberger, "Efficiency Effects of Taxes on Income from Capital," in Krzyzaniak, *Effects of Corporation Income Tax*, pp. 107–17.

[234] This may be seen by subtracting the gross gain from the tax-induced shift of resources, $EFK_{y1}K_{y0}$, from the gross loss of $ABK_{x0}K_{x1}$, by noting the equality of $K_{x0}K_{x1}$ and $K_{y1}K_{y0}$, and then comparing like-sized triangles and areas.

One of the most interesting features of the basic Harberger model is the extent to which the incidence and the excess burden of the corporate profits tax may diverge from each other. Both are functions of the two elasticities of substitution between labor and capital in production in the two sectors and the elasticity of substitution between the two sector outputs in consumption. When the three elasticities are equal, the incidence of the tax falls equally on income from capital employed in the two sectors, but its excess burdens will vary widely and directly with the absolute value of the three elasticities.[235]

This simple analysis of one tax in a distortion-free economy has been extended by Harberger, with great theoretical elegance, to deal with the use of any number of different tax instruments in a world characterized by a wide variety of economic distortions.[236] In his model there are only excess burdens and distortions because each is analyzed with reference to a world in which the allocation of resources is optimal. One must be careful not to be led by this approach into the false assumption that unneutral taxes always worsen resource allocation. This is not an implication of the model, for explicit attention is given both to distortions that offset and to distortions that reinforce others. A distorted economic world, in other words, can be improved by adding distortions of the right kind. A less cumbersome approach is to take the real world, with all its imperfections, as the base of the analysis and deal explicitly with both the harmful and the beneficial allocational effects of taxation.[237] While deference to traditional terminology might suggest calling these the excess burdens and benefits of taxation, a punc-

---

[235] The welfare cost, for example, would be four times as great for elasticities of −1 as it would be for elasticities of only −0.25. See Harberger, "Efficiency Effects of Taxes on Income from Capital," p. 109.

[236] Arnold C. Harberger, "Taxation, Resource Allocation, and Welfare," in *The Role of Direct and Indirect Taxes in the Federal Revenue System*, A Conference Report of the National Bureau of Economic Research and the Brookings Institution (Princeton University Press, 1964), pp. 25–70, and "The Measurement of Waste," in American Economic Association, *Papers and Proceedings of the Seventy-sixth Annual Meeting, 1963* (*American Economic Review*, Vol. 54, May 1964), pp. 58–76. See also Robert L. Bishop, "The Effects of Specific and Ad Valorem Taxes," *Quarterly Journal of Economics*, Vol. 82 (May 1968), pp. 198–218.

[237] See, for example, Earl R. Rolph and George F. Break, "The Welfare Aspects of Excise Taxes," *Journal of Political Economy*, Vol. 57 (February 1949), pp. 46–54, reprinted in *Readings in the Economics of Taxation*, pp. 110–22.

tilious linguist would probably prefer a less glamorous designation such as allocational gains and losses. Whereas the harmful allocational effects of a tax are excess to the direct burdens, or incidence of the tax, beneficial allocative effects have nothing to be excess to but are simply separate and opposite to the direct burdens. The term *excess burden,* however, is not likely to disappear soon from the terminology of tax analysis. Until it does, it must be remembered that two excess burdens may be equal to none.

A second important feature of the generalized Harberger analysis is the extent to which welfare costs pyramid when more than one distortion applies to a given economic activity. In his welfare measures these costs vary with the square of the distortion, and in practice, therefore, policy makers should be careful to avoid adding one distortion to another of like kind. Another kind of welfare loss, which Taubman and Rasche call "complete resource misallocation,"[238] occurs when the economic lives of capital assets are not fixed, as is commonly assumed in welfare economics, but are sensitive to economic influences, as seems likely to be the case in practice. By affecting the right economic variables, tax policy would be quite capable of shortening economic asset lives. Unless this premature destruction of assets were justified by another preexisting distortion, the result would be not simply a misallocation of resources from superior to inferior uses but a shift from a positive to a zero social rate of return. In that sense the wastage would be complete.

Beyond analysis of the allocation effects of specific taxes the next logical steps for the theorist are to consider the use of taxation to control or eliminate adverse externalities,[239] and to attempt the ambitious task of designing optimal tax systems.[240] These attempts

[238] P. Taubman and R. Rasche, "Subsidies, Economic Lives, and Complete Resource Misallocation," *American Economic Review,* Vol. 61 (December 1971), pp. 938–45.

[239] See William J. Baumol, "On Taxation and the Control of Externalities," *American Economic Review,* Vol. 62 (June 1972), pp. 307–22.

[240] There has been a recent resurgence of interest in this topic. See A. B. Atkinson, " 'Maxi-Min' and Optimal Income Taxation," Discussion Paper 47 (University of *Economic Review,* Vol. 61 (March 1971), pp. 8–27, and "Optimal Taxation and J. E. Stiglitz, "The Structure of Indirect Taxation and Economic Efficiency," *Journal of Public Economics,* Vol. 1 (April 1972), pp. 97–119; Partha Dasgupta and Joseph Stiglitz, "On Optimal Taxation and Public Production," *Review of Economic Studies,* Vol. 39 (January 1972), pp. 87–103; Peter A. Diamond and James A. Mirrlees,

so far have had little impact on actual tax policy making, however. Whereas optimal economic efficiency apparently would require non-uniform commodity tax rates, both administrative simplicity and political neutrality point strongly in the opposite direction. Not only would it be costly to determine the initial set of optimal tax rates, but recurrent needs to adjust them to changing economic conditions might entail high maintenance costs as well. Even under the best administrative practice, uncertainties about the economic justification for tax rate differentials would probably exist, creating opportunities for power groups to seek to justify low rates on commodities of interest to them. These important tradeoffs have not been dealt with in the economic literature on optimal taxation.

A second difficult tradeoff, between economic efficiency and interpersonal equity, is created by the typical optimal tax rule that relatively high tax rates should be levied on commodities with low price or income elasticities of demand, many of which are necessities consumed mainly by low-income groups. While in principle this problem can be handled by adding distributional weights to the analysis so that a dollar of taxes imposes real burdens that are inversely related to income,[241] in practice the lack of any agreement on the relative weights robs the exercise of policy significance. On the other hand, if a federal negative income tax plan were in operation, adjustments could presumably be made in its basic allowances to counteract whatever undesirable regressive burdens an optimal system of federal commodity taxes would impose on the poor. Finally, as Leibenstein's development of the concept of "X-efficiency" has made clear,[242] numerous economists seriously doubt that the allocative

---

"Optimal Taxation and Public Production; I: Production Efficiency," *American Economic Review*, Vol. 61 (March 1971), pp. 8–27, and "Optimal Taxation and Public Production; II: Tax Rules," ibid. (June 1971), pp. 261–78; Avinash K. Dixit, "On the Optimum Structure of Commodity Taxes," ibid., Vol. 60 (June 1970), pp. 295–301; Abba P. Lerner, "On Optimal Taxes With an Untaxable Sector," ibid., pp. 284–94; James A. Mirrlees, "An Exploration in the Theory of Optimum Income Taxation," *Review of Economic Studies*, Vol. 38 (April 1971), pp. 175–208; James A. Mirrlees, "On Producer Taxation," ibid., Vol. 39 (January 1972), pp. 105–11; Eytan Sheshinski, "The Optimal Linear Income-tax," ibid. (July 1972), pp. 297–302; and J. E. Stiglitz and P. Dasgupta, "Differential Taxation, Public Goods, and Economic Efficiency," ibid., Vol. 38 (April 1971), pp. 151–74.

[241] See Diamond and Mirrlees, "Optimal Taxation."

[242] Harvey Leibenstein, "Allocative Efficiency vs. 'X-Efficiency,'" *American Economic Review*, Vol. 56 (June 1966), pp. 392–415; William S. Comanor and

inefficiencies that might be eliminated by comprehensive tax reform
are quantitatively significant.

## Empirical Analysis

The use of systematic, quantitative analysis of interindustry tax
differentials as a policy-making tool in this country was greatly
stimulated by rapidly rising state government needs for additional
revenue during the 1960s. In 1965 Legler and Papke applied differential impact analysis to the business tax structures of the state
of Indiana and the city of New York, and in 1969 Bahl and Shellhammer used input-output analysis to evaluate the business tax
structure of West Virginia.[243] The aim of such analyses is to measure the change that would be brought about in the distribution of
tax payments by industry group by the substitution of one equal-
yield tax for another. Since these comparisons are made without
any allowances for tax-induced changes in prices, outputs, or incomes, they are only a first, small step toward the elusive goal of the
tax analyst—the derivation of a comprehensive set of differential
incidence measures. They may, however, improve the policy maker's
ability to forecast future business tax revenues, to compare the
growth elasticities of alternative business tax structures, to assess
the relative impact of different tax policies on mobile and immobile
industries, and to estimate the extent to which state business tax
burdens are being or might be exported. In addition, when tax burdens levied at early stages of production are expected to be shifted
forward to later stages, as in the case of Indiana's and West Virginia's gross receipts taxes, input-output data and analyses are required to estimate the burden embodied in one dollar of final demand for the output of different industry groups.

---

Harvey Leibenstein, "Allocative Efficiency, X-Efficiency and the Measurement of
Welfare Losses," *Economica*, N.S., Vol. 36 (August 1969), pp. 304–09; and David
Schwartzman, "Competition and Efficiency: Comment," and Harvey Leibenstein,
"Competition and X-Efficiency: Reply," *Journal of Political Economy*, Vol. 81
(May/June 1973), pp. 756–64, 765–77.

[243] John B. Legler and James A. Papke, "Optimizing State Business Taxation: An
Application of Differential Impact Analysis," *National Tax Journal*, Vol. 18 (Sep-
tember 1965), pp. 240–46, and "Toward a Rationalization of State-Local Business
Taxation," in National Tax Association, *Proceedings of the Fifty-Eighth Annual
Conference on Taxation* (1966), pp. 541–51; and Roy W. Bahl and Kenneth L.
Shellhammer, "Evaluating the State Business Tax Structure: An Application of
Input-Output Analysis," *National Tax Journal*, Vol. 22 (June 1969), pp. 203–16.

These accomplishments leave unresolved the question of whether the use of differential impact analysis will in practice accelerate or retard the process of tax reform. By revealing the unneutralities of existing tax structures, such analysis should stimulate desires for change, but it may sharpen opposition to reform by revealing the anatomy of its differential impact, particularly to potential losers. The net outcome may simply be to strengthen the maxim that "old taxes are good taxes," and to confine structural tax reform to occasions involving major changes in total tax revenues. At the same time, by convincing people that old taxes are good only in comparison to new ones, the analysis may strengthen popular pressures for aggregate tax reduction. On the other hand, there is the possibility, dear to tax specialists, that better data and better analyses can lift public discussion of tax changes from the mere comparison of individual money gains and losses to the higher plane of the public good to be achieved by the use of more equitable and more efficient tax instruments.

Development of reliable measures of the efficiency costs of taxation would clearly be a major contribution to such enlightenment. Although the problems involved are massive, some progress has been made in this search, mainly by use of the theoretical framework developed by Harberger to deal with the incidence and efficiency effects of taxation. Harberger has been a major contributor to these endeavors. Early in the postwar discussions of federal tax reform, for example, he provided the provocative estimate that existing tax favors to mineral industries created a situation "in which it takes $2 million of capital invested in mineral exploration to produce as much product as $1 million of capital invested in other industries."[244] In 1959, for congressional hearings on revision of the federal income tax laws, he extended his purview to the whole corporation income tax and estimated its welfare costs for each of fifty-four industry groups for the 1953–55 period. The aggregated costs came to approximately $500 million, or slightly more than 2.5 percent of the total yield of the corporation income tax.[245]

[244] Arnold C. Harberger, "The Taxation of Mineral Industries," in *Federal Tax Policy for Economic Growth and Stability*, Papers Submitted by Panelists Appearing before the Subcommittee on Tax Policy, Joint Committee on the Economic Report, 84 Cong. 1 sess. (1955), p. 439.

[245] Arnold C. Harberger, "The Corporation Income Tax: An Empirical Appraisal," in *Tax Revision Compendium*, Compendium of Papers on Broadening the

This rough approximation, a pioneering measure of the excess burden of taxation, has been refined in a number of ways. Leonard Rosenberg extended the analysis to include the general property tax, the interindustry allocation of which was a major research project.[246] Using these allocations for forty-seven industry groups, with the income of unincorporated business in each group divided into its labor and capital components, Rosenberg placed the average annual welfare cost of the corporate profits and general property taxes in the 1953–59 period at $587 million, or just under 2 percent of the tax revenues collected. Harberger used these allocations in his two-sector model of corporate tax incidence to extend the analysis to all U.S. taxes on income from capital in the 1953–59 period and to investigate the effects on the welfare cost estimates of the use of different values for the three key substitution parameters.[247] The result was an interval estimate of efficiency costs of $1 billion–$3 billion a year (2.4–7.0 percent of the tax revenues involved), though Harberger preferred the narrower range of $1.5 billion–$2.5 billion a year.[248] Finally, Shoven and Whalley, in an analysis of differential tax incidence based on the Harberger-Rosenberg 1953–59 data, widened considerably the range of alternative estimates, mainly in the upward direction, from 2.2 percent of the tax revenue at the bottom to 11.7 percent at the top.[249]

Empirical estimation of the welfare costs of taxation is clearly in its infancy. Enough has been done, however, to indicate that it is a fertile field for fiscal research. Though many estimates are small enough to suggest that allocative efficiency in taxation may not be a significant policy issue, others are large enough to suggest that policy

---

Tax Base, Submitted to the House Committee on Ways and Means (1959), Vol. 1, pp. 231–36.

[246] Leonard Gerson Rosenberg, "Taxation of Income from Capital, by Industry Group," in Harberger and Bailey, *The Taxation of Income from Capital*, pp. 123–84.

[247] Harberger, "Efficiency Effects of Taxes on Income from Capital." The three parameters are the elasticities of substitution between capital and labor in production in the two sectors and the elasticity of substitution between the outputs of the two sectors in consumption.

[248] Ibid., p. 116.

[249] "A General Equilibrium Calculation of the Effects of Differential Taxation," pp. 306–07. In some of their calculations the authors also allowed for variation in the aggregate supply of labor, but since no measure of the value of leisure time was included in the welfare cost estimates derived in these cases, the estimates themselves are omitted from the range given here.

makers would be well advised to find ways of minimizing the potentially adverse allocational effects of taxation. Among the hazards to be avoided are high tax rates on products or factors subject to high elasticities of substitution, any piling of distortions on other distortions, and tax investment incentives that tend to shorten the economic lives of capital assets.

## Taxation and Economic Growth

In a time of deep concern about the potential perils of economic growth and of renewed interest in the classical theory of a stationary state,[250] a discussion of taxation and economic growth may seem anachronistic. The case for growth, however, is far from lost.[251] Though the topic may lack the glamor it had when the sluggish growth performance of the U.S. economy compared unfavorably with that of other advanced industrial nations,[252] growth still has wide appeal not only as a source of enrichment but even as a means of survival.

The relatively heavy U.S. reliance on direct taxes on income and profits and relatively light use of indirect taxes on sales or value added were in the postwar years suspected causes of the comparatively slow growth rate. That issue and others bearing on the optimal structure of federal taxation were the subjects of a conference of experts held at the Brookings Institution in October 1963.[253] Two months later, foreign tax experts held a similar conference on possible tax stimulants of economic growth.[254] The latter conference con-

[250] See, for example, Donella H. Meadows and others, *The Limits to Growth* (Universe Books, 1972); and Herman E. Daly (ed.), *Toward a Steady-State Economy* (W. H. Freeman, 1973).

[251] See William D. Nordhaus and James Tobin, "Is Growth Obsolete?" in *Economic Growth*, Fiftieth Anniversary Colloquium V (Columbia University Press for National Bureau of Economic Research, 1972); and Peter Passell and Leonard Ross, *The Retreat from Riches: Affluence and Its Enemies* (Viking, 1973).

[252] Between 1955 and 1962, U.S. real national income per capita grew at an average annual rate of only 1 percent, Italy's at 5.1 percent, Denmark's and Germany's at over 4 percent, and France's at 3.8 percent; Edward F. Denison, assisted by Jean-Pierre Poullier, *Why Growth Rates Differ: Postwar Experience in Nine Western Countries* (Brookings Institution, 1967), p. 18.

[253] *The Role of Direct and Indirect Taxes.*

[254] *Foreign Tax Policies and Economic Growth*, A Conference Report of the National Bureau of Economic Research and the Brookings Institution (Columbia University Press for National Bureau of Economic Research, 1966).

sidered so many tax instruments, applied under such widely differing economic and political circumstances, that very little general agreement could have been expected.[255] E. Gordon Keith in his summary reported that "schemes to encourage personal savings among lower income bracket individuals" were generally agreed to be "very costly and were not as a rule very effective." The majority of the participants felt that "special tax measures intended to encourage business saving and investment . . . had been effective not only in directing investment into certain favored sectors of industry but also in raising the general level of investment." As the conference progressed, the lack of knowledge about "the actual effects of specific tax measures on the savings and investment decisions of individuals and corporations" became more and more evident.[256] Since then, many theoretical and empirical research studies have been devoted to that area of uncertainty. The 1967 Brookings conference on investment tax incentives, though it "did not resolve the issue of the effectiveness of the tax incentives that were used," included analyses that were "substantially more sophisticated and comprehensive" than earlier studies and that went "a long way toward formulating the theoretical framework and developing the methodology for analyzing the effect of various economic factors on investment."[257]

Determination of the effects of tax policies on business investment is, of course, only the first step in the estimation of their effects on economic growth. How productive is new capital investment at the margin? How likely is it to produce sustainable rather than merely temporary increases in the rate of economic growth? To what extent will measured increases in growth rates be accompanied by unmeasured, and perhaps unmeasurable, environmental costs that should be taken into account? All of these difficult questions must be answered before the impact of taxation on economic growth, even by this one route, can be realistically assessed. As for the marginal productivity of business investment, the crucial unresolved issue is the extent to which advances in technical knowledge must be embodied in new capital assets before they exert an in-

---

[255] The countries covered were Japan, West Germany, Italy, the Netherlands, France, Sweden, and Great Britain.

[256] Ibid., pp. 36–37.

[257] Gary Fromm, "Introduction," in *Tax Incentives*, p. 1.

fluence on the rate of economic growth. In a highly influential paper testing the plausibility of the embodiment hypothesis, Solow estimated that a 1 percentage point increase in the aggregate growth rate could be achieved by an increase of only 2.5 percentage points in the fraction of national income saved and invested.[258] If the embodiment of technical advances occurs mainly in inframarginal investments, however, as suggested by Harberger, a 1 percentage point increase in the growth rate might require as much as a 10 percentage point increase in the saving-investment ratio.[259] The vast difference between these two estimates of the effectiveness of tax policies, combined with other uncertainties about the ability of different tax incentives to increase new investment substantially, might incline experts to look elsewhere for their growth policies were it not for greater uncertainties there. Moreover, Denison in comparing national growth rates concluded that "by any simple test . . . the United States has done less than Europe to stimulate growth by investment in nonresidential structures and equipment and inventories," and that this was "the only important field in which the United States was doing less."[260]

All things considered, investment tax incentives would be an important component of any set of national tax policies designed to stimulate economic growth. The other components can usefully be discussed in terms of three broad categories of tax policy suggested by E. Cary Brown: (1) structural changes that increase the level of taxation, both government expenditures and the aggregate level of employment being held constant; (2) structural changes that leave both the total amount of taxes collected and their distribution among different income and wealth groups unchanged; and (3) structural changes that alter the distribution of a given amount of tax revenue among different income and wealth groups.[261]

An increase in the level of federal taxation relative to the level of federal expenditures, which would increase the size of the full employment budget surplus (or decrease the deficit), would release

[258] Robert M. Solow, "Technical Progress, Capital Formation, and Economic Growth," in American Economic Association, *Papers and Proceedings of the Seventy-fourth Annual Meeting* (*American Economic Review*, Vol. 52, May 1962), pp. 76–86.

[259] *The Role of Direct and Indirect Taxes*, pp. 66–70.

[260] *Why Growth Rates Differ*, p. 343.

[261] *The Role of Direct and Indirect Taxes*, pp. 73–75.

resources from existing uses; it would be the task of monetary policy to see that those resources were redirected mainly into growth-stimulating activities. How successfully they might do this is a function in part of the ability of different tax plans to discourage household expenditures from going into relatively unproductive types of consumption rather than into saving, personal and business investment spending, and consumption that contributes to human capital formation.[262] The main candidates for addition to the present federal tax structure for this purpose would be a national retail sales tax, a consumption-type value added tax, or an expenditure tax.[263] In each case the most productive types of consumption could be protected by the use of exemptions and reduced tax rates. If in the most industrialized nations there is "very little, if any, gainful consumption at the margin in any household,"[264] few outright exemptions would be required for growth policy purposes. There would be distributional considerations, but any undesired, inequality-increasing effects of a broad-based consumption tax could presumably be handled both in the design of the tax itself and by appropriate concurrent changes in the structure of the federal individual income tax.[265]

[262] It is also a function of how successfully monetary ease, lower interest rates, and higher liquidity can stimulate capital formation.

[263] Because of its obvious administrative and compliance costs, expenditure taxation has been mainly a scholarly concern rather than an active interest of policy makers. However, Patrick L. Kelley has concluded that "in the context of highly developed societies, there seems little reason to doubt the possibility of effectively imposing an expenditure tax"; "Is an Expenditure Tax Feasible?" *National Tax Journal*, Vol. 23 (September 1970), p. 253. See also Richard E. Slitor, "Administrative Aspects of Expenditures Taxation," in Musgrave, *Broad-Based Taxes*, pp. 227–63.

[264] As Shoup suggests in *Public Finance*, p. 593. Gainful consumption is that which increases national output, either concurrently or subsequently, by more than the amount of the consumption; ibid., p. 592.

[265] For an individually self-assessed expenditure tax a progressive rate structure would be appropriate, and for either a retail sales or value added tax a credit-rebate arrangement tied to the individual income tax would be best. Joseph A. Pechman and Benjamin A. Okner have simulated the effects, on average federal tax rates of families at different 1972 income levels, of expanding federal tax revenues by $12 billion by several alternative income and sales tax plans. For the 75 percent of families with annual incomes below $17,000, an income tax surcharge, a uniform percentage point increase in all federal individual income tax bracket rates, and a broad-based value added tax (VAT) with a low-income credit would all impose approximately the same additional tax burdens. Above $17,000 the VAT burdens would be significantly below those of the two income tax plans, but these differentials could be offset by combining enactment of a VAT with suitable structural income tax reforms. Charles

Those growth-stimulating tax policies that alter neither the total amount nor the vertical distribution of tax revenues focus attention on the broad question of choice of tax base. Among the main alternatives—income, consumption, and wealth—the choice does not appear to be very important as far as economic growth is concerned. Apart from their differential distribution effects, income and consumption taxes have long been regarded as having roughly equivalent effects on incentives to work, and empirical evidence confirms that conclusion. Either a wealth tax or a tightly defined and administered gift and inheritance tax might be more favorable to work effort. The general absence of such levies from modern tax systems, however, precludes any direct empirical assessment of their impact on the work-leisure choice.

Evidence as to the differential effects of the three tax bases on household saving and business investment decisions is mixed. Econometric investment models are not yet able to predict definitively the effects of changes in rates of return or in the rental prices of capital assets. While there is no empirical evidence that a shift from income to consumption taxation would raise the personal saving rate significantly, economists differ in their interpretation of this situation. On the one hand, Harberger has argued that "it would not require a phenomenal responsiveness of savings to the net rate of return in order to generate a fairly significant welfare cost as a consequence of the distortion of the savings-consumption decision."[266] On the other hand, Robert Hall after analyzing the effects

---

L. Schultze and others, *Setting National Priorities: The 1973 Budget* (Brookings Institution, 1972), pp. 440–43.

Credit sales taxes are now an established feature of state revenue systems; see Advisory Commission on Intergovernmental Relations, *State-Local Finances: Significant Features and Suggested Legislation, 1972 Edition* (Government Printing Office, 1972), pp. 214–16. For an analysis of the first state sales tax credit, adopted by Indiana in 1963, see James A. Papke, "New Perspectives in Retail Sales Taxation," in National Tax Association, *Proceedings of the Fifty-Eighth Annual Conference on Taxation*, pp. 258–70.

[266] *The Role of Direct and Indirect Taxes*, p. 61. The distortion in question is the gap created by an income tax between the after-tax rate of return, which governs personal saving-consumption choices, and the before-tax rate of return, which should govern society's choice between aggregate investment and consumption. In terms of Harberger's measure of welfare costs the loss from that distortion would be $\frac{1}{2}\Delta S[t/(1-t)]$, where $\Delta S$ is the change in saving produced by a shift from consumption to income taxation, and $t$ is the rate of the proportional income tax. For a tax rate

of replacing the federal income tax by a federal sales tax that maintained the same level of aggregate demand concluded that "the argument from economic efficiency for a consumption tax is weak indeed. A careful examination of the life-cycle model of intertemporal equilibrium has shown that while there is an inefficiency associated with an income tax, its steady-state value is quite small, and can only be escaped by a temporary further reduction in consumption."[267] Samuel B. Chase, Jr., in his summary of the first NBER-Brookings conference concluded that though "few issues of substance were unanimously agreed upon . . . the proceedings of the conference, viewed in their entirety, provide little support for a major move in the direction of commodity taxation and away from income taxation."[268] For the present it appears that choices among alternative bases for U.S. taxation at the federal, state, or local level may rest on considerations other than the potential differential effects on economic growth.[269]

Growth-stimulating tax changes that alter the vertical distribution of income and wealth are perhaps the most important, and certainly the most controversial, of all. Many tend to increase inequalities in the distribution of income. Investment tax incentives do so because business and corporate source income is much more unequally distributed than the other major types of personal income; any significant reduction in work disincentives would probably require lower marginal income tax rates at the highest income levels; and a strong positive correlation between marginal propensities to save and family income levels would indicate that reducing tax progressivity might stimulate personal saving propensities sub-

---

of 33.33 percent, the welfare cost would be $\frac{1}{4} \Delta S$. Many other economists who doubt that private saving decisions reflect the real social rates of return available to the economy as a whole support government policies designed either to narrow the gap or to compensate for its effects on economic growth. See James Tobin, "Economic Growth as an Objective of Government Policy," in Walter W. Heller (ed.), *Perspectives on Economic Growth* (Random House, 1968), pp. 99–110.

[267] Robert E. Hall, "Consumption Taxes Versus Income Taxes: Implications for Economic Growth," in National Tax Association, *Proceedings of the Sixty-First Annual Conference on Taxation* (1969), p. 144. See also Albert Ando and Franco Modigliani, "The 'Life Cycle' Hypothesis of Saving: Aggregate Implications and Tests," *American Economic Review*, Vol. 53 (March 1963), pp. 55–84.

[268] *The Role of Direct and Indirect Taxes*, p. 313.

[269] For further analysis of the economic effects of taxes on income, consumption, and wealth see Goode, *The Individual Income Tax*, Chap. 3.

stantially. The one potentially positive contribution is in diverting consumption to human capital formation. Since opportunities for increasing economic growth by such means exist mainly at the lowest income levels, income-equalizing policies, such as a negative income tax, are called for.

It appears, therefore, that tax rates under a growth-stimulating policy would be negative at the lowest income levels, becoming positive and increasing steadily as family income rose, but moderating or flattening out as disincentive-prone levels were reached. The total U.S. tax-transfer system is, in fact, in general accordance with this pattern. Viewing government transfer payments as negative taxes, the Musgraves estimated for 1968 that the following percentages of income were paid in federal, state, and local taxes by families with incomes below $10,400 a year:[270]

| Income | Taxes as percentage of income |
|---|---|
| Less than $4,000 | −64.3 |
| $4,000–5,700 | 9.1 |
| 5,700–7,900 | 23.4 |
| 7,900–10,400 | 28.6 |

The estimated tax burden rose to 32 percent of incomes between $12,500 and $17,500 and to 36 percent of incomes above $92,000.

These estimates, to be sure, depend critically on the assumptions made about the incidence of the various taxes, and especially the corporate income, general property, and social security payroll taxes. The Musgraves calculated the tax burdens under different incidence assumptions. The estimates given in the foregoing tabulation allocated the corporate tax half to consumers and half to recipients of capital income, the residential property tax to tenants and homeowners, the business property tax half to consumers and half to recipients of capital income, and the payroll tax on employers to consumers. Other calculations assumed the corporate tax to be borne by shareholders, the property tax to be allocated entirely to recipients of capital income, and the employer share of the payroll levy to be shifted backward to workers. Under these assumptions the tax-transfer system appears considerably more progressive: the net tax rate on families with incomes between $4,000 and $5,700, for example, would fall from 9.1 percent to 4.7 per-

[270] Musgrave and Musgrave, *Public Finance in Theory and Practice*, pp. 368–73.

cent, and the rate on incomes above $92,000 would rise from 36 percent to 63 percent. Conversely, if both the corporate and property taxes were assumed to rest on consumers, average tax rate progression would be reduced, particularly at the higher income levels. For the $4,000–$5,700 income group, for example, the net tax rate would be 10 percent and above $92,000 it would barely be 27 percent.[271]

The progressivity of the U.S. tax system, and hence the possible tradeoffs between redistributional tax policies and growth tax policies, clearly depend critically on tax incidence. Until some of the uncertainties about incidence are resolved, this particular tax policy issue is likely to remain highly controversial. Human investment may therefore be a more attractive growth target for tax policy than business investment,[272] and changes in the structure of business investment may be less controversial than changes in its total amount. In addition, the ability of accelerated depreciation and investment tax credits to reallocate business funds among alternative uses appears to be less open to question than their ability to increase the aggregate amount of business investment.

## Conclusion

Though much has been accomplished in the theoretical and empirical analyses of the economic effects of taxation in the last two decades, few definitive answers to important policy questions have been obtained. There is room for both quiet satisfaction and a firm resolve to push ahead into the many difficult areas of fiscal research, particularly those dealing with the magnitudes of the key structural parameters of tax policy. One might dispute James Buchanan's assertion that some years ago public finance was "a dull, unimaginative, extremely limited, and almost irrelevant subdiscipline," but it is easy to agree wholeheartedly with his judgment that it is today "one of the most exciting areas in political economy."[273]

[271] Ibid., p. 370.
[272] For a criticism of the federal income tax treatment of educational expenditures see Goode, *The Individual Income Tax*, pp. 82–93.
[273] Buchanan, "Discussion," in *Public Expenditures and Taxation*, Fiftieth Anniversary Colloquium IV (Columbia University Press for National Bureau of Economic Research, 1972), p. 63.

# Public Expenditure Budgeting

PETER O. STEINER

# Public Expenditure Budgeting

THE BURGEONING LITERATURE by economists on the theory and practice of public expenditures is already the subject of several bibliographies and of at least four major attempts at survey and synthesis. To Otto Eckstein's pioneer survey have recently been added those by Prest and Turvey, Harberger, and Marglin.[1] I do not propose to render these papers obsolete by an encyclopedic survey, nor to sift for the nugget of revealed truth in this large literature. I intend instead a somewhat broader but necessarily personal statement of the conceptual issues that underlie the analysis of the political-economic process of reaching and implementing public expenditure decisions. My chief prejudice is the belief that more progress has been made in understanding the technical issues than the conceptual ones, and that therefore it is the latter that deserve extended discussion.

At any point in history—say, the United States in 1969—it is

[1] Otto Eckstein, "A Survey of the Theory of Public Expenditure Criteria," in *Public Finances: Needs, Sources, and Utilization* (Princeton University Press for the National Bureau of Economic Research, 1961), pp. 439–504; Alan R. Prest and Ralph Turvey, "Cost-Benefit Analysis: A Survey," *Economic Journal,* Vol. 75 (December 1965), pp. 683–735; Arnold C. Harberger, "Survey of Literature on Cost-Benefit Analysis for Industrial Project Evaluation," in *Evaluation of Industrial Projects,* United Nations Industrial Development Organization, Project Formulation and Evaluation Series, Vol. 1 (United Nations, 1968), pp. 229–46; and Stephen A. Marglin, *Public Investment Criteria; Benefit-Cost Analysis for Planned Economic Growth* (Cambridge: Massachusetts Institute of Technology Press, 1967).

clear that the society has decided that certain activities are legitimately performed by governments. By long tradition many services are provided by various levels of government and are paid for by funds raised through exercise of the police powers. Others are left to the private sector. Even in the face of the significant debate about the proper dividing line between the private and public sectors, there is a large, relatively stable, and broadly uncontroversial governmental sector of this economy, and of every other economy.

In order to focus on certain critical issues, I shall suppress some real distinctions and create some arbitrary ones. The most important simplification made here is to treat government as a single cohesive force, thus neglecting intergovernmental transfers as well as conflicts of authority and philosophy among federal, state, and local governments. The most important complication is to pretend that the theory of public expenditure policy is in reality two very different sets of propositions. One may be called the theory of the marginal public expenditure. It takes as given the legitimacy of government activity, and is concerned with how the public decision maker chooses among competing demands for his limited resources. The other set of propositions may be called the theory of the public interest, and concerns the way in which demands for public activity arise, are articulated, and are legitimized.

This is a separation of convenience, not of fact. For example, every marginal decision to expand some public program into a new area implies a legitimate public purpose in that area; often, proposed discrete extensions pose questions of public interest. Similarly, making a marginal decision rationally requires an objective function, the arguments for which relate directly to various aspects of the public interest.

There is one decisive reason for treating the theories separately. It is, simply, that at this time the available theories are of very different levels of adequacy in the two cases. For the marginal decision a well-developed, highly articulated, and largely uncontroversial set of theories exists and awaits practical implementation. But with respect to the nature of the public interest, theorists are primitives in the sophisticated world of public decision makers. Theorists know how to choose between two public housing proposals but not whether public housing is right and proper, while bureaucrats and senators have no difficulty in principle in deciding when public housing is required, but lack fine devices for choosing among alternative schemes of public housing. Indeed they usually do not wish to consider very many alternatives.

The first part of this essay deals with what I consider to be the difficult and controversial theory of the public interest; the second with the theory of the marginal decision; and the third briefly with the relation between these theories and present budgetary practice. Many other issues of necessity are ignored. In particular because of limits of space and competence the emphasis is heavier on new program decisions than on levels of operation of current programs, and on expenditure policies rather than on repayment and reimbursement policies.

# THE THEORY
# OF THE PUBLIC INTEREST

DEFINITION OF THE PUBLIC INTEREST is genuinely difficult because the notion embodies at least two implicit distinctions. One is between collective action and individual action, the other between public (that is, governmental) action and private action. Each is important. It is necessary to ask what it is that persuades members of a group to seek a collective solution to a problem rather than to rely solely on individual action. It is also necessary to ask whether collective desires merit public support, public indifference, or public hostility. Finally, if collective desires are in some sense legitimized, the appropriate form of collective action remains a question. There is no simple dichotomy between individual private activities and collective public action. Instead there are various kinds of collectivities —clubs, unions, churches, and political parties, as well as governments; and there are various degrees of public involvement from outright prohibition of certain activities, to taxes or subsidies, to direct public provision of services.

The *desire* for collective action, which underlies many demands for public provision of goods and services, arises when a group feels it cannot achieve its objectives unaided. But mere demands, however genuine, are not enough. Aid to the needy aged (or unattractive prostitutes) may be the only effective device by which this portion of the population may be assured a subsistence level of living; price supports may provide farmers (or racetrack touts) with protection against excessive competition that would be unavailable without collective action; a program to place a man on the moon by 1970 (or to commit genocide) can be visualized only as a collective program. Each of these problems transcends individual solution and thus gets either collective solution or none at all; but by itself that does not render them legitimate activities of government.

Moreover, the required use of collective action is not only not sufficient to define public activities, but also not strictly necessary. Governments may be asked to provide education, housing, transportation, and recreation even though private alternatives exist. The demand may rest upon considerations of efficiency, but it may also reflect captious preference or even prejudice. What leads to the choice of public provision from among alternative means of meeting particular ends?

Casual observation suggests that the public interest may be served by providing or encouraging provision of a variety of goods or services, and by nonprovision or discouragement of others. The former goods and services may be loosely defined as vested with the public interest, or as public goods.

## The Nature of Public Goods

Serving the public interest may take many forms: provision of goods, subsidization of their provision by private means, enactment of laws that impede or prohibit their provision or constrain the form in which they are provided. The focus here will be on policies that involve public expenditures. It should be remembered that choice among alternative available means is always an element in important policy issues.

The goods and services provided by public expenditures or encouraged by public policies can be described and classified in a number of different ways. Though "public goods" are spoken of as a single category, any review of public policies shows great diversity. Some kinds of public goods are provided only publicly because there exists no reasonable private alternative way of providing them. This can happen (as in the case of national parks, national defense, or space research) because there is no private mechanism to pay for these goods, or it can happen (as in the case of sewage disposal or justice) because compulsory use of the good by all is required to permit its enjoyment by any group. Other public goods, such as public housing or public education, may be functionally similar to available private alternatives, but qualitatively different in ways that ▪ society prefers. Still other public goods may differ from private ones only in the distribution of beneficiaries and costs.

If the proper domain of public expenditure policy is public goods, their definition becomes vital. The concept has been defined in many ways, and for diverse purposes, and it is not surprising that definitions motivated by purposes other than understanding the rationale and process of public expenditure policy are not wholly satisfactory.

"A *public good* is any good or service which is *de facto* provided for or subsidized through government budget finance."[2] This definition is neat but not helpful. It does not name the attributes of a potential good or service which a policy maker should take into account in deciding whether to provide the goods. In this definition "publicness" is wholly a matter of legislative designation, not of any characteristic of the good or service.

In many ways, an intrinsic definition based upon technical characteristics of goods or services would be desirable. The perfect collective consumption good provides such a definition. An impressive array of economists have so defined public goods.[3] Dorfman has recently written:

There are certain goods that have the peculiarity that once they are available no one can be precluded from enjoying them whether he contributed to their provision or not. These are the public goods. Law and order is an

[2] William C. Birdsall, "A Study of the Demand for Public Goods," in Richard A. Musgrave (ed.), *Essays in Fiscal Federalism* (Brookings Institution, 1965), p. 235.

[3] These include Paul A. Samuelson, "The Pure Theory of Public Expenditure," *Review of Economics and Statistics*, Vol. 36 (November 1954), pp. 387–89; Robert H. Strotz, "Two Propositions Related to Public Goods," *Review of Economics and Statistics*, Vol. 40 (November 1958), pp. 329–31; Howard R. Bowen, "The Interpretation of Voting in the Allocation of Economic Resources," *Quarterly Journal of Economics*, Vol. 58 (November 1943), pp. 27–48; Albert Breton, "A Theory

example, and there are many others too familiar to make further exemplification worth while. Their essential characteristic is that they are enjoyed but not consumed, [and that their benefits are derived] without any act of appropriation.[4]

This kind of very narrow definition was designed to demonstrate that there may be a type of activity that is socially desirable but that will not be achieved by the private market unaided. It serves well the purpose of showing the existence of public goods. It can prove a hindrance, however, if it leads to the view that goods which conform to it are the only class of goods which government can legitimately provide. In fact, examples are hard to find, and the great bulk of nondefense public expenditures covers goods and services that do not meet the definition. Roads, schools, welfare payments, recreational facilities, housing, public power, and irrigation, among others, are important classes of public expenditures that some can be precluded from enjoying, that can be consumed in whole or in part, and that technically can be made subject to user charges. The concept of the perfect collective consumption good, while sufficient to justify public expenditure, is not necessary nor does it embrace much of what public expenditure policy concerns. It does, however, identify certain characteristics such as nonconsumption, nonappropriation, and the existence of externalities that may give a good its public goods aspect.

Externalities are very important, as has been recognized for a long time. Knut Wicksell (himself citing earlier authority) put it eloquently in 1896:

If the community or at any rate a sizeable part of it has an interest in a particular utility accruing to an individual, then it would clearly be unreasonable to allow the creation of that more general utility to depend solely upon that individual: he might not value the state activity highly enough to make the sacrifice of paying the required fee or charge, or else ignorance may cause him or poverty force him to do without the service.

---

of the Demand for Public Goods," *Canadian Journal of Economics and Political Science*, Vol. 32 (November 1966), pp. 455–67; and R. Dorfman, "General Equilibrium with Public Goods," in J. Margolis and H. Guitton (eds.), *Public Economics: An Analysis of Public Production and Consumption and their Relations to the Private Sectors* (Macmillan, 1969).

  [4] Ibid.

Herein lies the chief justification of the modern demands for free or very cheap process of law, elementary education, medical care, certain public health measures, etc.[5]

While they are important, it would be easy to follow externalities too far. Does any good which produces an externality become a public good no matter how incidental the externality? Few goods do not meet this test and thus this definition fails to provide guidance as to which goods ought to be candidates for public provision, just as it fails to explain which goods are publicly provided.

Since standard definitions are not fully satisfactory, let me try a new one: *Any publicly induced or provided collective good is a public good.* A collective good in this definition is not necessarily a collective consumption good. Collective goods arise whenever some segment of the public collectively wants and is prepared to pay for a bundle of goods and services other than what the unhampered market will produce. A collective good thus requires that there be (1) an appreciable difference in either quantity or quality between it and the alternative the private market would produce, and (2) a viable demand for the difference.

Collective goods may be privately or publicly provided. Cooperatives, unions, vigilante organizations, country clubs, car pools, and trade associations are all examples of private organizations that arise in response to collective demands for private collective goods or services. When the coordinating mechanisms for providing a collective good invoke the powers of the state, it is here defined as a public good. This definition requires that a public good meet the tests of a collective good. Notice that public provision by itself does not create public goods. This definition is virtually implicit in the discussions of Head, Musgrave, Olson, Weisbrod, and Margolis.[6] It provides an

[5] Knut Wicksell, "A New Principle of Just Taxation," reprinted in Richard A. Musgrave and Alan T. Peacock (eds.), *Classics in the Theory of Public Finance* (Macmillan, 1958), p. 98; translated from *Finanztheoretische Untersuchungen* (Jena: Gustav Fischer, 1896).

[6] John Graeme Head, "Public Goods and Public Policy," *Public Finance*, Vol. 17, No. 3 (1962), pp. 197–219; Musgrave, *Theory of Public Finance;* Mancur Olson, Jr., *The Logic of Collective Action* (Harvard University Press, 1965); Burton A. Weisbrod, "Collective-Consumption Services of Individual-Consumption Goods," *Quarterly Journal of Economics*, Vol. 78 (August 1964), pp. 471–77; and Julius Margolis, "Secondary Benefits, External Economies, and the Justification of Public Investment," *Review of Economics and Statistics*, Vol. 39 (August 1957), pp. 284–91.

analytic framework for considering the various sources of public goods.

A most important aspect of this definition is that it makes publicness not an all-or-nothing attribute, but one that may apply merely to particular aspects of a good. While there are cases (for example, national defense) in which the choice is between public provision and no provision, and it is thus argued that the good is entirely a public good, the more common situation is for goods to comprise a variety of services, only some of which have the attributes of collective goods. Given sufficient importance, these aspects of collective interest may lead to public provision of either these aspects or the entire good, including its noncollective aspects. Thus provision of smog control or river purification attacks a particular externality of private production. In contrast public housing provides individuals with services they would otherwise have purchased privately, along with the distinctive public services that public housing is supposed to entail.

Such mixed goods test and stretch definitions. Public education and public housing reflect both quantitative and qualitative differences from the comparable privately produced or producible goods. If the differences are intended and desired, they constitute public goods in this definition. In Olson's phrase, "the achievement of any common goal or the satisfaction of any common interest means that a [collective] good has been provided for that group."[7]

This somewhat vague notion of public goods can be filled out by a more detailed classification of different types of public goods.

## A Classification of Public Goods

I have, in effect, defined the vector of public goods as a vector of differences between the goods and services the private economy is motivated to provide and the goods and services the public wants, is willing to pay for, and expects its government to assist it in achieving.[8] This is, to an important degree, a normative definition,

---

[7] *Logic of Collective Action*, p. 15. The word in brackets is "public" in the original. Elsewhere in his book Olson refers to groups other than political states. But it is clear that the notion of a public good as provided by a government, as used here, is also intended.

[8] The identification of the public is deferred for the moment.

and much of the debate about the appropriate elements of the public goods vector is a normative debate. But there is a positive aspect as well: What is it about particular goods and services that makes them candidates for public consideration? What is it that makes certain activities the traditional province of governments?

It seems worthwhile to distinguish three types of public goods: (1) those arising from intrinsic, perhaps technical, characteristics of specific goods that result in externalities that are not effectively marketed; (2) those arising from imperfections in market mechanisms, rather than in the nature of the goods or services themselves; (3) those arising from concern with the quality or nature of the environment rather than aspects of particular goods or markets. These become, in order, increasingly elusive, but it is impossible to capture the flavor of actual government expenditure programs without all of them.

## Public Goods Arising from Nonmarketable Services of Particular Goods

The precondition for a discrepancy between public wants and private supplies lies in the existence of externalities (or, as they are sometimes called, spillovers or third-party effects). Any time provision of a good or service yields side effects the value of which is not reflected in the prices of the outputs sold or the resources used, external economies or diseconomies are produced. There can be many reasons for such externalities: Private producers may use resources they do not consider scarce, or produce by-products that they do not consider valuable because they cannot control and market them. Familiar examples are discharges of noxious wastes into water or air; downstream navigational or flood control consequences of a private power dam; civic beautification or uglification incident upon building of private golf courses, factories, or slaughterhouses. Because some of the resources used or outputs produced are not correctly valued by the market, there is every reason to expect the market to misuse them. Thus, simply for efficiency's sake, collective concern and public action may be required to allocate resources in accord with true valuations. Whether such externalities (which must surely be present to some extent in every good) justify public notice and action depends upon the benefits to be achieved measured against the costs of interference. People will disagree about the costs of interference or the proper cutoff level; but these are matters different from the nature and size of the externalities.

The perfect collective consumption good is really an extreme case of externalities: All of the output is regarded as individually unmarketable; all of the benefits are external. The outputs of those goods from which one cannot be excluded as a consumer—and thus for which one cannot be compelled to pay his share of the cost of provision—play a large role in the thinking of those who have been concerned to derive a legitimate role for public activity. Defense, public health, law and order, and hurricane watches are familiar examples. The common practice of listing a few examples (and not pressing them very hard) and adding, "There are many other examples"[9] is close to fraudulent. If nonexcludability implies no one can conceivably be excluded, the list of such goods is short indeed. One need not police the ghetto nor defend Alaska. Television signals can be scrambled so as to exclude those who will not buy the unscrambler. Movie houses, concert halls, hospitals, and colleges all use walls to exclude those who will not meet the requirements placed upon their use.

Collective goods may arise because exclusion would be relatively costly rather than because it is impossible. If at any moment this cost is above a certain level, there may be no effective private supply of the good. But in other cases the cost of exclusion may be annoying rather than prohibitive and potential consumers may urge public action merely to avoid bearing the costs. Put differently, the cost of arranging exclusion may be an avoidable externality.

Implicit in this discussion is an important attribute of the public collective good: the willingness to appeal to the police power of the state. One can slide in imperceptible steps from situations where there is no viable alternative means of providing the good, to cases where the alternative seems unnecessarily costly, to cases where the alternative, while not very costly, is simply judged to be less desirable, and finally to cases where the alternative differs only in who pays for it.

There is real purpose in downgrading the distinction between inability and unwillingness to provide a good privately. If a practical definition of specific collective consumption goods and services is to

---

[9] See, for example, Richard G. Lipsey and Peter O. Steiner, *Economics* (Harper & Row, 1966), p. 497.

be established, it seems difficult to escape the view that a judgment is required about reasons for turning to the political process and the coercive power of the state, rather than dealing with the second-best solution. These reasons must be judged meritorious by the social decision processes. *If this is so, collective consumption goods are defined by, as much as they define, the exercise of legitimate governmental decision processes.*

Among the positive issues that underlie the normative debate about whether a particular collective good ought to be publicly provided are (1) whether private market alternatives to public provision are impossible, impractical, merely costly, or simply unwanted; (2) why the market solution is unsatisfactory to members of the group and to society as a whole; and (3) what the identity of the group of beneficiaries is. The last deserves comment.

A collective good need not provide joint benefits to all members of a society, only to some subgroup. But which group? The larger the group the more persuasive its demand for public action is likely to be, or (put differently) the less willing its members will be to accept a costly alternative. There are bases other than size for weighing the merits of the demands of any group, and these may vary over time. Importers, farmers, labor unions, small businessmen, and minority groups are among the identifiable groups that have asked and received special treatment. Today, for example, our society seems more responsive to the demands of the underprivileged than to those of the wealthy; a half century ago it was clearly otherwise.

One reason many collective consumption goods lead to demands for public provision is because the potential willingness to pay of different consumers cannot be tapped by private suppliers. Weisbrod, in an important paper, suggests a further source of values for which there is no market: option demands.[10] Consider several examples. I value the existence of Yellowstone Park, despite the hope that I never have to visit it again; I value the Everglades because I may want to visit them, even though I probably will not. Similarly, I value a first-rate tuberculosis sanatorium, although in all probability I shall never need its services. Were any of these threatened with ex-

[10] Weisbrod, "Collective-Consumption Services of Individual-Consumption Goods." Millard F. Long has recently challenged Weisbrod's concept in "Collective-Consumption Services of Individual-Consumption Goods: Comment," *Quarterly Journal of Economics*, Vol. 81 (May 1967), pp. 351–52.

tinction I should be the loser, but there is no market in which my willingness to pay for the option to use them can be translated into revenue to the providers.[11]

Weisbrod's most suggestive example concerns the standby availability of transport. How much is it worth to the New York-Washington air travelers to have a good rail alternative in case of snow or strike? Suppose that it is worth enough to justify the rail service, but that the railroad has no way of being reimbursed by those whose option demands are critical to continuation of the services. In these circumstances, the public good may be provided by the government's insistence that the railroad's passenger service be maintained with or without subsidy. In this view governments may not have been irrational in trying to preserve passenger train service even in the face of the inability of the carriers to develop a set of user charges that succeed in covering costs.

### Public Goods Arising from Market Imperfections

In practice there can be no sharp distinction between market failure caused by technical characteristics of particular goods and market failure caused by market imperfections. Inability to handle externalities, for example, may be regarded as a shortcoming of existing markets rather than as the absence of markets for specific services. But a distinction suggests additional sources of unsatisfactory private market performance that generate demand for public collective action. Efficient markets frequently presuppose adequate information, timely adjustment, sufficient competition, and modest transaction costs. The absence of any of these may motivate replacement of market determination by nonmarket provision, or supplementation of markets with ancillary public goods.

INFORMATION. Suppose all conditions for ideal resource allocation are satisfied except that market signals are systematically not read or are misperceived by economic actors. An allocation of goods and resources will occur, but it will, in general, differ from an allocation based on adequate and accurate information. Information may be a

[11] Option demands are not really a brand new concept. They are, in a sense, much like consumers' surplus: They arise because the price charged for the good or service is below the maximum each buyer would be willing to pay. Thus the option to buy at a low future price has present value. Weisbrod's insight is not in identifying option demands, but in recognizing that they are a significant source of demand for public action.

collective good (and thus generate a demand for its public provision) because even if there is a well-articulated private desire to have information, there may be no effective market in which to buy it efficiently.[12] It may also be a public good because the externalities of having misinformed traders may be judged to be socially undesirable.

TIME LAGS. If resources respond to market signals surely but slowly, the market process may prove an expensive way to achieve resource shifts. If physicists are in short supply, their price may be expected to rise and this may motivate additional youngsters to undertake education leading to careers as physicists. Since education is a slow process, available physicists may earn high rents over long periods due to the long supply lags. It may well be that public policy can increase the supply of physicists more quickly and more cheaply by fellowships, research grants, and other means than the unaided market.[13] If increases in the supply of physicists, but not increased incomes of existing physicists, are desired results, then such programs supply public goods.

A large and growing literature is concerned with the extent and causes of factor immobility. Education is but one of the sources; others include unemployment rates, prejudice, and institutional barriers to greater mobility, such as seniority and pension rules and state laws affecting eligibility for relief. Whenever markets work to reallocate resources too slowly, a collective demand to supplement or to replace the market mechanism may arise. Retraining programs, moving allowances, public employment services, and even attacks on prejudice may be public goods if they serve to reduce the lags that the market economy produces to the point that society finds tolerable.

MONOPOLY POWER. Noncompetitive imperfections require little

[12] George J. Stigler, in "The Economics of Information," *Journal of Political Economy*, Vol. 69 (June 1961), pp. 213–25, provides a conceptual analysis of the costs and benefits of obtaining information. Lester G. Telser, in "How Much Does It Pay Whom To Advertise?" *American Economic Review*, Vol. 51 (May 1961), pp. 194–205, deals with the problem of buying information in the form of advertising as a joint product with news, entertainment, and so forth.

[13] A study by J. Kenneth Little, *A Survey of Federal Programs in Higher Education* (Department of Health, Education, and Welfare, 1962), supplies some evidence on the incentive effects of subsidies to scientists and other academic personnel.

comment. Public activities to encourage or compel competitive behavior, or to replace monopolistic, private supply by public provision, are further sources of public goods.

TRANSACTION COSTS. It has been seen that an important aspect of collective goods concerns the inability of the market to translate potential willingness to pay into revenues. Related is the situation where the private market is technically able to collect revenues, but at a high cost. Toll collection on interurban roads and urban bridges may or may not be both feasible and efficient, but intra-urban toll roads would surely involve intolerably large collection costs and time losses. Because the transaction costs of high speed intra-urban travel as a private good are prohibitive, if it is to exist at all it must be a public good. Metering costs may be justified for commodities of high unit value, such as gas and electricity, but not for sewage (and, in some areas of high population density, for water).

Where these high transaction costs inhere in the particular service they are simply an externality; where they reflect the institutional arrangements of the market they are a potential additional source of collective concern. The higher cost of attempting to gear a pricing system to an individual's willingness to pay is a repeated source of turning away from the market. Suppose for many goods willingness to pay increases at least proportionally with income. With a few exceptions most private services are not provided on a basis that reflects income, because of the enormous administrative costs that such pricing would entail. If such a basis of payment is appropriate, reliance on the income tax, and thus on state provision, may suddenly appear desirable.

## Public Goods Arising out of Concern
## with Environmental Quality

Up to this point public goods have been discussed in terms of market failure—failure because of either the absence or the imperfections of private markets. This is the grand tradition of classical economics. But even perfectly functioning markets for *all* goods and services would not eliminate the desire for market interference. Men may choose to reject market solutions to allocative problems with respect to the distribution of income, the nature or quality of goods produced, or the patterns of consumption that markets produce.

The most compelling examples of collective public goods appear to be national defense, law and order, and public health. What is their particular appeal? Is it that they are collective consumption goods? So is television. The appeal is not in the specific planes, rockets, soldiers, policemen, vaccines, or nurses that are their elements, for each of these can be readily provided as private goods to private users, but rather in the fact that they are part of and condition the environment of the society. Even the criminal who detests the legal framework is affected by it. Looked at this way these goods suggest other things that affect the environment and thus create externalities not linked to particular goods: the literacy rate, the level of unemployment, the incidence of crime, the pace of technological progress, and, importantly, the pattern of distribution of income and wealth.

DISTRIBUTION OF INCOME.[14] Accept this assertion: It is fully feasible to charge users for use of parks and playgrounds, to charge parents for school bus service and school lunches, to charge fishermen for fishing privileges. Suppose in each of these cases that there is sufficient willingness to pay and ability to collect to assure private provision of parks, playgrounds, school buses and lunches, and fishing opportunities. Should these functions be left to private provision?

There are two issues here rather than one. Does concern focus merely on the distribution of income or on the pattern of consumption? When subsidized public housing is provided to the urban poor, is the aim to make available more or better housing to users who would be excluded by private provision (or who would exclude themselves)? Or is it rather to increase their share of national consumption, and the choice of giving them public housing instead of a cash income supplement is motivated by some other consideration? (One might use indirect means, for example, in order not to impair the self-respect of the recipients.)

It is sometimes argued that purely redistributional objectives which reflect dissatisfaction with the initial patterns of ownership of wealth and resources ought to be satisfied by income transfers rather

[14] For a recent effort to work out the implications of income distribution for public investment planning, see A. Myrick Freeman III, "Income Distribution and Planning for Public Investment," *American Economic Review,* Vol. 57 (June 1967), pp. 495–508.

than by provision of goods and services, in order not to distort resource allocation. This familiar argument does not persuade, if one
regards as legitimate a desire of a society to interfere with the pattern of consumption that would result from market determinations.
A society may choose to affect income distribution and the pattern
of consumption jointly. Provision of housing, education, milk, or
recreation to underprivileged children may be a public good because
of the externalities which children so treated bestow upon others.
Public policies designed to aid small business, the family farm, the
needy aged, and the slum child all reflect rejection of market determination, rather than denial of the possibility of market determination.

It is, of course, not clear that all actual interferences reflect a
positive intention both to redistribute income and to change consumption patterns. In the United Kingdom (by way of contrast with
the United States), fishing rights are sold, and fishing is an upper-
class form of recreation. On the other hand, virtually all Scottish
golf courses are owned by municipalities and subsidized out of tax
receipts, and in Scotland golf is a working-class recreation. But if
some consumption distortions are fortuitous, others are intended.

NATURE AND QUALITY OF OUTPUT. The quality and nature of some
goods and services are of public concern, quite independent of any
distributional considerations. Often the nature of the good or service
is affected—for better or for worse—by who provides it. Government newspapers differ from private ones, public television and
radio from commercial broadcasting, a system of public schools from
a private school system, private from public research and development. In some of these examples the two kinds of goods may
coexist; in others an exclusive choice is made. But in all cases a
choice among qualitatively different outputs may and can be made;
the qualitative difference of public from private provision constitutes
a public good or a public bad.

### Public Goods: A Summary View

I have stressed the pluralistic nature of the sources of collective
demands as arising from technical characteristics of particular
goods, from market imperfections and failures, and from other divergences between collective and individual values. The time is long

since past when the primary need is to define public goods merely in order to establish the prima facie case for some public interference with private markets; what is sought instead is a framework for debate about whether particular activities merit inclusion in the public sector.

It seems to me useful to identify in each case the source of the alleged collective concern. Is the source a major qualitative difference between public and private provision, or is it merely a wish for incremental output, arising in response to a neglected externality? In this distinction often lies an important policy choice between public provision and a less fundamental public restructuring of private incentives. Similarly one wants an indication of whether public concern is fixed on the specific good or service or on the environment in general. There are more ways to reduce overall unemployment than there are ways to retrain Appalachian miners. Again the relevant alternatives are affected by the real objects of policy. Frequently at issue is whether redistributional policies achieved by provision of specific goods and services bring about changes in consumption patterns deliberately or incidentally.

The basis of *collective* concern having been established, it is worth establishing the basis of *public* concern. Who are the alleged beneficiaries, and what is their claim to recognition? What second-best alternative do they face if their claims are rejected?

Defining as specifically as possible the vector of differences between a private good and its public alternative is a critical part of the public decision-making process. Neither de facto definitions (such as Birdsall's) nor neat but narrow ones (such as that of the perfect collective consumption good) prove very helpful for the crucial problem of defining the scope of the public sector.

## Sources of a Public Interest: Alternative Views

To convert a collective interest of some group into the public interest requires a distinct act of legitimation. How does it occur? Views differ with respect to both what is aggregated and the requisite degree of consensus.

The discussion among economists about the public interest is surprising in its defensive tone, as if there is some disloyalty in find-

ing a role for extramarket forces in the economy. Perhaps because
of this defensiveness, a great deal of the economists' discussion has
revolved not around the issue of how to define the public interest,
but rather around how to demonstrate that there is at least a minimal role of government activity that clearly benefits everybody.
Much of welfare economics consists of such a possibility theorem.
Possibility theorems are fine in their way. Misinterpreted, however,
they may greatly limit the scope of the phenomenon whose possibility they are devised to establish. This has been the problem and
the fate of formal welfare economics.

### The Point of View of Individual Utility

Those who hold this view consider the public interest of a society
as simply an appropriate aggregate of the private interests of the individuals who make up the society. Each individual is assumed to
seek his own utility (or satisfaction) by pursuing all avenues open
to him. Assume, as a rough distinction, that he draws satisfaction
from the consumption of two kinds of goods, private goods and collective goods. (He may, of course, derive utility not only from his
own consumption but from the status of others, rejoicing in either
their good fortune or their bad.) The individual's wants, as reflected
by his utility function, may be distinguished from his effective demands, determined by his utility function *and* the constraints, such
as income, that bind him.

For private goods there is a market through which individuals
can make known their effective demands for goods; in the context of
an enterprise system, private producers are induced to meet these
demands whenever their aggregate warrants. The situation of collective goods differs in that private markets fail to respond to real effective demands. Thus *collective action* is required to satisfy *individual
demands*. Governmental devices can provide the form of the collective action that substitutes for private markets in channeling resources to meet the aggregate of individual demands.[15] (So far as
the individual's utility depends upon consumption by others, he is
unlikely to be able to do much to satisfy his preferences except

[15] For the purpose of the ensuing discussion, it is convenient to talk as if public
goods are jointly enjoyed by all. If $X$ is the quantity of a public good, each member of society is assumed (for the moment) to be in a position to enjoy all $X$
units.

through government. Here is further motive to look to government.) In this attractively symmetrical view, government activity enables people better to achieve their objectives.

These assumptions have settled an issue of principle (Is there a legitimate role for government?) without having answered the practical question of which public goods the society should provide. Granted that individuals have demands for collective goods, how should their preferences be aggregated to determine whether the total welfare is sufficient to justify the total cost? Is this answer affected by the system of taxes used to raise the funds? These are among the critical questions of welfare economics.

UNANIMITY: THE DE MINIMIS VIEW. Figure 1 depicts a simple society, which consists of three persons whose demands (in terms of utility) for units of public good $X$ vary.[16] The tax burden on each individual (measured in utility terms) is known for any quantity of the public good. In the figure, the horizontal axes are identical and measurable. The vertical axes are not comparable, and may be mere ordinal scales.

Clearly, if some quantity of a new public good had the happy property of adding at least as much to the utility of each individual as his contribution to the cost detracted from it, the good would be desirable. Such is the case for quantity $X_A$ in Figure 1. Any output less than $X_A$ would disadvantage everybody. A totally de minimis view of the public interest would limit it to cases meeting this requirement because, while it is conceivable that there are some goods that satisfy this criterion, there cannot be many. In a multiperson economy, if even one had a demand curve that lay everywhere below the tax contribution disutility line, no positive quantity of output would command unanimous consent.

Most public activities imply (often intentionally) a redistribution of income which leaves some worse and some better off. This would be the case in Figure 1 with any output greater than $X_A$. Whatever the merit of establishing as desirable at least the quantity $X_A$, any implication that exactly $X_A$ is desirable seems quite unwarranted. Few economists are content to rule out any change merely because it has redistributional consequences. To do so invests

---

[16] Without loss of generality at this stage, quantities of a single public good $X$ are dealt with instead of the choice of a vector of public goods.

## FIGURE 1. Utility Demands of Hypothetical Individuals for an Economic Good

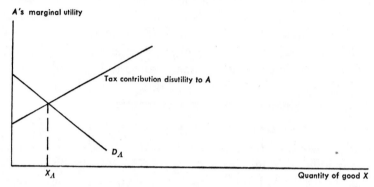

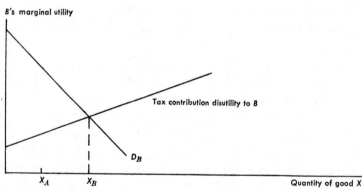

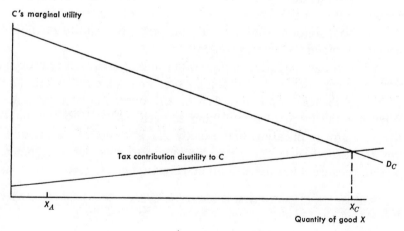

the initial distribution of society's resources with an overriding sanctity. Nor can the difficulty be avoided by assuming that the utility function of an individual includes as an argument preferences about the distribution of income. For, unless an implied redistribution were to be regarded as desirable by everyone, there would be no unanimous consent to a policy that embodied it.

The struggle of formal welfare economics to escape this dilemma has been tortured and fruitless. The Kaldor-Hicks compensation principle, wherein a change that benefited some but not all was justified if the gainers could compensate the losers, not only encounters technical ambiguities but also implies an inherent neutrality toward redistributional consequences.[17]

Nor am I persuaded of the case for neutrality toward redistribution in allocational decisions on the ground that redistribution of income can be accomplished directly if it is desired. Social inertia is such that this would give too much weight to the current distribution of income, and would serve in practice to limit the possibilities for redistribution.

Clearly an operating rule that said, "Provide no public good if it changes the distribution of income" would be paralyzing. But if redistributions are permitted, there is no reason why some cannot be regarded as desirable and others as undesirable.

RETREAT FROM UNANIMITY. Some reckoning of gains and losses is needed if all proposals are not to be rejected. A requirement that decisions be based on individual utility functions implies either the assignment of weights to the utility of individuals or ability and willingness to measure and compare individual utilities. Interpersonal comparisons are potentially unattractive, unless they are themselves subject to well-defined rules of procedure.[18] Such rules might be for-

[17] Tibor Scitovsky, in "A Note on Welfare Propositions in Economics," *Review of Economic Studies,* Vol. 9 (November 1941), pp. 77–88, demonstrated an inconsistency in the principle in the case in which price changes occurred. Several writers have questioned the use of potential compensation; see William J. Baumol, *Welfare Economics and the Theory of the State* (2nd ed., Harvard University Press, 1965); Ian Malcolm David Little, *A Critique of Welfare Economics* (2nd ed., London: Oxford University Press, 1957); and Charles F. Kennedy, "The Economic Welfare Function and Dr. Little's Criterion," *Review of Economic Studies,* Vol. 20, No. 2 (1953), pp. 137–42.

[18] Edward C. Banfield, in " 'Economic' Analysis of 'Political' Phenomena: A Political Scientist's Critique" (paper prepared for Harvard University Seminar on

mulated. For example, one may take a strict majoritarian view. In terms of Figure 1, this would lead to provision of the quantity $X_B$, since $B$ is the member of society with the median preference. But there is nothing inherently just or appealing about a rule that leads to dominance by the median effective demand of the society; indeed, without protection for minorities it would seem offensive to most people.

The major objection to a utility-consensus view of social welfare functions is that it is nonoperational and thus does not provide guidance to the decisions of real societies. Certainly decisions are taken with less than unanimous consent. Certainly many public goods provide benefits in excess of their contributions only to very small minorities of the society, but are provided with the evident acquiescence of sizable majorities. Some might argue that, ex post, individuals are thus revealed to value the benefits which accrue primarily to others. But this rationalization can be applied to every actual expenditure and thus leads back to a de facto definition: Whatever the government does is revealed to be desired by the people.

Thus if formal welfare economics does not go beyond individual utility functions, it fails because it justifies either too little or too much of public expenditures. Viewed from the vantage point of welfare economics, public decisions about public goods appear to be impossible to make.[19] Fortunately, other economic views are possi-

---

Political-Economics Decisions, March 1967; ditto), suggests the following as an extreme parable about a society that can make accurate interpersonal comparisons of the subjective states of individuals $A$ and $B$: "If $A$'s preference is for putting $B$ into a gas chamber, then 'bliss for the whole universe' is served by his putting him there, provided only that $B$'s loss of satisfaction at being put there is less than $A$'s at putting him there. Even if $B$ claims that his loss of satisfaction will be at least as great as $A$'s gain of it, the just and equitable society will tell him that he is mistaken and put him there anyway in the 'good cause of adding more to the rest of mankind's (that is to say, $A$'s) well-being.' If perchance $A$ and his friends constitute 51% of the population and $B$ and his friends only 49%, the matter will be simple indeed."

[19] This is, of course, a conclusion of Arrow's "General Possibility Theorem": "If we exclude the possibility of interpersonal comparisons of utility, then the only methods of passing from individual tastes to social preferences which will be satisfactory and which will be defined for a wide range of sets of individual orderings are either imposed or dictatorial." Kenneth J. Arrow, *Social Choice and Individual Values,* Cowles Foundation for Research in Economics at Yale University, Monograph 12 (2nd ed., John Wiley & Sons, 1963), p. 59. For discussion and criticism of this famous proposition, see especially Little, *A Critique of Welfare Economics;*

ble: Economists are saved the humiliation of abandoning as barren a fertile field. It is the wasteland of welfare economics, not the reality of public decision making, that is the mirage.

PRESSURE GROUPS AS PREFERENCE-AGGREGATING ORGANIZATIONS.[20] Suppose that each individual has, in addition to his personal evaluation of any proposed activity, a view of it as a member of any one of a number of groups (such as a social club or trade union) to which he belongs. If he is willing to be bound by the consensus of the members of the group, there is a much greater possibility of consensus, first, because a significant clustering of views is likely to emerge, and, second, because logrolling among groups can create collections of activities that command dominant majorities. Suppose people are prepared to accept and to be taxed for things they consider socially worthwhile—such as (say) foreign aid, wars on poverty, and higher pay for Senators—even though they cost many individuals more in income forgone than they contribute to their individual utilities. They accept these programs as part of a package which they find adds to their own utility on an all-or-nothing basis.

The view that social choices may rest on collective values arrived at by caucus rather than by simple aggregation is more than an escape from the general impossibility of deriving a social welfare function from individual values. It has positive merit in that it embraces a view of the individual which many find descriptively accurate and analytically helpful. In this view an individual functions in a pluralistic sense with loyalties, commitments, and valuations at many levels: to himself, his family, his church, his neighborhood, his employer—and possibly also to his race, religion, class, country, and political party. The pluralistic view is the heart of sociology, social anthropology, and much of economics.[21] If it is accepted, it suggests that individuals will be prepared to act on collective issues without inevitably asking explicitly: What's in it for me? They may ask instead: What's in it for the Negro—or the farmer—or the working

and Gordon Tullock, "The General Irrelevance of the General Impossibility Theorem," *Quarterly Journal of Economics*, Vol. 81 (May 1967), pp. 256–70.

[20] See David B. Truman, *The Governmental Process* (Knopf, 1957), for an extended discussion of groups in the political process.

[21] The term "institutional economics" is so narrowed by usage that I avoid it here, though clearly the insight that institutions mold as well as serve individuals is central to my point.

man? If they do, they invite an analysis of the views of political pressure groups, which usually have highly articulate spokesmen and well-defined programs they are seeking to enact.

### The Point of View of Willingness to Pay

The difficulties of deriving an ordering of aggregate preference based on individual utilities arise from the incommensurability of the utility indexes of individuals. Without unanimity of views or rules for assigning weights, consistent decisions become impossible.

A second approach is to ask how much an individual is willing to be taxed for a given collective good, rather than how much he values it. The difference between these approaches may seem small but it may alter considerably the view of the scope of the public interest. In the first place, there is a substantial difference between a positive preference for some activity and a toleration of it, as the well-known political literature on the use of veto power makes clear. Second, the metric of value of the activity has been shifted from the inherently unmeasurable *utility* to the discernible, and interpersonally comparable, *willingness to pay*. To be sure, something is lost, in that the willingness of a given person to pay reflects his situation, particularly his income and wealth. One must, therefore, be all the more wary about distributional biases toward the status quo.

When applied to the collective consumption good, this approach leads to the so-called pure theory of public expenditure. Consider Figure 2, a diagram in what may be called the Bowen-Samuelson tradition.[22]

Figure 2 differs from Figure 1 in that the vertical axis is measurable and is comparable across individuals. $D_A$, $D_B$, and $D_C$ represent the quantities of $X$ (a public good that all can enjoy jointly) that each of the individuals would be willing to support as a function of price. The total marginal cost (assumed constant) is shown by $MC$, and the cost per individual is shown as $MC_\alpha$. (For simplicity a tax structure is assumed such that each citizen pays one-third of the

---

[22] Bowen, "The Interpretation of Voting"; and Paul A. Samuelson, "Diagrammatic Exposition of a Theory of Public Expenditure," *Review of Economics and Statistics*, Vol. 37 (November 1955), pp. 350–56. A better historian of thought might define it as the Sax-Wicksell-Lindahl-Musgrave-Bowen-Samuelson . . . tradition, to recognize the apparently valid theorem that no one ever has an original idea. Samuelson is diligent in identifying his predecessors and Musgrave provides admirable summaries of earlier views. In an earlier day, theories of this type were called "voluntary exchange" theories.

**FIGURE 2.** Willingness of Hypothetical Individuals to Pay for an Economic Good

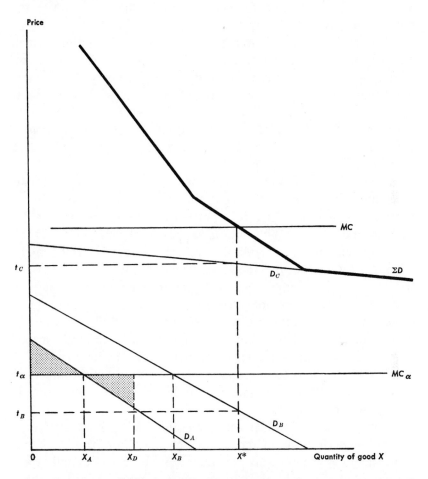

cost.) At one level the results are as in Figure 1: At quantities up to $X_A$, all three citizens are selfishly delighted to have the good produced; at quantities from $X_A$ to $X_B$, citizens $B$ and $C$ are happy, but the desired level of $A$ has been exceeded. Only citizen $C$ wants more than $X_B$, and he would like $X_C$ (a quantity so large it is not shown on the diagram).

But since the analysis deals with revealed willingness of individuals to pay, not noncomparable levels of pleasure and pain, it can be carried further.

Because the demands are complementary, the effective aggregate demand is the vertical sum of the positive portions of $D_A$, $D_B$, and $D_C$ and is shown by $\Sigma D$.[23] The output $X^*$ represents the intersection of $\Sigma D$ and $MC$, and occurs somewhere in the interval $X_A$ to $X_C$—on either side of $X_B$ according to the manner in which the curves are drawn. ($X_D$ may be neglected for the moment.)

$X^*$ represents the Bowen-Samuelson optimal solution, which has the following logic: For all quantities below $X^*$ there is an aggregate willingness to pay equal to more than the cost of each marginal unit; for all quantities beyond there is no such willingness. Thus there exists a tax policy which would involve taxes at levels to cover marginal costs, and leave all citizens satisfied. According to the figure, $C$ must be taxed $X^*(t_C)$; $B$ must be taxed $X^*(t_B)$, and $A$ is left untaxed.

"Existence of tax policy such that . . ." sounds very much like the compensation principle once again. And it is subject to a similar objection. If the tax structure is not (or should not be) malleable, there is no bliss in the $X^*$ solution. Suppose each citizen is taxed the lump sum amount $t_\alpha(X^*)$. At the uniform tax rate $t_\alpha$ (which might be in effect if all three had the same income, family size, and so on), two of the three taxpayers get more than they are willing to pay for and are coerced to provide what only $C$ wants. If $C$'s needs are in some sense more meritorious than those of $A$ and $B$, this may be appropriate, but why then stop at $X^*$? One cannot escape the distributional question, unless one insists on regarding it as irrelevant. If $X$ involves aid to the needy aged, one may take a view of the effects of the coercion different from that one would have if it involves providing a civic yacht harbor.

Nor are these difficulties with the optimal solution merely symptoms of imperfections in the taxing schema. Citizens have social values about appropriate tax policies too. Suppose $X$ is a public playground. If $A$ is a rich misanthrope and $C$ a poor Samaritan, there is no compelling reason why $C$ should carry most of the tax burden, even though he is apparently willing to do so. Society may prefer to coerce $A$ in order to relieve $C$ of part of his burden.

[23] Both Bowen and Samuelson use this device. See Bowen, "Interpretation of Voting," and Samuelson, "Diagrammatic Exposition of a Theory." Notice that it is the complementary nature of their consumption, not its publicness, that makes vertical summation appropriate. For example, peak and off-peak demands for the same capacity, while private, are complementary, and vertical addition is appropriate. See Peter O. Steiner, "Peak Loads and Efficient Pricing," *Quarterly Journal of Economics,* Vol. 71 (November 1957), pp. 585–610.

I have argued here that the $X^*$ solution is not compelling with respect to the *quantity* of a public good to provide. Does it serve the lesser but still important purpose of deciding whether to provide the good at all? Surely there must be some collective willingness to pay before the government will provide the service. Unfortunately the Bowen-Samuelson condition does not answer this question either. On the revenue side it neglects the consumer surplus that might lead an all-or-nothing choice to be affirmative.[24] On the cost side it is concerned only with marginal costs.

Notwithstanding these difficulties, some have argued that this approach offers the following rule as a usable rough guideline to public decision making: If, in aggregate, effective demands exceed cost, the service should be provided whether or not payment is exacted. Unfortunately this opens the door to game-strategic behavior. Suppose payment proportional to demand is not to be required. Any group that knows it will not be asked to pay more than a fixed share can exaggerate its valuation of a service it desires. For example, in Figure 2, a vertical upward shift in $D_c$ can increase $X^*$ to any desired level. If, on the other hand, proportional payment is to be required, every group will have an incentive to understate its real valuation as long as others value the service enough to get it provided.

## The Point of View of an Aggregate Social Welfare Function

Society is necessarily made up of individuals, but it need not be a simple aggregate of them. It may be that the interdependencies between people and their interactions are more important than the individual value structures. Nations, races, even football teams, acquire personalities and modes of behavior. While a search for collective values until recently has been more congenial to political scientists and sociologists than to economists, an increasing number of economists are moving toward the view that individuals voluntarily yield certain coercive powers to a government which is charged to discover, articulate, and implement social priorities, or collective wants.

This collective view is broader than previous ones, but not necessarily competitive with them. It may be that social priorities are in-

---

[24] This is the familiar proposition that a discriminating monopolist may profitably produce a commodity even though average cost lies everywhere above the demand curve.

deed arrived at by some aggregation process. But there are other possibilities. Political theory has long been concerned with the legitimacy of government and with the nature of the social contract among citizens or between a government and its citizens.

In this approach a collectivity, society, may be fruitfully considered an independent entity possessing its own value orderings.[25] In Rothenberg's view, if I understand it, social valuation, as opposed to solely individual valuation, is an existent reality.[26] This view has the great pragmatic value of inviting the search for revealed social priorities without insisting on a single source of them. If priorities with respect to income distribution, for example, are established and consented to by the citizens, then the distributional consequences of particular public decisions become "benefits" or "costs" instead of barriers to either clear thinking or clear action. The formidable measurement issues—of quantifying the benefits and assessing the costs—remain, but a major hurdle has been crossed. Here one is aggregating not across individual utility or willingness to pay, but across individual political influence and tolerance. While to some extent the existing distribution of political power and influence is thus vested, it is often argued that this is more nearly the result of a social contract than is the distribution of wealth.[27] The degree of consent that is required is whatever the political process demands.

I find this view of the problem both congenial and fruitful. It does not dispense with the individual and individual values, for one must ask how the political process articulates the public interest, but it does recognize that most individuals have a large range of things they will accept without withdrawing from the system, and that they

---

[25] There is some danger that this view will be misinterpreted as embracing the organistic conception of the state that has provided the intellectual defense of fascist governments. That is clearly not the intention of the writers cited here.

[26] ". . . We may consider treating the Social Welfare Function for a particular society as the very same values embodied in those strategic social decision-making processes within the society which valuate the kinds of social states pertinent to the economic problem, and thus . . . we consider treating the social ordering (or social preference scale) as the ordering of social states which results from the operation of those processes." Jerome Rothenberg, *The Measurement of Social Welfare* (Englewood Cliffs, N.J.: Prentice-Hall, 1961), p. 318.

[27] James M. Buchanan and Gordon Tullock, in *The Calculus of Consent* (University of Michigan Press, 1962), develop an ingenious "economic theory of constitutions" in which individuals find it advantageous to agree in advance to certain rules even though they may work to the individual's disadvantage on occasion.

will vent their approval or disapproval in some sort of orderly political process. It does not lead, inherently, to either a minimal or maximal role for government. It does not exclude distributional questions from policy, nor does it endow the existing distribution of income with overriding status. What it lacks is any clear indication that one situation is superior to another in a wholly unambiguous sense. This does not mean that whatever society does is desired; rather it means that particular public decisions can be shown to be valid only in terms of particular value judgments. It tends to pose issues of public policy in terms of whether society does in fact hold certain value judgments rather than in terms of the demonstrable inherent legitimacy of certain activities. Some will regard this as retrogression. I am not so inclined. Economists have long sought a "calculus of consent,"[28] but in the search have found it easier to derive a lower bound to public activities than to define their proper domain. The discussion of public expenditure policy, if it is to be fruitful, must go beyond this.

The central issue in this debate is not one of the logical correctness of looking at social choices as an aggregation of individual values or as a two-step procedure in which collective values are first agreed on—some way, any way—and then used to make social choices. Any perfectly understood aggregate behavior can be decomposed into its disaggregated elements. It is instead a matter of research strategy. Is insight more likely to be achieved one way than the other? If there is stability in aggregate social values (just as with aggregate consumption functions), then basing policy on such aggregate values (or aggregate consumption functions) is likely to work. My own view is that at this stage in the development of economic science there is more insight and less bias in the third view of the public interest than in either of the others. Many will disagree.

## Articulation of the Public Interest

There are divergent views about how the political structure articulates social priorities and the extent to which *process* determines outcome. It is helpful to start with a dichotomous classification that overstates differences in points of view. In one view the political pro-

[28] The phrase is Buchanan's and Tullock's. See n. 27.

cess is a market-like mechanism that coalesces the views of the members of the society. Here the political process is a facilitating and implementing one, not intrinsically a formative one. An efficient government, like an efficient market, quickly and accurately translates inherent preferences into explicit consensus. Just as a market may perform a mapping function (since people discover their preferences best by confronting real alternatives), so an efficient government serves to help people discover as well as fulfill their collective preferences. In principle (though, of course, not necessarily in practice) one should be able to simulate such a process, and simply add a government sector to a general equilibrium model of the society. Government (in this view) is a decision maker only in the limited sense of a reactor to and processor of signals it receives. A properly functioning government will arrive at an optimal decision set without exercise of independent judgment.

The second view is that while individual social preferences clearly exist and play a role, they are so inchoate, ambiguous, or conflicting that the political process is required to forge a public interest; and it does so with substantial discretionary choice. Without knowledge of the motives of the governors, and of the political process itself, there is no indicated solution nor accurate prediction of governmental action. In this view, if a government sector is created, it must be assigned objectives, procedures, and decision makers. The role of the preferences of individuals is to constrain or otherwise affect public decision makers, and the way this occurs must be made explicit.

The differences between the approaches are important not only in terms of the information each requires in order to permit prediction of outcomes, but in terms of determining whether comparative static analysis is possible or must be replaced by a genuinely dynamic model of political decisions.

## Government as a Quasi-Market

In all market-type analyses of the political process, voting is the means by which individual values are translated into action decisions. Bowen's pioneer article is of this type.[29] If it is assumed that the tax burden of any public expenditure on each individual is

---

[29] Bowen, "The Interpretation of Voting."

known to him, and that everyone votes in a system of simple majority rule, the outcome of elections can be predicted. For example, if preferences are assumed to be those shown in Figure 2, with a tax burden of $MC_\alpha$ per person, it can be predicted that quantity $X_B$ will be provided by majority vote. Neglecting the effect of the tax structure on political choices,[30] it is the median preference that dictates the outcome of majoritarian voting. More generally, the result of an election in this model depends wholly upon the pattern and variance of the preferences of voters and the structure of taxes. The result may, but need not, yield the Bowen-Samuelson optimal quantity $X^*$ (in Figure 2 it does not). This quantity is based upon aggregate willingness to pay and thus, if tax burdens are equal, it depends upon the mean rather than the median willingness to pay. Bowen believes that the institutional facts are that voters' preferences are symmetrically distributed, and that thus median and mean will coincide. I know of no evidence to confirm this conjecture. Bowen does not suggest that a referendum on each proposed decision actually is the decision procedure, but rather that it is a procedure that might be used, and one whose results are approximately achieved by the institutions of democratic government.

A much more elaborate but broadly similar theory is presented by Downs, to whom government consists of men who like the emoluments and perquisites of their jobs and whose goal is reelection, or reappointment by elected officials.[31] The government is thus motivated to maximize its political support. It is interested in a citizen's vote, not his welfare; to get his vote, however, it must cater to his view of his welfare. Were it not for uncertainty, Downs' model would be fully mechanistic and predictable.[32]

[30] The usual technique is to assume tax rates are pre-fixed, perhaps by a prior election. As noted by Wicksell, Samuelson, and others, if it is assumed that voters' preferences are also used as the basis for setting taxes—on the benefit theory of taxation—unfortunate game-theoretic considerations enter the voting procedure: It becomes in the interest of each individual to pretend a lower degree of interest in the public good than he has. For this reason alone, the separation of the tax and expenditure issues, followed by Bowen in "The Interpretation of Voting," by Dorfman, in "General Equilibrium with Public Goods," and by others, is helpful. The assumption does not seem to do violence to the facts.

[31] Anthony Downs, *An Economic Theory of Democracy* (Harper & Row, 1957).

[32] Uncertainty creates some scope for leadership, and for errors that give politics an interesting dynamic. It is not possible to pursue them here. See Downs, *Economic Theory of Democracy*, esp. Chaps. 5–8.

A less mechanistic model is offered by Maass. His explanation is to a major degree a two-stage political market theory. In the first stage the voters choose "men who, in their personal capacity, and in virtue of their character, are fitted to discharge the task of deliberation and discussion at the parliamentary stage."[33] In the second stage, these officials are held accountable for their political acts by the need to seek periodic reelection.

Maass's model gives more freedom to the politician than does Downs's: Officials are not necessarily maximizing the probability of reelection by every move, only by their overall performance. At the very least they are constrained only to be aware of their constituents' sensibilities. Indeed, if they regard their mandate as sufficiently general they have the need as well as the opportunity to crystallize their constituents' values. Here Maass verges into a creative or formative view of government and the definition of public interest.

Market theories can be criticized from within or from outside the market framework. Most critics of the votes-as-market-signals approach to analysis of the political process have sought a more substantial discretionary role of government; these are considered below. Within the market-analogy framework, Arrow, Black, and Buchanan have questioned the ability of such a quasi-market system to translate inherent preferences into rational social priorities, as well as its efficiency.[34]

Arrow's well-known demonstration of the paradox of collective choice is so simply illustrated that it bears repeating:

| Individual | Preference ordering |
|---|---|
| I | $A \Rightarrow C \Rightarrow B$ |
| II | $C \Rightarrow B \Rightarrow A$ |
| III | $B \Rightarrow A \Rightarrow C$ |

[33] The words are those of Ernest Barker, *Reflections on Government* (London: Oxford University Press, 1942), quoted with evident approval by Arthur Maass, "System Design and the Political Process: A General Statement," in Maass and others, *Design of Water-Resource Systems* (Harvard University Press, 1962), p. 569.

[34] Arrow, *Social Choice and Individual Values;* Duncan Black, *The Theory of Committees and Elections* (Cambridge: Cambridge University Press, 1958); and James M. Buchanan, "Individual Choice in Voting and the Market," *Journal of Political Economy,* Vol. 62 (August 1954), pp. 334–43.

Even if each of the individuals has no difficulty ordering his preferences among three competing possibilities, *A, B,* and *C,* there may be no clear collective preference. In the example, clearly, two-thirds prefer *A* to *C,* and two-thirds prefer *C* to *B.* Thus if they first choose between *B* and *C* and then between *A* and *C, A* will command a majority. But two-thirds prefer *B* to *A* and a different order of choice can produce any one of the results.[35] Black and Rothenberg, among others, have explored the theoretic consequences of alternative voting and balloting schemes in producing outcomes, and both discover a purely political dimension to the politics of consent.[36] This will be explored further below.

Buchanan, in the second of two papers stimulated by Arrow, identifies some important weaknesses in the market analogy.[37] He accepts the voting process as analogous to the market mechanism, but is wary about drawing welfare implications from the analogy. Buchanan believes that good inheres in the efficiency of decentralized market decisions and is concerned lest the loose analogy with voting suggest that it, too, is efficient and good. He points out these differences: (1) Voting involves an extra dimension of uncertainty: Consequences follow the collective vote, not the individual vote; therefore the voter may not vote his own best interests because he underestimates the possibility of the decision impinging on him. Indeed, since in a collective vote there is a diffusion of responsibility for the collective decision, the individual may act in the mass as he would never act individually. A man may vote for Prohibition, capital punishment, or U.S. participation in a war, while at the same time he would not abstain from alcohol, invoke the death sentence, or urge his son to enlist in the army. (2) In voting, the individual is influenced by his sense of participation in social choice. A vote for

[35] The theorem proved is that transitivity in all individual orderings is not sufficient to assure a collectively transitive set of choices.

[36] Black, *Theory of Committees and Elections;* and Jerome Rothenberg, "A Model of Economic and Political Decision Making" (paper prepared for Harvard University Seminar on Political-Economic Decisions, March 1967; ditto).

[37] Buchanan, "Individual Choice in Voting and the Market." The first paper, "Social Choice, Democracy, and Free Markets," *Journal of Political Economy,* Vol. 62 (April 1954), pp. 114–23, makes an important point that is not of concern here. It deals with the distinction between a consistent social welfare function and a set of consistent decisions. In showing that it was not necessarily possible to reach the first, Arrow does not prove that a consistent social welfare function is a necessary condition for consistent decision making.

open housing need not imply willingness to live in a racially mixed neighborhood. Many of the most ardent supporters of such laws have exercised their option to move farther away from integrated neighborhoods. Dahl and Lindblom speak of voting as broadening the sense of identification;[38] Buchanan notes that the effect may be for ill as well as for good. Men may be willing to do collectively unto others what they would not do individually or consent to have done to them unless done to all.[39] (3) In voting, the individual is often faced with indivisible votes for mutually exclusive choices. He cannot make marginal choices, or much influence the definition of candidate or issues. Often he votes for candidates some of whose policies he disapproves. Thus the mandate of a winning candidate is readily misinterpreted. (4) Minority votes are wasted, whereas even minority preferences exert influence in the market. If fear of wasting votes leads voters to support their second choices, even actual votes for candidates may fail to reflect the strength of the support the candidates' views have.[40] Nonvoting, an alternative form of expression, is not easily interpreted. (5) Typically, voting provides equality of influence of individuals, instead of reflecting command over resources. Bowen is wrong: The weighting of individual choices in the marketplace is different from that in the polling booth. Buchanan here goes well beyond saying that some remarkable coincidences would be required to assure that the distributions of political and economic influence were perfectly correlated. He adopts, I think, a view of Frank Knight's that market votes are in some sense superior to political votes.[41]

[38] "On the whole, the process of making market choices tends to narrow one's identification to the individual or, at the most, to the family. The process of voting, on the other hand, with all that it presupposes in the way of discussion and techniques of reciprocity, tends to broaden one's identifications beyond the individual and the family." Robert A. Dahl and Charles E. Lindblom, *Politics, Economics, and Welfare* (Harper, 1953), p. 422.

[39] Julius Margolis offers yet a different view of this problem. See "The Structure of Government and Public Investment," in American Economic Association, *Papers and Proceedings of the Seventy-sixth Annual Meeting, 1963* (*American Economic Review*, Vol. 54, May 1964), pp. 236–42, and discussion, pp. 250–57. A man may be willing to pay his share of a joint venture only if he can force his reluctant neighbors to do the same. In this view a vote is an offer to sign a social contract if enough others also sign. Marglin also makes this point.

[40] This phenomenon may be found in the market too. If buyers can be persuaded to accept second best, their true preferences may not be effective.

[41] Frank H. Knight, in "The Meaning of Freedom," in Charner M. Perry (ed.), *The Philosophy of American Democracy* (University of Chicago Press, 1943),

These critiques by Arrow and Buchanan serve to warn against too quick acceptance of an analogy of the political process with the market process. The practical question is whether the two situations are enough alike that the economist's techniques of analysis and his theorems about market behavior can be applied directly and fruitfully to political decision making. My answer after reading in the political-market literature is "no." Individual citizen-voters both influence and constrain political choices; but they do so within limits sufficiently broad that attention to choices *within the limits* needs, deserves, and repays effort.[42] The important issue is, of course, the breadth of the limits. In the arena of political choices, the limits seem to be of such width that attention cannot be confined to those imposed by voters' preferences. All of the following contribute to a substantial discretionary role of government: the variance in the views of individuals; the infrequency of choices by voters and the availability to them of many bundles of policies among which to choose; the lack of emotional commitment to some views, which protects a political leader who opposes them from being declared anathema; the inchoate, uncertain, and changeable nature of many voters' preferences; the negotiations that pressure groups can and do carry on with governments; and finally the influence that in fact political leaders can exert on their followers on many issues. If these things are true, the choice set of the government, while constrained by voters' preferences, may be far from singular.

*Government as an Organic Chooser of Ends*

Dorfman presents a suggestive model of the public sector that is close to the market-analogy models, while explicitly introducing governmental choice.[43] He returns to an older view of the world in which individual views are oriented to and expressed by socioeconomic pressure groups. The government is in a sense a coalition of

---

points out that individuals may be unequally constrained by voting from utilizing their "normally available capacities for action." Evidently Knight feels that unequal constraints are more unfair than unequal initial distributions of wealth.

[42] The issue is reminiscent of the debate of an earlier era about economic and collective-bargaining theories of wages. Reder's synthesis of the competing Dunlop and Ross views was that supply and demand considerations set limits within which collective bargaining takes place. Melvin Reder, "The Theory of Union Wage Policy," *Review of Economics and Statistics*, Vol. 34 (February 1952), pp. 34–45.

[43] Dorfman, "General Equilibrium with Public Goods."

such blocs that cooperate in order to provide public goods. The constraint of coalition requires that no group be treated so badly as to be moved to withdraw its support. In Dorfman's terminology each group has a potential voters' surplus: the excess of its self-perceived benefits from provision of the public good over the group's contribution to its provision. The imposed constraint is that this voters' surplus must be nonnegative for each group. But the government has multiple possibilities beyond this since it can weight the interests of the different groups unequally. Dorfman notes that differences in political parties constitute in effect differences in weighting schemes, and members of the party in power have substantial freedom to pursue their own preferences, and to compete for the right to govern, by catering to those groups that can generate sufficient support to keep them in power.

What is refreshing in this formulation is, first, the explicit statement of the constraint; second, the identification of governors as a group with ends of its own and some ability to pursue them; and, third, the recognition of intermediate groups as a focus for articulating and coalescing individual values.

It is more difficult to accept the basic conclusion that Dorfman believes his model suggests: that it will lead to a downward bias in public expenditure relative, say, to the Bowen-Samuelson optimal level. Were the constraint to be applied literally, *and marginally,* to each unit of public goods, it would constitute a demand for unanimous consent and the conclusion would follow at once. In terms of Figure 2, $X_A$ constitutes that level of output for which the marginal voters' surplus of all groups ($A, B,$ and $C$ now represent groups) is positive, and corresponds to the minimal level of public expenditure of the kind agreed to by everyone. Under this interpretation, Dorfman's theorem of a downward bias in public expenditure would result from implied unanimous consent of groups with different preferences. Dorfman intends another (and more plausible) interpretation: that the decision concerns a discrete increment, and that the voters' surplus must be nonnegative over this increment. In Figure 2, the output $X_D$ is the level at which the voters' surplus of group $A$ becomes zero. There are two problems with this interpretation. The first is that there is no theoretical reason for the chosen level of $X_D$ to be less than, or even as little as, $X^*$, as the contrived Figure 3 illustrates. Here the constraint does not apply to any group until output $X_D$, which is greater than $X^*$. In Dorfman's model it is perfectly pos-

**FIGURE 3. Willingness of Hypothetical Groups to Pay for an Economic Good**

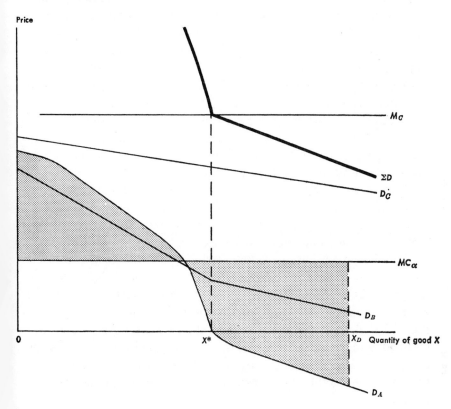

sible for the government to weight the views of group *C* heavily enough to choose level $X_D$. Thus the downward bias is not theoretically deducible. Dorfman regards the downward bias as an empirical, not a logical, matter: "For any single public good, there are likely to be groups that have a very low desire for it from the very outset."[44] This leads at once to the second difficulty: How are the units of goods subject to the constraint to be defined? Once the marginal unit is abandoned for the incremental package (as is necessary to avoid the de minimis solution), may not the definition of the package include many goods? If it may, the constraint implies merely that in its total program the government leaves no group with an aggregatively negative surplus; this may well imply an excessive

[44] Ibid.

rather than a deficient level of public expenditures, as the government compensates otherwise dissident groups by including something which offsets their low desire for the goods that the government itself cherishes. Choice of the policy package is an integral part of Dorfman's theory. Logrolling is not only possible but likely (even if it is not strictly necessary), and a good part of the art of government becomes the definition of acceptable packages. The upward bias of logrolling on the level of expenditure seems to me far more important than the downward bias Dorfman stresses.

A further but less basic question about Dorfman's model concerns the alleged need for unanimity among groups. Given constitutional safeguards of minorities, is not a majority coalition sufficient?[45] If the governing group has positive preferences about programs, may it not be expected to take political risks to achieve them? Indeed, having a small but genuinely hostile opposition may be important in maintaining group solidarity.

The surviving insight in this model is the view of the decision maker as one who pursues his own objectives (or perhaps those of the group he spiritually comes from) by his artistry in forging the political coalition that keeps him in power. The problem is to define the real preferences of the governor, the extent to which he is constrained, and the extent to which he perceives either his objectives or his choices. Brandl regards neglect of these problems as the major source of the inability of economists to comprehend public decision making.[46]

The possibility of predicting political behavior on the basis of class, of platform, or of party seems to be a largely unresolved question of the new political science. In nineteenth-century Britain it was possible to infer a politician's views from his education and class; it seems less possible in twentieth-century America. To predict behavior accurately by party affiliation is more likely, but since parties are themselves shifting coalitions, much of the problem remains. Hotelling's famous paper, "Stability in Competition," sought to explain the similarity of Republican and Democratic platforms of 1928 as a po-

[45] I would add an implicit revolutionary constraint: No sizable group should be so disadvantaged as to be motivated to begin an open rebellion which has an appreciable probability of success or a high cost of suppression.

[46] John E. Brandl, "On Budget Allocation in Government Agencies," *Review of Social Economy*, Vol. 25 (March 1967), pp. 29–46.

litical search for the greatest coalition.[47] But as Arthur Smithies was to point out, 1936 was another story. So too, one might contrast 1960 with 1964.

A more direct view of governmental search procedures can be represented by work of Maass and Major.[48] Here the legislative process is viewed as centrally concerned to discover what agreement on objectives can be reached. Partly this is a matter of bringing together elected spokesmen for individuals and groups, but more basically it is a genuine search. The process of discussion is critically involved in a mapping function; it poses issues that permit both legislators and their constituents to discover their views about objectives. It may thus permit (via compromise and persuasion) the development of agreement on public objectives, which can serve for a time as the social objective function. This view continues to disquiet many economists, for it leaves a large element of slack within the governmental decision process that is not readily understood in terms of inputs into governmental decisions. Thus the ability to predict government decisions is limited.

Rothenberg has an enormously elaborate model designed to remove this element of slack.[49] Unfortunately it defies concise description. To quote his summary, in part, "the legislative process is seen as an *n*-person, non-zero sum, repeated cooperative game of strategy, for which no general solution exists . . . unfortunately, manipulation of the model to elucidate its complications is beyond the scope of the present paper." I confess to being skeptical. Game theory, here as elsewhere, seems to provide a vocabulary for discussing a multiplicity of outcomes rather than a tool for predicting particular outcomes.

One aspect of Rothenberg's model picks up a strand that has characterized the work of Duncan Black over two decades: the influence of the institutional rules of legislative decision on the outcome of the decision process.[50] This fascinating literature is ne-

[47] Harold Hotelling, "Stability in Competition," *Economic Journal,* Vol. 39 (March 1929), pp. 41–57.

[48] Maass, "System Design and the Political Process"; and David C. Major, "Decision-Making for Public Investment in Water Resource Development in the United States" (Harvard University, Graduate School of Public Administration, Harvard Water Program, August 1965; mimeograph).

[49] Rothenberg, "Model of Economic and Political Decision Making."

[50] Black, *Theory of Committees and Elections.*

glected here only because the chief question now addressed is the choice of policies within a relatively fixed institutional framework, not the influence on choices of changes in the institutional framework.

Banfield, like Maass and Black, is a political scientist, but unlike them he is profoundly skeptical of the utility of the type of analysis that characterizes economics: the solution of constrained maximization problems.[51] His central point is that in the articulation of social values, the techniques of economics do not merely fail to predict behavior (because more information is required about individuals' values, or the nature of the constraints, and so on) but rather that they are inherently biased and are bound to mispredict. In Banfield's view, the alternating and intertwined activities of discussion, of struggle, and of arbitration constitute the heart of the decision process and exhibit such variance in possible outcomes that they dominate the problem of explaining political behavior. To neglect these in favor of the inputs into the political hopper is to neglect the major sources of variance in favor of the minor ones. In effect Banfield argues that the limits placed on decision makers by individual preferences are so wide as to be of no real interest.

This view might be expected to lead Banfield toward the Black and Rothenberg analyses of process, toward the work of Schelling and others on the strategy of conflict, or perhaps toward the organizational theorists.[52] Here, too, however, Banfield is pessimistic almost to the point of nihilism. His pessimism seems extreme, but it underlines the absence as yet of a compellingly effective set of predictive theories. Banfield's view that politics, and thus also the prediction of its outcomes, is an art rather than a science, may prove right; at this stage neither the economists nor most political scientists seem prepared to abandon the search for an explanation of public decision making.

## Evaluation of Alternative Views

This extended discussion of alternative views on the nature of and means for articulating the public interest clearly reveals no con-

[51] Banfield, " 'Economic' Analysis of 'Political' Phenomena."
[52] Thomas C. Schelling, *The Strategy of Conflict* (Harvard University Press, 1960).

sensus. Indeed, it is relatively easy to demonstrate why each approach is deficient. While one of these theories may with slight changes prove adequate, there is greater likelihood that we will have to await a more profound insight. It seems to me of prime importance, however, to distinguish between the present inadequacy of our theories and the presence of a phenomenon. Things need not be understood to exist; substantial agreement on certain social priorities may exist despite our inability (at any point in time) adequately to derive them from basic principles. Suppose today we cannot *derive* from individual values a consistent set of social valuations that enables us to say. "There is a clear collective demand for this activity." Are we constrained to act as if it does not exist, or settle for the logic of the lowest common denominator of acceptable action—that which will command unanimous consent? To answer "yes" makes the society a prisoner of its ignorance. It is less elegant, but not less scientific, to take as a starting point for evaluating social actions the revealed objectives of society instead of the derived ones.

The matter can be put more strongly. Suppose one could prove that in some fundamental sense the prediction of social values is impossible from basic information about individuals and their political representatives. Would it then be necessary to quit the analysis of public decision making? I think not. One might take the nature of social valuations as revealed by past actions and assume that such preferences have some stability. In other words it might be possible to infer dominant collective social priorities from social actions and the repudiation or nonrepudiation of them by the electorate.[53]

In the United States today it is hard to avoid the belief that there is a strong collective preference for certain public goods such as public aid to education, for improved highways, for a redistribution of income benefiting the elderly and the urban poor. Are these only today's choices of today's individuals, or are they a reliable indicator of how Americans are likely to feel next year or even ten years hence? There is evidence of stability in some choices, and gradual change in others. In any period there are highly debatable issues that get resolved and stay resolved for generations. Agreement on them may not be unanimous, but it is sufficient that legislators of each party are content to let them lie. Today the debates about mini-

---

[53] For such an attempt, see Birdsall, "A Study of the Demand for Public Goods."

mum wages and social security—even Medicare—seem remote and (in this sense) resolved. The appropriate level of the programs may be an issue, but their existence is not likely to be subject to any serious challenge. On the other hand, there is no strong evidence of similar preferences for or against integrated housing or schools, for foreign aid to nonaligned or eastern countries, for domestic gun control, or for international disarmament. At any time some issues are genuinely unresolved, and for others the degree of consensus is uncertain.

Evidence on these matters is available even in the absence of analytic solution. Not only do elections provide some information about revealed preferences but enormous quantities of attitudinal information can be collected by the techniques of survey research. Theorists tend, erroneously, to denigrate stability and regularity in the absence of comprehensive theory. Men successfully and repeatedly circumnavigated the globe using theories now regarded as naive and wrong. Today the tides along the Bay of Fundy can be predicted with enormous accuracy, but little is understood of their differences from place to place. Closer to home, the aggregate effects of a tax cut can be more accurately predicted than its incidence.

These arguments are not meant to minimize or disparage the progress of the purely theoretical debate. Even failures are more promising now, and the emptiness of the new welfare economics has been left a long way behind. Most encouraging is the genuine joint dialogue among social scientists of different fields as well as different persuasions.

## The Problem of Weighting

It is increasingly the practice to treat the public interest (or social welfare) as a function with several arguments. For example, following Marglin,[54] one might write

$$U = U(Z_1, Z_2, Z_3, \cdots, Z_n)$$

where the $Z$s are different aspects of the public interest, such as economic efficiency (or contribution to national income), the pattern

[54] Stephen A. Marglin, "Objectives of Water-Resource Development: A General Statement," in Maass and others, *Design of Water-Resource Systems*.

of income distribution, the rate of economic growth, balance-of-payments equilibrium, economic stability, national security, and freedom. Whether one considers these as different aspects of a one-dimensional index of utility, or as different dimensions of a multidimensional concept, is more than a semantic issue. If, for example, $Z_1$ and $Z_2$ are readily comparable in terms of a cardinal measure of their contribution to utility (for example, market value of electric power and market value of irrigation water), they can easily be elements of a scalar measure of welfare. Their relative weights are given by the common yardstick used for measuring them. If on the other hand $Z_1$ and $Z_2$ represent efficiency and freedom, each of which may be supposed to be meaningfully defined and ordinally measured, no simple yardstick may be available for comparing them. Thus the problem of tradeoffs between these separate dimensions of a public interest vector remains to be solved. Because noncomparability, or difficulty in comparison, is a feature of many public choice problems, it seems to me convenient to regard the public interest as genuinely multidimensional, and thus explicitly to consider conflicts among objectives.

The number of dimensions and their definition are matters of analytic and operational convenience. Because there are many different sources of public interest, there will be many forms of a proximate contribution to public welfare. Whether it makes more sense to combine different effects into a single dimension than to treat them as separate dimensions of the public interest depends upon whether one believes there is an acceptable cardinal measure of their contribution to public welfare. If there is one, it makes sense to combine them; if there is none, it is better to keep them separate.

With a one-dimensional objective there is a simple decision rule. If, for example, one is concerned solely with contribution to national income, it is conceptually easy to choose between a dam in Oregon and a retraining program in West Virginia. But if one cares as well about who gets the income, this simple rule becomes simplistic. Given multiple objectives, it is inevitable that individual proposed actions will affect more than a single dimension. Inevitably also the objectives will often conflict. The definition of a multidimensional objective function neither creates nor resolves the conflicts; instead it identifies them.

The central aspects of choosing policies in face of multiple objectives are how to define an appropriate measure of each objective, and how to resolve conflicts among objectives.

A very simple, indeed trivial, theorem says that if weights are left unspecified, any policy $A$ may in general be made to appear less or more desirable after the fact than an alternative $B$ (which may easily be "not $A$"), by specifying which objective is implicitly the important one. This theorem is important only because it is neglected so frequently.

Many forms of implicit weighting exist in practice. It is almost routine in lay discourse to argue that because a proposed policy advances *some* object of social policy, it is desirable ("The war on poverty will improve the distribution of income"). Or to agree that because it retards some other object it is undesirable ("The war on poverty extends the role of government and thus reduces individual freedom"). Neither of these statements tells us whether the war on poverty is desirable.

Somewhat subtler is the implicit neglect of certain objectives by assuming the dominance of others. Much of the economist's traditional emphasis on efficiency has had the effect of giving it a very high weight relative to growth or distribution. Joseph Schumpeter, always treated as a giant with respect to his theories of development and cycles, is still regarded as a crank with respect to his views on monopoly, because he challenged orthodoxy by arguing that static efficiency considerations are overweighted relative to growth.

If objectives are genuinely multidimensional and not immediately comparable, some solution to the weighting problem is implicit or explicit in any choice, and that solution reflects someone's value judgment. Put formally, it is now accepted in principle that the choice of weights is itself an important dimension of the public interest. This choice is sometimes treated as a prior decision which controls public expenditure decisions (or at least should do so), and sometimes as a concurrent or joint decision, an inseparable part of the process of choice.

*Weight Selection Viewed as a Prior Decision*

Several widely divergent views of the public decision process have in common a tenet that important aspects of the weighting decision should be regarded by the decision maker as given to him. Two of these virtually assume lexicographic ordering of certain objectives. In lexicographic ordering, objective 1 is dominant, but in case two choices are equivalent in terms of objective 1, choice is made upon the basis of objective 2, and so on. (Listing in alphabetical order is the best-known lexicographic procedure.)

One view that is virtually lexicographic in effect is that efficiency, as measured by private market allocations, is the dominant criterion. If a project is efficient in this sense, it (or some substitute) is worth undertaking; otherwise it is not. Once a project is so legitimized, the decision maker is welcome to examine other, secondary objectives in project selection or design. This appears to be the view of McKean, Harberger, and Mishan when they insist that the correct (really, the only correct) rate for discounting future benefits and costs and for assessing the opportunity costs of public funds is some specified measure of the marginal productivities of capital in the private sector.[55] (The discount rate as an implicit weighting device will be treated below.) This view solves much of the weighting problem by assumption and makes many otherwise difficult decisions easy. Those who hold this view are repeatedly appalled at the obvious outrages performed by the public sector, and the apparent acquiescence therein of otherwise sensible people.

A different but no less arbitrary lexicographic view is that public budgets for particular activities reflect dominant social choices, and that while efficient allocation of the funds *within* the budget is appropriate, efficiency considerations should not determine the size of the total budget. Probably the boldest statement of this view is my earlier work; and it will be expanded below.[56]

While neither of these forms of solution-by-assumption of the weighting problem is likely to prove literally satisfactory in all situations, either might provide insight into how the public decision mak-

[55] Roland N. McKean, *Efficiency in Government Through Systems Analysis, with Emphasis on Water Resources Development* (John Wiley & Sons, 1958); Harberger, "Survey of Literature on Cost-Benefit Analysis"; and Edward J. Mishan, "Criteria for Public Investment: Some Simplifying Suggestions," *Journal of Political Economy,* Vol. 75 (April 1967), pp. 139–46. An alternative interpretation is discussed on pp. 292–94 below.

[56] Peter O. Steiner, "Choosing Among Alternative Public Investments in the Water Resource Field," *American Economic Review,* Vol. 49 (December 1959), pp. 893–916.

ers regard their actions as constrained by a society's underlying consensus view of key issues they face.

An alternative to taking weights as inherently given is to regard them as an explicit prior decision. It is conceivable to imagine the political system having a procedure whereby decision is reached on, then announcement made of, a fixed set of weights that will be controlling in choosing among income, income distribution, and so on. No one suggests this is the procedure used, although both Chenery and Marglin urge this as a real possibility for economic planners. Chenery, for example, suggests the planners announce a national income equivalent to balance-of-payments effects, thus making for a fixed tradeoff.[57]

While more or less accepting the view that weighting decisions are relatively stable and preexisting, Eckstein, Haveman, and Weisbrod, among others, do not wish to assume them nor to expect political leaders to articulate them.[58] Instead they suggest attempting to infer the weights by an analysis of past choices. Eckstein suggests looking at an issue such as differential tax rates, in which a decision on distribution is at the heart of congressional intent, in order to discover implied values that congressmen hold. Haveman applies this approach to evaluating water resource investments with respect to a multidimensional objective. These approaches are suggestive, even if one is unwilling to go all the way and take congressional actions as perfectly revealing social consensus.

Weisbrod deals with a two-dimensional objective function covering efficiency and income distribution. He suggests that every example of choice of a less efficient alternative over one that is more efficient implies a minimum implicit weight to the redistribution that is involved. His hope is that analysis of many decisions would reveal a weighting scheme. The hazard here is that any irrational choices, any mistaken estimates of efficiency, and any nonincluded objectives

[57] Hollis B. Chenery, "The Application of Investment Criteria," *Quarterly Journal of Economics,* Vol. 67 (February 1953), pp. 76–96; and Marglin, *Public Investment Criteria.* One is not limited in principle to linear relationships. Chenery's tradeoff at time *t* could be a variable function of the size and sign of balance-of-payments disequilibrium at time *t*.

[58] Eckstein, "Survey of the Theory of Public Expenditure Criteria"; Robert H. Haveman, *Water Resource Investment and the Public Interest* (Nashville: Vanderbilt University Press, 1965); and Burton A. Weisbrod, "Income Redistribution Effects and Benefit-Cost Analysis," in Samuel B. Chase, Jr. (ed.), *Problems in Public Expenditure Analysis* (Brookings Institution, 1968)

would all be imputed as distributional benefits. But the real test of Weisbrod's suggestion will depend upon whether it produces a clear and consistent pattern of implicit values. To my knowledge, it has not been tested as yet.

Yet another approach to weighting of objectives is to regard certain objectives as constraints. Suppose $U = U(Z_2)$ is maximized subject to $Z_1 \geq Z_1^*$. Then until the constraint is satisfied, $Z_1$ has a high priority, and after it is satisfied $Z_1$ has a shadow price that reflects the price paid in assuring its achievement. This traditional approach to allocational problems is often useful. It may, however, prove difficult to define which objectives are to be regarded as genuinely constraining.

### Weights as the Outcome of Political Process

The discussion above treated the appropriate weighting scheme as a preexisting condition for the decision process. Dahl and Lindblom, Braybrooke and Lindblom, and Maass, Major, Banfield, and Eckstein, among many others, regard weights as generated by the *process* of decision. In this view the political process addresses weighting problems not abstractly but in a case-by-case confrontation. In each case the decision about what to do forces a discussion, or compromise, or struggle among competing objectives. To Maass the essence of the legislative process is the making of choices among conflicting objectives. The decisions will be made upon the basis of the information (or prejudices) available, and the scope for the analyst in affecting the decision will be reasonably to identify the choices. Eckstein expresses the strong view that administrators and project analysts should not arrogate the weighting process and bury the choices within a single measure of benefit.[59] (The academic literature reveals no dissent.)

This whole area strikes an analyst as untidy. It is clear that choices among objectives must be made, and that the political process must somehow make them. There appears, however, to be indecision about whether it does so within narrowly confined limits of

[59] Dahl and Lindblom, *Politics, Economics, and Welfare;* David Braybrooke and Charles E. Lindblom, *A Strategy of Decision* (Macmillan, 1963); Maass, "System Design and the Political Process"; Major, "Decision-Making for Public Investment in Water Resource Development"; Banfield, " 'Economic' Analysis of 'Political' Phenomena"; and Otto Eckstein, *Water-Resource Development* (Harvard University Press, 1958).

underlying consensus, or with substantial discretion. Is the alternative to the invisible hand the responsible arm or the visible paw? Perhaps more important is the source of such discretion as does exist: Is it simply variance in underlying views, is it ignorance or indifference on the part of the citizen, or is it an explicit delegation of authority by the electorate? Answers to these questions critically affect subsequent research strategy. Banfield's nihilism seems to reflect the view that discretion arises from such deep underlying ignorance, indifference, or both, that no effective limits are imposed on the wondrous ways of politicians. At the opposite extreme, if politics is conceived as a mere veil that masks a variety of underlying views, a key to understanding the outcome is to study the variance of the views. Downs, and to a lesser extent Lindblom, embodies this view. It has important precursors in an older political science literature on interest groups.[60]

What is particularly disturbing is the virtual absence of disposition on the part of either economists or political scientists to engage in an empirical study of the decision process that will resolve these areas of debate. The large literature is almost entirely theoretical and assertive. Yet survey data about public attitudes on issues exist and provide some sort of a base. Similar data about ex post public reaction to political decisions and procedures might be developed. In fact such evaluative questions are now asked, but only about things like a major war or the overall performance of a president or a party. While I do not wish to say more about its design in this essay, a study of how decisions are reached and the extent to which they are responsive to public opinion is worth undertaking; it seems more promising than another decade of assertions in resolving differences.

## The Discount Rate as a Weighting Device

Characteristically, choice among alternatives involves choice among time paths as well as among quantities and qualities. A staggering literature concerns the correct way to allow for time, that is, to define a measure that permits rational choice among alternative

[60] An admirable summary with an extended bibliography is found in Truman, *Governmental Process.*

timestreams.[61] What is novel in my discussion here is treating this as a debate about the nature of the public interest. Much of the debate about the discount rate really reflects a division over two questions: (1) What is the effective way to handle multidimensional objectives? (2) Should efficiency considerations play a dominant role in the weighting procedure? The discussion which follows is meant to demonstrate that the essential debate rests upon differences in viewpoint, not upon technical issues. This accounts for economists' failure to come to agreement on what appear, superficially, to be simple technical matters.

One great technical debate is now resolved. The criterion for choosing between competing projects is, ceteris paribus, the higher present value, defined as:

$$PV = \sum_t \frac{B_t - C_t}{(1 + r)^t},$$

where $B_t$ and $C_t$ are benefits and costs at time $t$, and $r$ is an appropriate discount rate.[62]

The issue that is unresolved concerns what discount rate is to be used in calculating present value. Here there are two major schools: Harberger, Hirshleifer, McKean (and others) opt for some kind of marginal cost of capital; Feldstein, Marglin, and I (among others), for some kind of explicit measure of social time preference. While it has become fashionable to distinguish these views as "social opportunity cost" and "social time preference," the terminology is misleading; all are concerned with the opportunity cost of time preference.

In order to explore the differences in point of view, it is helpful to deal with a very simple example. The basic numbers are shown in Table 1. Suppose the government plans to spend $100 on either of

[61] An exhausting, but not exhaustive, sample of references is marked by asterisks in the bibliography section entitled, "Selected General References," pp. 343–53.

[62] An earlier view argues for the rate-of-return criterion. For each project one might compute the value of $r$ for which $PV$ was zero. This is the internal rate of return. One of Irving Fisher's great insights was to notice that for *independent* projects, comparison of the internal rate of return with the cost of capital provided a rational choice criterion. Its disadvantages, which have been noted by many and are ably summarized by Harberger in "Survey of Literature on Cost-Benefit Analysis," become decisive in choosing among alternative (and very possibly interdependent) projects, the characteristic problem of public expenditure policy.

**TABLE 1. Hypothetical Example Comparing Opportunity Costs of Time Preference of Two Projects Serving the Same Objective**

| Characteristic | Project A | Project B |
|---|---|---|
| Cost of project | $100.00 | $100.00 |
| Physical output (units) | | |
| Year 1 | 30 | 0 |
| Year 2 | 0 | 33 |
| Value of output (1 unit = $3.80) | | |
| Year 1 | $114.00 | 0 |
| Year 2 | 0 | $125.40 |
| Present value evaluated at: | | |
| 6 percent | $107.50 | $112.50 |
| 10 percent | 103.60 | 103.60 |
| 11 percent | 102.70 | 101.60 |
| 15 percent | 99.10 | 94.80 |

two projects, $A$ and $B$, each of which serves an underlying objective but in so doing produces a different timestream of benefit. $A$ produces 30 units of physically defined output after one year, and none thereafter; $B$ produces 33 units at the end of two years and none thereafter. Notice that at this point a unit of output has not been valued, nor an opportunity cost of the $100 specified. Can anything be said?

Clearly the present value of $A$ (in physical units) is $30/(1 + r)$ and of $B$, $33/(1 + r)^2$. For any discount rate greater than 10 percent, the present value of $A$ is greater; for a rate less than 10 percent, the present value of $B$ is greater; and if the rate equals 10 percent, the present values will be equal. The time preference school would argue that if society's rate of time preference in receiving benefits is greater than 10 percent per annum, project $A$ is preferable, *and if Congress is committed to choosing one or the other,* it should choose $A$. If the rate is less than 10 percent, it should choose $B$. *It should be especially noted that this decision is independent of the value per unit (in dollars or in utility) of a unit of output.*

Adding a monetary measure of the value per unit of output superficially changes nothing. With $z$ representing the value of a unit of benefit a comparison of the present value of $A$—$30z/(1 + r)$— with the present value of $B$—$33z/(1 + r)^2$—would still turn only on the value of $r$. Monetary valuations play two roles: to permit comparisons of unlike units of output, and to introduce some implicit additional alternatives.

To consider the second of these, an arbitrary value of $3.80 is assigned to $z$, and present values of projects $A$ and $B$ are then computed at various interest rates. The results are shown in the last four lines of Table 1. It is of course true that $A$ has a higher present value than $B$ for all discount rates greater than 10 percent. But somewhere between 11 and 15 percent (actually at any rate greater than 14 percent) the present value of even the preferred project falls below $100, the cost of the project.

If $z$ accurately measures the tradeoff between dollars and public benefits, an additional requirement that the present value of benefits must exceed the present value of costs ($100 in this example) is a requirement of absolute merit, with which no one can sensibly disagree. *The use of z thus invites consideration of the implicit alternative of doing neither.* But the condition is an important one. There are many situations in which values of $z$ are assigned with no expectation that their absolute size is a sensible measure of benefits. (The reasons for doing so are discussed below.) In such cases the test of absolute merit, implied by the subsidiary rule that benefits be greater than costs, loses its meaning. Sometimes the question of absolute merit is irrelevant because it has been predetermined by congressional assertion. If the relevant question is not whether to produce some benefit stream but how best to do it, only the relative size of the present values matters. This is always affected by the size of the discount rate.

The central issue must now be faced. How should the discount rate be chosen? Is it necessary for society to assign a particular value to the discount rate, or is this itself an element of collective choice? In particular, is it rational for society to assign a discount rate that differs from the private rate of return? To be specific, stay with the example and suppose the private rate is greater than 10 percent, say 15 percent. Would it be rational to choose a rate of less than 10 percent?

The apparent inefficiency in such a choice is simply illustrated. Suppose that the social rate of time preference is 6 percent. If present values are computed with 6 percent, the choice will fall to project B which produces benefits of $125.40 after two years. At 6 percent this yields a present value of $112.50, nicely greater than the cost of the project. But the $100, if put into the private sector, could produce $100(1.15)(1.15) = \$132.25$ in two years and this is greater than the benefit produced by project $B$. Thus if $z$ is accurately assigned, the choice of $B$ is inefficient. This is shown in the row of present values where the rate is 15 percent: The present value of the return does not exceed the cost. *The use of the private rate of return as the discount rate and insistence on a present value in excess of current cost insure consideration of the implicit alternative of leaving the money in the private sector.* To its proponents, this is decisively important. If $z$ is a perfect, or at least an unbiased, measure of the dollar merit of public benefits, there can be no quarrel. If one objects that the private output may be qualitatively different from that of project $B$ and that society may prefer the public output, the reply of the private-rate school is that assigning a value to $z$ has taken account of the social valuation of differences in benefits. The real issue here is how confident one is that the levels of $z$ accurately measure the qualitatively different outputs of private and public sectors. Can units of education be accurately compared with sports cars? It is at least possible that the $z$s reflect an adequate measure of qualitatively different *public* outputs and permit comparison of similar but different outputs of $A$ and $B$, but at the same time provide an inadequate measure of either $A$ or $B$ relative to sports cars.[63] Where large qualitative differences between either $A$ or $B$, on the one hand, and the private alternative goods, on the other, are involved, the assertion of the absolute merit of $A$ or $B$ and a determination of their relative merit may be more honest (and more subject to political ratification) than attempts to assign $z$. (In the example, raising $z$ to $4.50 causes both $A$ and $B$ to have merit compared to leaving the $100 in the private sector.) *Use of the private discount rate relies crucially on the faith that z is as accurate a measure of benefit between private and public sectors as it is within either sector.*

Those who insist on the use of the private discount rate implic-

[63] I am not invoking a unique discontinuity here. In statistics there are many cases in which a measure becomes increasingly unsatisfactory as circumstances vary. In such cases it is necessary to identify a threshold beyond which confidence is too small to permit reliance on the measure for decisions. Index numbers become increasingly unreliable as one departs from the weighting base; in regression the standard errors of estimate grow at an increasing rate as the independent variables deviate further from their means, and so on.

itly have the required degree of faith in the ability to impute benefits to the differences between public and private goods. These differences, however, are usually qualitative and require difficult imputations. Perhaps surprisingly, the staunchest advocates of the private discount rate are also those who are most skeptical about the adequacy of imputed benefits. When, as with McKean, this skepticism leads to unwillingness to include most imputed benefits, it introduces a marked downward bias into estimation of the present values of public projects.[64] It is nonmarket benefits that usually provide the main incentive for collective action. Indeed, if only market benefits are counted and the private discount rate is used, most projects that then promise positive present value will appeal directly to private development. The public-goods issue will arise only for a limited class of goods, particularly the perfect collective consumption goods.

In some ways the presence of the alternative of doing neither project has clouded the issue. If the private market discount rate in the example had been 11 percent, all would agree that one of the public projects should be undertaken. Using 11 percent as the discount rate leads to the choice of $A$, while the social time preference rate of 6 percent leads to $B$. The relative merits of $A$ and $B$ are seen differently even though either is preferred to leaving the money in the private sector. If there is a rational basis for a difference between public and private time preference, is there any reason why the latter should distort the structure of a purely public choice? Advocates of the private rate would say "yes," on the ground that the public project $A$ will produce $30z$ ($114) in one year. This is more than the $111 that $100 will produce in the private sector. If this $30z$ ($114) is then reinvested in the private sector at 11 percent, it will be worth $114(1.11)$, or $126.54, at the end of year 2, which is more than the $33z$ ($125.40) of project $B$. (It is important to notice that it does not produce $30z(1.11)$, or $33.3z$ physical units, since the units of the public good are not produced by the private sector.) Thus the first year, but not the second year, of public projects has merit. Put differently: The combination of project $A$ for the first year plus a private project for the second year appears superior to either project $B$ or a two-year private project. This is the rationale

---

[64] Roland N. McKean, "The Use of Shadow Prices," in Chase (ed.), *Problems in Public Expenditure Analysis.*

behind the case for myopia in public decisions.[65] Even though absolute merit is not initially at issue, this argument again depends critically upon the accuracy of $z$ in equating private and public benefits. This is because a mixed private-public alternative is implicitly introduced.

To summarize, the use of private opportunity cost as the discount rate rests upon a basic belief in the ability to find an adequate yardstick for comparing very different types of benefits—in other words, for defining a one-dimensional objective function by defining an appropriate set of weights in the form of a value-of-output measure. Harberger states the conclusion thus:

> The solutions reached by Eckstein, Marglin and Steiner are all subject to a single, decisive criticism: they may lead to results in which the rate of return to investments in the public sector lies below that which could be obtained by placing the same funds at the disposal of the private sector, or by investing directly in private sector type activities.[66]

This is compelling if, but only if, there is a one-dimensional measure of rate of return from diverse activities, and if the throw-off (or yield) of benefits can always be reinvested at the private rate. The essential difference in points of view that prevents me, at least, from accepting the Harberger view lies in rejecting one or both of the implicit premises.

In this debate, the possibility that the social rate of discount may be below the private marginal productivity of capital is not at issue. Harberger, for example, explicitly recognizes it. Clearly the two rates represent different things: One is a collective social preference in which people, not dollars, vote or have their preferences otherwise considered; the other is a concept of effective demand for capital. What *is* at issue is whether public policies should serve to equilibrate them. McKean, for one, would decrease public budgets so as to equate them; Harberger would use public policy to expand private investment to bring the private rate down to the public one. I have been content to regard budgets as assigned, to some degree, by predetermined preferences for nonefficiency dimensions, and to evaluate within those budgets using the social discount rate.

---

[65] For a full and emphatic attack on this view, see Stephen A. Marglin, "The Social Rate of Discount and the Optimal Rate of Investment," *Quarterly Journal of Economics,* Vol. 77 (February 1963), pp. 95–111.

[63] Harberger, "Survey of Literature on Cost-Benefit Analysis," p. 25.

## Summary: The Role of Efficiency

Economists traditionally place major emphasis on the efficient allocation of resources, and much of the debate about public interest is also so phrased. This is particularly, but not exclusively, the case when dealing with the portion of the debate concerning the discount rate. This essay has stressed a multidimensional objective function rather than one involving only efficiency. Economists who disagree with this approach are not likely to do so on the grounds that efficient use of resources is the only sensible objective of social policy, nor on the grounds that efficient use of resources will never conflict with other objectives. Instead they may argue, first, that any worthwhile objective can be incorporated within an efficiency framework by an appropriate set of measurements of benefits and costs. Thus efficiency can embrace the maximization of a utility function that may have several arguments. Or they may argue, second, that objectives like income redistribution not conveniently and conventionally included within the efficiency framework can and should be satisfied by lump-sum taxes and transfers that do not serve to distort resource allocation.

Since either one of these arguments is, if correct, sufficient, the case for efficiency seems powerful and it has many adherents. Nevertheless, many economists, including this one, do not find these arguments persuasive.

The first argument has already been discussed at some length and constitutes a highly important question of research strategy. If there is a multidimensional objective structure, can it be compressed effectively into a single dimension by assignment of a measure of benefits? My view is that, while such a compression is possible, it is not desirable, because it leads to the submergence of real issues behind a facade of faulty measurements. Bias can run either way—by overvaluing intangibles (see, for example, the characteristically shoddy imputation of secondary benefits), or by neglecting as benefits those differences in the vector of public and private goods that are not readily measured. There is, of course, no inherently correct way to handle the problem of what is the best form of response to difficulties in accurate measurement. I would rather measure only what I have confidence in measuring with some accuracy and leave issues involving magnitudes not accurately measured to be decided by explicit choice. It may be easy to choose between defense and education at a given time even though it is hard to express a price that equilibrates them.[67] If one does not use a uniform system of valuations (it is argued here that one need not), there is a danger that one will make some inconsistent decisions. But if one uses badly biased data, one risks making consistent but faulty decisions. As has been said in another connection, it may be better to be vaguely right than precisely wrong.

The second defense of efficiency fails to prove compelling if one believes that approximate lump-sum transfers cannot be made, that they cannot be made without high transaction costs, or that they will not be made. These are factual questions, but there is no substantial doubt about the facts. It might, for example, be possible to achieve indirectly for underprivileged urban residents what direct public action now provides through urban redevelopment and various poverty programs. But it is unlikely that in a political context the same results would have been achieved. The current effort to replace a myriad of welfare programs by a negative income tax will test the ease or difficulty of achieving by taxes or transfers what might otherwise be provided by direct public action. Whether for good or ill, it is frequently easier to do things one way than another. To limit the public policy maker to allocationally neutral tools constrains him and thus changes the nature of the results he achieves. Whether the change is large (as I believe) or small is a factual matter on which one day the facts may be decisive.

Obviously the question, "What is the public interest?" has no simple answer. Asking it invites the sort of smile reserved for small children and benign idiots. Let me end this discussion with some wholly personal assertions. There is a role for measurement, a role for analysis, and some need for explicit decision making. Decision makers are ill served when these roles are blurred. One such blurring occurs if we submerge real decision making among competing objectives into a mere measurement problem by giving the advice,

[67] Obviously, once the dividing line between them is set, an implicit (shadow) price exists. But the price may be very different a few years hence. The argument here is that it may be easier to make the decision (and thus imply the price) than in some objective sense to assign the price and thus determine the decision. Only at a purely formal level are these equivalent.

"Assign benefits and costs and then pick the optimal set of projects."
This provides too little help. One of the economist's most potent
functions is honestly to identify and separate that which can be accurately measured and compared from that which involves such hero-
ics of assumption that actual measurements are but concealed
preferences. The advantage of articulation of real choices over assignment of measures that appear to obviate them is that it makes the
decisions explicit and subject to review. But identification of the
scope for explicit choice does not mean unconstrained choice for administrators. Within particular dimensions, departures from the
efficient solution ought to be identified and justified.

All sorts of decisions do get made and not all of them are sensible. The analyst's role, in my conception, is to force an articulation
of the proximate objectives served and of the conflicts among them.
I should be willing to regard open decisions so arrived at by elected
(or otherwise responsible) public officials as a reasonable approximation to the collective values that we call the public interest. At
present so many issues and conflicts are concealed, both among objectives and among alternative means, that the discretion of the policy maker is augmented beyond what is necessary or desirable.

## THE THEORY OF MARGINAL PUBLIC EXPENDITURE CHOICES

THE THEORY OF MARGINAL public expenditure decisions is usually
discussed in the literature as benefit-cost analysis. Unfortunately the
phrase has acquired different meanings and different overtones for
different people. At one extreme, benefit-cost analysis becomes thoroughly trivial; at the other, genuinely misleading. To define the sensible middle ground requires disposing of the extremes.

This way lies triviality: Suppose all desirable consequences of
some action are defined as benefits, and all undesirable consequences as costs. A decision maker desiring to maximize welfare is
advised to choose among possible courses of action in such a way as
to maximize the difference between benefits and costs, and is given
the following rules of optimizing behavior: Undertake any project

for which, at some level of output, benefits exceed costs (in other words, for which the benefit-cost ratio exceeds unity), and push that project to the point at which the increase in benefits equals the increase in costs (marginal benefits equal marginal costs).

If this is what benefit-cost analysis means, it is simply a definition of rational behavior. It applies equally to any decision: of a man to marry or to commit suicide, of a firm to produce or to collude, of a government to tax or to engage in war, of a politician to run for office or to put his nephew on the payroll, of a poker player to cheat or to draw to an inside straight. Its very generality suggests that it is unlikely per se to offer specific guidance. Moreover, if rationality is to be assumed, benefits greater than costs for any positive action may be inferred. But since this is true of every action it explains none.

If denigrating this purely formal set of rules for optimizing behavior as a schoolboy's exercise in elementary calculus is too harsh, it is only because there is insight in such exercises, and many decisions have been made that would have benefited from it.[68] But without more, this framework is virtually empty. Its widespread use in legislative enactments, in bureaucratic practices, and in theoretical and empirical research suggests that there is more.

Whether this framework helps in policy decisions depends upon how clearly one can define the decision maker, his objectives, and the relevant dimensions and consequences of his choices. It depends also on the definition and measurement of benefits and costs, and upon the myriad linkages between decisions and consequences. It is widely believed that the framework has proved useful at least in forcing some articulation of objectives, proximate and ultimate, and in providing a frame of reference for defining and quantifying the measurable merits and demerits of particular programs.

It is because benefit-cost analysis can prove helpful that it runs the hazard of misleading, for the deductive rules of optimizing behavior rest upon identification of all marginal benefits and costs, and measurement of them in terms of their net effect on the objectives. If costs and benefits are defined to cover a biased subset of the consequences of an action, or if the measures employed bear but a super-

---

[68] The basic mathematics is explicated in many places. For a competent presentation, see Jack Hirshleifer, James C. DeHaven, and Jerome W. Milliman, *Water Supply: Economics, Technology, and Policy* (University of Chicago Press, 1960), pp. 152–74.

ficial resemblance to the correct ones, there is no significance for optimizing behavior of a benefit-cost ratio greater than unity. The
optimizing-decision rules depend upon the measurements of benefits
and costs embodying all consequences, direct and indirect, open and
hidden. The analytically relevant benefits and costs are implicitly and
completely defined by the objective function of the decision maker.

Obviously one must settle for less than this in the real world. But
incomplete or imperfect information must be distinguished from
bias. If, for example, the definitions of what are to be included and
how they are to be measured become subject to administrative or
legislative determination or interagency compromise, they no longer
provide any necessary guide to optimal decision making. There is
more than a little belief that legislative requirements for benefit-cost
calculations have had greater impact on the justification of projects
decided upon than on the choice of projects to be justified, and that
systematic bias does occur. Marglin, for example, ends his brief history of benefit-cost analysis by observing that "benefit-cost analysis
was introduced as a means of project 'justification' alone (this word
is used in the U.S. government literature), not as a tool for project
planning; in American practice (as distinct from theory) it often
has served as window dressing for projects whose plans have already
been formulated with little if any reference to economic criteria."[69]

Benefit-cost analysis as an applied subject must seek its way between the trivial and the fraudulent. Without prejudging the planning-programming-budgeting system (PPB), which is discussed
below, it is fair to say that earlier federal agency benefit-cost calculations have been regarded from both within and outside the government with varying degrees of skepticism, ranging from a grain of
salt to open cynicism.

The major academic discussions of public decision making have
found it useful to utilize the benefit-cost vocabulary in examining
real questions of project design and selection.

Because benefit-cost analysis has been so thoroughly and recently surveyed,[70] comment here is limited to a few issues that seem
to be important yet relatively neglected. Immediately below I suggest

[69] Marglin, *Public Investment Criteria*, p. 18.

[70] Eckstein, "Survey of the Theory of Public Expenditure Criteria"; Harberger,
"Survey of Literature on Cost-Benefit Analysis"; Marglin, *Public Investment Criteria;* and Prest and Turvey, "Cost-Benefit Analysis."

a model of the decision-making procedure that links the broader issues of the public interest to the narrower ones of project design and
selection.

## A Sequential Model of Public Decision Making

No matter how decisions actually get made, the outcome of
public expenditure decision making indicates that each of the following has been decided: (1) the total level of public expenditures;
(2) the relative sizes of the major programs of public expenditures,
such as defense, space, foreign aid, poverty; (3) the set of specific
projects which will constitute a program, hence also the rejection or
postponement of other projects; (4) the designs of accepted projects
which are to be implemented, hence the rejection or postponement
of alternative designs.

Many different choice procedures might have been employed,
and a variety of theoretical models might serve to represent the process or to predict its outcome. It is particularly important to make
the distinction between a virtually simultaneous determination of
answers to the above questions, and a genuinely sequential procedure. If it is sequential, an iterative procedure might lead in the end
to results that are independent of the sequence, in which case a simultaneous model (although descriptively inaccurate) would prove
analytically sufficient for predicting outcomes. On the other hand,
the results of a sequential procedure may depend crucially upon the
sequence, and thus not converge toward the results of a simultaneous
determination model. In such a model it is possible for value judgments or even errors made at one stage to exert a significant effect
on the final decisions.

The standard decision model of the economist is a simultaneous
determination model. In the presence of a cardinally measurable objective function and perfect knowledge of the effect of any decision
on the level of welfare, an optimal set of decisions is assured by the
conditions that the marginal public expenditure dollar has a benefit
equal to the marginal private expenditure dollar (thus assuring the
correct total public expenditure level), and the marginal benefit of
public expenditure dollars is the same across programs, projects,
and project elements. It is hardly necessary to explicate this model
for economists; indeed, if one had either a single-dimensional social

objective function, or a set of measurement devices capable of reducing all interobjective conflicts to a single metric, only such a model would make economic sense, and the economic theory of public expenditures would be genuinely trivial. If decision makers failed to observe the canons of optimizing behavior, they would have to be educated. Only measurement issues would remain to be settled.

## The Case for a Sequential Model

By now it must be apparent that I reject this simultaneous determination model. In particular, it seems to me that prior decisions as to the total level of expenditure and the relative size of major programs largely constrain the selection of projects and designs, rather than being determined by them or simultaneously with them. While this might reflect an outrageous nonoptimality in the decision procedure, it may instead reflect a conscious decision to regard the levels of budget as matters of higher priority. I argue thus not on normative grounds (though in fact I believe this is as it ought to be) but on the positive grounds that this sequencing does in fact happen, precisely because procedures have been chosen that ensure its happening. Such feedbacks as are allowed are limited in number and attenuated in effect.

Before the form and implications of a particular sequential procedure are explored, a rationale may be suggested for its use in preference to a simultaneous determination. Obviously the total budget is the sum of its parts. But values that are largely independent of its composition may be attached to the total, first, because the total budget is an important fiscal tool and thus an important element in stabilization policy, and, second, because it is taken as an index of the role and scope of government in the life of the society.

Empirically it is apparent that Americans value stabilization as a public objective. (My guess is we value it below defense and above other public goods.) It is unreasonable to expect that stabilization policies are assigned benefits and costs which are directly comparable to benefits and costs of specific public goods. It is also unreasonable to insist (as Musgrave would) that stabilization needs be handled by tax adjustments rather than expenditure variations.[71] (If it showed nothing else, the 1966–68 debate between President Johnson

[71] Musgrave, *Theory of Public Finance.*

and the Congress about the 10 percent income tax surcharge showed this.) For these reasons alone the total budget decision may be taken as exogenous for most marginal decisions about public goods. Whatever the real alternative to a particular public project may be, it is seldom the transfer of funds to or from the private sector.

Between the political parties no less than among economists there are different and strongly held preferences about the size of the role of government. These preferences tend to invest the level of total (nondefense) expenditures with a symbolic significance as a measure of the quality of the society. They reinforce stabilization considerations and further diminish the probability that the inherent merits of a particular project will much affect the size of the total budget.

Whether, among major budget categories (as distinct from the total budget), choices are largely insulated from marginal interprogram decisions is probably more debatable. There seems to be little dissent from the proposition that defense needs appear to be determined within narrow limits without regard to the opportunity costs of other goods forgone.[72] If interest on the national debt, space expenditures, veterans' programs, and international affairs, each of which seems to enjoy an important degree of insulation from other programs, are excluded, that portion of the budget which is subject to interprogram marginal choices is less than a third of all federal expenditures. Sixty percent of this remainder is devoted to health, labor, and welfare, including payments of social security benefits. The rest, less than 15 percent of total federal expenditures, covers agriculture (including price supports), commerce, transport, housing, education, and general government. Even if this 15 percent were fully substitutable among programs, which clearly it is not, it would be a small part of total federal expenditures, and a smaller part yet of all government expenditures. Even without a precise line between insulated and competitive programs, it seems clear that significant insulation exists.

The issue is not whether or where benefit-cost analysis is ap-

---

[72] For a discussion of the complexities involved in estimating the opportunity costs of defense expenditures, see Frederic M. Scherer, *The Weapons Acquisition Process: Economic Incentives* (Harvard University, Graduate School of Business Administration, Division of Research, 1964).

propriate. There is no question that it is appropriate and helpful at the level of project design and selection. Rather, the question is whether these decisions are made in such a way that they determine the total budget and its major divisions, or whether they represent the much less basic set of decisions of how to allocate resources within a more or less rigidly prespecified budget category. As a positive matter of the facts of political life, it is hard to avoid the conclusion that it is the latter, narrower role that is left to economic analysis.

## Stages in Decision Making

For purposes of analysis, government may be visualized as consisting of three kinds of decision makers ultimately responsible to the voters: a President, a Congress, and Executive Agencies which work for the President but are also responsible to Congress. It may be assumed that society has four objectives: Defense $(D)$, Income Redistribution $(R)$,[73] Economic Stability $(S)$, and Efficiency $(E)$, and that there are the following stages in decision making:

STAGE I: PRESIDENTIAL PROPOSAL. The President recommends to the Congress a variety of programs that he desires, for Congress to approve or disapprove in principle. Each program will, he asserts, make a positive contribution to defense or income redistribution, or both. He also recommends a total budget and a level of budget deficit that will either promote economic stability or lead to an approximately known destabilizing effect. Thus, in essence, he proposes initial weights for $D$, $S$, and $R$.

STAGE II: CONGRESSIONAL REVIEW. Congress accepts some of the President's suggestions and rejects others. For those it accepts, it authorizes approximate amounts to be appropriated, which are more likely to be below than above the requested amounts. This known bias leads to some inflation of original requests. Congress knows this, but does not really object, since it values the nominal watchdog role it plays as much as the real one.[74] The program authorizations that come out of Congress at Stage II are likely to be somewhat, but

[73] A simplifying proxy for the whole discretionary nondefense budget.
[74] If there were no genuine water in budget requests, congressmen would feel themselves rubber stamps, or would be forced to make changes that could cause them political harm.

not strikingly, different from those made to it by the President, both in total amount and in the relative weights for $D$, $S$, and $R$. Since they have no appreciable staff, the amount of real initiative that resides in legislatures is debatable. But even in a counterpunching stance, in which they merely prune unevenly a somewhat overstated budget, legislatures can and do make some changes in weights. These changes are likely to be larger the less strongly the President and his wing of his party control the Congress.

Congress recognizes that these preliminary authorizations are not fully binding, on it or on anyone else, but expects implementing proposals not to go over the budgeted amount by more than 10 percent. It knows that ultimately it will face pressure from the President to increase the total budget.

In Stages I and II, the President and Congress assert (or refuse to assert) key social priorities with respect to the broad objectives $D$ and $R$. (In an expanded list one would redefine redistribution to include many aspects, such as farm price supports, social security, wars on poverty or crime, aids to education, and so on; and defense to include military programs, space programs, foreign aid, and the like.) In so asserting they do more than make a preliminary assignment of relative weights to be given to the objectives of redistribution and defense. They also, often, imply minimum amounts of expenditures and weights for these objectives. Here Dorfman's notion of the viable coalition plays its role. The minimum guarantees are those necessary to prevent alienation of any important subgroup. If these minimum amounts are in aggregate very nearly as large as the total authorized amounts, the discretion is of a different kind from what it is if they are well below them. Presidential and congressional assertions of basic social priorities are, of course, subject to periodic review and indirect ratification or rejection by the voters.[75]

---

[75] This raises again the issue discussed earlier (p. 275) about how tightly voters hold the reins. I prefer here to regard voters' control as Jefferson's "consent of the governed" rather than voters' sovereignty. The difference between consent and determination arises if voters will consent to a reasonable variety of alternative outcomes. Consent is a threshold, not a maximizing concept. One critic of this view argues that the difference is not great because the transaction costs of trying to do more than consent are prohibitive; thus exercise of consent *is* maximizing behavior. But the difference is great from the point of view of public officials. They acquire discretion under the consent procedure that they would not have as mere agents for maximizing voters.

Many potential weighting issues are brushed aside at this stage. Marginal efficiency considerations have so far been ignored. This means that at least minimum levels of public activities of various sorts may be expected to be quite independent of such things as the opportunity cost of capital, public or private, or the levels of prices and wages. I do not here commit the elementary error of neglecting the distinction between averages and margins. There are some marginal tradeoffs between programs considered in the model at a later stage (Stage III). But the point is that some controlling decisions are made and at the later stages may very well bind in such a way that marginal equilibrating adjustments cannot be made. For example, however undesirable or inconvenient the basic farm program may be in a given year, the legislative commitment to it exists. To argue, as some will, that this means that the benefits of the basic level have been judged greater than the opportunity cost of other, forgone objectives is to sacrifice insight to after-the-fact consistency. It neglects the fact that there are real things at stake, for the future as well as the present, in congressional battles about creation or rejection of new public programs.

STAGE III: PROJECT DESIGN. Executive agencies must now design specific projects to implement proposed programs. Given approximate scales of approved programs (from prior years as well as from congressional authorizations), executive agencies in Stage III design program elements (or projects) from among a great variety of possibilities. Ultimately each agency will come up with a reduced set that constitutes its proposed program, which is arbitrarily assumed to have an aggregate cost of the authorized amount plus 15 percent.

In this task each executive agency is considered to be both highly competent and highly conscientious. It serves its conception of the objectives of the agency's programs. The defense agency will suggest the best set of defense projects that it can for the maximum sum expected to be available to it. (It will probably be unconcerned with redistributive or stability objectives.) The redistribution agency will suggest the best set of redistributive projects that it can for the expected maximum budget, although it may well neglect defense or stability considerations. This is not to say that individual agencies are monolithic; their objectives may be several and they will have to assign weights among their multiple objectives—for example, in the water resources field, flood control versus irrigation and power. But an agency makes its choices on whatever basis seems internally adequate to it. It ranks projects according to *its* objectives and *its* weights, rather than according to a set of weights that is in any sense common to, or selected by, all agencies. Subject to its given objectives and to its estimated budget, maximization of efficiency is the sole criterion used in recommending projects. This is the realm of agency-perceived efficiency—but only intraprogram efficiency, subject to the (assumed) budget constraints. The motivation for efficient allocation comes from the need to economize the agency's expected budget in order to achieve its objectives. (In general these objectives are probably not very different from those intended by the President and Congress in establishing the program, but there is some room for discretion here as well.)

Stage III yields a proposed set of projects for each program. Programs are characteristically somewhat overbudgeted, and it is possible but not essential that, within programs, projects are ranked as to relative merit.

STAGE IV: THE PRESIDENTIAL BUDGET. A presidential review agency, which may be called the Bureau of the Budget, now prepares a final budget to send to Congress. Its major review function is to combine the programs of individual agencies into a total program that is consistent with the President's stabilization objectives and with his view of the political realities. By this time a tax program is undoubtedly well developed, and the tolerable overall size of budget is likely to be known within very narrow limits. This stage represents a feedback in that this is a second round of presidential recommendation; however, it consists typically of applying a total expenditure constraint to a series of agency budgets. While such trimming as may be required might be used systematically to reconsider sizes of major programs (and thus to revise interprogram and interobjective weights), it is more realistic to assume that cuts are, in fact, either proportional or haphazard with respect to these matters. At this stage neither the time nor the information to make systematic marginal comparisons is available. Moreover, there may be real reluctance to reopen a number of issues which are implicitly settled by relative program sizes.

In this view, Stage IV is not used for revising major prior decisions about detailed choices; instead it embodies largely a scaling operation in which uncoordinated project proposals are made consistent with other constraints in the least controversial way.

STAGE V: CONGRESSIONAL CHOICE OF FINAL BUDGET. From the executive budget proposals, Congress selects particular subsets of projects, subject to its previous guarantees. In so doing, it also determines the size of the total budget and the level of deficit.

Out of Stages III and IV come to Congress a proposed set of projects, possibly ranked as to relative merit within programs. The analytical economist would be pleased if, in this final stage, Congress recognized that in every marginal decision it faced three marginal effects—on $D$, $R$, and $S$. If Congress did so, it would recognize that in recommending the marginal $100 million for defense, it was either forgoing the marginal $100 million for redistribution or adding $100 million to the budget deficit. If Congress behaved this way and if the marginal sacrifices in all lines were then equated within the committed budget limits, the iterative procedure would produce the Pareto-efficient solution corresponding to a preassigned set of weights for $D$, $R$, and $S$.

Even in this simple case, and assuredly in more complex ones, it is not necessary or likely that Congress in Stage V will consider simultaneously the whole matrix of tradeoffs among programs and between marginal projects and the total budget. Nor is it necessary that it follow the agency's ranked list in any particular program. Because the procedure followed can greatly affect the weights given to various objectives and the role of efficiency, it is worth extended discussion. Alternative models are possible.[76]

*Congressional Choices*

The nature of congressional choices will depend upon the times in two senses: One is the responsiveness of congressmen to war or peace and prosperity or depressions, and the other the biennial change voters make in the composition of Congress. The second is vitally important in preserving the constraint of individuals' values on discretionary choice, as discussed above, but it may be neglected

[76] Maass, in "System Design and the Political Process," and Major, in "Decision-Making for Public Investment in Water Resource Development," present a model of political decision making which differs from, but which can be interestingly compared to, the one presented here.

in the present context. For illustrative purposes, consider three (non-exhaustive) prototype situations among which economic circumstances and congressional preferences differ. In each case—wartime, cold war, peacetime unemployment—a particular pattern of congressional preferences is assumed; this ignores the fact that Congress is a conglomerate of individual congressmen rather than a monolithic body.

WARTIME. Congress is assumed to give lexicographic priority to defense needs. As between stability and redistribution it has no strong a priori preference ($D{\Rightarrow}S; D{\Rightarrow}R$). It is convenient to assume that Congress sets the defense appropriation first. Will it accept the whole list of defense projects? Not necessarily. It may decide that some projects lack absolute merit, either because the tentative budget was too high ("waste in the military"), or because of biases within the defense agency (such as interservice rivalry). Further it may question the judgment of the executive agency about military strategy and other matters. It may add to, delete from, or change the nature of projects approved, but it is more likely to grumble and make small changes than to make large ones. In this case, the significant changes it does make are motivated almost exclusively by its perception of *defense* considerations.

The realistic assumption that this wartime defense budget is uncomfortably large implies pressure on either the nondefense (here, the redistributive) budget, or the total budget, or both. But the redistributive budget has a minimum level. It is likely that redistributive programs in aggregate will have to be cut nearly to this minimum level, and the total budget will be the sum of the merit-based defense budget and a minimum redistributive budget. This results characteristically in a destabilizing total budget.

Because the total available budget for redistributive programs is likely now to be narrowly fixed in amount, and is insufficient to fund all the proposed projects, much will have to be cut and thus there is room for arbitrary action by Congress. Which projects will be selected? If there is a realm for purely political, and economically capricious, choices, it is here. Even if Congress received ranked projects, it has no need to follow the rankings. To the extent that the lists of projects submitted by the agencies are themselves relatively homogeneous in benefits per dollar, a capricious choice will involve relatively small efficiency losses. To the extent that the benefits vary greatly within a given agency or among agencies, the losses may be larger. But whatever choices are now made—studied or capricious, efficient or inefficient—the congressional reranking that now takes place is likely to be irreversible. In the more complex real world (where redistribution is a vector), many congressional redistributional values are implemented by individual project selection. Year after year certain types of projects are funded, and others cut or postponed.

COLD WAR. Assume a situation such that congressional choices are virtually lexicographic, and run in order from stability to defense to redistribution $(S \Rightarrow D \Rightarrow R)$.

This case differs from the previous one chiefly in that the acceptable total budget may be heavily influenced in advance by stabilization criteria. This implies more serious scrutiny of the defense budget, including eliminating, curtailing, or postponing some projects that would have been funded in wartime. In a strictly lexicographic ordering, redistributive programs are likely to bear the brunt of the desire for stabilization and to be deeply affected in aggregate by the prior decisions on defense. Since a cold war is also likely to involve inflationary forces, much cutting is required (and thus much discretion is created) in the proposed redistributive budget.[77] If one replaces lexicographic ordering by strong preferences, the overall budget constraint imposed by stability considerations may force some explicit incremental choices between defense and redistributive programs. (Parenthetically, it may be worth exploring the hypothesis that these situations reveal more about congressional choices of weights for redistribution versus defense than do the other cases.) But the extent of interprogram comparisons need be neither greater nor more systematic than Congress wishes to make it; and Congress is better qualified to make decisions than to engage in fact-finding studies. In any event, the tight total budget created by the cold war leaves Congress with many decisions to make. Whatever its decisions it may modify further the interobjective weights. Because

[77] A major political choice is between use of a tax reduction and an expenditure increase to achieve a specified net budget deficit. This involves an important choice that itself has redistributive consequences. Since I want to neglect it, I shall assume tax rates and structure fixed.

many of these final decisions are made ad hoc, and sometimes in haste, there is no guarantee that the ultimate de facto weights are carefully or explicitly assigned.

PEACETIME UNEMPLOYMENT. The assumptions in this case are of substantial unemployment and a disposition to use fiscal policy to remedy it. It is, moreover, supposed that the mix of tax cuts and expenditures to be used has been decided upon and will involve a substantially expanded level of nondefense expenditures. Congressional preferences put first priority on stability, with the choice between defense and redistribution not well articulated $(S{\Rightarrow}D; S{\Rightarrow}R)$. Here budget constraints are loosened and a wide variety of new, expanded, or previously postponed projects can be undertaken and may be actively sought. These circumstances provide the President and the agencies with the opportunity for proposing a great variety of programs and projects that vary in their incidence and in their contribution to other goals of society. There is great discretion, particularly at the presidential and executive agency levels. Congress by instinct and habit is better equipped to restrain than to create—a task for which, in any case, it has insufficient staff—and its role in active choice is apt to be subordinate. Some programs or projects will be attacked by some congressmen, and Congress may curtail them. But these are more likely to be symbolic acts than vital rearrangements of the interprogram weights of the executive branch. Even if Congress is to a degree out of sympathy with the President, it will probably find it difficult to alter very much because it cannot easily create a viable alternative expenditure program to coalesce the opposition.

## Implications for Benefit-Cost Analysis of the Sequential Model

The merit of this fairly elaborate sequential model is not merely that it bears some descriptive similarity to real institutions, but that it leads to some implications that are important if they may be taken to characterize the real decision process.

A basic implication is that many important decisions about the total budget and its major subdivisions are made without regard to the characteristics of individual programs or projects. They reflect assignments of weights among conflicting dimensions of the public interest. There is no reason why economists need refrain from bringing data to bear on those decisions, but I suggest that if they wish to influence the decisions they do so directly, not indirectly through the definition of benefits or costs of particular projects. One of the major postwar debates has concerned the proper size of the public sector in an affluent society.[78] The economists' debate might have been submerged in questions of how best to assign benefits to parks or costs to smog, or of how to determine the price differential that would equate a unit of private research with a unit of public research. But to submerge the real issue of social values in this way would have served only to prevent its careful discussion and debate. The central question was one of values, rather than of discount rates, computational formulae, or the proper measurement of particular benefits. A book such as *The Affluent Society* proves significant if it helps individuals to crystallize views of the public interest that have lain inchoate within them. The policy struggle in 1964 over whether a tax cut or an expenditure increase was the best road to a needed deficit provides a second example. The central issue would have been clouded rather than clarified by a detailed attempt to compare benefits from particular programs of expenditure with the benefits from particular tax cuts.

This implication, if it applies, both limits and liberates benefit-cost analysis. The benefit-cost estimator may regard his assignment to be the design of an appropriate choice procedure for selection of projects *within* a well-defined area, for which he will receive a budget. Thus he needs to judge the adequacy of his measures or his models for choice only in the context of optimizing within his budget; he can ignore the effects his choices might have on the total government budget or the tradeoffs between widely different types of programs. Such things may or may not be considered; but they will not be critically affected by his measurements. This means, for example, that what constitutes benefits in water resources, how such benefits should be measured, and how different timestreams should be evaluated, can be decided with reference to what is best for choosing among alternative projects in the water resources field and need not be the same as, or equivalent to, devices designed to choose between

[78] John Kenneth Galbraith, *The Affluent Society* (Houghton Mifflin, 1958); and Francis M. Bator, *The Question of Government Spending; Public Needs and Private Wants* (Harper & Row, 1960), among others.

alternative forms of missiles or to evaluate a subsidy to the merchant marine or to education.

This point may be made in a most controversial way: I see no reason why society cannot even have different rates of social time preference for different activities: perhaps very high for such defense-related public goods as ample supplies of domestic oil or a native merchant marine, high for income redistributive programs, but quite low for education or public health. This means it places a low value on future supplies of oil, but a high value on future health. If so the public may choose to subsidize medical research (despite a slow payoff) but leave the oil-shale industry to its own devices. Of course the same results could be achieved by imputing a very high value to medical discoveries and a low one to the oil produced after 1975, but it is not clear how such imputations should be made. If imputations are arbitrary for such interprogram comparisons, they can easily distort within-program choices.

Once it is decided that, at the margin, agricultural subsidies are not really competing with school construction, the need for a common metric disappears. One may choose among school construction projects in the way that makes sense for school construction without implying anything at all about which of two farm policies is superior.

The kind of sequential decision procedure described will not in general iterate to some inherent solution. If the budget makers reconsidered the total budget and its major subdivisions after the first round of project approval and then assigned revised budgets which led to revised programs, and so forth, the efficiency criteria which enter at the relatively late project evaluation stage would have a significant effect on the prior decisions. Without such feedbacks, or with highly attenuated feedbacks, efficiency becomes subordinate to the other dimensions of the public interest that determine the basic budgets. This is the situation actually encountered. The task of the agencies consists of efficiently using a predetermined budget, rather than determining the appropriate efficiency budget. Whether this somewhat limited role for efficiency represents progress or travesty is a value judgment about which individuals, especially economists, disagree.

A more technical implication of the proposition that sequence and process matter and affect the substance of choices is that the techniques of comparative static analysis are likely to fail to predict adequately. The dynamics of process, and its influence on substance, become important matters that are only beginning to receive serious attention by economists.[79]

# The Intraprogram Choice Set[80]

If programs are significantly insulated from one another, intra-program choices differ from interprogram choices. Since a program is both constrained and insulated by its budget, the definition of what *is* a program becomes important. The breadth of the set of projects that are considered to be in direct competition for funds must be viewed both cross sectionally and over time.

## Comprehensiveness of the Choice Set: Cross Sectional

The ultimate recommendations of an agency are a subset of possible programs. In making them, the agency will have explicitly rejected some alternatives and (equally important) implicitly rejected all projects not explicitly considered.

The advantage of breadth in the explicit choice set is that the likelihood of overlooking superior alternatives diminishes as the number of alternatives considered increases. Critics of particular public decisions complain more often that their preferred solutions were not in the choice set than that they were considered and rejected.[81] The wider the explicit choice set, however, the greater the required amount of benefit and cost calculation.

It is helpful to think of three subsets of projects: (1) a number of exceptionally attractive opportunities for achieving the agency's objectives; (2) some specific alternative projects that will be technically precluded by each of the projects of the first kind; and (3) a reservoir of feasible but less exciting expenditure possibilities.

[79] Maass, "System Design and the Political Process"; Rothenberg, *Measurement of Social Welfare;* and Peter O. Steiner, *On the Process of Planning* (Athens, Greece: Center of Planning and Economic Research, 1968).

[80] The notion here is of the appropriate predetermined budget category, whether it comprises the combined activity of many agencies or the activity of only a fraction of a single agency. I shall, however, speak of an agency as if it is the relevant aggregate.

[81] John Krutilla and Otto Eckstein provide a typical example in *Multiple Purpose River Development* (Johns Hopkins Press for Resources for the Future, 1958). They charge that the Hells Canyon decision was made between inferior alternatives.

When an agency recommends a particular project from within its choice set it may close a number of doors. The funds it uses might have been spent on other projects from within the choice set or from the reservoir of possible projects. Moreover, because of interdependencies among projects, the choice of project $A$ may preclude project $B$ even if funds are available for both.[82]

In order correctly to evaluate the opportunity costs of projects, it is useful to include in the choice set the major alternatives that will be precluded. It is thus usually desirable to include in the explicit choice set the first two subsets of projects mentioned above. The third subset may usually be excluded and dealt with by an appropriate charge for use of budget that reflects an estimate of the return from the reservoir of lesser opportunities. This budgetary charge is agency specific, and arises because the agency receives less funds than it could spend on meritorious projects. It will be less than the true opportunity cost of the preassigned budget if all the meritorious projects in the first set cannot be undertaken. The reason for not assigning the true opportunity cost at the start is that it is not known in advance which projects are to be left undone.[83] This opportunity cost is an outcome of, not an input to, the decision process.

The notion of a choice set, and selection among explicit alternatives, relieves some of the burden of assigning an opportunity cost to the funds used. Some reservation price is still required to reflect the current public alternative use of the funds for unspecified alternatives, but this price tends to be relatively low. The major forgone alternatives are within the choice set. Their opportunity costs will appear as the shadow prices of the constraints in the choice set.

The practical inability to reach correct allocation decisions by simply considering the absolute merit of individual projects is one of the striking characteristics of public decision-making problems, in contrast to much of private decision making. It is worth further discussion. It arises not because of the publicness of the projects but because of certain interdependencies and discontinuities that are more common in public goods than in private ones. It arises particularly where arbitrary budgets are binding, where the differences be-

---

[82] For example, see Steiner, "Choosing Among Alternative Public Investments."

[83] A worthwhile endeavor is the development of a generalized suboptimizing routine that iterates to an optimal solution in complex constrained choice problems. I have searched for one in vain.

tween best and second best are likely to be large, and where preclusive interdependencies are frequent.[84]

While such situations are uncommon in private markets, they abound in the public expenditure area, particularly with respect to new programs and capital expenditures. Budgets characteristically are virtually binding. Because government expenditure frequently is developing new areas, the discrete and discontinuous supramarginal choice is often identifiable, and best and second best may be far apart. Because public expenditures are biased toward situations where spillover effects are important, interdependencies become commonplace rather than exceptional.

A most serious, and probably warranted, criticism of agency decision procedures is that they tend to devote little or no effort to generating the alternatives among which they choose, but instead deal with a small and haphazardly chosen group of potential projects and spend great effort showing that each of them has, in some sense, absolute merit. The losses of efficiency in choosing from too restricted a set may be very large indeed. One of the advantages of large-scale computers is that they reduce some of the technical problems of choosing from broadly defined choice sets. When the will arises, there will be a way.

## The Choice Set over Time: Time Horizons

Many agencies deal with annual or biennial budgets and thus in any formal sense make decisions on an annual or biennial basis. Longer-range considerations, however, enter in two ways: by use of a positive discount rate in computing present values and by the time horizon that is implicit in the choice set used.

Since many current expenditures reflect production of public goods which will generate future benefits, it is clear that future times enter current decisions. Use of a positive discount rate in computing

---

[84] An example of private decision making in which such a situation exists concerns the professional football draft. A team approaches the annual player draft with a rigidly limited budget of high draft choices, particular personnel needs, and an arbitrary roster limitation. Moreover, it faces a supply of college football talent where the differences in value to it between the first and second available quarterback (or linebacker) may be very great. No matter how good the linebacker is, this football team cannot sensibly decide whether to draft the best linebacker on the first round without considering the alternative of drafting the reserve quarterback it also needs. See also note 85.

present values makes distant benefits diminish rapidly in present value. For example, if 6 percent is the relevant discount rate, the present value of $100 received *n* years hence diminishes from $50 to $10 to $1 as *n* increases from twelve to forty to eighty. The fact that a positive discount rate implies a time horizon is familiar. A different aspect of the time horizon that is less well understood needs to be stressed. It refers not to the duration or time profile of benefits from a single project, but rather to the fact that both new projects and new budgets will be generated in the future. But the expectations about the two need not be symmetrical for all time periods, and it can be quickly shown that optimal behavior varies as these expectations change.

Because every agency expects to have a budget in the next period and in future periods, it tends to regard a decision to leave certain projects undone as a postponement to a time when its funds will be replenished rather than as an outright rejection. Suppose it expects to receive *X* dollars a year forever. Suppose also that some projects are postponable and others are not. It may appear to the agency to be sensible to undertake the latter and postpone the former, even if the present value of the postponable projects is higher than the present value of the now-or-never ones. Whether this is sensible, however, depends upon the new projects that will emerge next year and thereafter.[85] A simple example will bring out the central issues.

Two projects (each costing $100) constitute the choice set of an agency that has a budget of $100 this year and expects the same budget next year. While the present value of *B* ($110) is higher than that of *A* ($105), *B* is postponable and *A* is not. Should the decision maker choose *A*, and plan to do *B* one period hence, when his budget is re-funded? This would prove a sensible answer if no new investment opportunities arose. If, on the other hand, a nonpostponable investment opportunity of type *A* appears *every* period, the superior project *B* is in danger of being postponed forever. One can make a variety of assumptions. For example, if a project costing $300 but leading to benefits of $600 is expected in period 3, the agency would do well to do neither *A* nor *B* in year 1 or 2, but in-

---

[85] The football draft analogy is again relevant. This year's decisions depend upon expectations about next year's crop of draftees, too. Indeed, future draft choices are currency in trading between clubs.

stead to hoard its resources. And so on. (When an agency regards its budget and its investment opportunities as equally representative of its future opportunities, either because both regenerate periodically, or because they expand or contract more or less together, it will be referred to as having congruent expectations.)

A major consideration in defining the choice set is to choose a set of projects and a time horizon which can reasonably be regarded as having congruent expectations. The appropriate time horizon is not determined by the budgetary period or process, but by the analyst's ability to foresee the nature of budgets and of future useful public expenditure opportunities. There is again no reason why these need be the same in one field as another. An emerging new program like the war on poverty may spawn many new projects every year and thus regenerate its investment opportunities with a short time horizon; the space exploration program may, by defining the man-on-the-moon project, have exhausted interesting possibilities for a generation. If the time horizon is not reasonably picked to reflect congruent expectations, an optimal choice and sequencing of expenditures will not occur.[86] There is no formula to dictate *how* an agency should decide what ought to be its horizon for planning projects; indeed, the literature leaves this issue wholly undiscussed.

### Constraints and the Choice Set

Constraints can be of various kinds and many have found it helpful to classify or categorize them.[87] Among a number of suggested categories are: financial (budgetary), distributional, political, administrative, legal, and physical constraints. In discussing constraints it seems desirable to distinguish two different kinds of questions. First, are the constraints immutable or can they be avoided or remedied? Second, do the constraints represent contemporary social values or are they regarded as institutional flaws which ought to be corrected?

[86] For discussion of the sequencing problem, see Harberger, "Survey of Literature on Cost-Benefit Analysis," pp. 243–45; Stephen A. Marglin, *Approaches to Dynamic Investment Planning* (Amsterdam: North-Holland Publishing Co., 1963), pp. 9–34; and Stephen A. Marglin, "Economic Factors Affecting System Design," in Maass and others, *Design of Water-Resource Systems*, pp. 171–92.

[87] See, for example, Eckstein, "Survey of the Theory of Public Expenditure Criteria"; Marglin, "Economic Factors Affecting System Design"; and Prest and Turvey, "Cost-Benefit Analysis."

The first question is straightforward. Certain constraints represent physical or economic realities. Competing alternative uses of the same physical space are necessarily incompatible. Alternative means to a single well-defined end are incompatible (in the sense of being redundant); other processes may be necessarily complementary, and so forth. Constraints of this sort may be viewed as both unavoidable and unremediable (in the current period if not for all time); while they complicate the choice procedure, they do not condition its character. Some other constraints (for example, what Eckstein calls administrative constraints and illustrates by defining a maximum possible rate of expansion of a program) are virtually of the same character, although conceivably they are potentially remediable. Yet other constraints, such as legal requirements or political considerations or budget limits, are immutable only if the choice is to leave them unchanged.

Here the second question, which is attitudinal, becomes important. One man's constraint may be another's objective. Consider, for example, a legal or political constraint which requires that a given percentage of a budget be spent in the southern states or for the benefit of some other worthy minority group. This may be viewed, on the one hand, as a revealed social preference about what ought to be. If so, it is not a limitation on what is possible but rather an opportunity to serve a high social objective. Alternatively the constraint may be viewed as an imperfection in the social or institutional fabric that is unfortunate and should be removed if possible or evaded if it cannot be removed.

These differences in attitudes have enormous operational significance for project design, for the form of project justification, and for actual project selection. To continue the example, one may (a) look for the best projects which happen to be in the southern states and give them a high priority; (b) relocate efficient projects to the South; or (c) stress (and perhaps imagine) southern features of projects located in the North.[88] The issue here is not different from that faced with respect to the budget constraint (see page 301): Does a binding constraint represent a higher social ordering or reveal a source of inefficiency?

[88] Haveman, in *Water Resource Investment and the Public Interest*, Chaps. 1–6, provides a detailed empirical study and evaluation of the selection of federal water resource projects in the South during the period 1951–62.

The nature of choices made, in the long run even more than in the short run, depends upon decisions by an agency as to which constraints it intends to honor in spirit and which it intends to erode or evade if possible. With one exception, mentioned just below, it seems hazardous to treat constraints generally as due to imperfections and to evade them if possible. To do so invites replacing systematic political value judgments by agency value judgments. Disputes about values ought, in my view, to be fought openly. An agency objecting to, say, a regional requirement ought to fight against it by showing the cost of the constraint rather than by changing project descriptions.

Political feasibility is often asserted as a constraint, but it is a troublesome notion. It can be used to dismiss competing alternative means to given ends, or to cause easy acceptance of the second best. Here the danger is that the soft constraint of political infeasibility will provide a rationalization for almost any indolence, inefficiency, or chicanery. The decisions about whether to live within a bad law or a particular set of attitudes, or instead to generate pressure to fight them, must be made. Assertions of political infeasibility tend more often to stop inquiry than to limit it to relevant alternatives.

## The Definition and Measurement of Benefits and Costs

Because opportunity costs always represent benefits of a forgone alternative, there is no theoretical distinction between benefits and costs. Indeed, both symmetry and elegance tempt the theorist to regard all decision problems as ones of benefit maximization subject to all resource constraints. The conventional use of costs reflects the pragmatic view that, for a great fraction of resources used, the acquisition price reflects value in the best alternative use. This is because, in a competitive world, price is the outcome of market contention among potential users. In fact, of course, it is not benefits that are difficult, and costs that are easy, to measure. Where market evaluations exist and are regarded as acceptable, measurement is easy, whether on the benefit or the cost side. Difficult cases occur where market evaluations are regarded as erroneous (and thus require correction) or where markets do not exist at all and thus imputations of values are required. It is relatively easy to measure both benefits and costs of a toll bridge; it is extremely difficult to measure the benefits or the costs of the Grand Canyon.

Dramatic advances have been made in the last decade in attacking formidable measurement issues.[89] That period has seen serious attempts to measure what earlier groups had regarded as unmeasurable, such as the value of life, leisure, health, and the quality of environment. This progress warns against regarding as inherently unmeasurable a number of aspects of public activity that have not so far been measured at all. Nevertheless, at this time the following remain largely unmeasured, if not unmeasurable: freedom, equity, justice, equality. The problem is not in quantifying *some* benefits or costs of these dimensions of welfare, but in achieving a reliable index of net benefits.

The variety of issues involved is staggering. Because two earlier Brookings volumes[90] go into these issues at length, the discussion here will be limited to a few dicta.

### A Few Debated Benefits and Costs

Some dimensions of public activity are troublesome because there appears to be no consensus as to whether they represent "goods" or "bads," whether they should play a positive, negative, or neutral role in analyses. One of these is public provision per se, as in public power, public housing, flood insurance, Medicare, and so on. Many major decisions taken are more heavily influenced by this issue than by any quantification of more tangible benefits or costs. The Hells Canyon and Tidelands Oil cases are representative of this kind of controversy. In each situation the proponents regarded public provision as a positive good, while the opponents regarded it as a distinct liability. Whatever the lip service given to efficiency considerations, there is little doubt that they were largely drowned out by the public-private issue.[91]

A second troublesome issue concerns the appropriate public val-

[89] A fair sample of leading (and easily accessible) studies is given in the section of the bibliography entitled, "Measurement Issues in Benefit-Cost Analysis," pp. 353–57.

[90] Samuel B. Chase, Jr. (ed.), *Problems in Public Expenditure Analysis* (Brookings Institution, 1968); and Robert Dorfman (ed.), *Measuring Benefits of Government Investments* (Brookings Institution, 1965).

[91] See Krutilla and Eckstein, *Multiple Purpose River Development*.

uation of risk.[92] Suppose two projects with the same expected value have different expected variances. Risk aversion, an observed and rational private attribute, would lead to preference for the project with the smaller variance. Should public values reflect private values and avoid or discount risk? Arrow argues that governments should be neutral toward risk because, in aggregate, society is better off self-insuring and maximizing expected values.[93] The argument is that riskiness imposes private rather than social costs. Death of a salesman, of a firm, of a venture, or of an industry may generate private disasters but, at worst, social problems; these problems can be more readily countered if national income is maximized. If one accepts this argument, it is difficult to avoid carrying the logic a step further and arguing that public authorities ought to have a risk-assumption preference just sufficient to offset the private bias against risk. Arrow's contention that there is no reason why the public authorities should have risk aversion can readily be extended to yield the view that they should regard private risk aversion as a social cost to be overcome in order that on net balance society becomes risk-neutral.

While Arrow's insight is helpful and important in defining an additional potential public good (risk assumption), there can, clearly, be national risks too great to bear with equanimity. A rational government may well pay a premium to avoid a risky defense policy; it may pay a premium to avoid the risk of an undiversified economy. (Notice that the risk of overspecialization of an economy is one that private enterprise may not be able to cope with.) Of course, a supranational government might willingly bear these risks. Quite apart from the constituency, risk aversion may be a rational public attitude if the costs of dealing with the disasters that do occur are large. There seems to be no general answer as to how to view risk. I share Arrow's rejection of the attitude that risk, per se, is to be avoided, but this seems to create no more than a rebuttable presumption for risk neutrality.

[92] This paragraph speaks of pure risk, not uncertainty. It is assumed that the benefits in year $t$ are some fully known probability distribution with an expected value $E(B_t)$ instead of a certain level $B_t$.

[93] Kenneth J. Arrow, "Optimal Public Investment Policy" (Discussion Paper No. 2, Resources for the Future Seminar on the Discount Rate for Public Investment, Washington, March 1965; mimeograph).

Uncertainty is also troublesome. Clearly, estimates of economic magnitudes become increasingly difficult with the remoteness of the period in which they occur, or with their remoteness from market experience. Many strategies for dealing with uncertainty have been suggested, none wholly satisfactory. At one extreme there are those who would neglect it, who regard the best estimates of benefits tomorrow and twenty-five years from now as equally accurate.[94] The objection to this is that the analyst can support his prejudices by the way he assigns magnitudes to uncertain outcomes; the hard facts can be diluted by the soft ones. A substantially opposite view would argue that there is a certain threshold of certainty required beyond which one should assign zero benefits and costs. A relatively mild form of this view would impose a time horizon of, say, ten, twenty-five, fifty, or one hundred years, beyond which benefits should be neglected.[95] A harsher form would neglect those imputed benefits and costs that stray too far from the certainty threshold of market-type phenomena.[96] The hazard of this approach is, of course, that the neglected items may be nonnegligible in their effect. Assigning zero as their value is as arbitrary and as potentially biased as assigning any other number. A third strategy is to assign a higher discount rate than would otherwise be appropriate. The underlying implicit theory requires that, as a rough matter, uncertainty increase exponentially with time and that in the absence of this corrective, there is a consistent bias to overestimate uncertain magnitudes.[97]

None of these solutions seems to me satisfying. A fixed and dis-

[94] The President's Water Resources Council, *Policies, Standards, and Procedures in the Formulation, Evaluation, and Review of Plans for Use and Development of Water and Related Land Resources,* S. Doc. 97, 87 Cong. 2 sess. (1962).

[95] For example, Report to the Federal Inter-Agency River Basin Committee, *Proposed Practices for Economic Analysis of River Basin Projects,* prepared by the Subcommittee on Benefits and Costs (1950), known as the Green Book; revised in Report to the Inter-Agency Committee on Water Resources by the Subcommittee on Evaluation Standards, *Proposed Practices for Economic Analysis of River Basin Projects* (1958), also known as the Green Book.

[96] McKean, "The Use of Shadow Prices."

[97] In *Water-Resource Development,* p. 88, Eckstein bases his recommendation of the use of an uncertainty premium upon such an argument: "From the moment a project is finished, it can be expected to become more and more obsolete as compared to the current state of technology, and as time passes, it will lag further behind current best practice for achieving the same purpose." This leaves me unmoved. Cannot the estimator build obsolescence into his estimates?

tant cutoff point is relatively benign, but it avoids the issue rather than solving it. Neglecting nonmarket benefits entirely assures drowning the baby. Use of an increased discount rate seems equally unsatisfactory, though it is often advanced. In the first place, uncertainties not related to time are not recognized. More importantly, in this solution, so far as the discount rate affects genuine choices among equally certain alternative time profiles of benefits and costs, those choices may be seriously distorted by changing the discount rate.

What then is the solution? A reasonably eclectic and frequently satisfactory tactic is to do a sensitivity analysis on particular uncertain elements of benefit and cost estimation to determine which ones critically affect the views of the merit of a project. Many uncertain magnitudes do not matter; those that do can be approached anew with the hope that ingenuity can narrow the range of uncertainty.

### Correction of Market Prices

Market prices of goods and factors obviate the need for subtle cost imputation when they reasonably approximate the marginal alternative uses of factors of production, and obviate the need for benefit imputation when they reflect the marginal valuation consumers place upon the goods. But these conditions do not always pertain; when they do not, correction of market information becomes important.

Discrepancy occurs, first, when some resources are substantially unemployed and the lags in mobility are great. The price of an employed unit of such a resource may greatly overstate the opportunity cost of utilizing otherwise unemployed units. Thus, for example, during a period of substantial unemployment, a public policy that, whatever its other effects, also serves to decrease unemployment may require not only the imputation of a nonmarket benefit—a decrease in the unemployment rate—but also a correction to its cost by a reduction in wage rates. Part, indeed perhaps all, of this wage may reflect no real resource diversion from other uses. To see clearly that such a correction may be appropriate, one need only consider the case where the alternative to the employment-inducing project is a direct transfer payment to unemployed workers. If unemployment compensation (or relief) is paid in the same amount as the wages, the total marginal product of employing the resource is a net benefit.

Labor is, of course, not the only resource potentially unemployed. Capital, machinery, land, water, and other resources can be idle in various degrees at various times. A careful evaluation should allow for variations in implicit supply prices even if the market fails to do so.[98]

A related, but perhaps less important, source of error in market prices concerns their noncompetitive character. So far as a market price includes a monopolistic rent or a government subsidy, it fails to reflect the alternative value of the resources used. Obviously in selected cases this may be important. The value of agricultural commodities subject to important subsidy cannot sensibly be used in estimating the value of publicly provided irrigation water for growing such crops, for this would lead to a significant overvaluation of irrigation water. Large subsidy programs are sufficiently well defined that the bias they introduce into market prices can be identified. Monopoly pricing is more difficult, and I would counsel neglecting it except where a convincing demonstration of lower alternative cost is plausible.

The correct treatment of taxes which become embodied in prices is easy only after one takes a firm stand on an unresolvable philosophic debate: Do taxes represent a transfer that should be regarded as unavoidable tribute or instead a payment for a set of government services needed and used in amounts roughly proportional to tax payments? Amounts of tribute should be excluded from prices, payments for service included. No guidance can be offered here on where truth lies, but it is wholly possible that a given individual will answer differently for different taxes. Surely there is more service to the payer in the gasoline tax than in the excise tax on cigarettes or furs.

Perhaps the most serious potential imperfection in market prices as measures of value is that they refer to current, marginal valuations. Most project benefits or costs involve discrete (and often large) increments of future goods and resources. To take an old but

[98] It took economists some time to accept these readily provable notions. The reason is their long preoccupation with a full-employment, competitive, equilibrium model in which the kind of discontinuity here implicit was not allowed to exist.

dramatic example, it was easy in principle to recognize that the average value of a large increment to the supply of electric power in the Tennessee Valley was in no real way related to the pre-TVA price of electric power; it was harder to find a sensible answer. This was so not only because the increase in supply was enormous, or because it occurred slowly in a region where many other changes were occurring, but also because, with lags, changes in supply prices generated new demands for electrical equipment and for electricity-using industries. Solving such problems demands case-by-case ingenuity.

*Imputation of Nonmarket Information*

Historically, benefit-cost measurement developed most rapidly in the water resources field in part because two of the principal outputs, power and water, had private market substitutes and were to be sold, whether privately or publicly developed. Nonmarket benefit estimation developed through attempts to assign benefits to the nonmarketable by-products of multipurpose hydroelectric projects the principal appeal of which to their sponsors was often their size and their publicness. Many early attempts to measure benefits of flood control, navigation, and recreation are in the literature.[99] The revived interest in benefit-cost analysis outside of the water resources field seems largely to have been a deliberate strategy of the Brookings Institution. The papers of the First and Second Conferences on Government Expenditures and Rothenberg's study of urban renewal constitute a remarkably large part of the new and imaginative literature.[100] What characterizes them as a group is, first, the recognition that it is desirable to tip the balance between the measured and unmeasured by attention to those aspects of the nonmarket benefits that are likely to prove large; second, the primacy they give to conceptualization of the nature of benefits and costs;

[99] The bibliographies in the books by Eckstein, *Water-Resource Development,* and McKean, *Efficiency in Government Through Systems Analysis,* contain many of these. Some of the more notable studies are listed under "Water Resources" in the bibliography section entitled, "Measurement Issues in Benefit-Cost Analysis," pp. 356–57. Other important contributions appeared from the late 1930s through the 1950s in the *Journal of Land Economics.*

[100] Chase (ed.), *Problems in Public Expenditure Analysis;* Dorfman (ed.), *Measuring Benefits of Government Investments;* and Jerome Rothenberg, *Economic Evaluation of Urban Renewal* (Brookings Institution, 1967).

and third, the way benefits and costs may vary as circumstances change. In short, there is a remarkable avoidance of techniques the only merits of which are expediency and ready availability of data. These studies, by and large, are searching where the going is rough.

Schelling, for one example, seeks to measure the value of a life, not of a livelihood, and makes real progress toward this goal by recognizing that a way must be found other than valuing the *identified* life.[101] The child in the well is priceless; but the price society will pay to reduce the probability of an air crash is not only finite but determinable. That the value of a life is not the same as the insurable livelihood is suggested by very different behavior with respect to insurance of principal wage earners and other family members. To take another example, Nelson's survey of earlier attempts to value *time* showed infinite variety of assignments of appropriate wage rates.[102] His own great contribution is to recognize that the time one saves may be valued differently according to who gets to spend it, and to who evelutes the saving. Both Schelling and Nelson complicate easier solutions—and in so doing give promise of finding measures that to a real degree approximate social values.

Ultimately the essential role of the economist is to provide proper benefit and cost measures to aid rational choice. Much work remains to be done.[103]

## Choice Models

The literature of benefit-cost analysis has had no shortage of specific models designed to summarize or encapsulate the whole process of economically rational selection. Identifiable models are associated with the names of (among others) Chenery, Eckstein, Feldstein, Harberger, Marglin, McKean, and Steiner. Still other models are implicit in the formulations of almost every theorist; and (as the later discussion demonstrates) the U.S. government has its own.

---

[101] Thomas C. Schelling, "The Life You Save May Be Your Own," in Chase (ed.), *Problems in Public Expenditure Analysis.*

[102] James R. Nelson, "The Value of Travel Time," in Chase (ed.), *Problems in Public Expenditure Analysis.*

[103] In "The Role of Alternative Cost in Project Design and Selection," *Quarterly Journal of Economics,* Vol. 79 (August 1965), pp. 417–30, I have pursued the attractive will-o'-the-wisp of alternative cost as a substitute for benefit measurement. The ultimate conclusion is that there is no general substitute.

It is neither necessary nor fruitful to reproduce them. Their central similarity and essential differences may be suggested by regarding each of them as a special case of a more general eclectic model. Choice models consist, first, in assigning a measure of net value to a specific proposed project and, second, in selecting a program from among the available projects.

### Valuation of a Specific Project

Let $V_i$ be the net value of the $i$th well-defined project. (The $i$ subscript is suppressed for the present.) $V$ may be viewed as consisting of a number of components, as follows:

$$(1) \quad V = G - p_1K_1 - p_2K_2 - p_3K_3 - \cdots - p_jK_j - \cdots - p_nK_n$$
$$= G - \sum_j p_jK_j,$$

where

$$G = \sum_t \frac{B_t - C_t}{(1 + r)^t},$$

and represents the present value of directly measured benefits and costs discounted at rate $r$; $p_j$ is the shadow price of the $j$th binding constraint; and $K_j$ is the number of units of the constrained resource used by the project.

Each of the $p_j$ and $r$ represents a form of opportunity cost, and the central differences among the valuation models arise in specifying what are the relevant (that is, nonzero) ones, and how their values should be assigned.

Harberger and others would define $r$ as the private marginal efficiency of capital, and include all benefits and costs in G.[104] The only constrained resource is current outlay, which is assumed to have as its best alternative use investment in the private sector. All of the $p$s are zero because there is no scarce resource the use of which has not been drawn into the $B$s and $C$s (benefits and costs).

The large group of theorists who assign the discount rate $r$ as a measure of social time preference must add at least one term to reflect the opportunity cost of funds used.

Eckstein regards total costs as constrained by the amount of money raised by taxes.[105] His valuation model is $V = G - p_1C$, where $p_1$ is determined by the opportunity cost of money raised by

[104] Harberger, "Survey of Literature on Cost-Benefit Analysis."
[105] Eckstein, *Water-Resource Development*.

taxation. A fuller discussion of its determination as a weighted average of forgone investment and consumption is the theoretical contribution of Krutilla and Eckstein in *Multiple Purpose River Development*, a book which is, however, more important for its empirical than its theoretical contribution.

Others who have followed Eckstein have preferred to regard only capital expenditures (or, alternatively, current year expenditures) as constrained, thus modifying Eckstein's formulation to $V = G - p_1K_1$, where $K_1$ is some specified portion of total costs.

More complicated models in the same spirit recognize multiple or alternative sources of constrained funds. If, for example, some funds, $K_1$, came from the private sector via taxation and some, $K_2$, from other public projects, then $V = G - p_1K_1 - p_2K_2$, where $p_1$ need not equal $p_2$. This is an important part of my valuation model.[106] Chenery would incorporate a term $-p_3K_3$ to represent the drain on foreign exchange reserves.[107]

The valuation expression in equation (1) is a genuinely eclectic formulation. This has some advantage over any particular specification of *the* relevant opportunity cost if, as I believe, the relevant constraints differ from project to project, from time to time, and from place to place.

What is the significance of the differences among models? As Dorfman said, almost in this context: "Quite clearly, the precise formula used for consolidating and expressing the results of the analysis is a relatively superficial matter: properly interpreted all the formulas lead to the same conclusions."[108] This view seems to me both

[106] Steiner, "Choosing Among Alternative Public Investments." The model set out by Stephen A. Marglin in "Economic Factors Affecting System Design" is in the Eckstein-Steiner spirit, but he notably advances the concept by a sophisticated discussion of the nature of the STP (social time preference) discount rate in "The Opportunity Costs of Public Investment," *Quarterly Journal of Economics*, Vol. 77 (May 1963), pp. 274–89, and "The Social Rate of Discount and the Optimal Rate of Investment," and by introducing dynamic considerations in timing of project starts, in *Approaches to Dynamic Investment Planning*. In "Net Social Benefit Calculation and the Public Investment Decision," *Oxford Economic Papers*, Vol. 16 (March 1964), pp. 114–31, Martin S. Feldstein, too, is in the spirit, but with further modification of the discount rate.

[107] Chenery, "Application of Investment Criteria." Chenery himself is concerned *only* with the foreign exchange opportunity cost, which is perhaps appropriate in the development context in which he considers the problem; that is, he writes, $V = G - p_3K_3$.

[108] Dorfman (ed.), *Measuring Benefits of Government Investments*, p. 8.

technically correct and potentially misleading when applied to different valuation models.

The sense in which it is correct is that any model can incorporate any relevant cost, if not in its direct cost then in its discount rate or in a constraint which binds; similarly if a benefit is not presumed through a generous budget, it may be explicitly included in measured benefits. Thus any model can be made equivalent to any other. But while different models can lead to the same result, they need not do so. Choice of $r$ and specification of the relevant $ps$ reflect different views of what the real and proper alternative uses of funds may be. They differ in what is embraced in the definition of benefits and costs; in what are regarded as the binding constraints; and in the nature of the critical opportunity costs. Differences in these respects prove important, not because it is impossible to translate from one framework to another, but because different benefits and costs seem to be of *primary* importance in different models and the "lesser" measurements that are neglected are different in the models.

This may be made explicit with respect to the opportunity cost of capital. In principle it is clearly possible that the relevant alternative to the expenditure on a particular project might have been *any* of the following: (1) return of funds to the private sector via tax reduction, thus augmenting alone or in some combination (a) private investment, (b) private consumption, or (c) private hoarding; (2) another very similar public project; (3) some highly different public program; (4) reduction of the money supply with no real primary effects; (5) an increase in foreign exchange reserves.

Within a Krutilla-Eckstein type model, for example, the course of least resistance is to assume that all funds have come from the private sector. The cost of, say, a diversion of funds from another type of public program could be included in the basic estimations, but it is unlikely that it would be. Alternatively a Harberger or McKean model, with its stress on use of private marginal efficiency of capital as a discount rate, is well equipped to measure diversion from private investment, but must be stretched to incorporate the others. At an opposite extreme, a simplified version of my model is well equipped to handle diversion from similar public projects, but invites neglect of the others. Chenery focuses on the exchange reserves and makes neglect of other opportunity costs easy.

The basic point is simply that the way in which a question is asked often structures the way it is answered. This reflects not a sly and sinister bias of the person posing the question, but rather his view of what the relevant issues are.

*Choice of an Optimal Program*

If every project is uniquely defined and if the decision maker's problem is to ratify or reject it, his problem is the specification of $x_i = 0$ or $x_i = 1$ in such a way as to maximize $\Sigma_i x_i V_i$. If the only relevant constraint is the budget constraint, this means ranking projects according to $V_i$ and implementing the list in order until the budget is exhausted. This oversimplifies the process in two critical ways: It neglects both the great varieties of interdependencies among projects and the design of particular projects. I have discussed the first issue extensively, in an attempt to provide an algorithm for handling complex interdependencies.[109] The second is well introduced by Maass.[110] These are important practical issues, but they need not be pursued here.

## Summary and Conclusion

Benefit-cost analysis, once the province of the bureaucrat, has enjoyed—or suffered through—a dozen years of attention from some of the leading gunners of economic theory. Where does it come out?

It seems clear that benefit-cost analysis has been elevated from a sacred incantation to a frame of reference for posing real issues of social values and their measurement. While much underbrush has been removed, the central problems of public decision making remain. Measurement of benefits and costs must follow (rather than substitute for) conceptualization of benefits and costs. Once available, such measurements prove helpful in policy decisions, but many aspects of public choices defy summary measurement. Two problems are now more clearly defined: the critical importance of interdependencies that complicate design and selection, and the importance of weighting different objectives in the objective function.

If there is a serious charge against the progress that the academic

[109] Steiner, "Choosing Among Alternative Public Investments."
[110] Maass and others, *Design of Water-Resource Systems.*

invasion of this area has achieved, it is that the mathematical structure of choice situations has been labored beyond the point of sensible return, and the confrontation of real problems with real data largely neglected. If the state of the art before 1950 was long on measurement and short on theory, the balance has been redressed and it is time to return to implementation.

# FEDERAL GOVERNMENT BUDGET PLANNING

SOME OF THE THEORETICAL QUESTIONS raised above have recently become of intensely practical concern to government administrators as a result of the introduction in 1965 of planning-programming-budgeting (PPB) throughout the federal establishment. The purpose here is not to anticipate either the success or the difficulties which the implementation of PPB will encounter, nor to trace the historical development of applied economic analysis culminating in the present budgeting approach. It is to review the conception and articulation of expenditure criteria in the current PPB instructions, to see to what extent they represent a movement toward theoretical criteria sounder than those enunciated in earlier federal statements, and to indicate whether they appear to offer operational guideposts to public decision makers.

The immediate precursor of PPB is clearly the program budgeting system initiated in 1961 by the Department of Defense.[111] More basically PPB represents the present stage in a continuing series of attempts to improve the measurement of government output, previous milestones of which included the program budgeting systems of the Tennessee Valley Authority and the Department of Agriculture during the 1930s and the Hoover Commission's proposals for performance budgeting during the 1950s. Benefit-cost analysis, as such, can be traced directly to the requirement of the Flood Control Act of 1936 that enunciated the now familiar standard that "the benefits to whomsoever they may accrue [be] in excess of the esti-

---

[111] Charles J. Hitch, *Decision-Making for Defense* (University of California Press, 1965).

mated costs. . . ."[112] Aside from the specific implication of distributional neutrality in this phrase, no criteria for defining benefits and costs were given in the 1936 Act. An interagency effort to reconcile differences which arose between departments resulted in publication in 1950 of *Proposed Practices for Economic Analysis of River Basin Projects.*[113] This document was extraordinary for its unprecedented, if not wholly successful, attempt to bring economic analytic techniques to bear upon the problems of government investment. It never attained official standing, however, and the Bureau of the Budget in 1952 adopted its own set of criteria for appraisal of river development projects in *Budget Circular A-47.*[114] In 1961, the Director of the Bureau of the Budget invited a panel of consultants, under the chairmanship of Maynard Hufschmidt, to assess the current criteria for river development. The resulting report apparently reflected more sophisticated analysis than the Bureau of the Budget was prepared to accept.[115] Subsequently, in 1962 a new interagency committee recommended policies, standards, and procedures, relating to cost allocation, reimbursement, and cost sharing in plans for use and development of water resources, which were approved by President John F. Kennedy.[116]

## Planning-Programming-Budgeting

Planning-programming-budgeting aims now to go much further than the water resources criteria in restructuring the process of analytic decision making. At the center of the PPB concept is the statement of objectives and alternative methods of meeting those objectives—what is to be done and why. These are to be formulated in terms of *major program issues.* Government agencies are instructed to group their activities in terms of a *program structure*

[112] 49 Stat. 1570. For adequate short histories of economic criteria proposed, see Major, "Decision-Making for Public Investment in Water Resource Development," pp. 23–54; and Marglin, *Public Investment Criteria,* pp. 15–18.

[113] Green Book.

[114] U.S. Bureau of the Budget, *Budget Circular A-47* (1952).

[115] Report of Panel of Consultants to the Bureau of the Budget, *Standards and Criteria for Formulating and Evaluating Federal Water Resources Developments* (1961), hereafter referred to as the *Consultants' Report.*

[116] *Policies, Standards, and Procedures in Formulation, Evaluation, and Review of Plans,* S. Doc. 97, 87 Cong. 2 sess. (1962).

that "facilitates comparisons of the cost and effectiveness of alternative approaches."[117] Within the program structure are some five to ten *program categories,* each of which represents a set of similar outputs and need not reflect the preexisting organizational structure of the agency (or group of agencies with common objectives) or types of congressional appropriations. Program categories are broken down into *subcategories* and *program elements,* which define more specific (and possibly competitive) outputs within the broad program categories. The following is an illustration of a program category, with subcategories and with elements of one subcategory, taken from a program memorandum of education programs of the Department of Health, Education, and Welfare, November 1, 1967:

*Category*
Education programs
   *Subcategories*
   Basic skills and attitudes
   Vocational and occupational skills
   Advanced academic and professional skills
   Individual and community development
      *Elements*
      Community services and continuing education
      Public library services
      Inter-library cooperation
      Public library construction
      Library and information science schools
      Research and development
      Educational television
   General research
   General support

PPB is built around three documents. First, there is a *program memorandum* which states the major recommendations of each agency to the President, and provides a rationale for each choice made "by identifying agency objectives in a measurable way, and comparing alternative programs in terms of their costs and who pays

---

[117] U.S. Bureau of the Budget, *Bulletin No. 68-9,* April 12, 1968, printed in *Planning-Programming-Budgeting; Budget Bureau Guidelines of 1968,* submitted by the Subcommittee on National Security and International Operations to the Senate Committee on Government Operations, 90 Cong. 2 sess. (1968), p. 2.

them, and their benefits and the group benefitted."[118] It can cover one program category, or cut across several. Program memoranda are intended not only to make explicit the long-range goals, but also to develop the strategy for implementing the program within the context of the current annual budget. The program memorandum is the summary justification of an agency's proposed program. At least nominally, the analytic basis of choices is stressed in the prescription for the content of the program memorandum.

The second document is the *special analytic study*. It is intended to provide the detailed analysis that underlies program decisions, and can be of two types: The first is intended to be initiated and completed within the year and to bear on the resolution of an issue for that current budget year. The second is directed toward developing "on a longer-run basis the conceptual understanding necessary to improve the data available, to evaluate the implications of agency objectives, and to provide an analytic basis for deciding future Major Program Issues. . . ."[119]

The third document is the *program and financial plan*. Called in the PPB instructions "the basic planning document of the agency PPB system," it is to present in tabular form the outputs, costs, and financing of all agency programs, for each program element, and for each of the seven years that it covers.[120] It is to incorporate three tables: Table I to show outputs and costs by program element; Table II, costs by program category and subcategory and, for the budget year, budget authority by program category and subcategory; and Table III, a translation of financial requirements from the program structure to agency appropriations.[121]

Table I is supposed to summarize the outputs expected from the activities of each program element. It is to set forth outputs and costs by program element utilizing "a quantitative measure of the end products or services produced by a program element. . . . Outputs in these terms might include the number of B-52 squadrons, number of workers trained, etc."[122]

[118] Subcommittee on National Security and International Operations, *Planning-Programming-Budgeting*, p. 5.

[119] Ibid., p. 2.

[120] Ibid., pp. 2 and 6.

[121] Ibid., p. 7.

[122] Ibid., p. 10.

Table II is supposed to make use of a "commitment classification," which is to "group financial data for programs according to the degree of control that can be exercised by the Executive Branch in the allocation of resources in the budget and future years. . . ."[123] The classification breaks down into programs controlled by statutory formulae; those controlled by workload level; market-oriented programs; new programs requiring legislation; administration commitments; programs controlled by level of appropriations, divided into construction and acquisition of major capital items and ongoing costs and minor capital items.

PPB is viewed as a continuous, year-round process, providing data for decisions incorporated in the annual executive budget and the annual legislative program of the President. As described in *Bulletin No. 68-9,* the process may be characterized in the following manner: In the first quarter of the year, the Bureau of the Budget notifies agencies of major program issues requiring program memoranda and suggests special analytic studies. From February through August, special studies and draft memoranda are prepared, submitted to the Bureau of the Budget, and returned to the agencies with comments by its staff. From July through September, the agency head is to make final decisions on his recommendations, the program memoranda are to be put in final form, and the program and financial plan is to be updated to reflect the current program decisions. These documents, as well as the annual budget and legislative programs, must be submitted to the Bureau of the Budget by September 30. From October through December, the Bureau reviews the agency submissions and, after discussions and negotiations with the agency, makes its recommendations to the President. Agency heads may, and often do, appeal some of the recommendations directly to the President. He then makes his decisions, usually during December, and these are communicated back to the agencies. In January the executive budget and legislative program are presented to Congress, and the agency is expected to update its program and financial plan to conform to the budget, for submission February 15 to the Bureau of the Budget.

So much for the *form* of PPB. What of its substance? In one sense it is impossible to predict its results in advance of an extended trial.

[123] Ibid., p. 12.

But, at least nominally, PPB embodies many changes in criteria and procedures from earlier directives, and potentially alters the substance of the decisions reached.

## Definition of Objectives

The Green Book and *Budget Circular A-47* focused almost exclusively on an efficiency objective. The *Consultants' Report* was highly critical of them on this account, objecting that the effect was to resolve interobjective conflicts by ignoring everything but efficiency. The consultants urged maintaining the distinction between objectives, on the one hand, and, on the other, rules of operating procedure which are used to guide the planners in carrying out the objectives. The *Consultants' Report* describes an idealized model of investment decision making similar to the Maass-Major model, but it recognizes that in practice broad objectives may be stated by Congress in such general or contradictory terms that the real policy decisions must be made at the agency staff level. In this respect PPB goes a long way toward accepting the recommendations of the *Consultants' Report*. Tentative guidelines issued by the Bureau of the Budget in 1966 observe that "perhaps the most difficult and important task of analysis of programs in the public sector is being clear on objectives and the contribution of specific programs to specific objectives."[124] The PPB instructions proceed with suggestions that the planner examine the following: the source of authority of the stated objective, its binding effect (whether a statute, an agreement with a congressional committee, a moral obligation, and so forth), whether there is room for interpretation, and whether the objective is operational. Implicit in these suggestions is the view that the government planner must have a clear understanding of the process by which objectives are decided upon.

Certainly the formal reports, particularly the program memoranda, described in the PPB system invite, if they do not compel, an explicit search for program objectives, and take for granted a multiple objective standard. Further, they require at least allegations about the extent to which particular programs meet the objectives. This is real progress. Whether in fact the program memoranda will produce clearer and more explicit statements of objectives than have

[124] U.S. Bureau of the Budget, *Program Evaluation Checklist* (March 29, 1966).

been previously made (in annual reports, budget requests, and so on) is as yet conjectural. Clearly the PPB instructions expect specific identification of the contribution of program activities to well-defined objectives.

## Assignment of Weights

For the most part the water resources standards left fuzzy the problem of determining relative weights among several objectives. As Haveman and others have pointed out, *Budget Circular A-47* and *Policies, Standards, and Procedures* mention income distribution, in addition to the emphasized objective of efficiency, but say virtually nothing about how to reconcile conflicts between the two.[125] In marked contrast, the *Consultants' Report* considers the problem explicitly, and its practical suggestion is that alternative plans be prepared which emphasize objectives in varying proportions. In this way policy makers choose the plan that most nearly embodies the relative objectives that they prefer.[126] An ideal method suggested by the consultants would involve attaching explicit weights to various components of a project, or maximizing one objective subject to the constraint of a specified level of attainment in another.[127] They recognize that this is demanding in that it requires (1) field-level planners to prepare additional alternative plans; (2) policy makers to decide on weights or constraints; and (3) reasonably speedy transmission of plans from the field level to the policy level and back again.

This sort of approach is implicit in the PPB instructions. In addition to reminders that priorities among objectives and programs should be made clear and "the relationship among related goals in different parts of the same agency or in different agencies" should be explicit,[128] *Budget Bulletin 68-9* calls for the preparation by agency staff of alternative programs which are to be compared in the program memoranda in terms of their costs and their achievement of the stated objectives.[129] In requiring submission of program memo-

---

[125] Haveman, *Water Resource Investment and the Public Interest.*

[126] *Consultants' Report*, p. 64.

[127] In *Public Investment Criteria*, Marglin elaborates this approach and discusses its implications for the application of specific criteria.

[128] U.S. Bureau of the Budget, *Program Evaluation Checklist*, p. 2.

[129] U.S. Bureau of the Budget, *Bulletin No. 68-9*, p. 2.

randa first to agency heads and policy-making staffs, and then to the
Bureau of the Budget and the President, who is to make the final
program recommendations to Congress, PPB provides a means for
policy makers to choose among alternative programs or modify suggested strategies—or both—so as to produce the desired mix of
weights on various objectives.

There is promise in the PPB system of an approach which can
make the assignment of weights more nearly explicit. I have argued
above that the issue is not whether efficiency should be given a
weight of near unity, but rather whether the weights of conflicting
objectives are to be chosen explicitly. PPB cannot predetermine the
ultimate weights Congress will assign; but it can influence the political process by which they are assigned through framing choices for
the policy makers in the executive branch which make clear the relative contribution of programs to specified objectives. Here again
PPB seems very constructive on paper.

### Appropriate Discount Rate

The problem of selecting a measure for comparing alternative
timestreams of benefits is treated rather cursorily in the Green Book,
*Budget Circular A-47,* and *Policies, Standards, and Procedures.*
Each simply recommends using the average rate of interest payable
on long-term government bonds over a sufficiently long period of
time to smooth the influence of cyclical fluctuations.[130] Only the
Green Book discusses the requirement for use of the government
borrowing rate. With allowances made for risks and uncertainty in
the estimates of benefits and costs, the appropriate time discount rate,
it argues, is "the risk-free return expected to be realized on capital
invested in alternative uses."[131] It regards the best approximation of
this rate to be a projected average yield, expected over the period of
analysis, in the absence of inflation or deflation, on such relatively
risk-free investments as long-term government bonds. It does not explain why.

---

[130] Green Book (revised), pp. 23–24; U.S. Bureau of the Budget, *Budget Circular
A-47,* p. 14; and *Policies, Standards, and Procedures in Formulation, Evaluation, and
Review of Plans,* S. Doc. 97, p. 12. The last of these permits a remarkable exception:
Adjustment may be made "when and if this is found desirable as a result of continu-
ing analysis of all factors pertinent to selection of a discount rate for these purposes."

[131] Green Book (revised), p. 24.

The PPB instructions appear to me to gain some ground simply by *not* specifying the rate of interest on any particular investment for use as a discount rate. Agency planners are advised to test the reasonableness of a chosen discount rate by determining whether it "reflects alternative uses of investible funds."[132] Unfortunately this sound but pious advice is unencumbered by suggestions on its implementation. A second criterion is suggested: Agencies should test the sensitivity of results of preferred programs to the choice of several discount rates. Obviously this would prove helpful, for it would distinguish clear from close cases.

Although it is difficult to say at this early stage in its development, PPB seems to be moving implicitly in the direction of a social time preference (in distinction to a social opportunity cost) viewpoint in the discount rate controversy. This is suggested by emphasis in the *Program Evaluation Checklist,* supported by examples in *Bulletin 68-9,* that multidimensional objectives are envisaged and that efficiency benefits are not regarded as necessarily dominant. It is further suggested by the discussion of the assignment of weights among different objectives and the evaluation of alternative programs with different product mixes. These are characteristic concerns of an approach that explicitly employs social time preference for comparing timestreams of benefits.

However, nothing in the instructions precludes the possibility that federal agencies under PPB may adopt a viewpoint that emphasizes predominantly the efficiency objective, or favor the use of a private capital market discount rate. Although this would be clearly at variance with past or current procedures and criteria, PPB instructions are sufficiently vague to be consistent with any discount rate. This has a distinct advantage over insistence on a foolish rate.

### Time Horizon

With its greater emphasis upon systematic planning, PPB appears to go much further than the water resource standards did toward a method of rationalizing projections of the future. *Policies, Standards, and Procedures* embodied and continued the approach of earlier water resources documents. Time entered only in the evaluation of particular projects. The period of time to be encompassed in

[132] U.S. Bureau of the Budget, *Program Evaluation Checklist*, p. 4.

an analysis of benefits and costs was the useful economic life of the structure or service. Because of difficulties in projecting far into the future, an upper limit of one hundred years was imposed.

The PPB instructions stress the need for an "explicit, time-phased decision strategy."[133] By relating current program decisions to long-range objectives, the program memorandum is intended to specify not only *what* is to be done and *why* it is preferred over alternative courses of action, but also *when* each phase of a project is expected to be completed.

This is again both sound and pious. Whether it is operational is not certain. It asks a great deal of program memoranda—and of their authors. It may, however, provide a more nearly rational method of planning. Government planners who look at alternatives over the required five-year period may more accurately establish the time period in which expectations about budgets and projects are congruent and hence in which certain sources of bias in expenditure decisions may be avoided.

Whether five years is the appropriate time period is an empirical matter. The appropriate time horizon will vary from program to program, and thus specifying an inflexible time horizon is questionable. But the requirement for a five-year plan certainly forces more consideration of time horizons than previous procedures suggested.

*Uncertainty and Risk*

Neither the PPB instructions nor the earlier water resources standards say very much about the treatment of risk or uncertainty. Both the Green Book and *Budget Circular A-47* suggested that an adjustment for uncertainty be made by reducing the expected life of projects or by introducing conservative estimates of benefits and safety margins in costs. The *Consultants' Report* observed, as have other critics,[134] that this treatment merely produces a downward bias in net benefits.

The PPB instructions again at least avoid the mistake of suggesting an untenable behavioral rule with respect to the treatment of un-

---

[133] Ibid., p. 6.

[134] See, for example, Otto Eckstein, "Investment Criteria for Economic Development and the Theory of Intertemporal Welfare Economics," *Quarterly Journal of Economics*, Vol. 71 (February 1957), pp. 81–85; and Haveman, *Water Resource Investment and the Public Interest*.

certainty. They recommend the use of sensitivity analysis to determine how crucially particular cost or benefit estimations affect program recommendations.[135] Given the state of the art, this is probably the most satisfactory tactic. On the problem of pure risk, the PPB instructions are silent. It would be inappropriate to infer a position of neutrality towards risk, since there are more plausible interpretations of silence. The central question about risk—when public risk aversion or risk taking itself becomes a benefit or a cost—seems to be unanswered at this early stage of PPB. But then it is also unresolved in the theoretical literature.

*Issues in the Measurement of Benefits and Costs*

At the heart of PPB analysis lie the problems of estimating benefits and costs. Other issues, such as the selection of a time horizon, the definition of objectives, or the specification of a discount rate, are in a real sense subsidiary to this ultimate task. The framers of the PPB instructions obviously recognize this and have stressed its importance. However, the chief deficiency of the instructions is that they are as yet too general and too vague. Little guidance is given to dealing with the difficult—often critical—specifics of benefit and cost estimation, and very little of present malpractice is noted or enjoined.

In its general approach, PPB seems clearly to have profited from the experience with the water resources standards. The distinction between primary and secondary benefits defined in the Green Book and *Policies, Standards, and Procedures* is mercifully omitted from the PPB instructions. Whether the framers of PPB criteria reacted to the criticism of the water resources definitions, or merely chose to avoid the technicalities involved in the application of these terms, is uncertain. The result, in either event, should be more nearly satisfactory criteria for judging benefits. It is now known that so-called secondary benefits are a mélange of nonefficiency benefits,

[135] U.S. Bureau of the Budget, *Program Evaluation Checklist*, p. 7. Break-even analysis, for example, can be used to show the values which an uncertain parameter must take on in order to achieve equivalence between alternative programs. The PPB approach is perhaps similar to that of McKean, who, in *Efficiency in Government Through Systems Analysis*, advised a "general case-by-case evaluation involving a description of contingencies, a schedule showing a possible range of outcomes, and an analysis of the public attitude toward the disutility (utility) of uncertainty."

products or services not properly included as benefits, and real but remote efficiency benefits.[136] PPB has recommended, much as the *Consultants' Report* has done, the identification of all objectives as concretely as possible and the assessment of the specific benefits and costs of individual projects as they pertain to the objectives.

Many other general recommendations, equally sound, are given in the PPB instructions. For example, government planners are counseled to define clearly their standards of performance, to be wary of overquantification of benefits and costs, and to use the willingness-to-pay criterion in evaluating the demand for goods or services. This good advice provides only a start. The remaining essentials of sound benefit-cost estimation are a genuine devotion to finding the best and most honest answers to the kinds of specific problems that arise in specific cases. More experience with such problems of analysis will, it is hoped, generate both greater skill in benefit and cost estimation and the motivation to use it imaginatively. Whether the government establishment attracts people, or motivates them, or even permits them to devote themselves to such tasks remains a question. Most of the innovations of past years have come from outside.

### An Evaluation?

Obviously an appraisal of PPB at this time is premature. It is an agenda, and we must wait for the minutes. Rather than appraise, I have tried to indicate the direction in which PPB is moving. In most instances PPB appears to have improved upon previous federal standards, either by simply avoiding useless complications or by adopting what the professional literature suggests to be sounder practices. But in other aspects of procedure, PPB has yet to propose operational criteria for expenditure decisions. Perhaps the most important and the most encouraging aspect of PPB is that it appears to be taken seriously by the Bureau of the Budget and by the agencies.[137] As the theoretical literature demonstrates, progress follows attention.

[136] *Consultants' Report,* pp. 25–30.
[137] See Charles L. Schultze, *The Politics and Economics of Public Spending* (Brookings Institution, 1968).

# Bibliography

## Selected General References[1]

Alchian, Armen A. "The Rate of Interest, Fisher's Rate of Return over Costs and Keynes' Internal Rate of Return," *American Economic Review*, Vol. 45 (December 1955), pp. 938–43.

*Arrow, Kenneth J. "Discounting and Public Investment Criteria," in Allen V. Kneese and Stephen Smith (eds.), *Water Research*. Baltimore: Johns Hopkins Press for Resources for the Future, 1966.

*————. "The Impact of the Private Capital Market." Mimeograph. Discussion Paper No. 1, Resources for the Future Seminar on the Discount Rate for Public Investment. Washington: RFF, March 1965.

*————. "Optimal Public Investment Policy." Mimeograph. Discussion Paper No. 2, Resources for the Future Seminar on the Discount Rate for Public Investment. Washington: RFF, March 1965.

————. *Social Choice and Individual Values*. Cowles Foundation for Research in Economics at Yale University, Monograph 12. 2nd edition. New York: John Wiley & Sons, 1963.

Bain, Joe S. "Criteria for Undertaking Water-Resource Developments," *American Economic Review*, Vol. 50 (May 1960), pp, 310–20.

————. "Water Resource Development in California: The Comparative Efficiency of Local, State, and Federal Agencies," in Allen V. Kneese and Stephen Smith (eds.), *Water Research*. Baltimore: Johns Hopkins Press for Resources for the Future, 1966.

————, Richard E. Caves, and Julius Margolis. *Northern California's Water Industry*. Baltimore: Johns Hopkins Press for Resources for the Future, 1966.

Baldwin, Robert E. "A Comparison of Welfare Criteria," *Review of Economic Studies*, Vol. 21, No. 2 (1954), pp. 154–61.

Banfield, Edward C. " 'Economic' Analysis of 'Political' Phenomena: A Political Scientist's Critique." Ditto. Harvard University Seminar on Political-Economic Decisions, March 1967.

---

[1] See also the section of the bibliography entitled, "Measurement Issues in Benefit-Cost Analysis," pp. 353–57.

* Works marked with an asterisk have special bearing on the subject of allowing for time in benefit-cost analysis.

Barker, Ernest. *Reflections on Government*. London: Oxford University Press, 1942.

Bator, Francis M. *The Question of Government Spending; Public Needs and Private Wants*. New York: Harper & Row, 1960.

Baumol, William J. "External Economies and Second-Order Optimality Conditions," *American Economic Review*, Vol. 54 (June 1964), pp. 358–72.

———. *Welfare Economics and the Theory of the State*. 2nd edition. Cambridge: Harvard University Press, 1965.

———, and Richard E. Quandt. "Investment and Discount Rates Under Capital Rationing—A Programming Approach," *Economic Journal*, Vol. 75 (June 1965), pp. 317–29.

Birdsall, William C. "A Study of the Demand for Public Goods," in Richard A. Musgrave (ed.), *Essays in Fiscal Federalism*. Washington: Brookings Institution, 1965.

Black, Duncan. *The Theory of Committees and Elections*. Cambridge: Cambridge University Press, 1958.

Bonnen, James T. "The Distribution of Benefits from Cotton Price Supports," in Samuel B. Chase, Jr. (ed.), *Problems in Public Expenditure Analysis*. Washington: Brookings Institution, 1968.

Bowen, Howard R. "The Interpretation of Voting in the Allocation of Economic Resources," *Quarterly Journal of Economics*, Vol. 58 (November 1943), pp. 27–48.

Brandl, John E. "On Budget Allocation in Government Agencies," *Review of Social Economy*, Vol. 25 (March 1967), pp. 29–46.

Braybrooke, David, and Charles E. Lindblom. *A Strategy of Decision*. New York: Macmillan, 1963.

Breton, Albert. "A Theory of the Demand for Public Goods," *Canadian Journal of Economics and Political Science*, Vol. 32 (November 1966), pp. 455–67.

Buchanan, James M. "Individual Choice in Voting and the Market," *Journal of Political Economy*, Vol. 62 (August 1954), pp. 334–43.

———. "Social Choice, Democracy, and Free Markets," *Journal of Political Economy*, Vol. 62 (April 1954), pp. 114–23.

———, and William Craig Stubblebine. "Externality," *Economica*, N.S., Vol. 29 (November 1962), pp. 371–84.

Buchanan, James M., and Gordon Tullock. *The Calculus of Consent*. Ann Arbor: The University of Michigan Press, 1962.

Buchanan, James M., and Milton Z. Kafoglis. "A Note on Public Goods Supply," *American Economic Review*, Vol. 53 (June 1963), pp. 403–14.

Burkhead, Jesse. *Government Budgeting*. New York: John Wiley & Sons, 1956.

Castle, Emery N., Maurice Kelso, and B. Delworth Gardner. "Water Resources Development: A Review of the New Federal Evaluation Procedures," *Journal of Farm Economics*, Vol. 45 (November 1963), pp. 693–704.

Chase, Samuel B., Jr. (ed.). *Problems in Public Expenditure Analysis*. Washington: Brookings Institution, 1968.

Chenery, Hollis B. "The Application of Investment Criteria," *Quarterly Journal of Economics,* Vol. 67 (February 1953), pp. 76–96.

Ciriacy-Wantrup, Siegfried von. "Benefit-Cost Analysis and Public Resource Development," *Journal of Farm Economics,* Vol. 37 (November 1955), pp. 676–89.

———. *Resource Conservation: Economics and Policies.* Berkeley: University of California Press, 1952.

Clark, John M. *The Economics of Planning Public Works.* Study made for the National Planning Board of the Federal Emergency Administration of Public Works. Washington: U.S. Government Printing Office, 1935.

Coase, Ronald H. "The Problem of Social Cost," *Journal of Law and Economics,* Vol. 3 (October 1960), pp. 1–44.

Colm, Gerhard. "Comments on Samuelson's Theory of Public Finance," *Review of Economics and Statistics,* Vol. 38 (November 1956), pp. 408–12.

Dahl, Robert A., and Charles E. Lindblom. *Politics, Economics, and Welfare.* New York: Harper, 1953.

Davis, Otto A., and Andrew B. Whinston. "Welfare Economics and the Theory of Second Best," *Review of Economic Studies,* Vol. 32 (January 1965), pp. 1–14.

Davis, Robert K. "Planning a Water Quality Management System: The Case of the Potomac Estuary," in Allen V. Kneese and Stephen C. Smith (eds.), *Water Research.* Baltimore: Johns Hopkins Press for Resources for the Future, 1966.

Davisson, William I. "Public Investment Criteria," *Land Economics,* Vol. 40 (May 1964), pp. 153–62.

Dorfman, Robert. "Basic Economic and Technologic Concepts: A General Statement," in Arthur Maass and others, *Design of Water-Resource Systems.* Cambridge: Harvard University Press, 1962.

———. "General Equilibrium with Public Goods." Paper to be published in the *Proceedings of a Conference on Public Economics, Biarritz, France, 1966,* by the International Economic Association; published in French in *Economie Publique, Biarritz, 2–9 Septembre 1966* (Paris: Centre National de la Recherche Scientifique, 1968).

——— (ed.). *Measuring Benefits of Government Investments.* Washington: Brookings Institution, 1965.

Downs, Anthony. *An Economic Theory of Democracy.* New York: Harper, 1957.

———. "An Economic Theory of Political Action in a Democracy," *Journal of Political Economy,* Vol. 65 (April 1957), pp. 135–50.

*Eckstein, Otto. "Investment Criteria for Economic Development and the Theory of Intertemporal Welfare Economics," *Quarterly Journal of Economics,* Vol. 71 (February 1957), pp. 56–85.

*———. "A Survey of the Theory of Public Expenditure Criteria," in *Public Finances: Needs, Sources, and Utilization.* Princeton: Princeton University Press for National Bureau of Economic Research, 1961.

*Eckstein, Otto. *Water-Resource Development*. Cambridge: Harvard University Press, 1958.

*Feldstein, Martin S. "The Derivation of Social Time Preference Rates," *Kyklos*, Vol. 18, Fasc. 2 (1965), pp. 277–86.

*————. "Net Social Benefit Calculation and the Public Investment Decision," *Oxford Economic Papers*, Vol. 16 (March 1964), pp. 114–31.

*————. "Opportunity Cost Calculations in Cost-Benefit Analysis," *Public Finance*, Vol. 19, No. 2 (1964), pp. 117–39.

*————. "The Social Time Preference Discount Rate in Cost Benefit Analysis," *Economic Journal*, Vol. 74 (June 1964), pp. 360–79.

Foley, Duncan K. "Resource Allocation and the Public Sector." Ditto. Harvard University Seminar on Political-Economic Decisions, March 1967.

Freeman, A. Myrick III. "Income Distribution and Planning for Public Investment," *American Economic Review*, Vol. 57 (June 1967), pp. 495–508.

————. "Six Federal Reclamation Projects and the Distribution of Income," *Water Resources Research*, Vol. 3 (second quarter 1967), pp. 319–32.

Galbraith, John Kenneth. *The Affluent Society*. Boston: Houghton Mifflin, 1958.

Graaff, Johannes de Villiers. *Theoretical Welfare Economics*. Cambridge: Cambridge University Press, 1957.

Gramm, Warren S. "Water Resource Analysis: Private Investment Criteria and Social Priorities," *Journal of Farm Economics*, Vol. 45 (November 1963), pp. 705–12.

*Harberger, Arnold C. "Survey of Literature on Cost-Benefit Analysis for Industrial Project Evaluation," in *Evaluation of Industrial Projects*. United Nations Industrial Development Organization, Project Formulation and Evaluation Series, Vol. 1. New York: United Nations, 1968.

Hartman, Lloyd M., and Don A. Seastone. "Welfare Goals and Organization of Decision-making for the Allocation of Water Resources," *Land Economics*, Vol. 41 (February 1965), pp. 21–30.

Haveman, Robert H. "Benefit-Cost Analysis: Its Relevance to Public Investment Decisions: Comment," *Quarterly Journal of Economics*, Vol. 81 (November 1967), pp. 695–99.

Head, John Graeme. "Public Goods and Public Policy," *Public Finance*, Vol. 17, No. 3 (1962), pp. 197–219.

Hicks, John R. "The Valuation of the Social Income," *Economica*, N.S., Vol. 7 (May 1940), pp. 105–24.

Hines, Lawrence G. "The Hazards of Benefit-Cost Analysis as a Guide to Public Investment Policy," *Public Finance*, Vol. 17, No. 2 (1962), pp. 101–17.

Hirsch, Werner Z. "Cost Functions of an Urban Government Service: Refuse Collection," *Review of Economics and Statistics*, Vol. 47 (February 1965), pp. 87–92.

\*Hirshleifer, Jack. "Investment Decision Under Uncertainty: Applications of the State-Preference Approach," *Quarterly Journal of Economics*, Vol. 80 (May 1966), pp. 252–77.

\*————. "Investment Decision Under Uncertainty: Choice-Theoretic Approaches," *Quarterly Journal of Economics*, Vol. 79 (November 1965), pp. 509–36.

\*————. "On the Theory of Optimal Investment Decision," *Journal of Political Economy*, Vol. 66 (August 1958), pp. 329–52.

\*————, James C. DeHaven, and Jerome W. Milliman. *Water Supply: Economics, Technology, and Policy*. Chicago: University of Chicago Press, 1960.

Hotelling, Harold. "Stability in Competition," *Economic Journal*, Vol. 39 (March 1929), pp. 41–57.

Hufschmidt, Maynard M. "The Methodology of Water-Resource System Design," in Ian Burton and Robert W. Kates (eds.), *Readings in Resource Management and Conservation*. Chicago: University of Chicago Press, 1965.

Johansen, Leif. "Some Notes on the Lindahl Theory of Determination of Public Expenditures," *International Economic Review*, Vol. 4 (September 1963), pp. 346–58.

Jorgenson, Dale. "Review: *Approaches to Dynamic Investment Planning*, by Stephen A. Marglin," *American Economic Review*, Vol. 54 (June 1964), pp. 427–29.

Kafoglis, Milton Z. *Welfare Economics and Subsidy Programs*. University of Florida Monographs, Social Sciences, No. 11. Gainesville, Fla.: University of Florida Press, 1961.

Kaldor, Nicholas. "Welfare Propositions of Economics and Inter-Personal Comparisons of Utility," *Economic Journal*, Vol. 49 (September 1939), pp. 549–52.

Kennedy, Charles F. "The Economic Welfare Function and Dr. Little's Criterion," *Review of Economic Studies*, Vol. 20, No. 2 (1953), pp. 137–42.

Kneese, Allen V., and Stephen Smith (eds.). *Water Research*. Baltimore: Johns Hopkins Press for Resources for the Future, 1966.

Knight, Frank H. "The Meaning of Freedom," in Charner M. Perry (ed.), *The Philosophy of American Democracy*. Chicago: University of Chicago Press, 1943.

Krutilla, John V. "The International Columbia River Treaty: An Economic Evaluation," in Allen V. Kneese and Stephen C. Smith (eds.), *Water Research*. Baltimore: Johns Hopkins Press for Resources for the Future, 1966.

————. "River Basin Development: Planning and Evaluation," *Journal of Farm Economics*, Vol. 40 (December 1958), pp. 1674–87, and discussion, pp. 1687–89.

Krutilla, John V. "Welfare Aspects of Benefit-Cost Analysis," *Journal of Political Economy*, Vol. 69 (June 1961), pp. 226–35.

Lindahl, Erik. "Some Controversial Questions in the Theory of Taxation," in Richard A. Musgrave and Alan T. Peacock (eds.), *Classics in the Theory*
\* *of Public Finance*. New York: Macmillan, 1958.

Lipsey, Richard G., and Kelvin Lancaster. "The General Theory of Second Best," *Review of Economic Studies*, Vol. 24, No. 1 (1956), pp. 11–32.

\* Little, Ian Malcolm David. *A Critique of Welfare Economics*. 2nd edition. London: Oxford University Press, 1957.

\* ————. "Social Choice and Individual Values," *Journal of Political Economy*, Vol. 60 (October 1952), pp. 422–32.

Long, Millard F. "Collective-Consumption Services of Individual-Consumption Goods: Comment," *Quarterly Journal of Economics*, Vol. 81 (May 1967), pp. 351–52.

Maass, Arthur. "Benefit-Cost Analysis: Its Relevance to Public Investment
\* Decisions," *Quarterly Journal of Economics*, Vol. 80 (May 1966), pp. 208–26.

\* ————. "System Design and the Political Process: A General Statement," in Arthur Maass and others, *Design of Water-Resource Systems*. Cambridge: Harvard University Press, 1962.

————, and others. *Design of Water-Resource Systems*. Cambridge: Harvard University Press, 1962.

Major, David C. "Decision-Making for Public Investment in Water Resource Development in the United States." Mimeograph. Harvard University, Graduate School of Public Administration, Harvard Water Program, August 1965.

Manne, Alan S. "Capacity Expansion and Probabilistic Growth," *Econometrica*, Vol. 29 (October 1961), pp. 632–49.

Marglin, Stephen A. *Approaches to Dynamic Investment Planning*. Amsterdam: North-Holland Publishing Co., 1963.

————. "Economic Factors Affecting System Design," in Arthur Maass and others, *Design of Water-Resource Systems*. Cambridge: Harvard University Press, 1962.

————. "Objectives of Water-Resource Development: A General Statement," in Arthur Maass and others, *Design of Water-Resource Systems*. Cambridge: Harvard University Press, 1962.

————. "The Opportunity Costs of Public Investment," *Quarterly Journal of Economics*, Vol. 77 (May 1963), pp. 274–89.

————. *Public Investment Criteria; Benefit-Cost Analysis for Planned Economic Growth*. Cambridge: Massachusetts Institute of Technology Press, 1967.

————. "The Social Rate of Discount and the Optimal Rate of Investment," *Quarterly Journal of Economics*, Vol. 77 (February 1963), pp. 95–111. See also comment by Robert C. Lind, "The Social Rate of Discount and the Optimal Rate of Investment: Further Comment," *Quarterly Journal of Economics,* Vol. 78 (May 1964), pp. 336–45; and Dan Usher, "The Social Rate of Discount and the Optimal Rate of Investment: Comment," *Quarterly Journal of Economics,* Vol. 78 (November 1964), pp. 641–44.

Margolis, Julius. "The Economic Evaluation of Federal Water Resource Development: A Review Article," *American Economic Review,* Vol. 49 (March 1959), pp. 96–111.

―――. "Secondary Benefits, External Economies, and the Justification of Public Investment," *Review of Economics and Statistics,* Vol. 39 (August 1957), pp. 284–91.

―――. "The Structure of Government and Public Investment," in American Economic Association, *Papers and Proceedings of the Seventy-sixth Annual Meeting, 1963 (American Economic Review,* Vol. 54, May 1964), pp. 236–42, and discussion, pp. 250–57.

―――. "Welfare Criteria, Pricing and Decentralization of a Public Service," *Quarterly Journal of Economics,* Vol. 71 (August 1957), pp. 448–63.

\* Massé, Pierre. *Optimal Investment Decisions: Rules for Action and Criteria for Choice.* Englewood Cliffs, N.J.: Prentice-Hall, 1962.

\* McKean, Roland N. "Cost-Benefit Analysis and British Defence Expenditure," *Scottish Journal of Political Economy,* Vol. 10 (February 1963), pp. 17–35.

\* ―――. *Efficiency in Government Through Systems Analysis, with Emphasis on Water Resources Development.* New York: John Wiley & Sons, 1958.

―――. "The Unseen Hand in Government," *American Economic Review,* Vol. 55 (June 1965), pp. 496–506.

―――. "The Use of Shadow Prices," in Samuel B. Chase, Jr. (ed.), *Problems in Public Expenditure Analysis.* Washington: Brookings Institution, 1968.

Minasian, Jora R. "Television Pricing and the Theory of Public Goods," *Journal of Law and Economics,* Vol. 7 (October 1964), pp. 71–80.

\* Mishan, Edward J. "Criteria for Public Investment: Some Simplifying Suggestions," *Journal of Political Economy,* Vol. 75 (April 1967), pp. 139–46.

―――. "A Survey of Welfare Economics, 1939–59," *Economic Journal,* Vol. 70 (June 1960), pp. 197–265.

―――. *Welfare Economics; Five Introductory Essays.* New York: Random House, 1964.

Mohring, Herbert. "Consumer's Surplus Benefit Measures." Ditto. Harvard University Seminar on Political-Economic Decisions, March 1967.

Musgrave, Richard A. *The Theory of Public Finance.* New York: McGraw-Hill, 1959.

―――, and Alan T. Peacock (eds.). *Classics in the Theory of Public Finance.* New York: Macmillan, 1958.

Nelson, James R. "The Value of Travel Time," in Samuel B. Chase, Jr. (ed.), *Problems in Public Expenditure Analysis*. Washington: Brookings Institution, 1968.

Novick, David. "The Department of Defense," in David Novick (ed.), *Program Budgeting*. Cambridge: Harvard University Press, 1965.

Olson, Mancur, Jr. *The Logic of Collective Action*. Cambridge: Harvard University Press, 1965.

Ott, David J., and Attiat F. Ott. *Federal Budget Policy*. Revised edition. Washington: Brookings Institution, 1969.

Pearman, Elizabeth H. *Bibliography on Cost-Benefit Analysis and Planning-Programming-Budgeting*. McLean, Va.: Research Analysis Corporation, 1966.

Peck, Merton J., and Frederic M. Scherer. *The Weapons Acquisition Process: An Economic Analysis*. Boston: Harvard University, Graduate School of Business Administration, Division of Research, 1962.

Pigou, Arthur C. *The Economics of Welfare*. 4th edition. London: Macmillan, 1932.

Prest, Alan R., and Ralph Turvey. "Cost-Benefit Analysis: A Survey," *Economic Journal*, Vol. 75 (December 1965), pp. 683–735.

Rakowski, Mieczyslaw F. (ed.). *Efficiency of Investment in a Socialist Economy*. Oxford: Pergamon Press, 1966.

Reder, Melvin. "The Theory of Union Wage Policy," *Review of Economics and Statistics*, Vol. 34 (February 1952), pp. 34–45.

Rothenberg, Jerome. "Conditions for a Social Welfare Function," *Journal of Political Economy*, Vol. 61 (October 1953), pp. 389–405.

————. *The Measurement of Social Welfare*. Englewood Cliffs, N.J.: Prentice-Hall, 1961.

————. "A Model of Economic and Political Decision Making." Ditto. Harvard University Seminar on Political-Economic Decisions, March 1967.

Samuelson, Paul A. "Aspects of Public Expenditure Theories," *Review of Economics and Statistics*, Vol. 40 (November 1958), pp. 332–38.

————. "Diagrammatic Exposition of a Theory of Public Expenditure," *Review of Economics and Statistics*, Vol. 37 (November 1955), pp. 350–56.

————. "The Pure Theory of Public Expenditure," *Review of Economics and Statistics*, Vol. 36 (November 1954), pp. 387–89.

————. "Pure Theory of Public Expenditure and Taxation." Mimeograph. Harvard University Seminar on Political-Economic Decisions, 1965.

Schaller, Howard G. (ed.). *Public Expenditure Decisions in the Urban Community*. Baltimore: Johns Hopkins Press for Resources for the Future, 1963.

Schelling, Thomas C. *The Strategy of Conflict*. Cambridge: Harvard University Press, 1960.

————. "The Life You Save May Be Your Own," in Samuel B. Chase, Jr. (ed.), *Problems in Public Expenditure Analysis*. Washington: Brookings Institution, 1968.

Schultze, Charles L. *The Politics and Economics of Public Spending.* Washington: Brookings Institution, 1968.

Schumpeter, Joseph A. *Capitalism, Socialism, and Democracy.* 3rd edition. New York: Harper, 1950.

Scitovsky, Tibor. "A Note on Welfare Propositions in Economics," *Review of Economic Studies,* Vol. 9 (November 1941), pp. 77–88.

Sen, Amartya K. "Some Notes on the Choice of Capital-Intensity in Development Planning," *Quarterly Journal of Economics,* Vol. 71 (November 1957), pp. 561–84.

Smithies, Arthur. *The Budgetary Process in the United States.* New York: McGraw-Hill, 1955.

Steiner, George A. "Program Budgeting: Business Contribution to Government Management," *Business Horizons,* Vol. 8 (Spring 1965), pp. 43–52.

Steiner, Peter O. "Choosing Among Alternative Public Investments in the Water Resource Field," *American Economic Review,* Vol. 49 (December 1959), pp. 893–916.

―――. *On the Process of Planning.* Athens, Greece: Center of Planning and Economic Research, 1968.

―――. "Peak Loads and Efficient Pricing," *Quarterly Journal of Economics,* Vol. 71 (November 1957), pp. 585–610.

―――. "The Role of Alternative Cost in Project Design and Selection," *Quarterly Journal of Economics,* Vol. 79 (August 1965), pp. 417--30.

Stigler, George J. "The Economics of Information," *Journal of Political Economy,* Vol. 69 (June 1961), pp. 213–25.

Strotz, Robert H. "Two Propositions Related to Public Goods," *Review of Economics and Statistics,* Vol. 40 (November 1958), pp. 329–31.

Telser, Lester G. "How Much Does It Pay Whom To Advertise?" *American Economic Review,* Vol. 51 (May 1961), pp. 194–205.

Thomas, Harold A., Jr. "The Animal Farm: A Mathematical Model for the Discussion of Social Standards for Control of the Environment," *Quarterly Journal of Economics,* Vol. 77 (February 1963), pp. 143–48.

Truman, David B. *The Governmental Process.* New York: Knopf, 1957.

Tullock, Gordon. "The General Irrelevance of the General Impossibility Theorem," *Quarterly Journal of Economics,* Vol. 81 (May 1967), pp. 256–70.

Turvey, Ralph. "On Divergences between Social Cost and Private Cost," *Economica,* N.S., Vol. 30 (August 1963), pp. 309–13.

United Nations, Department of Economic and Social Affairs. *A Manual for Programme and Performance Budgeting.* Sales No. 66.XVI.1. New York: United Nations, 1965.

U.S. Bureau of the Budget. *Budget Circular A-47.* Washington: Bureau of the Budget, 1952.

―――. *Bulletin No. 66-3.* Washington: Bureau of the Budget, October 12, 1965.

U.S. Bureau of the Budget. *Supplement to Bulletin No. 66-3.* Washington: Bureau of the Budget, February 21, 1966.

————. *Bulletin No. 68-2.* Washington: Bureau of the Budget, July 18, 1967. Superseded by *Bulletin No. 68-9,* April 12, 1968, printed in U.S. Congress, Senate Committee on Government Operations, Subcommittee on National Security and International Operations, *Planning-Programming-Budgeting; Budget Bureau Guidelines of 1968,* 90 Cong. 2 sess. (1968).

————. *Bulletin No. 68-9.* See *Bulletin No. 68-2.*

————. *Consultants' Report.* See U.S. Bureau of the Budget, *Standards and Criteria for Formulating and Evaluating Federal Water Resources Developments.*

————. *Program Analysis Techniques: A Selected Bibliography.* Revised edition. Washington: Government Printing Office, 1966.

————. *Program Evaluation Checklist.* Washington: Bureau of the Budget, March 29, 1966.

————. *Standards and Criteria for Formulating and Evaluating Federal Water Resources Developments* (known as the *Consultants' Report*). Report of Panel of Consultants to the Bureau of the Budget. Washington: Bureau of the Budget, 1961.

U.S. Department of Health, Education, and Welfare. *A Survey of Federal Programs in Higher Education.* Prepared by J. Kenneth Little. Washington: Government Printing Office, 1962.

U.S. Department of the Interior, Office of Water Resources Research. *Bibliography on Socio-Economic Aspects of Water Resources.* Prepared by H. R. Hamilton and others, of the Battelle Memorial Institute. Washington: Government Printing Office, 1966.

U.S. Federal Inter-Agency River Basin Committee. *Proposed Practices for Economic Analysis of River Basin Projects* (known as the Green Book). Report by the Subcommittee on Benefits and Costs. Washington: Government Printing Office, 1950. Revised in Inter-Agency Committee on Water Resources, Subcommittee on Evaluation Standards, *Proposed Practices for Economic Analysis of River Basin Projects* (also known as the Green Book) (1958).

U.S. The President's Water Resources Council. *Policies, Standards, and Procedures in the Formulation, Evaluation, and Review of Plans for Use and Development of Water and Related Land Resources.* S. Doc. 97. 87 Cong. 2 sess. Washington: Government Printing Office, 1962.

Weisbrod, Burton A. "Collective-Consumption Services of Individual-Consumption Goods," *Quarterly Journal of Economics,* Vol. 78 (August 1964), pp. 471–77.

————. "Education and Investment in Human Capital," *Journal of Political Economy,* Vol. 70, Supplement, "Investment in Human Beings" (October 1962), pp. 106–23.

————. "Income Redistribution Effects and Benefit-Cost Analysis," in Samuel B. Chase, Jr. (ed.), *Problems in Public Expenditure Analysis.* Washington: Brookings Institution, 1968.

Wellisz, Stanislaw. "On External Diseconomies and the Government-Assisted Invisible Hand," *Economica,* N.S., Vol. 31 (November 1964), pp. 345–62.

Wildavsky, Aaron B. *The Politics of the Budgetary Process.* Boston: Little, Brown, 1964.

Williams, Alan. "The Optimal Provision of Public Goods in a System of Local Government," *Journal of Political Economy,* Vol. 74 (February 1966), pp. 18–33.

## Measurement Issues in Benefit-Cost Analysis[2]

### Air Pollution

Herfindahl, Orris C., and Allen V. Kneese. *Quality of the Environment.* Baltimore: Johns Hopkins Press for Resources for the Future, 1965.

Michelson, Irving, and Boris Tourin. "Comparative Method for Studying Costs of Air Pollution," *Public Health Reports,* Vol. 81 (June 1966), pp. 505–11.

Ogden, Delbert C. "Economic Analysis of Air Pollution," *Land Economics,* Vol. 42 (May 1966), pp. 137–47.

Ridker, Ronald G. *Economic Costs of Air Pollution: Studies in Measurement.* New York: Frederick A. Praeger, 1967.

### Defense

Fox, Peter D. "A Theory of Cost-Effectiveness for Military Systems Analysis," *Operations Research,* Vol. 13 (March–April 1965), pp. 191–201.

Hitch, Charles J. *Decision-Making for Defense.* Berkeley: University of California Press, 1965.

———, and Roland N. McKean. *The Economics of Defense in the Nuclear Age.* Cambridge: Harvard University Press, 1960.

Quade, Edward S. (ed.). *Analysis for Military Decisions.* Chicago: Rand McNally, 1965.

Scherer, Frederic M. *The Weapons Acquisition Process: Economic Incentives.* Boston: Harvard University, Graduate School of Business Administration, Division of Research, 1964.

### Education and Training

Becker, Gary S. *Human Capital; A Theoretical and Empirical Analysis, with Special Reference to Education.* New York: Columbia University Press for National Bureau of Economic Research, 1964.

Borus, Michael E. "A Benefit-Cost Analysis of the Economic Effectiveness of Retraining the Unemployed," *Yale Economic Essays,* Vol. 4 (Fall 1964), pp. 371–429.

Bowman, Mary Jean. "Social Returns to Education," *International Social Science Journal,* Vol. 14, No. 4 (1962), pp. 647–59.

[2] See also, "Selected General References," pp. 343–53.

Hirsch, Werner Z., and others. *Spillover of Public Education: Costs and Benefits.* Los Angeles: University of California, Institute of Government and Public Affairs, 1964.

Hirsch, Werner Z., and Elbert W. Segelhorst. "Incremental Income Benefits of Public Education," *Review of Economics and Statistics,* Vol. 47 (November 1965), pp. 392–99.

Page, David A. "Retraining Under the Manpower Development Act: A Cost-Benefit Analysis," *Public Policy,* Vol. 13 (1964), pp. 257–67.

Schultz, Theodore W. *The Economic Value of Education.* New York: Columbia University Press, 1963.

Somers, Gerald G., and Ernst Stromsdorfer. "Benefit-Cost Analysis of Manpower Retraining," *Proceedings of the Seventeenth Annual Meeting, Industrial Relations Research Association,* 1964.

Swift, William J., and Burton A. Weisbrod. "On the Monetary Value of Education's Intergeneration Effects," *Journal of Political Economy,* Vol. 73 (December 1965), pp. 643–49.

―――. *External Benefits of Public Education; An Economic Analysis.* Princeton: Princeton University, Department of Economics, Industrial Relations Section, 1964.

―――. "Preventing High School Dropouts," in Robert Dorfman (ed.), *Measuring Benefits of Government Investments.* Washington: Brookings Institution, 1965.

―――. "The Valuation of Human Capital," *Journal of Political Economy,* Vol. 69 (October 1961), pp. 425–36.

*Highways*

Friedlaender, Ann F. *The Interstate Highway System; A Study in Public Investment.* Amsterdam: North-Holland Publishing Co., 1965.

Mohring, Herbert. "Urban Highway Investments," in Robert Dorfman (ed.), *Measuring Benefits of Government Investments.* Washington: Brookings Institution, 1965.

―――, and Mitchell Harwitz. *Highway Benefits; An Analytical Framework.* Evanston, Ill.: Northwestern University Press, 1962.

Walters, Alan A. "The Theory and Measurement of Private and Social Cost of Highway Congestion," *Econometrica,* Vol. 29 (October 1961), pp. 676–99.

*Outdoor Recreation*

Clawson, Marion. "Methods of Measuring the Demand for and Value of Outdoor Recreation." Paper presented at a meeting of the Taylor-Hibbard Club, University of Wisconsin, January 13, 1959. Resources for the Future Reprint No. 10. Washington: RFF, February 1959.

Daiute, Robert J. "Methods for Determination of Demand for Outdoor Recreation," *Land Economics,* Vol. 42 (August 1966), pp. 327–38.

Knetsch, Jack L. "Outdoor Recreation Demands and Benefits," *Land Economics,* Vol. 39 (November 1963), pp. 387–96.

Mack, Ruth P., and Sumner Myers. "Outdoor Recreation," in Robert Dorfman (ed.), *Measuring Benefits of Government Investments.* Washington: Brookings Institution, 1965.
Trice, Andrew H., and Samuel E. Wood. "Measurement of Recreation Benefits," *Land Economics,* Vol. 34 (August 1958), pp. 195–207.

## Public Health

Jahn, Julius A. "The Statistical Design and Analysis of an Experiment To Measure the Effectiveness and Costs of a Health and Welfare Program," *Proceedings of the Social Statistics Section of the American Statistical Association, 1965,* pp. 42–50.
Klarman, Herbert E. *The Economics of Health.* New York: Columbia University Press, 1965.
————. "Syphilis Control Programs," in Robert Dorfman (ed.), *Measuring Benefits of Government Investments.* Washington: Brookings Institution, 1965.
Weisbrod, Burton A. *Economics of Public Health: Measuring the Economic Impact of Diseases.* Philadelphia: University of Pennsylvania Press, 1961.

## Research and Development

Griliches, Zvi. "Research Costs and Social Returns: Hybrid Corn and Related Innovations," *Journal of Political Economy,* Vol. 66 (October 1958), pp. 419–31.
Grossfield, K., and J. B. Heath. "The Benefit and Cost of Government Support for Research and Development: A Case Study," *Economic Journal,* Vol. 76 (September 1966), pp. 537–49.
Lipetz, Ben Ami. *The Measurement of Efficiency of Scientific Research.* Carlisle, Mass.: Intermedia, 1965.
Renshaw, Edward F. "Atomic Power: Research Costs and Social Returns," *Land Economics,* Vol. 35 (August 1959), pp. 222–31.
Scherer, Frederic M. "Government Research and Development Programs," in Robert Dorfman (ed.), *Measuring Benefits of Government Investments.* Washington: Brookings Institution, 1965.

## Transportation

Foster, Christopher D., and M. E. Beesley. "Estimating the Social Benefit of Constructing an Underground Railway in London," *Journal of the Royal Statistical Society,* Series A, Vol. 126, Part 1 (1963), pp. 46–78, and discussion, pp. 79–93.
Fromm, Gary. "Civil Aviation Expenditures," in Robert Dorfman (ed.), *Measuring Benefits of Government Investments.* Washington: Brookings Institution, 1965.
Kuhn, Tillo E. *Public Enterprise Economics and Transport Problems.* Berkeley: University of California Press, 1962.

Meyer, John R., J. F. Kain, and M. Wohl. *The Urban Transportation Problem*. Cambridge: Harvard University Press, 1965.

## Urban Development and Services

Hirsch, Werner Z. "Toward Federal Program Budgeting." Processed. RAND Corporation Papers, P-3306. Santa Monica, Calif.: February 1966.

―――. "Quality of Government Services," in Howard G. Schaller (ed.), *Public Expenditure Decisions in the Urban Community*. Baltimore: Johns Hopkins Press for Resources for the Future, 1963.

Rothenberg, Jerome. *Economic Evaluation of Urban Renewal*. Washington: Brookings Institution, 1967.

―――. "Urban Renewal Programs," in Robert Dorfman (ed.), *Measuring Benefits of Government Investments*. Washington: Brookings Institution, 1965.

Stone, Peter A. "The Economics of Housing and Urban Development," *Journal of the Royal Statistical Society*, Series A, Vol. 122, Part 4 (1959), pp. 417–76, and discussion, pp. 476–83.

U.S. Advisory Commission on Intergovernmental Relations. *Metropolitan Social and Economic Disparities: Implications for Intergovernmental Relations in Central Cities and Suburbs*. Report A-25. Washington: The Commission, 1965.

## Water Resources

Dantzig, D. van. "Economic Decision Problems for Flood Prevention," *Econometrica*, Vol. 24 (July 1956), pp. 276–87.

Eckstein, Otto. *Water-Resource Development*. Cambridge: Harvard University Press, 1958.

Haveman, Robert H. *Water Resource Investment and the Public Interest*. Nashville, Tenn.: Vanderbilt University Press, 1965.

Hirshleifer, Jack, James C. DeHaven, and Jerome W. Milliman. *Water Supply: Economics, Technology, and Policy*. Chicago: University of Chicago Press, 1960.

Hufschmidt, Maynard M., and Myron B. Fiering. *Simulation Techniques for Design of Water-Resource Systems*. Cambridge: Harvard University Press, 1966.

Kneese, Allen V. *The Economics of Regional Water Quality Management*. Baltimore: Johns Hopkins Press for Resources for the Future, 1964.

Krutilla, John V., and Otto Eckstein. *Multiple Purpose River Development*. Baltimore: Johns Hopkins Press for Resources for the Future, 1958.

Regan, Mark M., and Elco L. Greenshields. "Benefit-Cost Analysis of Resource Development Programs," *Journal of Farm Economics*, Vol. 33 (November 1951), pp. 866–78.

Regan, Mark M., and E. C. Weitzell. "Economic Evaluation of Soil and Water Conservation Measures and Programs," *Journal of Farm Economics*, Vol. 29 (November 1947), pp. 1275–94.

Renshaw, Edward F. "A Note on the Measurement of the Benefits from Public Investment in Navigation Projects," *American Economic Review,* Vol. 47 (September 1957), pp. 652–62.

Selby, H. E. "Indirect Benefits from Irrigation Development," *Journal of Land and Public Utility Economics,* Vol. 20 (February 1944), pp. 45–51.

More comprehensive bibliographies on measurement issues in benefit-cost analysis can be found in U.S. Bureau of the Budget, *Program Analysis Techniques: A Selected Bibliography* (revised, 1966); Elizabeth H. Pearman, *Bibliography on Cost-Benefit Analysis and Planning-Programming-Budgeting* (McLean, Va.: Research Analysis Corporation, 1966); H. R. Hamilton and others, *Bibliography on Socio-Economic Aspects of Water Resources,* prepared by the Battelle Memorial Institute for the U.S. Department of the Interior, Office of Water Resources Research (1966); and Alan R. Prest and Ralph Turvey, "Cost-Benefit Analysis: A Survey," *Economic Journal,* Vol. 75 (December 1965), pp. 683–735.

# State-Local Finance
# and Intergovernmental
# Fiscal Relations

DICK NETZER

# State-Local Finance
# and Intergovernmental
# Fiscal Relations

LITTLE OF THE STUDY of public finance is not oriented toward policy prescription. Even so, the issues which have engaged the attention of scholars can be classified within the conventional "positive" and "normative" categories.

In the field of state-local finance, there are three sets of positive issues. The first concerns the determinants of the wide range of variation in subnational public expenditure which is observed within the United States (state-local expenditure per capita in the low state is about 40 percent below that in the median state; in the high state it is about 60 percent above the median, excluding Alaska in the comparison). This, of course, has a bearing on policy, since in an open national economy with a high degree of mobility there is, presumably, concern about major variations in the scope and quality of the public services provided.

The second set of issues deals with the distributional and allocational consequences of the revenue devices employed by the subnational governments. The distributional consequences to be analyzed include effects on vertical and horizontal equity (usually measured among and within income classes) and, sometimes, effects on the geographic distribution of after-tax income. The allocational consequences involve analysis of the effects on the composition of investment and consumption expenditure by sector and industry (to discover, for example, whether heavy taxation of housing, under the property tax, leads to allocational inefficiency) and of the effects of geographic differentials in state-local taxes on the location of economic activity.

Third, the intergovernmental fiscal transactions pose a similar set of questions. How do they affect the geographic distribution of income? In regard to resource allocation, do intergovernmental grants stimulate additional public sector expenditure or are they substitutive in effect?

A fourth set of issues, of lively interest in the recent past, is now regarded as more or less settled. These concern the role of state-local governments in economic stabilization. The literature includes some controversy over the extent to which state-local fiscal activities have tended to reinforce economic instability, in the Great Depression and more recently.[1] But there is little evidence that state-local governments have had a positive, purposeful countercyclical role.

On the normative side, the basic issues, of course, relate to the appropriate role of government in general in economic stabilization, income redistribution, and resource allocation (to use the Musgrave classification).[2] This fundamental issue is dealt with elsewhere in this volume. But if it is settled outside the confines of a discussion

[1] See, for the initial statements of the argument, Alvin H. Hansen and Harvey S. Perloff, *State and Local Finance in the National Economy* (Norton, 1944), and George W. Mitchell, Oscar F. Litterer, and Evsey D. Domar, "State and Local Finance," in Board of Governors of the Federal Reserve System, *Public Finance and Full Employment,* Postwar Economic Studies 3 (1945), pp. 101–30. More recent work includes Robert W. Rafuse, Jr., "Cyclical Behavior of State-Local Finances," in Richard A. Musgrave (ed.), *Essays in Fiscal Federalism* (Brookings Institution, 1965), pp. 63–121; Ansel M. Sharp, "The Behavior of Selected State and Local Government Fiscal Variables During the Phases of the Cycles, 1949–1961," National Tax Association, *Proceedings of the Fifty-Eighth Annual Conference on Taxation, 1965* (1966), pp. 599–613; and Frank E. Morris, "Impact of Monetary Policy on State and Local Governments: An Empirical Study," *Journal of Finance,* Vol. 15 (May 1960), pp. 232–49.

[2] Richard A. Musgrave, *The Theory of Public Finance* (McGraw-Hill, 1959), Chap. 1.

of state and local finance per se (as it must be), an important question with respect to expenditure theory remains: What is the appropriate distribution of functional responsibilities among the levels of government in a multilevel system of the type existing in the United States? There is a parallel question on taxation theory: What are the appropriate revenue systems for the subnational governments in a multilevel system? And, since it is unlikely that the ideal distribution of revenues will coincide with the ideal distribution of expenditure responsibilities, what are the appropriate systems of intergovernmental payments to mediate between the two sets of assignments?

In this essay the normative issues are employed as an organizing device, within which the evidence on the positive questions is discussed.

## Approaches to Fiscal Federalism

Most explorations of the fiscal theory applicable to a federal system have started with three fundamental assumptions, the validity of which can be readily demonstrated. First, it is assumed that the subnational levels of government will continue to be major providers of public services. This assumption does not require complete acceptance of the existing distribution of functional responsibilities, but only of the proposition that state-local government will continue to be important. In fact, this distribution has been a rather stable one for nearly twenty years; state and local governments have accounted for roughly 40 percent of direct general expenditure by all levels of government.[3] Excluding defense-related expenditure, the shares have remained roughly one-fourth federal, one-fourth state, and one-half local during this period.[4] To be sure, there have been major shifts during the twentieth century—a substantial expansion of the state government share of civilian public expenditure from about 1920 to the mid-1940s (mainly attributable to the predominant

[3] Direct general expenditure excludes intergovernmental payments, expenditure of utility and liquor monopoly systems, and social insurance operations. For a brief review of the historic trends, see George F. Break, *Intergovernmental Fiscal Relations in the United States* (Brookings Institution, 1967), pp. 2–8.

[4] If social insurance operations are included in civilian public expenditure (as perhaps they should be), the federal government share of the total is considerably higher—36 percent in 1965—and has been rising somewhat.

role of state government in highways, higher education, and public welfare) and a major increase in the federal share in the 1930s. But none of the three levels appears to be withering away.

A second assumption is that, in an open, complexly interrelated, and mobile society, there are important spillovers of costs and benefits from the fiscal operations of particular subnational units of government. In other words, there is a national interest in the performance of some of the public services provided by the subnational units and a regional interest in some of the public services provided by subregional units. Short of the withering away rejected by the first assumption, fiscal solutions are required by this set of phenomena.

A third assumption is that the distribution of revenue-raising capacity among the state and local units is highly uneven. This, of course, is so: The range in variation in per capita personal income among the fifty states is more than 2 to 1, and the range among the 3,000-odd counties in the United States is more like 5 to 1.[5] These disparities create problems of accommodating the wider geographic interest in the provision of specific types of public services (essentially, problems of efficient resource allocation), and of interpersonal equity.

*Equity in a Federal System*

Equity is a real problem, both in theory and in practice. Ideally, in a federal system, deliberate fiscal action to redistribute income should occur only at the central government level. Otherwise, as Musgrave says, ". . . distributional adjustments at the state level may come to be nullified by interstate movement, and serious barriers to an optimal location of economic activity may be imposed."[6]

However, action in the state-local sector in practice does have a substantial redistributive effect. In part, this is deliberate and conscious—in connection with public assistance, for example. But more often, the income redistribution is the net result of supplying public goods, providing merit goods (like education and health services) free of user charges, and political compromises in state-local tax policy. There is a fairly pronounced "pro-poor" pattern of expendi-

[5] For a comprehensive discussion of interstate variations in fiscal capacity, see Advisory Commission on Intergovernmental Relations, *Measures of State and Local Fiscal Capacity and Tax Effort* (the Commission, 1962).

[6] Musgrave, *The Theory of Public Finance*, p. 181.

ture incidence, combined with a moderately regressive pattern of state-local tax incidence. Most studies of state-local tax incidence have produced incidence curves of a modified reverse "J" shape: sharp regressivity at the very low incomes, proportionality over a fairly broad middle-income range, and a small degree of progressivity at the upper ends of the scale. This finding, of course, largely reflects the incidence of the property and sales taxes, dominant at the local and state levels, respectively.[7]

Those studies which have examined expenditure benefits generally find that average dollar benefits per family rise very slowly indeed as income rises (no matter what the basis of allocation).[8] The combined result is significant redistribution. For example, the Minnesota study found that expenditure benefits per family were at least twice as great as the tax incidence for families with incomes of less than $5,000.[9] Gillespie's nationwide study found that, as of 1960, the *net* benefits for income classes below $3,000 exceeded 25 percent of family money income before taxes.[10]

The findings of the empirical studies can be challenged in a number of respects. The theory of tax shifting is by no means a set-

---

[7] See, for example, O. H. Brownlee, *Estimated Distribution of Minnesota Taxes and Public Expenditure Benefits* (University of Minnesota, 1960); Richard A. Musgrave and Darwin W. Daicoff, "Who Pays the Michigan Taxes?" in Michigan Tax Study Research Staff, *Michigan Tax Study Staff Papers* (Legislative Committee, Michigan House of Representatives, 1958), pp. 131–83; University of Wisconsin Tax Impact Study Committee, *Wisconsin's State and Local Tax Burden* (University of Wisconsin, 1959); Levern Graves, "State and Local Tax Burdens in California," in David R. Doerr and Raymond R. Sullivan, *Taxation of Property in California* (California Legislature, Assembly, 1964); University of Maryland, College of Business and Public Administration, *Maryland Tax Study* (University of Maryland, 1965); Gerhard N. Rostvold, "Distribution of Property, Retail Sales, and Personal Income Tax Burdens in California: An Empirical Analysis of Inequity in Taxation," *National Tax Journal*, Vol. 19 (March 1966), pp. 38–47; Dick Netzer, *Economics of the Property Tax* (Brookings Institution, 1966), Chap. 3; Alan D. Donheiser, "The Incidence of the New York City Tax System," in *Financing Government in New York City*, Final Research Report to the Temporary Commission on City Finances, City of New York (New York University, Graduate School of Public Administration, 1966), pp. 153–207.

[8] See, for example, Brownlee, *Estimated Distribution of Minnesota Taxes*; Musgrave and Daicoff, "Who Pays the Michigan Taxes?"; Netzer, *Economics of the Property Tax*.

[9] Brownlee, *Estimated Distribution of Minnesota Taxes*, p. 2.

[10] W. Irwin Gillespie, "Effect of Public Expenditures on the Distribution of Income," in Musgrave (ed.), *Essays in Fiscal Federalism*, pp. 122–86.

tled matter. For example, some theorists hold that commodity taxes are largely shifted backward to the factors of production. Others argue that consumption expenditures, and, by implication, consumption taxes, should be measured in relation to permanent or long-term income rather than income received within a single year. Either approach would generally result in a more nearly proportional incidence pattern.

Also, the studies on the incidence of expenditure benefits are based on highly arbitrary assumptions. It is difficult, however, to devise alternative assumptions which do not yield findings that the poor receive more benefits per dollar of income than the rich. If this is so, state-local finance will be generally income-redistributive unless the incidence of state-local taxes is far more regressive than almost any theoretical or empirical investigator would agree.

As long as the state-local sector redistributes income (which is inevitable unless governments confine themselves to benefit taxes), equals will not be treated equally on a nationwide basis even though each unit of government operates in that manner within its own borders. As Buchanan has shown, the "fiscal residua"—taxes paid less benefits received from public expenditure—of individuals at a given income or welfare level will be more favorable in the higher-income jurisdiction.[11] That is, the higher-income state or community can provide more generous public services at no higher tax rates than obtain in poorer areas, or the same standard of public services at lower tax rates. Therefore, the fiscal system will provide a standing incentive for interarea migration, an incentive above and beyond that produced by the workings of the economic system.

Buchanan offers a solution which would treat equals equally on a national basis and thereby reduce fiscal pressures on the location of human and other resources. His solution equalizes fiscal residua by means of regionally discriminatory federal personal income taxes, higher in rich areas than in poor by the amounts necessary to achieve the equalization. There would continue to be differences in the levels of taxes, or of public services (if taxes are uniform), among the subnational units, but these differences, for individuals, would be washed out by differences in federal government tax burdens. Since many obstacles to this solution are posed by constitutional law and tradition, Buchanan's second-best solution is a system of equalizing general-

[11] James M. Buchanan, "Federalism and Fiscal Equity," *American Economic Review*, Vol. 40 (September 1950), pp. 583–99.

purpose grants, with neither matching requirements nor functional restrictions.

*External Effects*

The perception that allocation branch public services will be inadequately supplied by subnational governments because of their inability to capture, within their own boundaries, all the benefits from the expenditure, is an old one. It provided the basis for inter-governmental grants-in-aid enacted a century or more ago (the Morrill Act land grants to colleges are one example). Articulation of the idea in economic efficiency terms is more recent, as is development of quantitative evidence on the extent of spillovers and of their influence on expenditure decisions.

There is virtually no public service which fails to afford *some* benefits external to the jurisdiction which provides it, just as there are few taxes the economic effects of which are entirely confined to the area encompassed by the taxing unit of government. The real fiscal problem is created by the services in which the ratio of external to internal benefits is very high. Such services can, perhaps, be divided into two classes: services connected with human resource development, in which the spillovers stem from the interarea migration of persons and the generalized social and political benefits of a healthy, well-educated populace; and the provision of the infrastructure, environmental control, and research and development activities appropriate to an advanced society, in which the spillovers usually arise from the technological nature of the services themselves.

Education is, of course, by far the most important in the first group and it is here that the most extensive work of quantification has been done.[12] The usual conclusion is that "mobility of the United States population is such that the vast majority of financial returns from public elementary and secondary schooling are generally realized outside the school districts which provided the child's education."[13] The technological spillovers are even more obvious. Public

---

[12] See, for example, Burton A. Weisbrod, *External Benefits of Public Education: An Economic Analysis* (Princeton University, Department of Economics, Industrial Relations Section, 1964); Werner Z. Hirsch, Elbert W. Segelhorst, and Morton J. Marcus, *Spillover of Public Education: Costs and Benefits* (University of California at Los Angeles, Institute of Government and Public Affairs, 1964).

[13] Weisbrod, *External Benefits*, p. 62.

activities connected with air and water pollution control and water supply create benefits—or minimize governmental costs—over entire natural basins, which have little to do with state, county, and municipal boundary lines. The benefits from most governmental transportation services and facilities can be captured only within metropolitan or larger regions. In the absence of rigid residence requirements for users, which would produce substantial underutilization, many users of large park and recreational facilities (like state or national parks, forest preserves, and seashores) will come from outside the local, or even state, jurisdictions in which the facilities are located.

On a collective basis, the price of public services to voters in a community is equivalent to the local taxes and charges they pay (less any intergovernmental grants available). If they are rational, local consumer-voters will be willing to pay only for the benefits which are realized internally—that is, the value of the services to them. But, if benefit spillovers are important, such rationality means that services of the quality and quantity appropriate to generate external benefits—services that rational voters in a whole region or the entire nation would be willing to tax themselves to pay for—will not be provided. The extreme cases of this undernourishment of public services are found in the larger metropolitan areas, where highly fragmented local government structures with the attendant spillovers lead to

. . . an allocation of resources to collective consumption that is below the optimum level that would be indicated if all benefits of such consumption were appropriable in the spending community. . . . The inefficiencies in terms of underallocation of resources to the public sector, and the accompanying inequities, go a long way toward providing some understanding, if not explanation, of the major problems confronting metropolitan America.[14]

Without intergovernmental payments (or complete benefit-tax financing of the expenditure of the state-local sector), the undernourishment cannot be overcome and an efficient allocation of re-

[14] Harvey E. Brazer, "Some Fiscal Implications of Metropolitanism," in Benjamin Chinitz (ed.), *City and Suburb: The Economics of Metropolitan Growth* (Prentice-Hall, 1964), pp. 144 and 145.

sources to the public sector achieved, as long as the jurisdictions providing major public services cover areas smaller than those in which large portions of the benefits are realized. And this will continue to be the case as long as expenditure decisions are made for schools by local school districts, for arterial city streets by municipal governments, and for income maintenance programs by state governments.

Break has developed a theory of optimizing grants, designed to deal with the distortion of state-local expenditure decisions, and hence of resource allocation, occasioned by benefit spillovers.[15] Since the grants are intended to cope with the spillover problem, they must be restricted to programs which actually do have important external effects. The grantor government is appropriately concerned with the content and efficiency of the programs: "It is an essential part of the optimizing grant theory that all supported programs would be operated to the joint satisfaction of the grantor and the grantee."[16] Moreover, the grants should be open-ended, not limited to a specific annual dollar amount; a dollar ceiling will prevent realization of important external benefits. If, in most years, the aid allotment is exhausted (as is the case with regard to many federal grant programs), the grantor has in effect been paying for internal benefits. With a proper matching formula, the dollar ceiling is unnecessary as well as inefficient.[17]

In theory, the matching formula should be based upon the ratio of external to internal benefits; that is, the grantor and grantee governments should share in costs in proportion to this ratio. Since the spillover ratio is not uniform among state and local governments and the rates of return on additional expenditure are also variable, the matching proportion should also be variable. Break suggests recognition of interstate differentials in both income and tax effort. Rafuse suggests the need for refined analysis and formulas, if the grants are efficiently to elicit the desired expenditure response.[18] Fis-

[15] Break, *Intergovernmental Fiscal Relations*, Chap. 3.

[16] Ibid., p. 241*n*.

[17] See the discussion by Robert W. Rafuse, Jr., "The Efficiency of Conditional Grants-in-Aid," in Joint Economic Committee, *Revenue Sharing and Its Alternatives: What Future for Fiscal Federalism?* Joint Committee Print, 90 Cong. 1 sess. (1967), Vol. 2, p. 1059.

[18] Ibid., pp. 1053–59.

cal capacity is one factor here, but not the only one; cost and other demand-influencing factors specific to individual programs deserve consideration as well.[19]

It should be noted that the theory of optimizing grants is quite different from the common articulation of the case for intergovernmental grants, to the effect that grants are necessary to assure a nationwide (or statewide) minimum program level for a specific function.[20] The case for minimum-program grants rests on a merit-goods or welfare type of argument, while the optimizing-grant theory is more in keeping with an individualistic calculus. Proponents are saying, in the former case, "We believe that everyone in the country should enjoy at least this level of service X"; in the latter, "We are willing to pay taxes to support services in other states because we ourselves will eventually benefit from such services."

Were the minimum-program approach to be justified on the basis of externalities, it would be necessary to assume that external benefits cease to be generated by program levels in excess of the specified minimum; this is highly unlikely.[21] However justified, the minimum-program approach is difficult to apply, since (like other merit-goods services) it requires a consensus on the minimum program to be provided and some measurement of the varying costs of achieving such a program.

### A Model of Multilevel Finance

The optimizing-grant approach is consistent with a number of model systems involving efficiency solutions to the problem of multi-

---

[19] This is carried to the logical extreme by Robert F. Adams and Neil M. Singer, "Intergovernmental Fiscal Relations and Efficiency Analysis," in Joint Economic Committee, *Revenue Sharing and Its Alternatives: What Future for Fiscal Federalism?* Vol. 2, pp. 1060–68. Adams and Singer suggest that the external-internal benefit ratio be ignored and that instead federal grants, in effect, be auctioned to the units which can demonstrate the highest ratios of benefits to program costs, viewed from a national standpoint.

[20] This is, in fact, the almost universal rationale for state school aid of the foundation-grant type.

[21] Break, *Intergovernmental Fiscal Relations*, pp. 158–59. It should be noted that there is considerable interest in the states in moving from a foundation school aid program to a cost-sharing formula of the New York State type. In the latter, the aid percentage is inversely related to a measure of local fiscal capacity, with a relatively high per pupil ceiling (and no overall dollar ceiling for the grant program). In effect, this is an optimizing-grant program.

level finance.[22] Such models provide for systematic differentiation in the roles of the levels of government, based upon their vastly different coverages of economic flows: the federal government encompassing the whole of a single integrated economy; the states generally comprehending most intraregional economic relationships; and the local governments typically exposed to both intra- and interregional economic competition and possessing limited capacity to internalize the benefits of public expenditure.[23]

In this type of model, the subnational governments are confined to allocation branch activities, with spillovers accommodated by intergovernmental grants of the optimizing type. Stabilization and deliberate income redistribution activities are the province of the central government. This is, of course, only a partly accurate reflection of reality. There is a substantial element of deliberate redistribution in the finances of state and local governments, especially in connection with education and with nonfederal financing of welfare, health, and other poverty-linked services. In 1965–66, the state-local sector spent about $10 billion for welfare programs and for health and hospital services principally aimed at the poor; about 40 percent of this was financed with federal aid, while the remainder absorbed roughly 10 percent of both state and local tax revenues (and a much higher percentage in large central cities).[24]

The model would suggest a series of upward shifts in the respon-

---

[22] For example, Charles M. Tiebout, "An Economic Theory of Fiscal Decentralization," in *Public Finances: Needs, Sources and Utilization* (Princeton University Press for the National Bureau of Economic Research, 1961), pp. 79–96; Charles M. Tiebout and David B. Houston, "Metropolitan Finance Reconsidered: Budget Functions and Multi-Level Governments," *Review of Economics and Statistics,* Vol. 44 (November 1962), pp. 412–17; and Richard A. Musgrave, "Approaches to A Fiscal Theory of Political Federalism," in *Public Finances: Needs, Sources and Utilization,* pp. 97–122.

[23] Increasingly, this approach is disputed, on the grounds that what now exists is actually a "marble cake," rather than a "layer cake" federal system, in which the three levels of government are all involved to some extent in the financing and provision of all the major types of civilian public services. This has been rationalized by the argument that there are differences in consumer preferences as to the mix of government in the provision of services and that changes in this mix are part of the process of adjustment to achieve desired levels of public services. See Selma J. Mushkin and Robert F. Adams, "Emerging Patterns of Federalism," *National Tax Journal,* Vol. 19 (September 1966), pp. 240–47.

[24] Computed from data in U.S. Bureau of the Census, *Governmental Finances in 1965–66* (1967).

sibility for, or the financing of, such activities, or both: from local to regional (possibly metropolitan-area-wide arrangements but more likely the state government) and from regional to national, with federal grants, expansion of social insurance, and perhaps a negative income tax supplanting the major state-financed redistributive activities. Other upward shifts would also occur in connection with spillovers, with optimizing grants as the most frequent adjustment mechanism in regard to human resource development spillovers, but reallocation of functional responsibilities the frequent mechanism for dealing with technological spillovers. This is because a single regional unit for performance of the service is often suggested by the nature of the production function; for example, regional air pollution control machinery seems more sensible than an elaborate system of intraregional payments and penalties.

Beyond this, there is a theoretical case for the existence of a multiplicity of small governmental jurisdictions to provide and finance allocation branch activities without important externalities, even within such closely connected regions as metropolitan areas. Tiebout has advanced this argument in developing a model in which individuals reveal their preferences for public goods much as they do in the course of voluntary exchange in the private sector.[25] Under a set of restrictive assumptions, he views suburban communities as competing for residents by offering differing packages of public services combined with the tax rates required to finance the services; consumers choose among the communities on the basis of their relative preferences for goods and services collectively, vis-à-vis privately, provided.

Unfortunately, Tiebout's restrictive assumptions usually do not apply: Mobility and knowledge are restricted; externalities exist; and actual fiscal flows are complex and often unrelated to decisions of individual consumer-voters. Therefore, it is not surprising that the pattern of tax rates and expenditure levels the Tiebout thesis would lead one to expect—a high and positive correlation—is seldom observed in metropolitan areas.[26] But if the local jurisdictions actually did correspond to "natural" service areas for the provision of most

[25] Charles M. Tiebout, "A Pure Theory of Local Expenditure," *Journal of Political Economy*, Vol. 64 (October 1956), pp. 416–24.

[26] Indeed, the surprising thing is that this pattern is *ever* observed. But it is, for example, in regard to nonschool expenditures and taxes in upper-income Chicago suburbs (the presumed laboratory for Tiebout's observations). See Netzer, *Economics of the Property Tax*, pp. 125–31.

local services and if the financing devices were specific cost-based user charges, most of the advantages of the Tiebout solution could be realized. That is, the provision of services would be related to revealed consumer preferences.

The model system would include, in addition to optimizing grants connected with spillovers, another type of intergovernmental adjustment mechanism—general-purpose or unconditional grants. There are three arguments for this. The first is the Buchanan equity argument. The existence of subnational governments with major responsibilities in a national economy characterized by important geographic disparities in income and wealth requires equalizing efforts by the central government. Equalizing grants not tied to specific functions provide a mechanism for precisely this, not as a substitute for specific-purpose optimizing grants, but in addition to them.[27]

The second argument is what has been called the "fiscal imbalance" argument. In this model, expenditure responsibilities are allocated among the levels of government on the basis of scale economies, with constant returns to scale implying that the responsibility for a function should be assigned to the lowest level of government within which the bulk of the benefits can be internalized. By assumption (and in reality) this means a major continuing role for subnational governments on the expenditure side. On the other hand, revenue instruments are assigned to the level of government which can best administer them. There are two aspects to this arrangement: economies of scale in tax administration, which apply in an important degree to nearly all types of tax instruments; and the actual or potential mobility of objects of taxation within a single, open economy. Together, these considerations lead to an assignment of the most productive revenue sources to the central government, in theory as in practice. In practice, centralization of tax collection is less than theory would suggest, but nonetheless it is considerable.

It would be an unlikely coincidence if the ideal allocations of expenditure and revenue responsibilities matched precisely—if the appropriate revenue powers of state and local governments were sufficiently productive to finance their expenditure responsibilities, even

[27] For a succinct summary of the distinction between the rationales for the two types of grants, see Walter W. Heller and Joseph A. Pechman, "Questions and Answers on Revenue Sharing," in *Revenue Sharing and Its Alternatives: What Future for Fiscal Federalism?* Hearings before the Subcommittee on Fiscal Policy of the Joint Economic Committee, 90 Cong. 1 sess. (1967), pp. 111–17 (Brookings Reprint 135).

after spillovers had been accommodated by optimizing grants. It has been argued that, in reality, the situation is one in which the federal government has ample revenue sources and limited civilian expenditure responsibilities, leading to the necessity for tax rate reductions (or intergovernmental transfers) for stabilization goals, while the opposite is true for state-local governments, requiring continual state-local tax rate increases. The result is increasing utilization of the relatively less attractive tax instruments which the state-local sector has available to it. Moreover, it is argued that state-local use of even these instruments is circumscribed by actual or potential interarea competition for the location of taxable resources.

To the extent that this is an accurate description of the situation probable in theory (and observed in reality), the result is inefficiency in the sense of an undersupply of public services. As Break points out, if fiscal imbalance were the only problem, "the appropriate solution would not be grants-in-aid at all but some form of tax sharing whereby revenues were returned to the jurisdictions of origin."[28] But given the need for interarea equalization as well, an appropriately designed system of unconditional grants can handle both equalization needs and fiscal imbalance.

A third argument for unconditional grants goes back to externalities and income distribution problems. If, on the basis of spillovers and distributive considerations, there is a national interest in a wide range of local activities, and if the differential degrees of national interest in the specific activities are very hard to calculate or determine with any precision, then general-purpose grants can help economize on decision making. This formulation cannot, of course, provide a basis for specifying the structure of a program of unconditional grants. It merely suggests that unconditional grants justified on the first two bases should err on the side of generosity.

Such are the outlines of one model system. The remainder of this essay explores the theoretical and observed conditions that bear upon the appropriateness or validity of this formulation.

## The Responsibility for Public Services

The allocation of responsibilities for the provision of public services among the levels of government in the United States is the re-

[28] Break, *Intergovernmental Fiscal Relations*, p. 109.

sult of a long process of political accommodation to a changing economic and social environment. At the state-local level, there are in effect fifty different structures of expenditure responsibility, just as there are fifty different state-local tax structures. Tradition and inertia, even accident, have played a large part in shaping the observed outcome.[29] However, inertia and accident do not provide the entire explanation for the observed reality, and they provide no clue at all for prospective policy.

In concept, the responsibility for decision making on public expenditure should be distinguished from the responsibility for program execution; it is entirely possible to conceive of programs in which local governments are the direct providers of the service but act without decision-making authority, in a ministerial capacity, as agents of higher-level governments. In reality, in the American system, the executing level of government usually possesses a very wide range of decision-making authority within some set of very general rules, such as requirements for a merit personnel system and nondiscrimination rules. Since local governments possess no sovereignty vis-à-vis the states, the rules could be quite binding. But typically they are not. For example, in most states, education is formally a function of state government delegated to the school districts. Even so, the range of decision-making authority exercised by the school districts is usually very wide.

There is, however, some real sharing of decision-making authority in connection with functional grants-in-aid from higher to lower levels of government. And, generally, the higher the grant as a percent of total expenditure for the function, the greater the transfer of

---

[29] Perhaps the most striking illustration of the role of accident in the allocation of expenditure responsibilities can be found in the decisions about the respective roles of state and local governments in the federally aided public assistance programs adopted following the passage of the Social Security Act in 1935. The act required a wholly new set of subnational administrative and financial arrangements at the state-local level. But, at that time, in some states, the state governments were in much worse straits than the local governments, while in others the reverse was true. For example, New York City had just adopted a new sales tax while New York State was feeling the consequences of a highly income-elastic revenue system; meanwhile, in many other states, the state governments had adopted new sales taxes while their local governments were grappling with massive property tax delinquencies. As a result, in New York State, public assistance became a locally administered program with substantial local financing. In contrast, in Illinois and some other midwestern states, it became a state-administered program, with little or no local financing.

decision-making authority to officials and agencies of the higher-level government.

Analysis of the allocation of expenditure responsibility is thus simplified. It can be examined conveniently from two standpoints: (1) Which levels of government actually spend, purchase goods and services, and make transfer payments to individuals? (2) Which levels of government finance the activity?

*The Existing Division of Responsibility*

Musgrave's "budget branches" provide a useful framework for organizing this examination. This framework is illustrated in Tables 1 and 2, for 1927 and 1965–66, respectively, in which civilian public expenditure is assigned to either the stabilization, redistribution, or allocation branch, with education treated as a fourth branch which is partly an allocation branch (merit-good) activity. The assignment of individual activities to a specific branch is, of course, partly a matter of personal judgment, and it is further complicated because the Census Bureau's functional categories cover some diverse collections of activities. Nevertheless, the principal implications seem clear enough:

1. Since the 1920s, redistributive activities have increased greatly as a share of civilian public expenditure, for all levels of government combined and for each of the levels (although least for the state government level).

2. Both the direct provision of redistributive services and their financing are now dominated by the federal government, very much unlike 1927.

3. However, the subnational governments continue to have a significant role in the provision and financing of redistributive services, especially if education is considered to have a major redistributive component.

4. Stabilization activities, wholly absent in 1927, constitute a modest share of public expenditure in the prosperous mid-1960s, as perhaps is to be expected.

5. The increase in the federal role, which has occurred in all the branches, far outshadows the increase in the state government role.

6. The state level has now (in 1965–66) replaced the federal government as the least important of the three levels of government. Despite this, the relative importance of state government has in-

**TABLE 1. Percentage Distribution of Direct Civilian Public Expenditure, by Budget Branch and Level of Government, 1927**

| Type of distribution and level of government | Budget branch | | | |
|---|---|---|---|---|
| | Total[a] | Redistribution[b] | Education[c] | Allocation[d] |
| *Expenditure, by budget branch* | | | | |
| All levels of government | 100 | 7 | 22 | 71 |
| Level making expenditure | | | | |
| Federal | 100 | 6 | 1 | 93 |
| State | 100 | 19 | 1 | 80 |
| Local | 100 | 4 | 32 | 64 |
| Level financing expenditure | | | | |
| Federal | 100 | 6 | * | 94 |
| State | 100 | 14 | 17 | 69 |
| Local | 100 | 5 | 30 | 65 |
| | | | | |
| *Expenditure, by level of government* | | | | |
| Level making expenditure | | | | |
| All levels | 100 | 100 | 100 | 100 |
| Federal | 16 | 14 | * | 21 |
| State | 16 | 42 | 1 | 18 |
| Local | 68 | 44 | 99 | 61 |
| Level financing expenditure | | | | |
| All levels | 100 | 100 | 100 | 100 |
| Federal | 17 | 14 | * | 22 |
| State | 20 | 41 | 15 | 20 |
| Local | 63 | 45 | 84 | 58 |

Source: Based on U.S. Bureau of the Census, *Census of Governments: 1962,* Vol. 6, No. 4, *Historical Statistics on Governmental Finances and Employment* (1964); partly estimated.
* Less than 0.5 percent.
[a] Excludes national defense and international relations; veterans' services; liquor stores; employee retirement; interest on federal government debt.
[b] Includes public welfare; hospitals; health services (except federal direct expenditure, largely for research purposes); housing; social insurance except unemployment compensation, public employee retirement, and veterans' life insurance.
[c] Excludes higher education, which is assigned to allocation branch.
[d] All other expenditure.

creased during these four decades, a fact that can be almost entirely explained in one of two ways. In terms of direct expenditure, the explanation lies in increased allocation branch activity, notably for highways and higher education. In terms of financing, the explanation lies in the increased role of state governments in financing public schools. But, to a considerable extent, the states have become intergovernmental transfer mechanisms—receiving federal funds for their direct expenditure activities, while transferring state-collected revenue to the local governments to support local activities. As Table 3 shows, in 1966 the state governments retained an estimated $8 billion of their intergovernmental revenue for their own uses and transferred the other $4 billion, plus $13 billion from their own revenue sources (which totaled $34.5 billion), to local governments.

**TABLE 2. Percentage Distribution of Direct Civilian Public Expenditure, by Budget Branch and Level of Government, 1965–66**

| Type of distribution and level of government | Budget branch | | | | |
|---|---|---|---|---|---|
| | Total[a] | Stabiliza-tion[b] | Redistribu-tion[c] | Educa-tion[d] | Alloca-tion[e] |
| Expenditure, by budget branch | | | | | |
| All levels of government | 100 | 5 | 28 | 20 | 47 |
| Level making expenditure | | | | | |
| Federal | 100 | 9 | 51 | 3 | 37 |
| State | 100 | 8 | 21 | 4 | 67 |
| Local | 100 | * | 13 | 42 | 45 |
| Level financing expenditure | | | | | |
| Federal | 100 | 8 | 47 | 6 | 39 |
| State | 100 | 5 | 16 | 27 | 52 |
| Local | 100 | * | 10 | 34 | 56 |
| | | | | | |
| Expenditure, by level of government | | | | | |
| Level making expenditure | | | | | |
| All levels | 100 | 100 | 100 | 100 | 100 |
| Federal | 33 | 64 | 61 | 4 | 26 |
| State | 23 | 36 | 18 | 4 | 33 |
| Local | 44 | * | 21 | 92 | 41 |
| Level financing expenditure | | | | | |
| All levels | 100 | 100 | 100 | 100 | 100 |
| Federal | 43 | 72 | 73 | 12 | 35 |
| State | 27 | 28 | 16 | 36 | 29 |
| Local | 30 | * | 11 | 52 | 36 |

Source: Based on U.S. Bureau of the Census, *Governmental Finances in 1965–66* (1967); partly estimated.
\* Less than 0.5 percent.
[a] Excludes national defense and international relations; space research and technology; veterans' services; liquor stores; employee retirement; interest on federal government debt.
[b] Includes farm price support activities; unemployment compensation; employment security administration.
[c] Includes public welfare; hospitals; health services (except federal direct expenditure, largely for research purposes); housing; social security benefits; social insurance except unemployment compensation, public employee retirement, and veterans' life insurance.
[d] Excludes higher education, which is assigned to allocation branch.
[e] All other expenditure.

Another way of examining the existing distribution of expenditure responsibilities—both for decision making and for execution of programs—is to classify governmental functions according to the geographical scope of the benefits produced by public services. Break employs a three-way classification: (1) local services, with few important spillovers beyond the local level; (2) intermediate or regional services, with the spillovers from the local level largely confined to particular regions; and (3) federal services, with significant extraregional benefits.[30] If this classification is compared to

[30] Break, *Intergovernmental Fiscal Relations*, pp. 68–71.

**TABLE 3. State Government as a Mechanism for Intergovernmental Fiscal Transfers, 1966**

*(In billions of dollars)*

| Source of state government general revenue | Amount from source | Use of general revenue | | |
| | | Direct expenditures | Payments to local governments | Total general expenditure |
|---|---|---|---|---|
| Local governments | 0.5 | 0.5 | 0 | 0.5 |
| Federal government | 11.7 | 7.7 | 4.0 | 11.7 |
| State sources | 34.5 | 21.7 | 12.8 | 34.5 |
| Statistical discrepancy[a] | ... | −0.7 | 0 | −0.8 |
| Total[b] | 46.8 | 29.2 | 16.8 | 46.0 |

Source: Adapted from U.S. Bureau of the Census, *State Government Finances in 1966* (1967); partly estimated by author.
[a] Total expenditure and total revenue are not equal in any given year.
[b] Figures are rounded and will not necessarily add to totals.

data from the 1962 Census of Governments (using Census functional classifications), it is apparent that the political decisions taken over many decades have produced a distribution of responsibilities which does not conform well with the presumed scope of benefits. The regional role seems too small for most services with important regional spillovers, and the federal role too small for some significant services with nationwide spillovers. On the other hand, the federal role is a very considerable one in some services with few spillovers beyond the regional level, notably in highways, water supply, and urban planning and renewal.

For example, consider some of the functions Break classes as mainly intermediate or regional in scope of benefits. About one-half of the expenditure for *airports* is actually made by municipal governments, rather than regional entities; the remainder is made by regional special districts, state governments, and the federal government. Intergovernmental transfers somewhat expand the federal role, but not that of regional governmental agencies, such as states, counties, and special districts of wide geographic scope. Nearly all expenditure for *refuse disposal* is made by small-scope local units. The great bulk (two-thirds or more) of expenditure for *sewerage* and for *transit* similarly is the responsibility of municipal rather than regional units. The federal and state government roles in both these areas have expanded somewhat since the 1962 Census of Governments, particularly in regard to financing. But these regional functions continue to be largely a local responsibility. The *urban planning and renewal* functional responsibility is somewhat different in character—virtually completely local in execution and largely federal in financing, but with almost no regional participation.

Break classifies only a few civilian functions as essentially nationwide in scope of benefits. One is *education*. Yet most expenditure is done by small-area local units or, in higher education, by regional (state) governments; financing remains largely a local and regional responsibility. A second national function is *aid to low-income people*. If this is defined narrowly to embrace only public welfare, then execution is mainly in the hands of regional governments (states and counties), and financing is about one-half federal. Break's classification, and the model developed earlier, suggests that the present arrangement involves an inordinate amount of local and regional responsibility. However, the federal role has been increasing over time, especially if the definition is expanded to include social insurance, public housing, and antipoverty programs.

The distribution of responsibilities among levels of government changes constantly, although usually at a slow rate, in response to changing political perceptions of the geographic extent of particular public problems. But this analysis suggests a rather interesting change since the 1930s. Then (and in the 1920s to some extent) the perception of important spillovers of benefits beyond local jurisdiction boundary lines tended to produce a substantial regional (state) government response, whether the spillovers were (in Break's system) national or regional—in education, public assistance, and highways. Increases in the federal role also occurred, to be sure. More recently, the perception of spillovers has tended to produce a federal response, whether the spillovers are national or regional in nature. Compare, for example, highways, mass transportation, and urban planning and renewal with education and antipoverty programs; all have involved large new federal programs in the past decade. Indeed, one might argue that federal government energies (and funds) have been devoted to essentially regional-benefit programs, at the expense of national-benefit ones. Alternatively, it could be argued that the classification of benefits employed here, after Break, simply disagrees with the nation's appreciation of the way in which benefits accrue.

*Other Criteria for Expenditure Responsibility*

The extent of spillovers never has been and never will be the sole criterion for determining the allocation of program responsibility. There are two other major factors, one entirely economic in character and the other involving both economic and political considerations. The first is the question of economies of scale; the second is the bias in favor of local decision making, others things being equal.

SCALE ECONOMIES. There is a growing body of literature which has some bearing on the question of scale economies in state-local expenditure. Most of the empirical studies are concerned with the more general question of the determinants of variation in expenditure per capita (or per pupil, for schools).[31] Deductive reasoning suggests that there are likely to be few cases in which unit costs of state-local services decline as the size of jurisdiction rises, once a rather low threshold is passed. For the very smallest jurisdictions, the provision of even the most rudimentary services is expensive on a per capita basis—at least one policeman on duty around the clock; one teacher for every primary school grade level; access roads passable in all weather, and so on.

But beyond the thresholds, scale economies tend to be unlikely, for two reasons. First, most state-local functions continue to be very labor-intensive, although this may become less true. Second, the quality of the service provided may be diluted if single production sites are used to supply service over very wide areas; schools, fire and police stations, local parks and playgrounds, and welfare centers all offer examples. Such functions constitute what Hirsch has called services amenable only to horizontal integration. A larger jurisdiction simply includes more production units providing the same

[31] For a comprehensive review of the subject, see Werner Z. Hirsch, "The Supply of Urban Public Services," in Harvey S. Perloff and Lowdon Wingo, Jr. (eds.), *Issues in Urban Economics* (Johns Hopkins Press for Resources for the Future, 1968). For a summary of the empirical results, see Robin Barlow, "Multivariate Studies of the Determinants of State and Local Government Expenditures in the United States" (background material for the Ford Foundation Workshop on State and Local Government Finance, University of Michigan, June 1966; mimeo.). The Hirsch and Barlow papers provide the source (and citations) for most of the observations which follow. For a critical appraisal of the expenditure determinants studies, see Barry N. Siegel, "On the Positive Theory of State and Local Expenditures," in Paul L. Kleinsorge (ed.), *Public Finance and Welfare; Essays in Honor of C. Ward Macy* (University of Oregon, 1966), pp. 171–86.

kind of service.[32] These services dominate the state-local sector. However, there are some capital-intensive functions, such as water supply, sewage disposal, and most transport services, for which scale economies are real.[33]

The empirical studies tend to support the deductive argument that scale economies are rare, but their results are not entirely persuasive. The nature of the data and the primary goals of most of the studies—the discovery of expenditure determinants—have led to formulations which mix supply and demand factors, rather than isolate cost functions. In any event, the multivariate studies of expenditure determinants are marked by the almost complete absence of negative associations between the size of the jurisdiction served (usually measured by population) and expenditure per capita or per pupil for particular functions. On the other hand, there have been few findings that functional expenditures rise with scale. Positive associations have been found for schools in a few places and for police expenditure in even fewer. The more general finding is a lack of any significant correlation between size and expenditure level.

This does not necessarily prove the absence of scale economies, since it is so difficult to satisfy the ceteris paribus requirement, especially in regard to quality of service. Moreover, some of the studies do not treat population density as a separate factor. Density is strongly, but not perfectly, correlated with population size, and logic suggests that density is an additional indicator of scale. In numerous studies, it has been found to have significant associations with expenditure levels.

Significant negative correlations, suggesting the possible presence of scale economies, have been found in some broad-scale studies for education, highways, welfare, health and hospitals, and general control.[34] Positive correlations are less common, and are confined usually to fire and police protection; however, a number of studies have found positive correlations between density and total state-local

[32] Werner Z. Hirsch, "Expenditure Implications of Metropolitan Growth and Consolidation," *Review of Economics and Statistics*, Vol. 41 (August 1959), pp. 232–41.

[33] An ex ante study which employs engineering data to illustrate this point is Walter Isard and Robert E. Coughlin, *Municipal Costs and Revenues Resulting from Community Growth* (Chandler-Davis, 1957).

[34] "Broad-scale studies" here means those covering the entire country or large nationwide samples of governmental units.

or total local expenditure. One of the most careful analyses, based on engineering-type data rather than regression analysis, concluded that unit costs, when properly measured, rise with density for most types of public services provided in urban areas.[35]

The Kain findings, unlike those in most of the multivariate analyses, relate to scale economies in a relatively pure sense. In other studies, a significant explanation for some of the apparent indications of increasing costs with density lies in the effects of increasing urbanization upon the basket of public services, even within a single functional category, held to be essential by voters and legislative bodies. That is, *demand* for public services may be a function of urbanization. If this is so, the expenditure determinants studies cannot be used to demonstrate conclusively the existence of diseconomies of scale.

Thus, the empirical evidence on scale economies is not clear-cut. But the evidence does make it difficult to urge, on the basis of scale economies, radical upward shifts in the responsibility for major governmental functions. It can be argued, however, that the high degree of labor intensity now prevalent in most state-local activities is in part a sign of technological backwardness, which could be overcome in many cases if the size of jurisdiction were larger. That is, small units cannot or do not effectively utilize the equipment available even now, not to mention the technology likely to be available in the future. This is surely true of many activities with a large clerical component, such as the disbursement function in income transfer programs, revenue collection, licensing and regulation, and similar activities. It is also true of other kinds of activities which might use highly specialized equipment, such as highway maintenance by small local units and police communications.

Moreover, larger jurisdictions may be better able to hire high-quality technical and professional personnel, and at lower salaries, than smaller jurisdictions, because the nonmonetary advantages of the jobs are greater than they would be in smaller places. On the other hand, some talented people may respond in the opposite way, as is evident from the ability of relatively small suburban school districts to attract good administrators. Large size, in government, tends to

[35] John F. Kain, "Urban Form and the Costs of Urban Services" (Harvard University Program on Regional and Urban Economics, 1966; mimeo.).

be accompanied by complexity, political controversy, and employee unionization, factors which can produce real diseconomies of scale.

LOCAL DECISION MAKING. The bias in favor of local decision making can be explained on a number of bases. One is a merit-goods type of argument, to the effect that respect for the preferences of geographically concentrated minorities (local units of government), within a state or metropolitan area or within the nation as a whole, is a merit good, the provision of which yields satisfaction to the majority of the populace. That is, the majority is entirely willing to yield repeatedly on its preferences, in the interests of achieving this form of satisfaction. Local land-use controls within a metropolitan area, under which a collection of minorities makes decisions which are typically inimical to the majority, is a good example.

But this willingness to yield to minorities may be no more than a reflection of the absence of adequate arrangements for compensating overridden minorities.[36] Economists have long held that welfare and efficiency considerations could be reconciled in such cases by adequate money transfers. The real issue is adequacy of the compensation. If loss or damage is calculated on the basis of the market value of the property rights in question *to the majority* (the usual case—consider, for example, a road through a nature preserve), compensation will seldom be enough to effect reconciliation.

There is also a pure efficiency argument for local decision making. If the ratio of internal to external benefits is high, expenditure decisions will clearly be inefficient unless made at the local level. Logrolling for an oversupply of the services will tend to develop, in the hope that taxpayers elsewhere will bear the brunt of the costs. This surely explains, in part, the extensive federal participation in activities which are essentially regional-benefiting. But the efficiency argument can be carried further, in an analogy with the private sector. It has been asserted that local decision making yields a variety of public service levels and that this is a form of competition which enlarges consumer choice (if consumers are geographically mobile), or at the least permits experimentation.[37]

---

[36] The extensive literature on relocation of those displaced by public action affords numerous illustrations. See, for example, U.S. Congress, House Committee on Government Operations, *Metropolitan America: Challenge to Federalism*, A Study Submitted to the Intergovernmental Relations Subcommittee by the Advisory Commission on Intergovernmental Relations, 89 Cong. 2 sess. (1966), pp. 57–84.

[37] See, for example, Tiebout, "A Pure Theory of Local Expenditure."

The basic political argument for local decision making is, of course, the claim that local autonomy enlarges political participation and disperses political power, thereby strengthening democratic institutions in general. This, however, is a highly ethnocentric argument, one which ignores the experience of other democratic countries. Britain and the Scandinavian countries, for example, are unitary rather than federated democracies, with quite limited effective local government decision making. In Australia, state governments are far more important vis-à-vis the local units than in the United States. This suggests that a local government sector as important as that in this country is *not* a necessary ingredient of a truly democratic society. Moreover, in a pluralistic society, there is a good deal of scope for local participation through institutions other than the formal structure of local government per se.

Here again, the arguments are by no means conclusive. Perhaps the most that can be said is that the case for local decision making is not strong enough to overcome arguments for more centralization of decision making for purely redistributive services and for other activities, like education, with nationwide benefit spillovers. On the other hand, for many services, the case for more centralization on the basis of economies of scale is much too weak to overcome the arguments for local decision making.

## Conclusion

This review suggests that appropriate changes in the present allocation of expenditure responsibility involve both centralizing and decentralizing shifts. Both apply to the national government's role: more responsibility for redistributive activities and for education (on the basis of spillovers); less responsibility for regional-benefit activities like transportation and some resource development functions. For the regional governments, defined as states and local units covering comparatively large areas, the implications are a relatively reduced role in education and income redistribution, but on balance a much larger proportional role, through assumption of more functions with intraregional benefit spillovers from both the federal and purely local governments, and through transfer of some capital-intensive services from the local units.

A larger relative role for state governments is not necessarily required; in some cases, it would be equally desirable, or even preferable, instead to enlarge the responsibilities of large-area local government agencies (such as metropolitan-area-wide governments and authorities). But, in the light of the demonstrable political unpopularity of the latter solution in recent years, an expansion of the state government role may be the best solution. Indeed, it can be claimed that the state governments are the best substitutes for metropolitan area government that the United States has or is likely to get. For the very large metropolitan areas, state government may actually be a *superior* alternative to metropolitan government. And, in fact, some state governments, like those in California and New York, recently have become much more active in fields such as water supply and water quality, mass transportation, and parks and recreation.[38] Since the evolution of subnational government institutions and approaches in the United States involves a good deal of imitation of what is done in a few pioneering jurisdictions, this is perhaps the wave of the future.

## The Division of Revenue-Raising Responsibilities

Perhaps the oldest prescription in the literature of fiscal federalism is the doctrine of separation of revenue sources—the doctrine that each level of government should employ distinctive revenue instruments, not utilized by the other levels. In doctrinal neatness and in simplicity for taxpayers, this has obvious appeal. It has even more intellectual appeal if in fact the levels of government have differential economic and administrative advantages for particular types of taxes. This formulation parallels the idea of comparative advantage in the international division of labor.

A level of government, in this approach, should employ those taxes which it can most effectively handle and no others. A level which has no *absolute* advantage for any tax nonetheless should use the taxes it can handle least badly. And if the levels with some absolute advantage confine themselves to the taxes in which their advantages are greatest, tax sources will remain for use by the least-favored levels. Thus, the approach suggests use of the income tax by

[38] In part, greater activity has been associated with the creation of nominally metropolitan agencies which are in fact very closely tied to the state governments and which the Bureau of the Census quite rightly classifies as dependent agencies of a state government.

the federal government exclusively, of consumer sales taxes by the states, and of the property tax by local governments, even though it is conceivable (and perhaps probable) that the federal government can better handle *any* of these taxes.

The doctrine of separation of sources for years has had a bad name in public finance literature. But is there still some element of validity in the approach? Are there criteria which suggest confining the use of specific tax devices to particular levels? Or should the superior types of taxes—determined on the basis of traditional canons of taxation which apply to a unitary governmental structure—be utilized by each of the three levels of government to the extent required by its own budgetary decision making?

## Separation of Sources in Practice

Since 1787, the state-local sector has not levied tariffs and the national government has not used the ad valorem tax on property. But aside from these major exceptions, revenue sources have never been completely separated in this country. And the degree of tax overlapping has increased substantially in the past forty years. The two major exceptions aside, few significant revenue sources are not utilized by at least two levels of government. Increasingly, income taxes and a number of selective sales taxes (such as taxes on motor fuel, cigarettes, and telephone service) are being utilized by all three levels.

However, much effective separation of sources continues, if the analysis proceeds in dollar terms rather than in terms of the numbers of jurisdictions, small and large, using a particular revenue source. As Table 4 indicates, the bulk of federal revenues comes from income taxes and the bulk of local revenues from property taxes, and the two levels hold dominant positions with respect to revenue yielded by the respective tax forms. The state governments are in a similar position with respect to sales taxes of general application.

This, however, is separation of the sources defined in terms of the legal forms of taxation—the legal measures of tax liability. An alternative approach is to define the sources in economic terms. A classification along these lines (based on estimated allocations of reported revenue amounts) is presented in Table 5. Taxes on personal income and wealth transfers and on payrolls are, in dollar terms,

**TABLE 4. Dollar Amount and Percentage Distribution of Governmental Revenue, by Legal Form and Level of Government, 1965-66**

(Dollar amounts in billions)

| Legal form | All governments Amount | Percent | Federal Amount | Percent | State Amount | Percent | Local Amount | Percent |
|---|---|---|---|---|---|---|---|---|
| Total revenue | $225.6 | 100% | $141.1 | 100% | $43.0 | 100% | $41.5 | 100% |
| Taxes | | | | | | | | |
| Income | 92.3 | 41 | 85.5 | 61 | 6.3 | 15 | 0.5 | 1 |
| Sales and gross receipts | 33.7 | 15 | 14.6 | 10 | 17.0 | 40 | 2.0 | 5 |
| Property | 24.7 | 11 | ... | ... | 0.8 | 2 | 23.8 | 57 |
| Other, including licenses | 10.1 | 4 | 3.9 | 3 | 5.2 | 12 | 1.0 | 2 |
| Charges for services, and utility and liquor store revenue | 25.8 | 11 | 9.8 | 7 | 5.0 | 12 | 11.0 | 27 |
| Miscellaneous general revenue | 8.4 | 4 | 4.6 | 3 | 1.5 | 4 | 2.3 | 5 |
| Insurance trust revenue | 30.6 | 14 | 22.6 | 16 | 7.1 | 17 | 0.8 | 2 |

Source: U.S. Bueau of the Census, Governmental Finances in 1965–66 (1967), p. 20. Totals and percentage calculations are based on unrounded data; details may not, therefore, add to totals.


**TABLE 5. Dollar Amount and Percentage Distribution of Governmental Revenue, by Economic Source and Level of Government, 1965-66**

(Dollar amounts in billions)

| Economic source | All governments Amount | Percent | Federal Amount | Percent | State Amount | Percent | Local Amount | Percent |
|---|---|---|---|---|---|---|---|---|
| Total revenue | $225.6 | 100% | $141.1 | 100% | $43.0 | 100% | $41.5 | 100% |
| Taxes | | | | | | | | |
| Personal income and wealth transfers[a] | 64.1 | 28 | 58.5 | 41 | 5.1 | 12 | 0.5 | 1 |
| Consumption[a] | 34.2 | 15 | 9.1 | 6 | 11.2 | 26 | 13.9 | 33 |
| Payrolls[b] | 24.7 | 11 | 20.8 | 15 | 3.9 | 9 | * | * |
| Business income, activity, assets, and intermediate purchases | 48.7 | 22 | 31.7 | 22 | 5.8 | 13 | 11.2 | 27 |
| User charges[c] | 37.2 | 16 | 13.7 | 10 | 11.8 | 27 | 11.7 | 28 |
| Other[d] | 16.7 | 7 | 7.3 | 5 | 5.2 | 12 | 4.2 | 10 |

Source: Reclassification of data in Table 4, by author, based on underlying Census Bureau detailed data and other material. Totals and percentage calculations are based on unrounded data; details may not, therefore, add to totals.

* Less than $50 million, or less than 0.5 percent.

[a] Includes, in addition to sales and license taxes, property taxes on housing and consumer-owned motor vehicles.

[b] For social insurance purposes only; excludes government employee retirement systems.

[c] Includes highway user taxes and special assessments as well as charges for services, utility revenue, and liquor store revenue.

[d] Largely consists of revenue from minor unclassified tax sources, miscellaneous nontax general revenue, employee retirement fund contributions, and earnings on insurance trust fund investments.

very largely the province of the federal government. This is somewhat less true of taxes on business as such, including levies on business income, activity, assets, and intermediate purchases. Local governments have a sizable role in business taxation, largely because roughly one-half of property tax collections are derived from taxes on real and personal property used in business, both farm and nonfarm. Similarly, the large local role in the consumption tax field is related to property taxes on housing; in this classification the state government position in consumption taxation is no longer a distinctive one. User taxes and charges constitute another area of substantial overlap. However, the real overlapping applies only to highway user taxes, since by definition a government's revenue from user charges are for use of *its own* facilities.

Obviously, the degree of separation of sources is steadily being reduced, as income and sales taxes spread among both state and local governments. In the past two decades, this spread has made roughly 30 percent of the population subject to general sales taxes imposed by two levels and nearly one-tenth subject to individual income taxes imposed by three levels of government.[39] Despite this development, the composition of tax revenues of the state-local sector in the aggregate has remained relatively stable during the past fifteen years, after undergoing radical change during the 1930s (see Figure 1). Sales and income taxes, on the one hand, and the property tax on the other, each have provided 40–45 percent of total tax revenue in recent years.

There are at least three strands to the argument that some degree of separation of revenue sources is appropriate. Put another way, there are three types of criteria for judging which level of government can best handle a particular revenue source. One relates to the unequal distribution of taxpaying capacity among the states and among local units within a single state. A second relates to differences in administrative efficiency and in the feasibility of effective enforcement, if such differences are inherent among the levels of government. A third, which has some bearing on the administrative capacity issue, is that of effects of tax differentials on the location of economic activity.

[39] For a comprehensive account, see Advisory Commission on Intergovernmental Relations, *Tax Overlapping in the United States, 1964* (the Commission, 1964), and *Tax Overlapping in the United States: Selected Tables Updated* (the Commission, 1966).

**FIGURE 1. Distribution of State-Local Tax Revenue, by Major Type of Tax, Selected Years 1902–66**

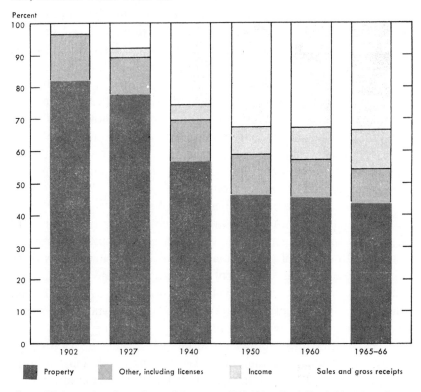

Source: U.S. Bureau of the Census, *Census of Governments: 1962*, Vol. 6, No. 4, *Historical Statistics on Governmental Finances and Employment* (1964), pp. 38–40; and *Governmental Finances in 1965–66* (1967), p. 18.

## Fiscal Capacity and Tax Effort

By itself, the unequal geographic distribution of a particular type of tax base does not necessarily argue for confining use of that form of taxation to levels of government with a wide geographic scope. Intergovernmental transfers *do* provide an adjustment mechanism which can accommodate this discrepancy. A high degree of inequality in tax base distribution combined with other defects in local administration may, however, suggest assignments of the tax to higher levels of government.

Moreover, if the differences in taxable resources are extreme enough, the tax in question is likely to be clearly inappropriate as a major means of financing functions amenable to local administration and decision making (for the very high rates necessary in some jurisdictions can produce deleterious effects on the location of economic activity). A hypothetical example might be the use of the retail sales tax as the primary element of local taxation for the support of municipal units in a metropolitan area. A municipality with a large regional shopping center is often surrounded by jurisdictions in which there is little retail trade at all. For example, in Bergen County, New Jersey, a 5 percent municipal tax on total retail sales in 1963 would have yielded per capita revenues of $468 in Paramus, the site of a cluster of massive regional retail centers; in six of the adjacent jurisdictions the per capita yield would have been $27, $42, $44, $55, $62, and $123, respectively.[40] For Paramus, the figure is more than double the present level of local taxation, but for the other places, the hypothetical sales tax yield is only one-quarter to one-half of present local tax yields.[41]

Per capita income differentials among and within states continue to be very large, no matter how income is measured.[42] Interstate personal income differentials dropped significantly during the Second World War, but since then there has been no trend toward greater geographic equality. The average deviation of state personal income per capita has been about 18 percent during most of the past twenty years, and the spread from the richest to the poorest state has narrowed very little.

Since the variation in income per capita is so great, the variation in taxable capacity is also large. The Advisory Commission on Intergovernmental Relations has made estimates of the yield of a standard representative tax system in the fifty states and the District of Columbia as of 1960.[43] The per capita yield ranged from 57 percent of the national average in the low state to 161 percent in the high state. But there were significant differences among the types of tax

[40] The six include all the adjacent places for which retail sales data are presented in U.S. Bureau of the Census, *Census of Business, 1963*, Vol. 2, *Retail Trade—Area Statistics*, Pt. 2, *Indiana to New York* (1966), pp. 32-3 and 32-8.

[41] Such disparities in taxable resources in connection with sales taxes result from the conventional allocation of the proceeds to the jurisdiction of sale rather than the jurisdiction of consumer residence. Since retail sales taxation is based on the idea of taxing consumers, the latter arrangement would be more consistent with the underlying philosophy. However, this arrangement is not used with regard to local sales taxation in this country.

[42] For a summary of trends in interstate differentials, their measurement and their significance, see Break, *Intergovernmental Fiscal Relations*, pp. 109–20.

[43] Advisory Commission on Intergovernmental Relations, *Measures of State and Local Fiscal Capacity and Tax Effort*, pp. 126–27.

**TABLE 6. Interstate Variation in the Per Capita Yield of Principal State and Local Taxes of a Representative Tax System, and in Selected Economic Measures, 1960**

(In percent)

| Type of tax and economic measure | Coefficient of variation |
|---|---|
| Total representative tax system[a] | 21.1 |
| Property tax | 27.2 |
| All nonproperty taxes | 21.1 |
| General sales | 19.8 |
| Selective sales | 18.4 |
| Individual income[b] | 35.0 |
| Corporate income | 23.5 |
| Economic measure | |
| Personal income, 1959 | 19.8 |
| Income produced, 1959 | 20.2 |
| Actual tax collections, 1960 | 19.7 |

Source: Calculated from data in Advisory Commission on Intergovernmental Relations, *Measures of State and Local Fiscal Capacity and Tax Effort* (the Commission, 1962).

[a] The representative tax system is one with provisions similar to those in effect in the majority of the states actually using the form of tax in 1960. Since the tax coverage and rates of the system are identical in all states, the variation in per capita yield among the fifty states and the District of Columbia is identical with the variation in the tax base per capita. The coefficient of variation equals the standard deviation divided by the mean.

[b] Because the representative individual income tax is progressive in rate structure, this is not, strictly speaking, a tax base measure; it is, however, a measure of fiscal capacity analogous to the tax base measures employed for other taxes.

in the representative system. The coefficients of variation are shown in Table 6.

Interstate variation is apparently lowest for the bases for consumption taxes, defined as the representative general sales tax (the base of which includes some intermediate business purchases) and the representative selective sales taxes, largely on liquor, tobacco, and gasoline. This is to be expected, in view of the relation of consumer expenditure to current income and since the rates of the selected excises are typically based on physical quantities rather than dollar value.[44] Interstate variation in the corporate income tax base,

[44] A general sales tax which covers neither housing nor food expenditure is likely to be proportional in incidence over most of the income range. The income elasticity of demand for physical quantities of liquor, tobacco, and gasoline, upon which most of the selective excises are based, is decidedly low. The elasticities are also low in terms of dollar expenditure for tobacco and for gasoline (except for the lowest income class) and are roughly unitary in these terms for alcoholic beverages. See National Industrial Conference Board, *Expenditure Patterns of the American Family* (the Board, 1965).

in contrast, is greater than the variation in personal income, and interstate variation in the yield of a representative (progressive rate structure) individual income tax is very large indeed, so large that it is difficult to conceive of a viable multilevel system in which state governments relied primarily on personal income taxes with a progressive rate structure.

The coefficient of variation for property taxes is an especially serious matter, because the property tax is not a state tax but a local one; the large interstate variation in the property tax base is compounded by large intrastate variations.[45] This can be seen most dramatically among local units within the larger metropolitan areas, where ranges in per capita values (excluding the extreme cases of industrial enclaves and resort communities) of 15 to 1 and more are not uncommon.[46]

TAX EFFORT. There is evidence that some of the major factors indicative of needs for public services are inversely related to taxable capacity. For example, the ratios of dependent to working-age population and the percentages of low-income households tend to be very high in the poor states and rather low in the rich states.[47] Within metropolitan areas, low property values per capita are usually found in jurisdictions characterized by large concentrations of poverty. And within metropolitan areas, variations in expenditures per capita are far smaller than variations in valuations per capita.

This should and does result in a wide range in effective tax rates among the jurisdictions in metropolitan areas; in the larger areas, ranges of 5 to 1 and 7 to 1 have been found.[48] Moreover, in the majority of cases, the high effort occurs in communities with low capacity and is sufficient to finance only relatively low levels of public expenditure.[49]

The relationship between per capita income levels and state-local tax effort, by states, is not nearly so strong.[50] There are both high-ef-

---

[45] The coefficient of variation in full value per capita among New York State's counties has been between 20 and 25 percent in recent years. See, for example, New York State Department of Audit and Control, *Comparisons of Revenues, Expenditures and Debt: 1949–1959,* Comptroller's Studies in Local Finance, No. 1 (1961).

[46] Netzer, *Economics of the Property Tax,* pp. 124–25.

[47] See Break, *Intergovernmental Fiscal Relations,* pp. 118–19.

[48] Netzer, *Economics of the Property Tax,* pp. 124–25.

[49] Ibid., pp. 124–30.

[50] See Break, *Intergovernmental Fiscal Relations,* pp. 134–35.

fort states (like California and New York) and low-effort states (New Jersey, Illinois, and Connecticut) among the rich states; among the poor, also, there are high-effort states (like Louisiana and Mississippi) and low-effort states (like Kentucky and Alabama). However, most of those with high effort, as measured by the ratios of state-local taxes to personal income, have per capita incomes below the national average and most low-effort states are relatively rich. Finally, the poorer states, almost without exception, have lower per capita expenditures than the richer states.

To the extent that high tax effort is in fact associated with low taxable capacity, therefore, there is a strong argument for intergovernmental transfers. But, where the association is exceptionally strong (as within metropolitan areas), there is also a case for reconsideration of the allocation of expenditure responsibilities, or the assignment of revenue devices among levels of governments, or both.

## Administrative Capabilities

It can be argued that few of the factors relating to differential capabilities for tax administration are inherent in the distinctions among the levels of government as such. One exception is the extent to which tax administration by subnational governments is complicated by the constitutional proscriptions on state taxation of interstate commerce. This apart, the real differences seem to relate to size, not to level of government. Scale economies, if they exist, relate to size of population or of tax base. Differentials in the ease of avoidance and evasion of specific types of taxes depend mainly upon the geographic size of the jurisdiction. However, by and large, size *is* systematically related to level of government: Only 5 of the 118,000 municipalities and only 16 of the 3,000 counties have populations over 1 million, while thirty-seven of the fifty states do.[51] Therefore, to a very considerable extent, to speak of size is to speak of level of government.

[51] U.S. Bureau of the Census, *City Government Finances in 1965–66* (1967), p. 7, *Current Population Reports,* Series P-25, Nos. 401, 404, and 407, "Estimates of the Population of Counties, July 1, 1966" (1968), and *Census of Governments: 1967,* Vol. 6, No. 1, *Popularly Elected Officials of State and Local Governments* (1968). The population data for municipalities are based on the 1960 Census of Population; other population data are for July 1, 1966. Excluded from the county government portion and included with municipalities are New York and Philadelphia, which have been substantially consolidated with the cities.

**TABLE 7. Expenditures for Financial Administration as Percentage of Revenue Collected by Central Tax Administration Agencies, by Size of Governmental Unit, Mid-1960s[a]**

| Population size group (in millions) | Number of governmental units[b] | Federal | State | City | County | All state-local[c] |
|---|---|---|---|---|---|---|
| | | \multicolumn{5}{c}{Level of government} | | | | |
| 5 or more | 14 | 0.7 | 2.0 | 1.4 | 6.0 | 2.0 |
| 2–5 | 22 | ... | 1.9 | 2.5 | 2.7 | 2.0 |
| 1–2 | 17 | ... | 3.0 | 3.3 | 5.1 | 3.3 |
| 0.5–1 | 64 | ... | 2.4 | 2.6 | 6.2 | 3.3 |
| 0.3–0.5 | 63 | ... | 3.5 | 2.9 | 5.5 | 3.8 |
| 0.1–0.3 | 277 | ... | 4.1 | 2.5 | 6.2 | 4.9 |
| Less than 0.1 | 20,636 | ... | ... | 3.3 | 7.4 | 4.3 |

Source: Computed from the following U.S. Bureau of the Census publications: *Governmental Finances in 1965–66* (1967); *State Government Finances in 1966* (1967); *City Government Finances in 1965–66* (1967); *Census of Governments: 1962*, Vol. 4, No. 2, *Finances of County Governments* (1964).

a. The denominator includes tax revenue plus other forms of revenue usually collected by tax collection agencies. The other forms include payroll taxes for Old Age and Survivors Insurance, railroad retirement (federal only), and unemployment insurance (federal and state governments); and water utility revenue (city governments).

b. Number of cities and counties in the category in 1960, and states in 1966.

c. Combines 1965–66 data for states and cities with 1962 data for counties. Other forms of local government (school and special districts) are not included.

SCALE ECONOMIES. It is obvious that there must be major economies of scale in tax administration, at least at the lower end of the size scale. Thousands of very small units of government would have to spend 5 percent or more of their tax revenues to support tax administration staffs of as few as four full-time employees. Although the quantitative evidence is inadequate, it suggests increasing returns to scale in tax administration for all major tax forms and across the whole range of size of governmental unit. One set of comparisons is that in Table 7, in which expenditures for financial administration, a broader concept than tax administration, are compared with revenue.[52] Although there are some irregularities (where the number of observations for a class of units is very small), the overall pattern—rapidly increasing costs as size of unit declines—is clear enough.

This is not simply a consequence of pure scale economies, but is partly a result of the forms of taxation typically used by larger units,

[52] The other elements of financial administration, including debt management, custody of funds, and budgeting and auditing, are likely to be *more* significant for the larger units. Thus, the evidence in Table 7 may in fact understate the case with regard to tax administration.

especially withheld income and payroll taxes; this variation in method no doubt provides a major explanation of the differences among the federal government, the states, and the county governments. However, scale economies are evidently present among states, among cities, and among counties. These levels do have roughly homogeneous tax systems. Counties are very largely confined to the property tax, and such differences as appear among the states do not systematically relate to state population size. Moreover, the larger units of government usually possess a wider array of taxes than the smaller units. The larger units, therefore, might be expected to show some diseconomies of scale on this account. But they do not; the lowest percentages in Table 7 are for the federal government and for New York City (which is the only component of the group with 5 million or more population within the city category), both of which have complex tax systems indeed.

Finally, there is some indication that the extent of scale economies would be even greater if it were possible to hold the *quality* of tax administration constant. Quality here is taken to mean the extent to which similarly situated taxpayers, as defined by the tax laws, in fact make similar tax payments. Few measures of quality in this sense exist, but there is one for the property tax—the dispersion of ratios of assessed values to sales prices around the median ratio within an assessment jurisdiction. The 1962 Census of Governments provided these data for single-family nonfarm houses, for 782 counties (or major cities with county-type responsibilities) in which a single agency does the assessing throughout the county (designated as Type A assessing organizations). The coefficient of dispersion was 22.6 percent for those with a 1960 population over 500,000, 22.5 percent for those over 50,000, and 31.3 percent for those under 50,000.[53] The superior quality in the larger places was achieved despite the fact that this accomplishment is more difficult in such places, in view of the heterogeneity of single-family houses with respect to age, type, accessibility, and price level.

STATE-LOCAL TAXATION OF INTERSTATE COMMERCE. The legal and economic issues involved here have received extensive attention in

[53] U.S. Bureau of the Census, *Census of Governments: 1962*, Vol. 2, *Taxable Property Values* (1963), Table 17. The figure for the thirty-seven areas over 500,000 was calculated by the author.

recent years.[54] It is worth noting at this point, however, that constitutional limitations complicate the administration of particular forms of taxation, notably state-local sales taxes and, particularly, taxes on business income. Unless a state is willing both to sacrifice the potential revenue from taxing out-of-state vendors and to expose in-state vendors to tax-free competition, it must devote administrative resources to the difficult task of discovering those interstate sales which are legally subject to its jurisdiction and enforcing tax liability. The latter may require collecting, via use taxes, from purchasers rather than vendors. But a major administrative argument for sales taxation is that taxing vendors affords a relatively inexpensive means of revenue collection.

There is, of course, no way that a state can refrain from taxing the income of interstate businesses, if it is to have a business income tax at all, since so much of business in the corporate form involves multistate corporations. States therefore must administer business taxes which require apportionment of the tax base among the states in which a firm conducts business. The existing administrative complexity can, perhaps, be best illustrated if it is compared with a hypothetical situation in which there were no constitutional barriers. In such a case, a wide variety of much simpler business tax instruments might be employed; for example, relatively immobile businesses would no doubt be subject to what amount to state export duties, rather than income taxes.

EASE OF EVASION AND AVOIDANCE. Differentials in the ease with which a tax can be illegally evaded are in part a reflection of quality of tax administration and in a sense, therefore, an aspect of scale economies. A small community cannot justify employment of revenue agents in numbers sufficient to eliminate evasion of sales or income taxes. The ease of evasion is also related to the interstate jurisdictional problem; there simply may be no lawful way to require out-of-state vendors to supply the information necessary for verifying tax liability.

But there is an additional factor. Smaller units of 'government typically levy a tax at a stage in the production-distribution-consumption process which allows more scope for evasion. For exam-

[54] For a summary, see Break, *Intergovernmental Fiscal Relations*, pp. 52–61.

ple, the smallest units generally can collect selective sales taxes only from retailers. Larger units, like the states and large cities, may utilize wholesalers and distributors as tax collectors; with fewer respondents, evasion is more unlikely. Finally, the federal government is likely to utilize producers and importers, with still fewer establishments. Generally, the evasion problem is significant only for relatively small units. However, recent experience with wholesale evasion of state cigarette taxes in the northeastern part of the country suggests that, for some types of taxes, only enforcement through collection from producers can really protect against evasion. This may imply federal administration.[55]

Avoidance of tax liability—distinguished from evasion by its legality—through shifting the taxable event or asset to another jurisdiction is similarly a problem mostly for relatively small jurisdictions. The extreme case, perhaps, is that of a gasoline tax levied by a small community, which can be avoided with little effort if there are adjacent tax-free areas. Obviously, avoidance of such taxes is closely related to geographic size of jurisdiction; the larger the size of the jurisdiction, the greater the nontax costs of avoidance, such as transport costs.

Since a critical factor is the relation of nontax avoidance costs to tax costs, even very small communities can reduce avoidance simply by keeping tax rates low enough. The device is widely used; the use of very low rates probably explains the persistence of a variety of easily avoidable (and otherwise objectionable) local taxes, often referred to as nuisance taxes. But very low rates produce trivial revenues, and even a whole cluster of low-rate nuisance taxes is likely to produce only minor revenue, but perhaps not minor administrative costs.

Another response to the avoidance problem, as well as to evasion and high administrative costs, is centralized tax administration, by a higher level of government, of a tax imposed by large numbers of lower-level governments within the wider jurisdiction. The oldest example of this is administration by a county of the property tax on behalf of all the units within it. County assessment and county col-

[55] However, the Advisory Commission on Intergovernmental Relations found that state collection of cigarette taxes at the manufacturers' level is both feasible and desirable. See Advisory Commission on Intergovernmental Relations, *State-Federal Overlapping in Cigarette Taxes* (the Commission, 1964), Chap. 6.

lection are the practices in most of the states. A newer example is the use of local supplements to a state sales tax, collected by the state government and remitted back to the jurisdictions in which the sales occurred. Such supplements are in virtually universal use in Illinois and California and in widespread use in seven other states.[56] In four more states, state administration is optional.

However, if such a tax supplement is very widely used by local governments and at uniform rates, it really amounts to an increase in the state tax, with the proceeds of the increase shared with local governments on the basis of source of collection. As such, it is not a truly local tax, but in reality an intergovernmental transfer device, the merits of which should be appraised on this basis. The administrative problems have been solved by effectively transferring the tax instrument to a higher level of government.

Where avoidance is of major proportions, the problem is not only the loss of revenue from that particular tax, but also the shift in the location of economic activity away from the taxing jurisdiction. The jurisdiction is concerned because the loss of economic activity can affect the bases of other types of taxes, as well as the material well-being of its residents. There is also a wider concern, from the standpoint of the national economy, with the consequences for the optimal pattern of location of economic activity.

## Tax Differentials and the Location of Activity

On the assumption that factors of production have considerable geographic mobility and that markets are, in general, reasonably competitive, there is some likelihood that locational decisions will entail departures from allocative optimality. That is, businesses, and perhaps individuals, will locate in places which do not involve maximum efficiency in the use of resources, rather than in the places with lowest overall costs, ignoring state-local taxes.[57]

Not all tax differentials are conducive to locational inefficiency,

---

[56] Sales tax supplements were authorized in three of these states during 1967 legislative sessions. Advisory Commission on Intergovernmental Relations, *State and Local Taxes, Significant Features, 1968* (the Commission, 1968), pp. 2, 117.

[57] This section is mainly a summary of the analysis in Netzer, *Economics of the Property Tax*, pp. 109–16, 122–24, and 131–32. For a comprehensive review of the evidence on this subject, see Advisory Commission on Intergovernmental Relations, *State-Local Taxation and Industrial Location* (the Commission, 1967).

even in theory.[58] Tax differentials which reflect differentials in the costs of public services consumed by businesses and individuals are hardly unneutral in this sense. Indeed, unless the taxes (or direct user charges) differ in such cases, locational inefficiency will result. Similarly, taxes in theory should contain an element of reimbursement to the community for any external diseconomies created by particular forms of economic activity (such as air and water pollution costs).

Moreover, above and beyond tax differentials stemming from such factors, there are other differentials which should not affect locational choice at all. These include taxes which fall on location rents, which "arise whenever the advantages of location at a particular site are sufficient to yield a return to the firm in excess of the return obtainable, all other things being equal, at alternative available sites."[59] In addition, if some factors of production are geographically immobile—such as important components of the labor supply and some types of natural resources for which there are few substitutes —taxes which fall upon the immobile factors will not cause locational shifts, although they may be otherwise objectionable.

It is a fair presumption that, in many cases, state-local tax differentials exceed the levels which can be described as locationally neutral for the reasons just advanced. But do they produce changes in location in reality, as in theory they should? State-local officials and legislators have been greatly concerned with interarea economic competition in framing tax policy, and in response a considerable literature has developed.[60] Most of the work takes a whole state as the unit of observation; thus, such studies have been addressed to locational effects among areas or regions, rather than effects within economic regions, such as metropolitan areas.

The general finding, with respect to interstate competition, is that "relatively high business tax levels do not have the disastrous effects often claimed for them."[61] In large part, this conclusion is re-

[58] See the elegant exposition by Harvey E. Brazer, "The Value of Industrial Property as a Subject of Taxation," *Canadian Public Administration*, Vol. 55 (June 1961), pp. 137–47.

[59] Ibid., p. 139.

[60] Much of this is reviewed in John F. Due, "Studies of State-Local Tax Influences on Location of Industry," *National Tax Journal*, Vol. 14 (June 1961), pp. 163–73.

[61] Ibid., p. 171.

lated to the fact that state-local taxes are so small an element in business costs, even in business cost differentials at alternative locations. No doubt the finding is valid in general, but there are three possible reservations.

First, most of the studies are too aggregative to uncover the marginal cases in which tax differentials are in fact the only significant cost differentials; such cases surely exist. Second, as state-local tax levels rise relative to total income and output, these marginal cases will become more frequent. And, of course, these levels have been rising sharply. For example, in 1965–66, revenue from the major state-local taxes on business amounted to 4.2 percent of national income originating in corporations, sole proprietorships, and partnerships in 1965; a decade earlier the corresponding figure was 3.1 percent.[62] Third, tax differentials may reinforce, rather than offset, other cost differentials and help precipitate probable locational shifts at an earlier date. It seems possible that this has occurred in states with high business taxes, such as Minnesota, Wisconsin, and Massachusetts.

There is an important distinction between interregional and intraregional location effects. Tax rate differentials may not be important enough to offset the major cost differentials between regions, but can easily be far more significant within a single region, like a metropolitan area, where other cost differentials are often relatively minor. The real problem appears to lie in the position of older central cities within the large metropolitan areas. Powerful economic forces have been leading to dispersal of economic activity from central cities to outlying sections.[63] Tax differentials generally reinforce this trend, since, in most larger metropolitan areas in the North and

---

[62] Major business taxes include estimated property taxes on business assets. corporation income taxes, state license taxes on corporations in general and occupations and businesses, the Michigan value-added tax, and unemployment insurance payroll taxes. Calculated from U.S. Bureau of the Census, *Governmental Finances in 1965–66* (1967), *State Government Finances in 1966* (1967), and *Census of Governments, 1962,* Vol. 6, No. 4, *Historical Statistics on Governmental Finances and Employment* (1964); U.S. Department of Commerce, Office of Business Economics, *The National Income and Product Accounts of the United States, 1929–1965, Statistical Tables* (1966).

[63] For a summary of the evidence, see John F. Kain, "The Distribution and Movement of Jobs and Industry," in James Q. Wilson (ed.), *The Metropolitan Enigma* (Chamber of Commerce of the United States, 1967), pp. 1–31.

East, effective property tax rates are higher in the central cities.[64] Moreover, the central cities are more frequent users of nonproperty taxes than are the outlying jurisdictions.[65] A recent study of New York City's finances provides fairly clear evidence that the major business tax differentials in that area actually have stimulated movement of economic activity away from the central city.[66]

In contrast to the probable impact of intra-area tax differentials on business location decisions, residential location decisions of individuals within metropolitan areas are apparently not very sensitive to tax differentials. One survey of high-income individuals suggests almost complete insensitivity to local tax differentials.[67] In part, this can be explained by the fact that the user-charge component of local tax payments is a large one for individuals in dormitory suburbs. Another explanation is the deductibility of local tax rate differentials for purposes of the federal individual income tax.[68]

Nonetheless, there is a significant, if indirect, set of locational effects of local taxes among the outlying jurisdictions in metropolitan areas. The larger American metropolitan areas are characterized by four conditions which are conducive to these indirect effects: (1) there are a large number of separate and relatively small governmental units; (2) these governments are responsible for the provision and a major part of the financing of costly public services; (3) their main revenue source is the property tax, the base of which is closely related to land uses within each tax jurisdiction; (4) these local governments are entrusted with considerable powers over land use patterns.

The result is an almost irresistible temptation to plan land use for fiscal ends—to zone out land uses with unfavorable tax-expendi-

---

[64] Netzer, *Economics of the Property Tax,* pp. 118, 122–24.

[65] For an overall comparison of tax differentials for manufacturing in one metropolitan region, see Alan K. Campbell, "Taxes and Industrial Location in the New York Metropolitan Region," *National Tax Journal,* Vol. 11 (September 1958), pp. 195–218.

[66] See the papers by Leslie E. Carbert, James A. Papke, William Hamovitch, and Henry M. Levin in *Financing Government in New York City.*

[67] Robin Barlow, Harvey E. Brazer, and James N. Morgan, *Economic Behavior of the Affluent* (Brookings Institution, 1966), pp. 169–70.

[68] See Benjamin Bridges, Jr., "Deductibility of State and Local Nonbusiness Taxes under the Federal Individual Income Tax," *National Tax Journal,* Vol. 19 (March 1966), pp. 1–17; and Bridges, "Allowances for State and Local Nonbusiness Taxes," in Musgrave (ed.), *Essays in Fiscal Federalism,* pp. 187–234.

ture ratios and zone in those with favorable ratios. Obviously, this "fiscal mercantilism" cannot work for *all* governments in an area. The effort to plan land use in this manner does, however, affect locational patterns. And it is highly unlikely that efficient patterns of land use in metropolitan areas, in the broadest sense, are those that maximize the current fiscal position of individual governments.

One final note with regard to locational influences of taxes: Whether or not empirical studies can isolate tax influences on location, policy makers clearly fear the potential effects, and these effects are therefore a real factor in tax policy at the state and local level, even if their fear is not justified by the evidence. Moreover, tax policy is one of the very few instruments subnational governments have at hand to influence economic development within their jurisdictions. It is of little use for students of public finance to dismiss this as nonrational behavior.

### An Appraisal of the Major Tax Instruments

The preceding discussion characterizes some of the criteria which are appropriate for analyzing the allocation of revenue sources among the levels of government. This section contains a summary appraisal of the major state-local revenue instruments on the basis of these criteria, as well as the conventional criteria—equity and allocation effects, other than those connected with location —which apply to taxation at any level of government.[69]

[69] There are only a few recent comprehensive appraisals of the major state-local taxes on a nationwide basis. Among them are John F. Due, *State Sales Tax Administration* (Chicago: Public Administration Service, 1963); Daniel C. Morgan, Jr., *Retail Sales Tax* (University of Wisconsin Press, 1964); Clara Penniman and Walter W. Heller, *State Income Tax Administration* (Public Administration Service, 1955); Netzer, *Economics of the Property Tax;* and Advisory Commission on Intergovernmental Relations, *The Role of the States in Strengthening the Property Tax* (the Commission, 1963), and *Federal-State Coordination of Personal Income Taxes* (the Commission, 1965).

Some of the best analyses have been done in connection with major tax studies in individual states and cities, such as Michigan Tax Study Research Staff, *Michigan Tax Study Staff Papers; Report of the Governor's Minnesota Tax Study* (University of Minnesota, 1956); University of Maryland, College of Business and Public Administration, *Maryland Tax Study;* California Legislature, Assembly Interim Committee on Revenue and Taxation, *A Program of Tax Reform for California* (California Legislature, Assembly, 1965), and various preceding publications; California Legislature, *Report of the Senate Fact Finding Committee on Revenue and Taxation* (California Legislature, Senate, 1965), and various preceding publications; and *Financing Government in New York City.*

INDIVIDUAL INCOME TAXES. In most respects, individual income taxes appear to be a superior revenue source for state government use, although, as noted earlier, not as the primary revenue source because of the highly unequal taxable capacity if a progressive rate structure is employed. At the state level, there are no serious problems of administration. It is difficult to believe that personal income tax differentials among the states can significantly affect locational decisions of either individuals or businesses.[70] Personal income taxes, of course, are more nearly neutral in other resource allocation effects than are most types of taxes—largely neutral among types of factor rewards and neutral with respect to the disposition of consumer income. As for equity considerations, it has been argued that progressive rate taxes are inappropriate for subnational governments and that income redistribution actions should be confined to the central government. However, the moderate rates and moderate degrees of progression (combined with federal deductibility) which exist make state income taxes only a minor redistributive factor in practice.[71]

Until quite recently, the states could be divided into income tax states and sales tax states, depending upon which of the two major forms of state taxation had been adopted or emphasized when the need for broad-based nonproperty tax revenue became apparent. Indeed, a fair number of the larger states used only one of the two tax forms, and proposals for adoption of the other gave rise to major controversies. Increasingly, however, revenue needs have blurred this easy classification. At the beginning of 1968, thirty of the fifty states employed both general sales taxes and personal income taxes of general application. One of the others (New Hampshire) used neither form of taxation; five (the largest of which is Oregon) used only the income tax; and fourteen used only the sales tax. This last

[70] In part, this conclusion rests on the assumption that the relatively few individuals who have large state income tax liabilities possess scarce talents which permit them to realize income differentials which offset personal tax differentials in the high tax states. However, the higher salaries paid a few key officers and employees are likely to be of trivial consequence to any firm.

[71] New York State's income tax is a relatively high one and fairly progressive. Despite this, the difference in state tax liability as a percent of total income (after taking into account federal deductibility) between a family with a $5,000 income and one with a $50,000 income is only about three percentage points. See also the discussion in Joseph A. Pechman, *Federal Tax Policy* (Brookings Institution, 1966), pp. 211–14.

**TABLE 8. Relative Dependence of State Governments on Sales and Income Taxation, 1967**

*(Number of states)*

| Ratio of general sales tax revenue to total state tax revenue (in percent) | Ratio of individual income tax revenue to total state tax revenue (in percent) | | | | |
|---|---|---|---|---|---|
| | No income tax[a] | 0–19 | 20–29 | 30 and over | Total |
| No sales tax[a] | 2 | 0 | 1 | 5 | 8 |
| 0–19 | 1 | 1 | 1 | 3 | 6 |
| 20–29 | 2 | 4 | 5 | ... | 11 |
| 30–39 | 8 | 6 | 3 | ... | 17 |
| 40 and over | 4 | 3 | 1 | ... | 8 |
| Total | 17 | 14 | 11 | 8 | 50 |

Source: U.S. Bureau of the Census, *State Government Finances in 1967* (1968), pp. 20 and 22.
[a] Includes states with taxes of limited application and states collecting a new tax for only a small part of the fiscal year. See Advisory Commission on Intergovernmental Relations, *State and Local Taxes, Significant Features, 1968* (the Commission, 1968), p. 12.

group included some good-sized industrial states, like Pennsylvania, Illinois, Ohio, and New Jersey.[72]

The convergence is more apparent than real, however. Only a few of the thirty states with both types of taxes apply personal income taxes at the high rates characteristic of the purely income tax states. The use of moderate or even nominal rates, which produce only small percentages of state government revenue, is the common pattern in these thirty states. As a result, there is the clear distinction among the states suggested in Table 8.

Whether a state falls in one category rather than another seems to be partly a result of historical accident (for example, which tax was constitutionally valid during a financial crisis) and partly a reflection of differences in voters' attitudes toward the imagined incidence of the respective forms of taxation. Other explanations are difficult to find. It is interesting to note that relatively heavy reliance on the income tax at the state government level tends to be associated with relatively heavy reliance on the property tax in total state-local revenue systems.[73] Moreover, the states with both high property taxes and high income taxes tend to spend relatively more

[72] In Pennsylvania and Ohio *local* income taxation is widespread. Advisory Commission on Intergovernmental Relations, *State and Local Taxes, Significant Features, 1968*, pp. 12–13, 45–46.
[73] See Netzer, *Economics of the Property Tax*, pp. 94–95.

than states with high sales taxes; this may suggest that preference for redistributive taxes is associated with preferences for public over private goods.

For local governments, the income tax is not nearly so attractive an instrument. For small units, the administrative problems can be formidable. Differences in taxable capacity are large, moreover. And unless cities in metropolitan areas can tax commuters and residents on a more or less equal basis, high rates could induce high-income people to move to tax-free suburbs. For the very largest cities, the income tax is perhaps superior to some of the tax alternatives, especially if commuters are taxed; in practice, use by central cities of the income tax can be ascribed to inappropriately heavy assignment of responsibilities to the cities (especially for redistributive services) and inadequate intergovernmental assistance for these functions.

CONSUMER SALES TAXES. Here, too, state government use of the tax instrument rates high by most criteria. Except for the interstate sales problem, administrative difficulties are not serious, by and large. Because states generally cover large geographic areas, sales tax differentials seldom can have significant effects on the location of retail trade. Because consumption spending differs among the states less than any other economic measure, bases for sales taxes are less unequally distributed than bases for any other major type of tax.

However, the implication is that consumer sales taxes can be regressive among income groups, which is in fact often the case. But it need not be so. The regressivity of the conventional retail sales tax can be moderated in one of two ways. In six of the forty-four states with sales taxes, per capita refundable credits against individual income taxes are allowed for sales taxes paid, in effect making the first few hundred dollars of taxable consumption expenditure exempt from the sales tax.[74] These credits can convert the sales tax to a proportional or even mildly progressive tax.

The other approach is to exempt from taxation types of consumer expenditure which are especially important in the budgets of low-income families. Thus, fourteen of the thirty-eight sales tax states not using the tax credit device exempt food from the sales tax.

---

[74] If there is no income tax liability, the taxpayer can apply for a refund. Advisory Commission on Intergovernmental Relations, *State and Local Taxes, Significant Features, 1968*, pp. 33–37.

Half the sales tax states exempt prescription drugs and a few exempt selected types of clothing.[75] Exemption of food from the sales tax base can make the tax more or less proportional, since expenditure for housing (which largely escapes the sales tax) and for food are rather income inelastic, at least with respect to current income.[76]

The tax credit approach is a relatively new one, and has the advantage that its moderating effect on regressivity does not depend on the actual consumption patterns of specific low-income families, which can vary widely. One disadvantage, however, is that the sales tax credit works only if *all* individuals and families, including those with very low or negative incomes, file income tax returns in order to claim the cash refunds due them. On the other hand, the food exemption approach has an administrative disadvantage too. It is easier to administer a sales tax if all sales by a retail establishment are taxable than if some are taxable and others are not.

The regressivity of the tax is also affected by the extent to which its coverage has been extended beyond the sale of tangible personal property, to include various kinds of consumer services. By and large, services other than housing become more important in family budgets as income rises; thus wider coverage of services tends to make the tax less regressive. It also reduces the allocational unneutrality of the sales tax, in affecting the relative after-tax prices of the various objects of consumer expenditure. Nearly all state sales taxes apply to such services as restaurant meals and hotel rooms. Roughly half of the state sales taxes cover consumer utility bills, admissions and amusement services, and automobile rentals. But only a few of the taxes apply to personal care services (like those in barber and beauty shops); repairs and alterations of clothing; appliance and automobile repairs; parking and garage charges; and laundry and dry cleaning services.[77]

As a local revenue source, sales taxes present problems of administration and of unevenly distributed bases, which are particularly serious for very small jurisdictions. The administrative difficulties and, equally important, the administrative costs can be drastically

[75] Ibid., pp. 1, 2, 27.

[76] See Donheiser, "The Incidence of the New York City Tax System," pp. 166–71.

[77] Advisory Commission on Intergovernmental Relations, *State and Local Taxes, Significant Features, 1968*, pp. 19–26.

reduced if the state government administers the local sales taxes together with the state sales taxes. At the end of 1966, local sales taxes were used in sixteen states, fourteen of which had state sales taxes. In eight of the fourteen, the local sales taxes were administered by the state for all the local governments involved, and in two for most of them.[78]

The locational effects can be significant for local governments in metropolitan areas, for both small and large places. A study of the New York City sales tax suggests that each percentage point of the tax has been responsible for a reduction of 6 percent in city retail sales of apparel and home furnishings and for diversion of these sales to tax-free suburbs.[79]

BUSINESS TAXES. As Table 5 shows, U.S. state and local governments are heavy users of taxes on business income, activity, assets, and intermediate purchases. In 1965–66, such taxes produced an estimated $17 billion of the total state-local revenue of $84.5 billion. The case for state-local taxes on business is weak in theory, and weaker still in regard to some of the major forms of business taxation actually employed. One pragmatic argument is that businesses are convenient tax collection devices, so convenient that business taxation is popular at all levels of government and in most countries. Moreover, there is at least one intellectual argument for using this convenient collection device. Part of the economic activity carried on within a state is reflected not in income received by residents of the state (which is taxable under personal income taxes), but in undistributed corporate profits and dividends paid to nonresidents. A state corporate income tax can reach this segment of income originating within the state.

At the *state* level, the major business taxes are those on corporate income (and related license taxes) and on intermediate business purchases. These tax bases are unequally distributed among the states. Business tax differentials surely have more potential for adversely affecting the location of economic activity than do differen-

---

[78] See Advisory Commission on Intergovernmental Relations, *Tax Overlapping in the United States: Selected Tables Updated*, Tables 44 and 46.

[79] Henry M. Levin, "An Analysis of the Economic Effects of the New York City Sales Tax," in *Financing Government in New York City*, pp. 664–68.

tials in state taxation of personal income or consumption. In any event, not only the rates of business income taxes but also the method of apportioning the income of interstate businesses and the extent to which state laws governing retail sales taxes cover intermediate business purchases have been major issues of state tax policy in recent years.

State sales taxes differ considerably in coverage.[80] Business purchases can amount to as much as one-third of the total sales tax base and as little as one-tenth; in most states, the figure probably is in the 15–25 percent range—nearer the upper end where food is exempt. The basic difference among the states relates to the underlying legal principle employed to define taxable retail sales. In most sales tax states, the exempted sales of goods for resale are defined to include only those items which become physical ingredients of goods which are later resold. In a smaller number of states, anything which is directly used in the production of goods for resale is exempt from the sales tax. Although these principles are applied in different ways, there is a general pattern. Where the physical-ingredient rule is the principle, sales of industrial machinery and equipment are customarily taxed, which is not the usual case under the direct-use rule. Also, fuel used in industrial processing is more often taxed under the first rule than under the second.

Nearly all the sales tax states, whatever the basic rule, tax sales of equipment and supplies for offices, stores, and construction. But only a minority tax sales of business-type services. The services most commonly taxed are printing and the rental or lease of machinery and equipment. Only a few states tax storage, repair, and maintenance services, and the like.

Policy on these matters involves the resolution of the customary conflict between the revenue yield from the taxation of business purchases and the presumed benefits to economic growth from exemption of business purchases. On a more abstract level, however, it is not hard to make an adverse judgment: Taxation of intermediate business purchases is not supported by the rationale for the sales tax as a consumption tax, and taxation of *some* types of business inputs but not others is allocationally unneutral.

---

[80] Much of this discussion is based on Morgan, *Retail Sales Tax,* Chap. 2.

One argument for inclusion of business purchases in the tax base is that additional exemptions make it more difficult effectively to enforce the taxation of sales of related consumer-type goods and services. Offsetting this argument is another: A considerable portion of taxable business purchases may consist of interstate purchases of machinery and equipment. If the vendors have no establishment in the state, the sales tax on such transactions can be enforced only through audit of the purchasers, which is an expensive form of tax administration.

The taxation of interstate sales (of both producer and consumer goods) has been a major issue in state tax policy, with concern expressed about both the avoidance of tax liability in some cases and the inequitable overtaxation of sales in others. The apportionment of the income of multistate corporations among the states for state income tax purposes has posed another major administrative issue. Both the gravity of the problems and the nature of the remedies raise questions. A major study of these issues was made by the Willis Subcommittee of the House Judiciary Committee. Its proposals, which are still under discussion, called for radical remedies indeed.[81]

Any business tax, at any level of government, is suspect on equity grounds, for its incidence is not clear and is probably unknowable. An equity defense might be based upon the benefit theory, that is, business activity benefiting from public services should be taxed to pay for them. But direct and obvious benefits can be far more readily recouped through explicit user charges than with the clumsy instruments of business taxation. Business taxes might be conceived of as charges for the indirect benefits of organized government—a social overhead charge. However, it is hard to see why this charge should be related to the levels of profits, or intermediate purchases, or assets. The only rational measuring rod would seem to be the scale of activity of a firm, namely, its value added.

Taxation on a value-added basis has the collateral virtue of allocational neutrality, an advantage signally absent in the more conventional American forms of business taxation. The value-added tax is neutral with respect to both the form of business organization and

[81] State Taxation of Interstate Commerce, H. Rept. 1480, 88 Cong. 2 sess. (1964), Vols. 1 and 2; H. Rept. 565, 89 Cong. 1 sess. (1965), Vol. 3; H. Rept. 952, 89 Cong. 1 sess. (1965), Vol. 4. For a discussion of these issues, see Break, Intergovernmental Fiscal Relations, pp. 52–61 and 232–38.

the composition of factor inputs. However, value-added taxation would not avoid the administrative or locational problems in state taxation of business enterprise.[82]

The major *local* business tax is that on business property. It suffers from every defect of state business taxes, in an aggravated form. Tax bases are exceedingly unevenly distributed among taxing jurisdictions; tax differentials appear to have discernible adverse effects on location patterns within metropolitan areas; and the unneutral allocational effects, sometimes among competing industries, are not minor.[83] Moreover, the administrative problems are great because the theoretical and practical difficulties of measurement require the business component of the property tax to be levied essentially on the basis of a set of proxies for the market value of the properties involved, some of which are relatively close parallels to it but many of which are not.[84]

To deal with some of these problems, the Advisory Commission on Intergovernmental Relations has recommended that state governments take over administration of the property tax on industrial and commercial property. Under this plan, taxes from existing business property would be distributed to the taxing units in which the property is located, but taxes collected from future additions to the business property tax base would be pooled for metropolitan-area-wide use—for example, for an area-wide school tax district.[85] This arrangement would reduce both disparities in tax bases (markedly, over time) and the adverse effects on location patterns. It is a decidedly radical proposal.

THE RESIDENTIAL PROPERTY TAX. Close to half of all property tax revenue is derived from taxes on housing, household goods, consumer-owned motor vehicles, and utilities serving domestic consum-

[82] For a discussion of some of the difficulties, see Douglas H. Eldridge, "Equity, Administration and Compliance, and Intergovernmental Fiscal Aspects," in National Bureau of Economic Research and Brookings Institution, *The Role of Direct and Indirect Taxes in the Federal Revenue System* (Princeton University Press, 1964), pp. 141–204. Ronald B. Welch, in his comments on the Eldridge paper in the same volume (pp. 208–15), is optimistic about the administrative feasibility of value-added taxation and its suitability for state use.

[83] For evidence on the last point, see Netzer, *Economics of the Property Tax*, pp. 22–27.

[84] Ibid., p. 169.

[85] See Advisory Commission on Intergovernmental Relations, *State-Local Taxation and Industrial Location.*

ers; housing accounts for the great bulk of it. In most respects—administration, locational effects, unequal resources, for example—the deficiencies of the property tax on housing are less serious than those of business property taxes. However, it can be argued that the defects of the housing tax are at least as serious as those of alternative forms of local taxation. Attainable standards of administrative quality, for one thing, seem very low.[86]

In the aggregate, the housing property tax is not terribly regressive, nor does it seem to have really adverse allocational effects, in the sense that the very high effective rates, when converted to sales-tax equivalents, deter consumption of housing. Property taxes on housing typically amount to 20–25 percent of housing expenditure or housing costs, excluding the property tax.[87] As noted earlier, the lack of adverse consumption effects in suburban communities is not difficult to explain. Moreover, for owner-occupants, heavy property taxes are offset by important federal income tax advantages, in the form of deductibility of payments for interest and property taxes and the tax-free nature of the imputed income.[88]

None of this, however, applies to central cities, the housing stock of which contains a large proportion of tenant-occupied housing. Housing property taxes appear to be sharply regressive in central cities.[89] As sales-tax equivalents, the rates are often well above 25 percent.[90] The federal income tax offsets are not available to renters. And the tax-public service nexus is far from clear to residents of central cities, where, unlike the suburbs, the property tax finances a substantial volume of redistributive expenditures. As a result, it can be argued that the housing property tax affords a significant obstacle to increases in consumption of housing in central cities and to the needed rebuilding of much of the housing stock in the large old central cities.[91]

None of the strictures on the property tax, whether on business

[86] Netzer, *Economics of the Property Tax,* pp. 19–20, 177–80.

[87] Ibid., Tables 2–7 and 2–8, pp. 29–30.

[88] For a quantification of this, see Dick Netzer, "Housing Taxation and Housing Policies," in Adela Adam Nevitt (ed.), *The Economic Problems of Housing* (St. Martin's Press, 1967), pp. 123–36, especially p. 133.

[89] See Donheiser, "The Incidence of the New York City Tax System," pp. 171–79.

[90] Netzer, *Economics of the Property Tax,* Table 5–6, p. 106.

[91] Ibid., pp. 74–85.

or housing, applies to the not insignificant portion of the tax which rests on land values. As Henry George held, taxes on land values fall upon a true economic surplus, and therefore alter neither the use of specific sites nor the location of economic activity. Their result is to reduce land values. This public appropriation can be justified on the grounds that the major part of the value of land is attributable to population growth, community development, and public improvements, none of which is a result of the enterprise of individual landowners.

Therefore, the idea of much heavier local taxation of land values enjoys considerable (and growing) attractiveness. Lower taxation of improvements and heavier taxation of land would probably tend to foster desirable rebuilding of cities and desirable patterns of land use in general. There are differences of opinion as to the administrative feasibility and short-term economic effects of a radical move in this direction, but the long-term advantages seem great.[92]

USER CHARGES. Strong arguments are advanced for heavier reliance on user charges (and tax devices which are essentially like user charges in character) by *all* levels of government. This, therefore, is one of the few revenue sources in regard to which the local level does not suffer major disadvantages.

User charges clearly satisfy equity requirements, if the service involved has the appropriate characteristics, notably divisibility among consumers, the absence of important externalities, and the presence of the exclusion principle (use of the service by some consumers denies it to others). Appropriate user charges would be locationally neutral, and considerations of the distribution of taxable capacity are irrelevant here. There are no general administrative problems, although devising administrable charging schemes is not easy in all cases. The positive argument for user charges is that they promote allocation efficiency: Resources are devoted to providing the affected public services only in the quantities users want and will pay for.

As Table 5 shows, state and local governments now receive over one-fourth of their total revenue from user taxes and charges. Nevertheless, there are two types of deficiencies in present reliance on user charges: They are often not employed at all when warranted,

---

[92] Ibid., pp. 197–212. See also James Heilbrun, *Real Estate Taxes and Urban Housing* (Columbia University Press, 1966).

and they are often applied in an inappropriate manner. Air and water pollution is a good example of failure to apply user charges where they clearly make sense. By and large, the construction and operation of sewerage systems and sewage treatment facilities are financed in the United States by local property taxes. Some places have sewer service charges of one kind or another, but they are by no means in the majority. Yet here is a case where the specific actions which give rise to public costs are easy to identify. The benefits of water or air pollution control may be very broad, but the sources of the public costs are highly individual. Moreover, it is not impractical to apply charges that have some relationship to the costs occasioned. This has been done in the Ruhr basin in Germany for many years.

Conventional highway financing illustrates the inept use of user charges. Gasoline taxes and licenses have some relationship to the amount of use of the highways by all users as a group and by individual users over long periods of time. But flat charges of this kind cannot possibly discourage people from freely using the very high-cost roads at the very high-cost periods. There is no discrimination among the parts of the road system depending on their cost to the public, including the costs of congestion.

One of the most serious obstacles to effective utilization of pricing devices in financing public services can be traced to the traditional justification for user charges (and analogous taxes) on the basis of benefits received. The benefit principle, however, is concerned not with allocation but with equitably spreading the costs of public goods among individuals. But this principle is inappropriate for allocation branch decisions on the financing and provision of services with a substantial private character. Efficiency in allocation requires that prices (or other types of charges) and the level of services provided be determined on the basis of the marginal *costs* of the services. More often than not, there is little correspondence between benefit-determined charges and cost-determined charges.

Vickrey has done extensive work on this problem. In a major paper,[93] he contrasts benefit and cost solutions for a number of urban services, and advances imaginative, and reasonably workable, cost-based charging schemes. A number of these schemes involve

---

[93] William W. Vickrey, "General and Specific Financing of Urban Services," in Howard G. Schaller (ed.), *Public Expenditure Decisions in the Urban Community* (Johns Hopkins Press for Resources for the Future, Inc., 1963), pp. 62–90.

charges based on site characteristics, such as land area and frontage; in effect, they are offered as substitutes for the existing benefit-justified taxation of the value of land and improvements, that is, the property tax.

## Conclusions

The existing distribution of revenue sources and the existing revenue structures of individual governments appear to have numerous deficiencies. But the taxes exist, and they produce large amounts of revenue. Therefore, the policy implications of this review would seem relevant to proposals for future increases in revenue, rather than to proposals for dismantling existing structures and starting over again. In this light, what are the conclusions?

1. The case for moderately increased state government utilization of individual income and general consumer sales taxes is a good one, especially in those states now employing relatively low rates.

2. The case for increased state use of any type of business taxation, except possibly the conversion of some existing business taxes to a value-added form, is a very poor one.

3. The case for increased local government use of most major tax forms is weak, with two significant exceptions: First, some of the objections to heavier local use of sales and income taxes would disappear were the local unit one that comprehends all or most of a metropolitan complex. In some areas, this situation could be readily achieved by expanding the county government role. But in the larger, multicounty (in some cases, interstate) metropolitan areas, its achievement is much more difficult. In effect, such a course of action would be an alternative to an enlarged state government role in financing services with a regional scope. But, as indicated earlier, it seems an unlikely alternative, the reverse of recent trends. Second, there are persuasive arguments for much heavier local taxation of land values.

4. There is a strong case for greater reliance on user charges and similar devices, employed in a sophisticated manner. This case applies particularly to the local level, but not exclusively. To the extent that the states increasingly substitute for metropolitan government in the provision of regional services—many of which, like transportation services, are clearly appropriate for user charge financing—state governments can be more effective practitioners of user charges.

# The Intergovernmental Transfer System

The earlier analysis of the allocation of expenditure responsibilities by level of government suggests that a fair degree of reallocation might be appropriate. The direction of the indicated reallocation is, in the main, a centralizing one—more direct federal provision of income-redistributive services, especially income maintenance payments, and more direct state, or regional government, provision of services with a regional scope. Such reallocation might be thought to imply a lessening of the needs for intergovernmental transfers. However, the analysis of the allocation of revenue-raising responsibilities also suggests centralization. On balance, therefore, this analysis of ideal multilevel systems implies more, not less, intergovernmental payments, an implication which of course is in keeping with recent as well as long-run trends in the American federal system.

## Functional Grants

The theory of optimizing grants calls for expansion of federal functional grants for activities which are assigned to state-local governments but which involve important spillover benefits of national scope. The converse of this is the elimination or reduction of federal grant programs for public services the benefits of which are geographically more confined, since large federal grants for such services will lead to local decisions to expand expenditure inefficiently.

The major national benefit services which are now, and probably always will be, assigned to the state-local sector include research and human resource development, notably education and manpower training, and health and social services other than income maintenance. Federal grants now finance only a relatively small part of total public expenditure for education and by no means all of the other human resource development activities. Moreover, as Table 9 shows, present federal grants are by no means confined to these fields. Aids for education, research, and redistributive services in fiscal 1967 accounted for 63 percent of total federal grants-in-aid. Another 5 percent of federal grants is for services which state-local governments provide essentially as agents for the federal government, in areas where the responsibility is clearly a federal one—economic stabilization, defense, services to veterans and Indians, and so forth.

**TABLE 9. Federal Grants-in-Aid to State and Local Governments, by Type of Activity, Fiscal 1967**

| Type of activity | Dollar amount (in millions) | Percent of total |
|---|---|---|
| Education and research | 2,732 | 18 |
| Elementary and secondary schools[a] | 1,715 | 11 |
| Other | 1,017 | 7 |
| Direct aid and services to low-income families | 6,834 | 45 |
| Public assistance (including medical) | 3,926 | 26 |
| Other[b] | 2,908 | 19 |
| Transportation and other regional-scope activities | 4,879 | 32 |
| Highways | 4,009 | 26 |
| Other[c] | 870 | 6 |
| Areas of primary federal responsibility[d] | 700 | 5 |
| Employment Security Administration | 518 | 3 |
| Other | 182 | 1 |
| Total | 15,144 | 100 |

Source: *Special Analyses, Budget of the United States, Fiscal Year 1968,* "Special Analysis J," Table J-10, pp. 157–61. Figures are estimates; they are rounded and will not necessarily add to totals.

[a] Includes activities under the Elementary and Secondary Education Act and aid to schools in federally affected areas.

[b] Main activities include antipoverty programs, most health grants, low-rent housing, surplus food programs, and area economic development programs.

[c] Includes water pollution control, other land and water resources activities, airports and urban transportation aids, and urban planning and renewal activities.

[d] Includes activities concerned with defense, economic stabilization, and groups and areas which are special federal charges: veterans, Indians, territories, Alaska, and the District of Columbia.

But nearly a third of federal grants—almost $5 billion in 1967 —was for transportation and for resource and urban development activities with benefits which seldom spill over regional boundaries, at least not to any major extent.[94] The theory calls for regional, not federal, financing of such activities and probably for regional administration as well, via state government or metropolitan-type agencies. Federal intervention in these areas seems a consequence of

[94] Federal transportation grants are dominated by grants for the Interstate Highway System and other intercity roads. It is often argued that these (and other) transportation facilities do involve substantial interregional benefits, warranting large-scale federal financing, because of defense and postal uses of the facilities and because of large indirect social benefits. But the latter can be realized only by *someone's* use of the facilities (and are therefore reflected in private transport costs and product prices) and the former could be reimbursed were the federal government to pay ordinary state highway user taxes and charges. See Break, *Intergovernmental Fiscal Relations,* pp. 70–71, for a succinct statement of the position advanced here.

the common failure (except in the case of highways) to apply regional financial or administrative solutions. Leaving urban planning and renewal decision making to individual local government jurisdictions is an example of this common failure. And federal functional grants for such purposes will probably continue to expand as long as regional solutions are not applied.

One essential element of the theoretical prescription, therefore, is a great enlargement of the regional government role in regional affairs, either directly or by state grants-in-aid to the local governments administering regional services. At present, state aid for regional services provided by local governments probably accounts for no more than 20 percent of total local expenditure for these services; nearly all of the aid is for highways, and a significant proportion of state highway aid is used for purely local-benefit roads, thereby promoting inefficient expenditure patterns.

Some figures, based on 1966 revenue and expenditure patterns, indicate more clearly the ideal arrangements for functional grants. Federal school aids should have been perhaps $10 billion higher, providing for federal-state-local percentage shares in school financing of 40-40-20, rather than the actual 10-40-50 shares; a continued large state role in school financing is surely suggested by the important regional as well as national spillovers of benefits from education.[95] Federal grants for health and welfare purposes (aside from public assistance) should have been perhaps $2 billion higher. Direct federal administration would have relieved the state-local sector of $2.5 billion in public assistance expenditures financed from state and local sources.

Offsetting this, federal grants for highways and other regional services should have been reduced by nearly $5 billion. Thus, there should have been net additional federal financing of $9 billion to $10 billion in civilian public expenditure, not counting the effects of any scheme of unconditional federal balancing and equalizing grants.

On balance, this set of changes in federal funding would require more state government financing, but substantially less local government financing of civilian public expenditure. Furthermore, the indicated needs for local-to-state shifts in the handling of regional services would increase the fiscal requirements of state governments

[95] Since most population migration is over short rather than long distances, it is clear that some of the benefits of education must be regional in scope.

still more. In total, the states would have required perhaps $7 billion above and beyond the $43 billion they raised from their own sources in 1966. It cannot be maintained that this increment is beyond the capabilities of appropriate state revenue systems, but such shifts would surely reinforce the argument for unconditional federal grants to the states. Moreover, since under these arrangements local government revenue requirements would have been as much as 40 percent below their actual 1965–66 revenues, the case for unconditional grants would be a strong one, whether or not the states passed through any of these federal funds to their local units.

FUNCTIONAL GRANTS AND INNOVATION. Innovation in the provision of public services contributes to benefit spillovers, and hence constitutes an argument for functional grants. Truly experimental programs and approaches tend to lower the money and nonmoney costs of emulation in other places. Moreover, the failure rate of experiments may be high, and other jurisdictions benefit from this lesson, as well. The innovation argument, therefore, can justify federal grants for experimentation and demonstration programs in services which, when established, have regional or even local, rather than national, benefits. However, such grants are likely to be modest in dollar terms.

Furthermore, such grants make sense only if they do in fact stimulate additional efforts by the recipient government, rather than substitute for expenditure of funds that lower-level governments would in any case make. The evidence on the stimulative versus substitutive effects of grants-in-aid is mixed. Those studies of the determinants of state-local expenditure which have considered federal aid as an independent variable have found that it is strongly stimulative.[96] On the other hand, some studies have found that state aid is more substitutive than stimulative, especially in connection with school aids.[97] In part, of course, this is by design; state aid schemes are often intended to replace local property tax support of local services, with stimulation only an incidental factor.

[96] See, for example, Seymour Sacks and Robert Harris, "The Determinants of State and Local Government Expenditures and Intergovernmental Flows of Funds," *National Tax Journal,* Vol. 17 (March 1964), pp. 75–85.

[97] See George A. Bishop, "Stimulative Versus Substitutive Effects of State School Aid in New England," *National Tax Journal,* Vol. 17 (June 1964), pp. 133–43.

*Balancing Grants*

The case for unconditional grants—a case which applies to both federal-to-state grants and state-to-local grants—has two elements. The first is that the revenue-raising abilities of the higher-level governments, in an appropriate multilevel revenue system, are great compared to expenditure responsibilities appropriately assigned to them; the reverse is true for the lower levels. As noted above, a rearrangement of federal-state-local expenditure responsibilities, together with functional grants on the basis of the optimizing-grant theory, would make this element of the case for unconditional federal-to-state grants much stronger.

The second element of the case is the inequality of fiscal resources among the lower-level jurisdictions. Perhaps this would be of less moment were the existing functional grants strongly equalizing in effect. But such is not the case for federal grants. As Break shows, some federal functional grants do have significant equalizing effects, but they are offset by grant programs with opposite effects; the result is that per capita federal grants are more or less proportional to state per capita income.[98] At the state-to-local level, the equalizing effects of functional grants are usually more noticeable. Most state school aid (69 percent of total state functional grants in the school year 1966–67) is disbursed on the basis of reasonably effective equalization formulas.[99] Another one-fifth of state functional grants are for health, hospital, and welfare services, with built-in equalizing effects.

There is, consequently, an argument—under the theoretical structure employed here—for sizable unconditional federal grants to the states. They should be sizable, because the interlevel fiscal imbalance is large, and they should have important equalizing effects. A large number of variants of plans for unconditional grants have been advanced since the development of the Heller-Pechman pro-

[98] Break, *Intergovernmental Fiscal Relations*, pp. 120–27; see especially Table IV-7, p. 127.

[99] Perhaps the major deficiency in the characteristic formulas is the understatement of the costliness of providing school programs of equivalent effectiveness in the large central cities, which often show up as low-need, high-resource areas as a result.

posal in 1964; this is not the place to examine them in detail.[100]

The states now make significant unconditional payments to local governments ($1.4 billion in 1967).[101] But these are much more balancing than they are equalization grants, because most of them involve the sharing of the proceeds of selected state taxes, with distribution on the basis of the origin of the tax collections. When the shared tax is a progressive income tax distributed to the taxpayer's place of residence (as in Wisconsin), the high-income dormitory suburb is a major beneficiary. State general-purpose aid need not be provided in this way, however: Twenty years ago, New York State shifted from a system of tax sharing based on origin to one of per capita aid, which at present has a significant equalizing character. This is surely an area in which competitive emulation of one pioneering state by others would be an effective demonstration of the continued value of state government as an arena for social experimentation.

[100] The most comprehensive discussion of unconditional federal grants can be found in the Hearings of the Subcommittee on Fiscal Policy of the Joint Economic Committee in July and August 1967 and the materials prepared for those hearings, both of which were published under the title, *Revenue Sharing and Its Alternatives: What Future for Fiscal Federalism?* cited in note 27 above. See also Break, *Intergovernmental Fiscal Relations*, pp. 107–64.

[101] U.S. Bureau of the Census, *State Government Finances in 1967* (1968), p. 8.

# Index of Names

Aaron, Henry, 159n, 165n, 220n
Adams, Robert F., 370n, 371n
Aliber, Robert Z., 154n
Andersen, Leonall, 62n, 65, 66, 67, 68, 69, 70, 71, 72, 73, 76, 96
Anderson, W. H. Locke, 215
Ando, Albert, 43n, 65n, 78n, 89, 90, 114n, 235n
Arrow, Kenneth J., 262n, 272, 275, 321
Atkinson, A. B., 225n

Bahl, Roy W., 227
Bailey, Martin J., 152n, 199, 212n, 229
Banfield, Edward C., 261n, 280, 287, 288
Barker, Ernest, 272n
Barlow, Robin, 160n, 182n, 183n, 184, 200, 381n, 402n
Barzel, Yoram, 160n
Baumol, William J., 144, 203n, 222n, 225n, 261n
Beck, Ralph A., 162n
Becker, Gary S., 181n
Bergstrom, Theodore, 160n
Bhagwati, Jagdish N., 222n
Bhatia, Kul B., 197
Bird, Richard M., 209n
Birdsall, William C., 245n, 281n
Bischoff, Charles W., 54, 92n, 94, 204n, 212n, 216, 217, 218n

Bishop, George A., 419n
Bishop, Robert L., 224n
Black, Duncan, 272, 273, 279, 280
Blinder, A. S., 45n, 52n, 69n, 71n, 100n
Boatwright, B. D., 212n, 219
Boskin, Michael J., 169n, 189n
Bossons, John, 176n
Bowen, Howard R., 245n, 264n, 266, 267, 270, 271, 276
Bower, Richard S., 144n
Bradford, David F., 222n
Brainard, William, 95n, 96
Brandl, John E., 278
Branson, William H., 48n, 111n
Braybrooke, David, 287
Brazer, Harvey, 145n, 160n, 163n, 182n, 183n, 184, 200, 368n, 400n, 402n
Break, George F., 182, 184n, 187n, 224n, 369, 370n, 374n, 391n, 397n, 410n, 421n
Breton, Albert, 245n
Bridges, Benjamin, Jr., 402n
Brinner, Roger, 101n
Brittain, John A., 149, 169–72, 173, 175, 196n, 199n
Brown, C. V., 183n, 185
Brown, E. Cary, 11n, 13–14, 17, 21, 43n, 64n, 78n, 90, 111n, 114n, 210n

423

# General Index